GROC'S CANDID G
TO

CRETE
and
Mainland Ports

For the package & villa holiday-maker,
backpacker & independent traveller,
whether journeying by air, car, coach, ferry-boat
or train

by
Geoffrey O'Connell

Published by

**Ashford, Buchan
& Enright**
1 Church Road
Shedfield
Hampshire
SO3 2HW

CONTENTS

ILLUSTRATIONS

Readers must not forget that prices are given as a guide only and relate to the year in which this book is researched. In recent years not only lodging and 'troughing' costs, but all transport charges have escalated dramatically. The increased value of most other currencies to the Greek drachmae has compensated, to some extent, for these apparently ever-rising prices.

In an effort to keep readers as up-to-date as possible, regarding these and other matters, the **GROC'S GREEK ISLAND HOTLINE** is available. *See* elsewhere for details. The series is now in its eighth year of publication and I would appreciate continuing to hear from readers who have any additions or corrections to bring to my attention. As in the past, all correspondence (except that addressed to 'Dear fifth', or similar endearments) will be answered.

I hope readers can excuse errors that creep (well gallop actually) into the welter of detailed information included in the body text. A pretty feeble excuse is to advise that in order that the volumes are as up-to-date as possible, the period from inception to publication is kept down to some six months, which results in the occasional slip up...

The cover picture of a church bell-tower, beside the road between Sfinari and Stomio, on the west coast of Crete, is reproduced by kind permission of GREEK ISLAND PHOTOS, Willowbridge Enterprises, Bletchley, Milton Keynes, Bucks.

The Candid Guides
unique
'GROC's Greek Island Hotline'

Available to readers of the guides, this service enables a respondent to receive a bang up-to-the-minute update, to supplement the extensive information contained in a particular Candid Guide.

To obtain this paraphrased computer print out, covering the Introductory Chapters, Athens, Piraeus & Mainland Ports, as well as any named islands, up to twenty five in number, all that is necessary is to:-

Complete the form, enclosing a payment of £1.50, and send to:-

Willowbridge Publishing, Bridge House, Southwick Village, Nr Fareham, Hants. PO17 6DZ

Note: The information will be of no use to anyone who does not possess the relevant, most up to date GROC's Candid Greek Island Guide. We are unable to dispatch the Hotline without details of the guide AND which edition. This information is on the Inside Front Cover.

Planned departure dates......................................

....

Mr/Mrs/Miss..

of...

....

I possess: I require:
GROC's Greek Island Guides   Edition   GROC's Greek Island Hotline
to:...............................   ....

....

....

....

....

....

and enclose a fee of £1.50. Signature.........................
Date.................
I appreciate that the 'Hotline' may not be dispatched for up to 7-10 days from receipt of this application. Please also enclose a large SAE.

GROC's Candid Guides
introduce to readers

Suretravel '90

A comprehensive holiday insurance plan that 'gives cover that many other policies do not reach', to travellers anywhere in the world. In addition to the more usual cover offered, the

SURETRAVEL HOLIDAY PLAN

includes (where medically necessary):
24 hour World Wide Medical Emergency Service including, where appropriate, repatriation by air ambulance.

Additionally, personal accident, medical and emergency expenses EVEN while hiring a bicycle, scooter or car.

An example premium, in 1990, for a 10-17 day holiday in Greece is £13.50 per person.

Note: all offers & terms are subject to the Insurance Certificate Cover

For an application form please complete the cut-out below and send to:
Willowbridge Publishing, Bridge House, Southwick Village Nr Fareham, Hants. PO17 6DZ

Mr/Mrs/Miss..Age..............

of...

....

I request a **SURETRAVEL** application form

Date of commencement of holiday.....................Duration..............

Signature..Date............

INTRODUCTION

This volume is the third edition of Crete, one of seven books in the very popular and proven series of the GROC's Candid Guides to the Greek Islands. The rationale, the *raison d'etre* behind their production is to treat each island grouping on an individual and comprehensive basis, rather than attempt overall coverage of the 100 or so islands usually described in one volume. This, for instance, obviates skimping the various regions of Crete in amongst an aggregation of many other, often disparate islands. In fact, due to the sheer size of Crete, it is treated as a separate case.

It is important for package and villa holiday-makers to have an unbiased and relevant description of their planned holiday surroundings, rather than the usual, extravagant hyperbole of the glossy sales brochure. It is vital for backpackers and ferry-boat travellers to have, on arrival, detailed and accurate information, at their finger tips. With these differing requirements in mind, factual, 'straight-from-the-shoulder' location reports have been combined with detailed plans of the island's major cities, towns and ports, as well as topographical, regional maps.

Amongst the guides generally available are earnest tomes dealing with Ancient and Modern Greece, a number of thumbnail travel booklets and some worthy, if often out-of-date books. Unfortunately they rarely assuage the various travellers' differing requirements. These might include speedy and accurate identification of one's location, and immediate whereabout's, on arrival; the situation of accommodation; as well as the position of a bank, the postal services and or tourist offices. Additional requisites probably embrace a swift and easy to read resume of the settlement's main quarters, cafe-bars, tavernas and restaurants; detailed local bus and ferry-boat timetables; and a full regional narrative. Once the traveller has settled in, then and only then, can he or she feel at ease, making their own finds and discoveries.

I have chosen to omit lengthy accounts of the relevant, fabulous Greek mythology and history. For the serious student, these aspects of Greece are very ably related by authors far more erudite than myself. Moreover, most island's have a semi-official tourist guide, translated into English, and for that matter, French, German and Scandinavian. They are usually well worth the 300 to 500 drachmae (drs) they cost; are extremely informative in 'matters archaeological'; and are quite well produced, if rather out of date, with excellent colour photographs. Admittedly the English translation might seem a little quaint (try to read Greek, let alone translate it), and the maps are often unreliable, but cartography is not a strong Hellenic suit!

Each **Candid Guide** is finally researched as close to the publication date as is possible. On the other hand, in an effort to facilitate production of this volume, it has been found necessary to omit any information that requires waiting until the springtime of the year of publication. These details, which include up-to-date air, ferry-boat and train fares, are often only available as late as April or May. They are now 'punched' into the **Hotline**, for particulars of which read on. Naturally, any new ideas are incorporated but, in the main, the guides follow a now well-proven formula with a layout designed to facilitate quick and easy reference. Part One introduces the island group to the reader - in this case the island of Crete; Part Two details the more usual, relevant mainland ports that a traveller may utilise to reach the group - in the respect of Crete, Piraeus and Githion; and Part Three marks the commencement of the individual island descriptions - in the case of Crete, the particular chapters being mainly based on the major, northern coastal cities and towns.

The exchange rate has fluctuated rather more gently in recent years. At the time of writing the final draft of this guide, the rate to the English pound (£) was hovering about 259drs. Unfortunately prices are subject to fluctuation, usually upward, with annual increases varying between 10-20%. For the time being, the drachma has ceased to devalue sufficiently to compensate for these uplifts.

Recommendations and personalities are almost always based on personal observation and experience, occasionally emphasised by the discerning comments of readers or colleagues. They may well change from year to year, and, being such personal, idiosyncratic judgements, are subject to different interpretation by others.

The series incorporates a couple of still innovative, unique services which have evolved over the years. These are:

GROC's Greek Island Hotline: An absolutely unrivalled service available to readers of the Candid Guides. Application enables purchasers of the guides to obtain a summary detailing all pertinent, relevant comments and information, that have become available since the publication of the particular guide - in effect, an up-to-date update. The Hotline is constantly being revised and incorporates bang up-to-the-moment intelligence. A payment of £1.50 (plus a large SAE) enables a respondent to receive the paraphrased computer print-out in respect of the various guides, with an upper limit of twenty five islands, in addition to Athens, and the relevant mainland ports. An interested reader only has to complete the form requesting the Hotline, enclose the fee and post to Willowbridge Enterprises, Bridge House, Southwick Village, Nr Fareham, Hants PO17 6DZ.

Travel Insurance: A comprehensive holiday insurance plan that 'gives cover that many other policies do not reach....' See elsewhere for details.

The author (and publisher) are very interested in considering ways and means of improving the guides, and adding to the backup facilities, so are delighted to hear from readers with their suggestions. Enjoy yourselves and 'Ya Sou' (welcome).

Geoffrey O'Connell 1990

1 PART ONE
Introduction to Crete (Kriti)

There is a land called Crete in the midst of the wine dark sea. Homer in The Odyssey

VITAL STATISTICS The island is approximately 264 km long, & averages some 55 km in width, with an area estimated at 8,200 sq km & a population of just below 500,000.

SPECIALITIES Yoghurt (from a tub); tighanites - pancakes covered with honey & sesame seeds; Cretan wines of note, which include *Minos, Gortinos & Kissamos*; *Mandareeni* - a tangerine liqueur; raki or tsikoudhia - a (more) lethal ouzo; herbal tea; honey; embroidery; Nikos Kazantzakis, author of amongst other books, *Zorba the Greek*; the Cretan men's mountain 'uniform' of headscarf, black shirt, old fashioned jodhpurs & riding boots.

RELIGIOUS HOLIDAYS & FESTIVALS include: (in addition to the Greek national celebrations): two weeks before Lent, a carnival celebrated throughout the island; 25th March at the Churches of Prasas (Iraklion County) & Apokorona (Chania County) - Annunciation of Our Lady; First Sunday after Easter at the Monasteries of Vrondisi & Zaros (Iraklion County) and Neo Chorio & Apokorona (Chania County) - St Thomas; 23rd April at the Monastery of Ag Georgios Epanosifi (between Archanes & Charakas, Iraklion County) - a religious feast & celebratory mass; 20th-27th May, Chania City - anniversary of the Battle of Crete; 26-27th May, Chora Sfakion - anniversary of the Declaration of the 1821 Revolution; 24th June - island-wide bonfires - birthday of St John the Baptist; Flasarna (Nr Kastelli, Chania County) - a moveable tomato fiesta (dependent on when they ripen, of course!); 1st-15th July, Dafnes (Iraklion County) - wine festival & folk art exhibition; 2nd-10th July, Sitia & Kornaria - cultural & artistic festivities; 13th-18th July, Voukolies (Chania County) - cultural and artistic events; 15th-30th July, Rethymnon - wine festival; 16th-31st July, Rethymnon - handicraft exhibition; 15th-17th July, Voni (Nr Thrapsano, Iraklion County) - religious fair; 19th-22nd July, Sitia - raisin festival; 29th-31st July, Archanes - painting & handicraft exhibition; 28th July-10th August, Vamos - cultural & artistic events; 13th-15th August, Archanes - festival; 12th-15th August, Anogia (Rethymnon County) - cultural & artistic festivities; 13th-20th August, Perama (Rethymnon County) - raisin festival; 15th August, religious fairs in many villages, including Mochos (Iraklion County), Neapolis, Meskla (Chania County), Alikampos, near Vryses (Chania County), Armeni (Rethymnon County), Chrysoskalitissa, near Stomio (Chania County), Spili (Rethymnon County) & Akoumia, near Melambes (Rethymnon County) - Assumption of Virgin Mary; 13th-15th August, Neapolis - festivities; 25th August, Amari (Rethymnon County) - religious fairs, St Titus day; 27th August, Vrondisi Monastery (Iraklion County) & Vryses (Chania County) - religious fair, St Fanourios; 29th August, Kournas & Chionna site (both in Chania County) - religious fair, St John the Baptist; 1st-10th September, Gavalochori (Chania County) - folklore manifestations; 14th September, Alikianos, Varypetro (Chania County)

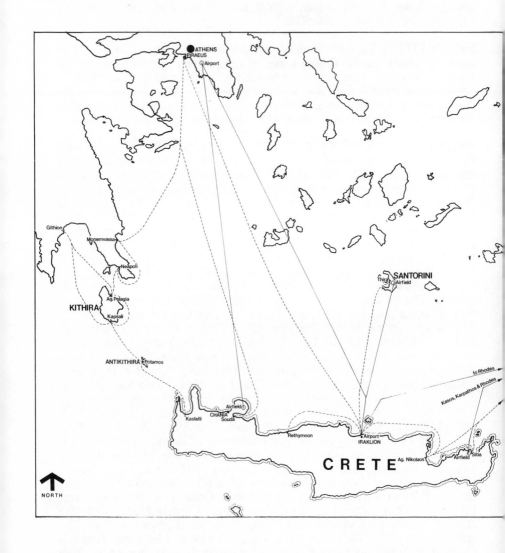

Illustration 1 Crete & the Aegean Sea

& villages around Mount Idha - religious fairs, Raising of the Holy Cross; 7th October, Monastery of Gouverneto (Chania County) - St John the Hermit; third Sunday of October, Elos (Chania County) - chestnut festival; 8th November, Arkadhi Monastery (Rethymnon County) - anniversary of the 1866 holocaust, folklore dancing in Rethymnon town; 11th November, Iraklion - religious procession for patron saint of the town, St Menas; 4th December, Ag Varvara (Iraklion County) - St Barbara; 6th December, Agios Nikolaos (Lasithi County) - St. Nicholas.

Crete is not so much an island, more a land in its own right. It is very much what you make it, with extreme contrasts offering almost every type of scenery and terrain imaginable: from the date palm clad, sandy beach shore of Vai, in the north-east, to the winter-snow clad mountains in the south-west; from the modernity of the National Highway, that skirts most of the north coastline, to the uncertain, almost indistinguishable donkey tracks that penetrate the interior vastness; from the lowland, polythene covered greenhouse squalor that edges some of the vast Messara Plain, to the simple, agricultural simplicity of the Omalos mountain plain; from the dusty, urbane, worldly-wise city of Iraklion to the comparative country town calm of Kastelli; from quiet, orderly, business-like Neapolis to the industrial squalor of Timbaki; from the relatively peaceful, seaside charm of Sitia, to the package tourist frenzy of Agios Nikolaos; from fly-blown, bedraggled Lendas, to the simple, naive allure of Keratokambos; from the over-exploited cave dwellings of Matala to the almost idyllic fishing village of Mochlos; from the disjointed sprawl of Ierapetra to the bustling, beautiful alpine mountain town of Spili; and the simple Minoan remains of Kato Zakros, to the heavily restored, ancient city of Knossos.

Due to the extremely clement weather, the island has a long tourist season stretching from the beginning of April to the end of October. A number of areas have been subject to massive exploitation by the holiday industry, but whatever the requirements, Crete, perhaps more than any other situation in Greece, if not Europe, can surely fulfil every person's wishes. Be they for a sophisticated, self-contained luxury dream hotel, or the rural simplicity of a small pension, either one situated on a craggy, granite mountainside, or edging a sun drenched beach. Activities can encompass the extremes of hedonistic sunbathing, the quiet bustle of investigating ancient religious buildings, to brisk mountain walking. Crete's complicated and convoluted past is matched by an almost embarrassing wealth of archaeological remains and historical sites. Both require a lot more than a passing and light-hearted enquiry, to even scratch the surface.

Much is made of the Cretan's independent, steadfast, fiery nature and the exuberance of their welcome. Despite this friendliness, it is expecting too much, in the comparatively short time available to most travellers, to experience more than the usual reception afforded to the vast majority of holiday-makers. The latter now number some 1,000,000 per year, mostly concentrated in the summer months. Certainly Cretans suffer fools less gladly than most of their fellow countrymen, on the other islands.

Visitors' requirements vary considerably - from a two week package holiday, via those of an independent traveller, wishing to break loose of the fetters usually associated with 'organised' tourism, to that of the 'dedicated' drop-out, planning on eking out a summer on one or other of the beaches, where the authorities turn a blind eye...

Most travellers arrive on Crete, at the north coast airport or harbour of either Iraklion or Chania. More intrepid voyagers may dock at the ports of Kastelli, in the north-west, Agios Nikolaos or Sitia, in the north-east, or even Sitia airport.

Due to the geographical spread and spacing of the major northern towns (Ag Nikolaos, Chania, Iraklion, Kastelli, Rethymnon and Sitia), and taking into account the mountain ranges that form the east to west barriers, it is more comprehensible to split the guide into a number of regions based on the aforementioned locations. The adventurous may cover some of these areas, those with sufficient time and inclination, might see them all. The time available to a great majority of tourists will not allow more than a detailed visit to a few selected towns, or a more cursory inspection of rather more places. Time is not the only controlling factor, and account must be taken of the available lines of communication. The first-time visitor may well not appreciate that, with no trains, a bus service that only radiates out from the town centres on the north coast, and many roads that were not constructed with modern day traffic in mind, daily distances covered can be comparatively small. Added to these strictures is the extremely mountainous nature of much of the land.

Crete has sufficient accommodation to cope with all but the height of season influx, unlike many small islands, where *Rooms* may be at a premium for much of the year. The sheer size and amount of accommodation available makes it physically impossible to stay in, or even call on more than a percentage of them, in the larger towns. Thus, I have, on occasions, only listed those places that caught my fancy (for some reason or another), as well as noting the frequency of accommodation in locations, where it is less easily available. The same reasoning and approach applies to dining out.

Crete, once extensively forested, is now only lightly wooded, which may well be something to do with the island's comparative shortage of fresh water. There is an abundance of flora, seen at its best after the spring rains, some of which are indigenous to Crete, including the 'all healing' Cretan 'dittany', from the mint family of plants. Wild life includes the very interesting 'Kri-Kri' (Agrimi), a species of mountain goat, but no other creature of note, although there are supposed to be scatterings of scorpions, but no snakes. The bird life makes Crete an ornithologist's delight, the most imimpressive of the genre surely being the majestic birds of prey.

For the statistically minded, the average monthly temperatures and rainfall of Crete are:

	Jan	Feb	Mar	Apr	May	Jun	Jul	Aug	Sep	Oct	Nov	Dec
Average air temp C°	12.3	12.5	13.8	16.8	20.4	24.4	26.4	26.4	23.6	20.3	17.2	13.9
F°	54	54.5	57	62	69	76	79.5	79.5	74.5	69	63	57
Average sea surface C°	15.2	15.4	16	18.7	20.6	24	25.9	25.6	23.1	22.4	18.9	16.1
F°	59	60	61	65.5	69	75	78	78	73.5	72	66	61
Average days of rain	14	12	7	4	3	1	-	-	2	5	8	14

Maps *Clyde Surveys Ltd*, of Reform Rd, Maidenhead, Berkshire, SL68BU. (Tel   0628 21371) produce an excellent map of the island. A very good, 'home-grown' edition is produced by the *Efstathiadis Group*.

Symbols, Keys & Definitions Below are some notes in respect of the few initials and symbols used in the text, as well as an explanation of the possibly idiosyncratic nouns, adjectives and phrases, to be found scattered throughout the book.

Readers must accept that judgements of this or that location are carried out on whimsical grounds and are based purely on personal observation. The absence of any mention, has no detrimental significance and might, for instance, indicate that I did not personally inspect a particular establishment.

Keys The key *Tmr*, in conjunction with grids, is used as a map reference to aid easy identification of this or that location on port and town plans. Other keys used in the text include *Sbo* - 'Sea behind one'; *Fsw* - 'Facing seawards'; *Fbqbo* - 'Ferry-boat quay behind one'; *BPTs* - 'British Package Tourists' and *OTT* - 'Over The Top'.

GROC's definitions, 'proper' adjectives & nouns: These may require some elucidation, as most do not appear in 'official' works of reference and are used with my own interpretation, as set out below.

Backshore: the furthest strip of beach from the sea's edge. The marginal rim separating the shore from the surrounds. *See* **Scrubbly**

Chatty: with pretention to grandeur or sophistication.

Dead: an establishment that appears to be 'terminally' closed, and not about to open for business, but... who knows?

Donkey-droppings: as in 'two donkey-droppings', indicating a very small hamlet. *See* **One-eyed**.

Doo-hickey: an Irish based colloquialism, suggesting an extreme lack of sophistication and or rather 'daffy' (despite contrary indications in the authoritative and excellent *Partridges Dictionary of Slang*!).

Ethnic: very unsophisticated, Greek indigenous and, as a rule, applied to hotels and pensions. *See* **Provincial**.

(Ships) Galley Cooking: used to describe 'tired' rows of metal trays 'lurking' under the glass counters of tavernas, containing the exhausted, dried up, overcooked remnants of the lunch-time fare.

Gongoozle: borrowed from canal boat terminology, and indicates the state of very idly and leisurely, but inquisitively staring at others involved in some vital and busy activity.

Great unwashed: the less attractive, modern day mutation of the 1960s hippy. They are usually Western European, inactive loafers and layabouts 'by choice', or unemployed drop-outs. Once having located a desirable location, often a splendid beach, they camp under plastic and in shabby tents, thus ensuring the spot is despoiled for others. The 'men of the tribe' tend to trail a mangy dog on a piece of string. The women, more often than not, with a grubby child or two in train, pester cafe-bar clients to purchase items of home-made jewellery or trinkets.

Note the above genre appears to be incurably penniless (but then who isn't?).

Grecocilious: necessary to describe those Greeks, usually bank clerks or tour office owners, who are making their money from tourists but are disdainful of the 'hand that feeds them'. They appear to consider holiday-makers are some form of small intellect, low-browed, tree clambering, inferior relation to the Greek homo-sapiens. They can usually converse passably in two or three foreign languages (when it suits them) and habitually display an air of weary sophistication.

Hillbilly: similar to 'ethnic', but applied to describe countryside or a settlement, as in 'backwoods'.

Hippy: those who live outside the predictable, boring (!) mainstream of life and are frequently genuine, if sometimes impecunious travellers. The category may include students, or young professionals, taking a sabbatical and who are often 'negligent' of their sartorial appearance.

Independents: vacationers who make their own travel and accommodation arrangements, spurning the 'siren calls' of structured tourism, preferring to step off the package holiday carousel and make their own way.

Kosta'd: used to describe the 'ultimate' in development necessary for a settlement to reach the apogee required to satisfy the popular common denominator of package tourism. That this state of 'paradise on earth' has been accomplished, will be evidenced by the 'High St' presence of cocktail or music bars, discos, (garden) pubs, bistros and fast food. 'First division' locations are pinpointed by the aforementioned establishments offering inducements, which may include wet 'T' shirt, nightdress or pyjama bottom parties; air conditioning; space invader games and table top videos; as well as sundowner, happy or doubles hours.

Local prices: *See* **Special prices**.

Mr Big: a local trader or pension owner, an aspiring tycoon, a small fish trying to be a big one in a 'small pool'. Despite being sometimes flashy with shady overtones, his lack of sophistication is apparent by his not being Grecocilious!

Noddies or nodders: the palpable, floating evidence of untreated sewage being discharged into the sea.

One-eyed: small. *See* **Donkey-droppings**.

Poom: a descriptive noun 'borrowed' after sighting on Crete, some years ago, a crudely written sign advertising accommodation that simply stated POOMS! This particular place was basic with low-raftered ceilings, earth-floors and windowless rooms, simply equipped with a pair of truckle beds and rickety oilcloth covered washstand - very reminiscent of typical Cycladean cubicles of the 1950/60s period.

Provincial: usually applied to accommodation and is an improvement on Ethnic. Not meant to indicate, say, dirty but should conjure up images of faded, rather gloomy establishments, with a mausoleum atmosphere; high ceilinged, Victorian rooms with worn, brown linoleum; dusty, tired aspidistras, as well as bathrooms and plumbing of unbelievable antiquity.

Richter scale: borrowed from earthquake seismology and employed to indicate the (appalling) state of toilets, on an 'eye-watering' scale.

Schlepper: vigorous touting for customers by restaurant staff. It is said of a skilled market schlepper that he can 'retrieve' a passer-by from up to thirty or forty metres beyond the stall.

Scrubbly: usually applied to a beach or countryside, and indicating a rather messy, shabby area.

Special prices: A phrase employed to conceal the fact that the price charged is no more, no less than that of all the other bandits! No, no - competitors. **Local prices** is a homespun variation designed to give the impression that the goods are charged at a much lower figure than that obtainable elsewhere. Both are totally inaccurate, misleading misnomers.

Squatty: A Turkish (or French) style ablution arrangement. None of the old, familiar lavatory bowl and seat. Oh, no, just two moulded footprints edging a dirty looking hole, set in a porcelain surround. Apart from the unaccustomed nature of the exercise, the Lord simply did not give us enough limbs to keep a shirt up and control wayward trousers, that constantly attempt to flop down on to the floor, awash with goodness knows what! All this has to be enacted whilst gripping the toilet roll in one hand and wiping one's 'botty', with the other hand. Impossible! Incidentally, ladies should (perhaps) substitute blouse for shirt and skirt for trousers, but then it is easier (I am told) to tuck a skirt into one's waistband! A minor defect in the transition from Turkey, is that the close-to-the-floor tap, installed to aid flushing a squatty, is noticeable by its absence, in Greece. Well, it would be wouldn't it?

Way-station: mainly used to refer to an office or terminus in the sticks, and cloaked with an abandoned, unwanted air.

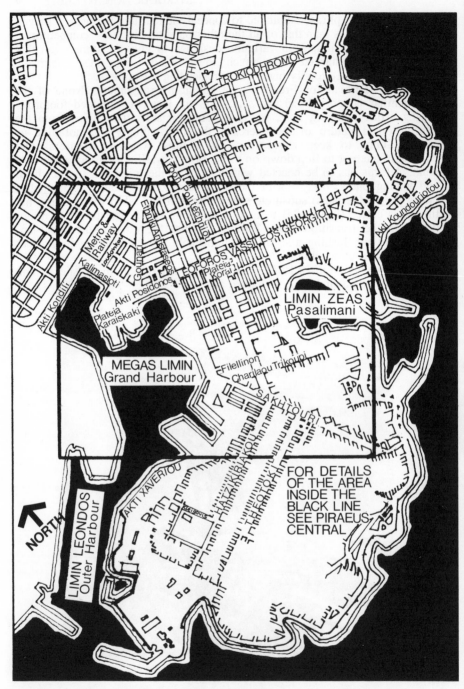

Illustration 2 Piraeus Port & Town

2 PART TWO
PIRAEUS (Pireas, Pireefs) & Other Mainland Ports including Githion

Fortune and hope farewell! I've found the port, you've done with me; go now with others sport.   From a Greek epigram

Tel prefix 01. Piraeus (Illustrations 2, 3 & 4) is the port of Athens and the usual ferry-boat departure point for most of the Aegean islands. This is a wearisomely large town and it's layout is confusing, on first acquaintance. One thing is for certain, and that is that the modern-day port bears very little resemblance to the Piraeus of old, as portrayed in the film *Never on a Sunday*. The bawdy seaport cafes, hashish dens, tavernas and seedy waterfront have been replaced by smart shipping offices, banks, tree planted thoroughfares, squares and parks. It has to be admitted that the sleazy south end of the parallel, canyon-like streets of Filonos and Notara are the 'Soho' of Piraeus, rich in low-life. I suppose fairly typical of this downtown area is the 'Clapcabana Cabaret' (which is probably what a client will get from overzealous attendance). Other hot-spots, not to be forgotten are the *Seamens Bar/Nightclub* and the *Moulin Rouge!* The other side of the coin is the very smart, rinky-dinky, east flank of the peninsula. This is edged by a neat Esplanade, as it chicanes, gently and leisurely rising and falling, following the cove, bay and harbour indented coastline.

Arrival at Piraeus will (usually) be by bus or Metro, unless approaching by sea. Then the choice of transport should be a ferry-boat, or hydrofoil (Well, it would be a long, tiring swim, wouldn't it?).

ARRIVAL BY BUS From Syntagma Sq (Athens), Bus No 40 arrives at Plateia Korai (*Tmr* C3), but in truth that is rather an over-simplification. For a start the bus is absolutely crammed, especially early morning, and secondly it is very difficult to know one's exact whereabouts. The first makes it difficult to leap up and down looking for telltale signs, whilst the latter is germane, as the bus hurtles on down to the south end of the Piraeus peninsula. The initial indicator, that the end of the ¾ hour journey is imminent, is when the bus runs parallel to the Metro lines. The next is crossing the wide avenue of Leoforos Vassileos Georgiou, after which signs for the Archaeological Museum indicate that it is time to bale out. From Plateia Korai, north-west down Leoforos Vassileos Georgiou (Yeoryiou) leads to the Main (Grand or Central) Harbour (*Tmr* B4); south-east progresses towards Limin Zeas (Pasalimani) Harbour (*Tmr* D3/4); and east makes off towards Limin Mounikhias (Tourkolimano) Harbour (*Tmr* E2). Limin Zeas is where the Hydrofoils (Flying Dolphins - *Ceres*) for all of the Argo Saronic dock (*Tmr* 26E4) - that is except for the Aegina island craft which berth (*Tmr* 24A/B3/4) alongside Plateia Astigos (Karaiskaki).

The Airport Express buses terminus on Plateia Astigos (*Tmr* 2A/B3/4); from Omonia Sq (Athens), Bus No 49 arrives at Plateia Themistokleous (*Tmr* 21B/C3); and a number of other services (including for instance Bus No 101) arrive at Kleisovis St (*Tmr* B/C5/6). From the latter, head north-east along Hatzikiriakou to Sakhtouri St, at which turn left, in a northerly direction, to reach the southern end of the Main Harbour waterfront.

ARRIVAL BY FERRY Re-orientate using the above information. Bear in mind that the various ferries dock all the way round the eastern periphery of the Grand Harbour, from the area of Plateia Astigos (*Tmr* 2A/B3/4) to a point south of the relatively new Passenger Ferry-Boat Terminal (*Tmr* 25B/C4). This facility is set in a pleasantly paved and landscaped section of Akti Miaouli.

ARRIVAL BY HYDROFOIL These *Ceres* hydrofoils, or flying dolphins, only service the Eastern Peloponnese and the islands of the Argo-Saronic. The Aegina island craft depart from a berth (*Tmr* 24A/B3/4) alongside Plateia Astigos (Karaiskaki). All the others dock at the south side of Limin Zeas Harbour (*Tmr* 26E4), a stiff ¾ hr walk, up and over the hillside of streets, from the Grand Harbour/Metro station. For those in a hurry, or simply worn out, it might just help to be reminded of the bus connection (No 905). These pass by Plateia Themistokleous on the way up Leoforos Vassileos Georgiou. Foot-sloggers will find it best to walk south along Akti Miaouli, as far as the Olympic Airline office (*Tmr* 8B/C3/4), at which turn left up Odhos Merarchias. This street ascends to Leoforos Vassileos Konstantinou (Iroon Politechniou), and then descends to the large, almost circular port of Limin Zeas. Here turn to the right, keeping on round to the far end of the harbour, where the hydrofoil quay is on the left.

ARRIVAL BY METRO The Piraeus Metro station (*Tmr* 1A/B2/3), the end of the line, is hidden away in a large but rather inconspicuous building, flanked by Plateia Loudovikou. It could well be a warehouse, an empty shell of an office block, in fact almost anything but a Metro terminus. Passengers emerge opposite the quayside, towards the north end of the Grand Harbour.

    Those catching a ferry-boat, almost immediately, might consider establishing a temporary headquarters. To do so, turn right out of the Metro building, cross the mainly paved Plateia Loudovikou to the waterfront, follow the Esplanade round to the left, and traverse Plateia Astigos (*Tmr* 2A/B3/4). This square is pleasantly shaded with trees, planted with bench seats, displays an old wooden railway carriage and is dominated by a tall, multi-storey waterfront building. Apart from size, it is noticeable for the advertising slogan that tops off the block. Set into the south, harbour-facing side are a number of cafe-bars, any one of which makes a convenient base camp. The importance of establishing a shore base, or bridgehead, becomes increasingly apparent whilst attempts are made to locate the particular ferry-boat departure point. But refreshments are not inexpensive at any of the harbour establishments. The Port police (*Tmr* 3A/B3/4) are located at the rear of the large Plateia Astigos building and must be regarded as favourites to dispense accurate information in respect of ferry-boats. Any knowledge received is best tucked away, for future comparison with the rest of the advice acquired!

    To obtain ferry-boat tickets, also turn right and left (Fsw) out of the Metro station and Square, to follow the quayside round in the direction of Odhos D Gounari, and beyond.

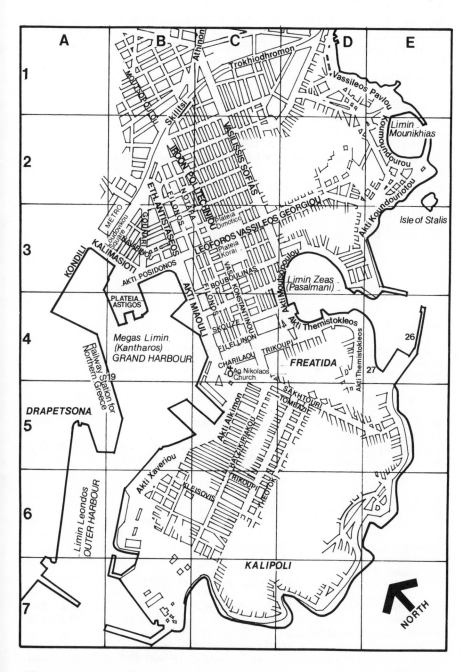

Illustration 3 Piraeus general

ARRIVAL BY TRAIN Peloponnese trains pull up at the same terminus building as the Metro (*Tmr* 1A/B2/3), whilst trains from Northern Greece 'steam' into the far (north-west) side of the Grand Harbour (*Tmr* 19A/B4/5). Incidentally the station for this latter terminal is almost like a country halt - even if it is plonked down alongside a squalid, industrial section of the waterfront. The stonework of the station building is picked out in red, there is a cafe-bar sign detailing an outline of the island of Crete, naturally enough the place name Piraeus is emblazoned along the front, there is a yellow post box, and the whole is topped off with a 'town hall' clock.

THE ACCOMMODATION & EATING OUT
The Accommodation Although I have never had to doss (or camp) out in Piraeus, I am advised that it is not to be recommended. There are just too many disparate (desperate?) characters wandering about.

Close by the Metro Station, are the:
Hotel Kentrikon (*Tmr* 29A/B3) (Class D) 16 Loudovikou Sq   Tel 417 9497
Directions: From the Loudovikou Sq entrance to the Metro building, turn left (*Sea to the right*). The hotel edges the square.
   All rooms share the bathrooms, with a single priced at 1500drs & a double 2000drs.

Hotel Ionion (*Tmr* 4B3) (Class C) 10 Kapodistrion   Tel 417 0992
Directions: Turn left from the Metro station (*Fsw*) along the quay road, Akti Kalimasioti, and left again at the first side street.
   The hotel, halfway up on the right, is noticeable by the prominent sign promising *Family Hotel and from now on Economical Prices*. But is it, with a single room, sharing a bathroom, charged at 2260drs & a double room, also sharing, 3525drs?

To the north-east of the *Ionion*, along the street and over the crossroads of Kapodistrion and Navarinou, is the:
Hotel Sparti (*Tmr* B3) (Class E) 18 Kapodistrion   Tel 411 0402
Directions: As above.
   Outwardly appears a 'bit-of-a-sleaze', but there cannot be any complaint about the 'share-a-bathroom' rates of 900drs for a single & 1500drs for a double, increasing to 1000drs & 1700drs (1st July-31st Oct).

The Delfini (*Tmr* 5B3) (Class C) 7 Leoharous   Tel 412 3512
Directions: As for the *Ionion*, but the second turning left.
   Singles cost 3500drs & doubles 4500drs, both with bathroom en suite.

The other side of the street to the *Delfini* is the:
Hotel Ikaros (*Tmr* B3) (Class E) 18 Leoharous   Tel 417 7094
Directions: As above.
   Only doubles, sharing the bathrooms, at a cost of 1600drs.

Hotel Elektra (*Tmr* 6B3) (Class E) 12 Navarinou.   Tel 417 7057
Directions: At the top of Leoharous St is the 'Esplanade parallel' Navarinou St, whereat turn right and the hotel is at the end of the block.
   Recommended as being comfortable, as well as convenient. During the season, a single room costs 1500drs & a double 1900drs (1st April-30th Sept), both sharing the bathroom.

Whilst in this neighbourhood, there are two smarter options. One is the relatively new *Hotel Acropole* (*Tmr* 30B3) (Class C, tel 417 4190), right at the junction of Navarinou and Gounari streets, and on   the right (*Fsw*). The other is across D Gounari St, on the north-east side of the Makras Stoas Market, the:
Hotel Triton (*Tmr* B3) (Class B) 8 Tsamadou   Tel 417 3457
Directions: As above,
A single room, sharing the bathrooms, costs 1900drs a night & with an en suite bathroom 2600drs, whilst a double room sharing is priced at 2800drs & en suite 3300drs.

At the 'opposite-end-of-the-rainbow' is the seedy, slovenly, but cheaper:
Hotel Aenos (Enos) (*Tmr* 31B2/3) 14 E Antistaseos   Tel 417 4879
Directions: From Odhos Navarinou cross over D Gounari St, along Odhos Tsamadou, as far as the junction with Ethniki Antistaseos, where turn left. The hotel is up the street, and on the right (*Sbo*).
An old Victorian style building, with high ceilings and bedrooms sharing the bathrooms. A single room costs 1000drs & a double 1500drs. On the way to the *Aenos*, along Ethniki Antistaseos St and on the corner of Tsamadou is another 'ancient', the *Hotel Kritikopoula* at No 21 Tsamadou (Class E, tel 417 5370). It has to be admitted that, in 1989, it had a rather 'dead' look about it.

For a rich (in numbers), if somewhat questionable sector, in and around the 'Old Quarter' of Piraeus, follow the quay road of Akti Posidonos and the waterfront of Akti Miaouli in a southerly direction, towards the Custom's office (*Tmr* 14B/C4/5). This passes by the:
Hotel Piraeus (*Tmr* B/C3/4) (Class D) 1 Bouboulinas   Tel 417 2950
Directions: As above, on the corner of the Esplanade and Odhos Bouboulinas.
A Victorian looking building, in which rooms, sharing the bathrooms,   cost 950drs for a single & 1330drs for a double.

Continuing south along Akti Miaouli, close by the Church of Ag Nikolaos is the outset of Leoforos Charilaou Trikoupi (*Tmr* C4). This   street runs east and is amply furnished with cheaper hotels, including the:
Capitol Hotel (*Tmr* 7C4) (Class C) Ch Trikoupi/147 Filonos   Tel 452 4911
Directions: As above and on the right, across the road from a cinema.
A single room costs 1800drs & a double room 2400drs, both with en suite bathrooms.

Ranged along Filonos St, which is wider and cleaner than the next, parallel street of Notara, are the:
Hotel Lux (Class E) 115 Filonos   Tel 452 0354
Directions: As above and on the right.
All rooms share the bathrooms, with a single priced at 790drs & a double 1130drs.

Hotel Adonis (Class D) 70 Filonos   Tel 452 0330
Directions: As above and on the left.
The minder is a gentleman of Far Eastern appearance, and the word is out that this establishment is popular with the more impecunious of the backpackers. A single costs 1100drs & a double 1600drs, both sharing the bathrooms.

Hotel Cavo (Class C) 79-81 Filonos   Tel 411 6134
Directions: As above and on the right, towards the north end of the street.
All rooms have en suite bathrooms, with a single costing 1950 drs & a double 2600drs.

Back down on Leoforos Charilaou Trikoupi, there are:
Glaros Hotel (Class C) 4 Ch Trikoupi   Tel 452 7887
Directions: As above.
Single rooms are en suite and start at 1700drs, while a double room, sharing a bathroom, costs 2020drs & en suite 2350drs. These charges rise, respectively, to 1870drs, & 2225/2585drs (15th June-31st Dec). A breakfast costs 325drs.

Serifos Hotel (Class C) 5 Ch Trikoupi   Tel 452 5075
Directions: As above.
A single room costs 1585drs & a double 2335drs, both with en suite bathrooms.

Santorini Hotel (Class C) 6 Ch Trikoupi   Tel 452 2147
Directions: As above,
All rooms have en suite bathrooms, with a single priced at 1700drs & doubles 2350drs, increasing to 1870drs & 2585drs (15th June-31st Dec).

The next side street off to the left of Leoforos Charilaou Trikoupi is Notara St, on which are sited the:
Hotel Atlantis (Class C) 138 Notara   Tel 452 6871
Directions: As above.
A single room is priced at 2200drs & a double 3000drs, all with en suite bathrooms.

Faros Hotel (Class D) 140 Notara   Tel 452 6317
Directions: As above.
All rooms have en suite bathrooms, with a single costing 1400drs & a double 1840drs, rising to 1450drs & 1940drs (1st July-31st Dec).

Hotel Ideal (Class C) 142 Notara   Tel 451 1727
Directions: As above.
All rooms have en suite bathrooms. A single costs 2500drs & a double 3100drs, increasing to 3500drs & 4400drs (1st June-30th Sept).

Again at right angles to Leoforos Charilaou Trikoupi, is Kolokotroni St, on which is, amongst others, the:
Aris Hotel (Class D) 117 Kolokotroni St.   Tel 452 0487
Directions: As above.
A single room, sharing a bathroom, is charged at 1130drs & with an en suite bathroom 1400drs. A double room, sharing, costs 1540drs & en suite 1900drs.

It will not go amiss to point out that a few of the accommodation opportunities here and abouts are nothing more than doss-houses for seamen and ladies of the night. Now please do not misunderstand me, I am of the opinion that most merchant men are the salt-of-the-air, but...!

For a complete change of ambiance, and price, those wishing to spend a leisurely time at Piraeus might consider staying on the east coast of the peninsula. It always seems to be sunny thereabouts (!), but the sheer volume of traffic that courses along the narrow road is a bit of a problem. From Limin Zeas Harbour, the Esplanade snakes along the coastal strip, passing the 'Town beach', **Stalis islet** close inshore, as well as the Royal Yacht Club of Greece and, on the inland side, the:

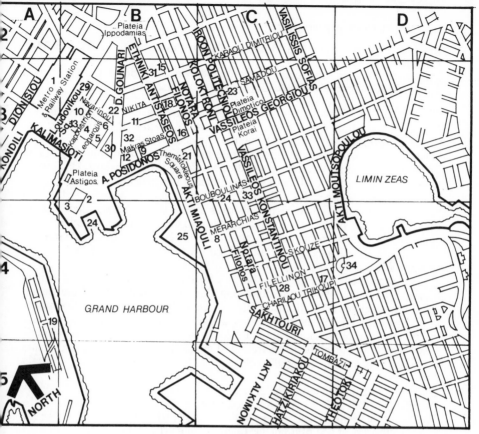

Tmr	
1A/B2/3	Metro & Peloponnese Railway Station
2A/B3/4	Plateia Astigos (Karaiskaki)
3A/B3/4	Port police
4B3	Hotel Ionian
5B3	Hotel Delfini
6B3	Hotel Elektra
7C4	Hotel Capitol
8B/C3/4	Olympic Airline Office
9B3	Macedonia & Thrace Bank
10	Bread shops
11B3	Main shopping St
12B3	J.S. Travel
13A/B3	Porto Ferry-boat Tickets
14B/C4/5	Customs Office
15B2/3	OTE
16B/C3	Ag Triada Cathedral
17C/D4	Archaeological Museum
18B/C3	Post Office
19A/B4/5	Northern Greece Railway Station Terminus
20E2	Delligiannis Taverna
21B/C3	Plateia Themistokleous
22B3	Ionian Bank
23B/C2/3	Town police
24A/B3/4	Aegina Hydrofoil dock
25B/C4	New passenger Ferry-boat terminal
26E4	Argo-Saronic/Peloponnese Hydrofoil dock
27D/E4	Naval Museum
28C4	Coin-op Launderette
29A/B3	Hotel Kentrikon
30B3	Hotel Acropole
31B2/3	Hotel Aenos
32B3	'Market' Square
33C3/4	'First Aid Station'
34C/D4	Ancient Theatre

Tmr = Town map reference
Fsw = Facing seawards
Sbo = Sea behind one
Fbqbo = Ferry-boat Quay behind one

Illustration 4 Piraeus inset

Hotel Cavo D'Oro (Class B) 19 Vassileos Pavlou Kastela   Tel 411 3742
Directions: As above.
Charges for their en suite rooms start off at 4800drs for a single & 6300drs for a double, increasing to 5700drs & 7560drs (1st May-31st Oct).

The Eating Out Piraeus is not noted for outstanding dining places around the Grand Harbour or the encircling terrain, despite the numerous restaurants, tavernas and cafes that line the quayside roads.
Apart from the cafe-bars ranged along the Plateia Astigos building (*Tmr* 2A/B3/4), the main streets, avenues and Esplanades are sprinkled with fast-food outfits. Some of the best value places are to found in and about the Makras Stoas Market Sq (*Tmr* 32B3). Returning to Plateia Astigos, a correspondent has confirmed that there is single storey, more modern building, to the rear of the one dominating the square. The latter contains a cafe snackbar, a waiting room and 'some of the cleanest loos in all of Greece'. Thus it is an ideal location for an 'on the spot, wash and brush up', before or after a ferry-boat trip.
To escape these generally lacklustre offerings, there are some excellent dining establishments spaced out along the eastern coastline of the peninsula, bounded by Akti Moutsopoulou (*Tmr* C/D3/4) and Akti Koumoundourou (*Tmr* E1/2) encircling (respectively) the Zeas and Mounikhias Harbours. The latter, more intimate location, with an 'off-the-main-drag', tree shaded, island harbour encircling Esplanade, has the tables and chairs of the various awning covered patios spread around the waterfront.

Especially recommended is the classy:
Delligiannis (*Tmr* 20E2) 1 Akti Koundouriotou.   Tel 413 2013
Directions: A very pleasant setting, in the 'pretty' part of Piraeus, up on the hill to the south-west of and overlooking Limin Mounikhias.
Apart from the position, the selection of food is excellent. There is outside seating, as well as that inside the look-alike for a high-class saloon bar. The service is quick, friendly and honest. For instance, enquirers will be advised that the 'souvlaki flambe' is nothing more than souvlaki on fire! 'Inside information' advises that the 'birds liver in wine' is delicious, despite being listed as a starter. The portions are larger than most main courses at other tavernas.

THE A TO Z OF USEFUL INFORMATION

AIRLINE OFFICE & TERMINUS (*Tmr* 8B/C3/4) The Olympic office is south and about halfway along the Esplanade, Akti Miaouli, on the corner of the junction with Odhos Merarchias. The office opens weekdays, between 0800-1900hrs, and Saturdays between 0800-1500hrs, but is closed on Sundays and 'idle days'.

BANKS The most impressive is the **Macedonia & Thrace** (*Tmr* 9B3), housed in a vast, imposing emporium which towers over the Esplanade Akti Posidonos. Should this establishment induce a state of awe, then in the same block is the **Commercial Bank**, which carries out all necessary transactions. Incidentally behind this 'Manhattan', tinted glass glitz hides away the Market. Around the corner, south along D Gounari St, and on the left (*Sbo*), is an **Ionion Bank** (*Tmr* 22B3). Bordering Plateia Loudovikou, the elongated square alongside the Metro Station (*Tmr* 1A/B2/3), is a **Credit Bank** (orange in colour) that deals in

Eurocheques and Visa transactions. A number of British banks have a presence, including Barclays, the Midland and the National Westminster, but they are at the International cruise liner, south end of the waterfront.

BEACHES There is a 100m long, broad stretch of beach (*Tmr* E2/3), between Zeas and Mounikhias Harbours, opposite Stalis islet. The shore is mainly pebble, with a sandy middle and backshore, and is fine for a bathe - if the general pollution of the bay can be ignored.

BREAD SHOPS They are quite widely spaced out, but one (*Tmr* 10A/B3) is conveniently situated by Loudovikou Sq. There are others: one almost directly across D Gounari St from the *Acropole* (*Tmr* 30B3), actually a General store; one on the corner of the junction of the side street, Odhos Dimothenous, and Akti Posidonos, to the west of the Macedonia Bank (*Tmr* 9B3), with yet another, only a few clothes shops further west on Akti Posidonos; and one more next door to the OTE (*Tmr* 15B2/3), on Karaoli Dimitriou St.

BUSES The two buses that circulate around the peninsula of Piraeus (in opposite directions) are the 904 and 905. The terminus for both buses is at Plateia Loudovikou (once Roosevelt Sq) alongside the Metro Terminus (*Tmr* 1A/B2/3).
No. 904 proceeds to Navarinou, Tsamadou, Leoforos Iroon Polytechniou, Chatzikyriakou, Ralli, Athanasiou, Akti Themistokleous, Akti Moutsopoulou, Lampraki, Leoforos Vassileos Georgiou. No. 905 proceeds to Navarinou, Tsamadou, Leoforos Vassileos Georgiou, Lampraki, Akti Moutsopoulou, Akti Themistokleous, Athanasiou, Ralli, Chatzikyriakou, Leoforos Iroon Polytechniou. Both buses 904 & 905 connect the Metro Station to the Zeas Marina Hydrofoil Quay (*Tmr* 26E4).
Plasteia Astigos (*Tmr* 2A/B3/4) is the 'Bus Sq' for the Express buses to both the West and East Airport Terminals. There is a Bus ticket office in the front of the large building bordering Plateia Astigos.
The 'Night Bus' No. 050 for Athinas or Akadimias Sts, Athens leaves from Sotirosdios/Filonos Sts, south of Plateia Themistokleous (*Tmr* 21 B/C3).

Trolley Buses
No 16   Drosopoulou (Ag Triada Cathedral, *Tmr* 16B/C3), Ag Ioannis Rentis (NE Piraeus suburb).

No 17   Skouze St, Akti Miaouli, Ag Georgios (NW Piraeus suburb).

No 20   Skylitsi (Neo Faliro), Leoforos Vas Pavlou, Akti Kountourioti, Leoforos Vas Georgiou, Akti Kondili, Drapetsona (W Piraeus suburb).

COMMERCIAL SHOPPING AREA There is a flourishing, noisy, busy Market and Market Square (*Tmr* 32B3), in the area bounded by Odhos Makras Stoas (behind the *Macedonia Bank*), and D Gounari St. Adjacent to the Market Square is an excellent Supermarket on the corner of Odhos Makras Stoas, useful for the shopper who cannot be bothered to visit the various Market shops and stalls. The right-hand (*Sbo*), south end of D Gounari St is awash with provisions stores, and Odhos Tsamadou (*Tmr* 11B3) is a main shopping street.
Towards the D Gounari St end of Navarinou St, on the north side of the road and close to the *Sparti*, is what I can only describe as a Drinks Supermarket (*Tmr* B3). Established in 1932, the choice and prices are absolutely excellent, if not unrivalled, and the owners/staff are most helpful. For those with a container,

they have a wide range of 'from the barrel' possibilities.
Prices in Piraeus are generally higher than elsewhere in Greece and shop hours are the 'standard' for large cities.

FERRY-BOATS Most island ferry-boats leave from the quayside that stretches between Akti Kondili (at the north end of the Grand Harbour), via Plateia Astigos and Akti Posidonos, round to Akti Miaouli (towards the south end of the Grand Harbour). As a general rule, the craft for Crete depart from the area of Akti Miaouli (*Tmr* B/C4), towards the south end.

Ferry-boat timetables (Mid-season)

Daily	Departure time	Ferry-boat	Ports/Islands of Call
Daily	1830hrs	Festos/N Kazantzakis	Iraklion.
	1900hrs	Kriti/Rethymno	Iraklion.
	1900hrs	Lissos/Aptera	Souda(Chania).
Mon	0830hrs	Daliana	Naxos, Ios, Santorini, Iraklion.
	1700hrs	Olympia	Paros, Amorgos, Astipalaia, Kalimnos, Kos, Nisiros, Tilos, Simi, Rhodes, Chalki, Karpathos, Kasos, Sitia(Crete), Ag Nikolaos(Crete).
	1930hrs	Arkadi	Rethymnon.
Tues	1300hrs	Daliana	Santorini, Iraklion, (& on to Karpathos & Rhodes).
Wed	1930hrs	Arkadi	Rethymnon.
Thurs	1600hrs	Daliana	Paros, Santorini, Iraklion (& on to Karpathos & Rhodes).
	1930hrs	Arkadi	Rethymnon
Fri	0900hrs	Ionian	Kiparissia(M), Gerakas(M), Monemvassia(M), Neapolis(M), Ag Pelagia(Kithira), Githion(M), Kapsali(Kithira), Antikithira, Kastelli.
	1300hrs	Olympia	Milos, Folegandros, Sikinos, Santorini, Anafi, AgNikolaos (Crete), Sitia(Crete), (& on to Kasos, Karpathos, Chalki & Rhodes).
	1845hrs	Ierapetra	Milos, AgNikolaos(Crete), Sitia(Crete).
	1930hrs	Arkadi	Rethymnon.
Sat	0800hrs	Aptera	Souda(Chania).
Sat	2000hrs	Knossos	Iraklion.
	2030hrs	Daliana	Naxos, Ios, Santorini, Iraklion.
Sun	0730hrs	Rethymnon	Iraklion.
	0800hrs	Aptera	Souda(Chania).

One-way fares: from 2488drs; duration from 12hrs (direct).

Also *See* the individual, north Crete city chapters, BUT NOTE that their details were 'culled' in 1989, whilst Piraeus has been finalised from early season 1990 information. Yes, well! Differences are noticeable. A 'for-example' is that this timetable only lists one Piraeus - Kastelli connection, but the Kastelli chapter lists two a week, which will be the case between June and September!

FERRY-BOAT TICKET OFFICES Without doubt, they are 'extremely thick' on the waterfront. Ticket sellers 'lie in wait', all the way from Akti Kalimasioti, past Plateia Astigos and along the Esplanade of Akti Posidonos, as well as along the various side-streets that branch off from them, more especially D Gounari and Ethniki Antistaseos.

My favourite offices continue to be the same two, geographically not far from each other, but poles apart in presentation and style. They are:

Jannis Stoulis Travel (*Tmr* 12B3) 2 D Gounari   Tel 417 9491
Directions: On the right (*Sbo*) of the outset of D Gounari St.

The owner, who has a rather disinterested air, is extremely efficient and speaks three languages, including English. Business has been good enough to allow the employment of a manager. The doors open Monday-Friday, between 0900-1900hrs, and Saturdays, between 0900-1430hrs.

His fast talking, ever-smiling, 'Speedy Gonzales' counterpart is now dressed in a sharp suit and occupies a carpeted, as distinct from a linoleumed, wall-to-wall stairway, alongside Akti Kalimasioti (*Tmr* 13A/B3). It has to admitted that my regard for the latter operator is entirely due to the fact that he was the man who sold me my first-ever Greek island ferry-boat ticket, more years ago than I am willing to concede.

There are 'batches' of ticket offices spaced out around the ground floor of the Plateia Astigos Building (*Tmr* 2A/B3/4), as well as a 'reader recommended' firm in the Metro Station concourse (*Tmr* 1A/B2/3). Those prospects aimlessly wandering along the quayside may be accosted by an enterprising vendor of tickets who lurks, from early morning, on Akti Posidonos.

It is probably best to make enquiries about the exact location of a particular ferry's departure point, prior to actually handing over cash for the tickets. It has to be admitted the vendors tend to refer to a ship's point of departure with an airy wave of the hand. When searching the quayside, do not go beyond the junction of Kondili and Kalimasioti, to the north, or the Port offices & Custom house (*Tmr* 14B/C4/5), to the south. A comparatively new facility is the Passenger Terminal (*Tmr* 25B/C4), to the sea-wall side of Akti Miaouli. The waiting room is up a shallow flight of steps, whilst the basement reveals evidence of an information/ Tourist police office, which, unfortunately, appears 'dead'.

HYDROFOILS (Flying Dolphins or Ceres) Apart from their 'speed of delivery', which is up to half as quick again as the quicker of the ferry-boats, these craft are well equipped with lavatories, a small snackbar, as well as central and aft viewing platforms. Unfortunately the speed has to be paid for, and the fares are in excess of double that of the same 3rd class ferry-boat tickets. Another general problem is that the hydrofoils are used by various package holiday firms, in order to transport their clients to, for instance, the Argo-Saronic islands of Poros, Hydra and Spetses. But the early bird should get a seat. A more specific point is that this service does not go any further south than Kithira island. On the other hand they can be used to pick up the particular ferry-boat, that runs down the eastern coast of the Peloponnese on its journey to Crete, at one of the jointly serviced mainland ports, or Kithira. The ports of 'cross-pollination' take in the Peloponnese harbours of Kiparissi, Gerakas, Monemvassia and Neapoli, as well as Ag Pelagia (Kithira island).

The Argo-Saronic/Peloponnese terminus (*Tmr* 26E4) is at Limin Zeas Harbour. It is conveniently overlooked by the patio of a large,   modern cafe-bar/ restaurant/zacharoplasteion, which is open during the essential hours of the Flying Dolphins' operation. Mind you it is not   inexpensive. A breakfast is served, but I have never been able to save enough to indulge this fancy... One plus point is that the ladies toilets are very clean, even if the gentlemens' is not so spotless.

Hydrofoil Timetable.

Day	Departure time	Ports/Islands of Call
Tues,Thurs Sat, Sun	0900hrs	Kiparissi, Monemvassia.
Tues, Sat Thur, Sun	0900hrs	Gerakas.
Tues, Sat	0900hrs	Ag Pelagia(Kithira), Neapoli.

One-way fares to:				
Kiparissi	3071	drs; duration	3hrs	35mins
Gerakas	3071	;	4hrs	5mins
Monemvassia	3857	;	4hrs	25mins
Kithira	4923	;	5hrs	30mins
Neapoli	4223	;	5hrs	45mins

HYDROFOIL TICKET OFFICES The main booking office (*Tmr* B/C3/4) is at No 8 Akti Themistokleous (Tel 452 7107), but tickets can be purchased at ticket huts, close to the departure point.

LAUNDRY There is a Coin-op Launderette (*Tmr* 28C4) on the 'up', or south side of Kolokotroni St, between Filelinon and Charilaou Trikoupi Sts, at No 133.

LUGGAGE STORE This facility has an incredibly garish hallway, and is on the north corner of the Plateia Astigos building (*Tmr* 2A/B3/4).

MEDICAL CARE Apart from the usual chemists, there is a 'First Aid Station' (*Tmr* 33C3/4), alongside a square bounded by Leoforos Vassileos Konstantinou (Iroon Politechniou), and the streets of Kolokotroni and Bouboulinas.

METRO *See* **Arrival by Metro, Introduction.** Purchasers of a ticket   must validate it in the ticket machine - or face a fine of 600drs.

NTOG Apart from the 'maybe-maybe not' office, in the basement of the Ferry-boat passenger terminal (*Tmr* 25B/C4), for details of which see **Ferry-boat Ticket offices,** there is, or was, a somewhat inconveniently situated facility at Limin Zeas Harbour (*Tmr* D3/4).   This is on the way round to the Hydrofoil dock, but if and when it functions, it only does so weekdays, between 0700-1500hrs.

OTE (*Tmr* 15B2/3) The office is north of the Post Office, on Karaoli Dimitriou St, close to Filonos St. It is open seven days a week, 24hrs a day.

PLACES OF INTEREST
Archaeological Museum (*Tmr* 17C/D4) Situated between Filellinon and Leoforos Charilaou Trikoupi Sts. Well laid out, with easy to identify   exhibits. Open daily, between 0830-1500hrs, but closed on Mondays, with entrance costing 200drs.

Ag Triada Cathedral (*Tmr* 16B/C3) The Cathedral was rebuilt in the early 1960s, having been destroyed in 1944. It has a distinctive, mosaic tile finish.

Battleship Averoff This legendary craft, dear to the Greek nation, is now located at the **Paleon Faliron Marina**, along the coast to the east of Piraeus. The Averoff was moored alongside the Naval School at Poros island, for some years. The boat and its fame perhaps, helps to illustrate the Greeks' need for tangible proof of their modern, military might. The Italian built warship was purchased in 1911, with the help of a bequest from the philanthropist George Averoff, who had made his money from the British, in Egypt. The vessel was rather out of date by the First World War, but joined in sea battles against the Turks, between 1912-13, at Eli and Limnos. During the Second World War it was loaned to the Allies and carried out escort duty in the Indian Ocean, to be 'pensioned off' in 1945. I wonder what the Greeks would have done with, say, the *Hood* or the *Ark Royal*? The ship can be viewed Tues-Sat between 0900-1230hrs, with entrance costing 50drs. Those intending to visit should note that these opening hours are subject to alteration.

Ancient Theatre (*Tmr* 34C/D4) Adjacent to the Archaeological Museum, close to Limin Zeas Harbour. The remains date from the second century BC.

Limin Zeas (Pasalimani) (*Tmr* D3/4) The semicircular harbour is of great antiquity, but is now lined by expensive, high-rise buildings. The port shelters fishing boats and caiques; provides a marina basin for the larger, modern yachts, some of them extremely expensive boats; contains a Hydrofoil terminal; as well as a base for yacht charterers. Immediately south of the harbour is a small triangle of sand and pebble beach. In addition to the NTOG office, there is a National Bank which transacts all exchange requirements. For some unknown reason, about half-way round the perimeter of the Esplanade, circling the harbour, is yet another old-time railway carriage on display. Our British Rail Southern Region travellers would probably be quite glad to commute in a piece of rolling stock of this modernity...! Excavations have shown that, in ancient times, there were several hundred boat sheds radiating out around the water-front. These were used to house the *triremes*, the great, three-banked warships.

The Naval Museum of Greece (*Tmr* 27D/E4) Tucked into a horseshoe of land bounded by the Esplanade Akti Themistoleous and the south end of Limin Zeas Harbour. Naturally, displaying varied exhibits of naval history, through the ages.

Limin Mounikhias (Tourkolimano or Mikrolimano) (*Tmr* E2). From Limin Zeas, continue north-east along the constricted, winding, coast hugging Esplanade. The road passes the bathing beach, in the lee of tiny, inshore Stalis islet, and the signposted turning down to the Royal Yacht Club of Greece. The main road circles about 50m above the attractive, intimate, quayside promenade that edges the semi-circular, old Turkish harbour. The picturesque waterside is tree shaded and 'chattily' ringed with awning covered patios of the cafe-bars, tavernas and restaurants, the latter forming a backcloth to the multi-coloured sails of the assembled yachts crowded into Limin Mounikhias. Racing yachts are believed to have slipped their moorings for regattas in Saroniko Bay, as far back as the 4th century BC, as they do to this day.

The Hill of Kastela overlooks the harbour and has a modern, open-air, marble amphitheatre, wherein theatre and dance displays are staged, more especially during the Athens Festival.

Parks There are a number of greenswards. One of these is a narrow garden area, more an enclosure, bounded by the streets of Merarchias and Kolokotroni, wherein are some deer and goats, 'banged up' in pens.

Illustration 5 The Peloponnese

POLICE
Port (*Tmr* 3A/B3/4) Tucked away behind the Plateia Astigos building.
Tourist & Town (*Tmr* 23B/C2/3) To the north of Plateia Dimotico, in amongst various other Municipal buildings and offices.

POST OFFICE (*Tmr* 18B/C3) The main office is on the corner of Tsamadou and Filonos Sts, north-west of the Cathedral. There is another office in the Metro (Tmr 1C1/2) concourse, but rather hidden by some stalls, and only open between 0730-1415hrs.

RAILWAY STATIONS *See* Arrival by Metro & Arrival by Train.
Metro (Underground) (*Tmr* 1A/B2/3).
'Steam' Station 1 (*Tmr* 1A/B2/3) The terminus for the Peloponnese, which is on the far, north side of the Metro.
'Steam' Station 2 (*Tmr* 19A/B4/5) The terminus for Northern Greece, situated on the far, west side of the Grand Harbour.

TAXIS They rank at all the major places and squares.

TELEPHONE NUMBERS & ADDRESSES

NTOG (*Tmr* D3/4) Zeas Marina	Tel 413 5716
Port Authorities	Tel 451 1311
Taxi rank	Tel 417 8138

TOILETS There are some old fashioned, large 'door-gap', 'squatties' in the Metro concourse (*Tmr* 1A/B2/3).

The Peloponnese Port For Crete

GITHION (Githio, Gythion, Yithion) (Illustration 6) Tel prefix 0733.
This spacious, very clean, pleasant port is spread out along the west side of a bay, at the foot of Mt Larysion. In fact, it is perhaps rather larger than might be imagined, thus less intimate, but still retains a village ambiance. The north end, especially in the area of the Town Hall is very reminiscent of Ag Konstantinos on the west mainland coast, whilst the south end is similar to Paralia Kymi on Evia island east coast. Historically Githion was the port for the Spartan empire, and still is the harbourage for the once mysterious region of the Mani.* (*See* **Places of Interest, A To Z**).
* *Essential reading is* Mani by Patrick Leigh Fermor, Penguin Travel Library. *Also try* The Flight of the Ikaros Eagle by Kevin Andrew, Penguin.
   Mythologically of interest, around the 'corner' from the Ferry-boat Quay (*Tmr* 2D4), is the elongated, pine tree shaded islet of Kranai or Marathonisi, now joined to the Esplanade by a walled causeway. It is said that in a boat offshore of this islet, that unprincipled Paris (of Troy) had his wicked way with one Helen. Yes, she of the face that... In any case, back to the salacious bit, which was a teeny-weeny bit unchappish as Helen was married to another, one Menelaus. This was one of those acts of 'nooky' that had far-reaching effects, setting in motion the apocalyptic Trojan War. Despite its diminutive size, this islet experienced a remarkably expansive slice of history. For instance it was the site of the ancient city of Kranai; it was a Phoenician trading post; and the Spartans constructed the town of

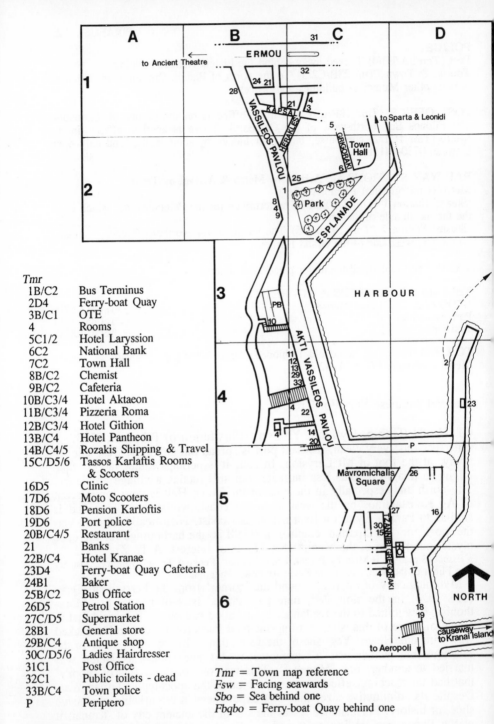

Tmr	
1B/C2	Bus Terminus
2D4	Ferry-boat Quay
3B/C1	OTE
4	Rooms
5C1/2	Hotel Laryssion
6C2	National Bank
7C2	Town Hall
8B/C2	Chemist
9B/C2	Cafeteria
10B/C3/4	Hotel Aktaeon
11B/C3/4	Pizzeria Roma
12B/C3/4	Hotel Githion
13B/C4	Hotel Pantheon
14B/C4/5	Rozakis Shipping & Travel
15C/D5/6	Tassos Karlaftis Rooms & Scooters
16D5	Clinic
17D6	Moto Scooters
18D6	Pension Karloftis
19D6	Port police
20B/C4/5	Restaurant
21	Banks
22B/C4	Hotel Kranae
23D4	Ferry-boat Quay Cafeteria
24B1	Baker
25B/C2	Bus Office
26D5	Petrol Station
27C/D5	Supermarket
28B1	General store
29B/C4	Antique shop
30C/D5/6	Ladies Hairdresser
31C1	Post Office
32C1	Public toilets - dead
33B/C4	Town police
P	Periptero

Tmr = Town map reference
Fsw = Facing seawards
Sbo = Sea behind one
Fbqbo = Ferry-boat Quay behind one

Illustration 6 Githion

Las, with many shrines and temples, the archaeological remains of which are still extant. Perhaps most interesting is the enduring structure that we would call a 'folly', but was actually a refuge tower, a life or death relic of the Mani of yesteryear. This has been restored and is scheduled to house a folk museum. It once belonged to the Mavronichalis family, who achieved notoriety as one of their number assassinated the first Greek president, Ioannis Kapodistras, in 1831.

ARRIVAL BY AIR The nearest airport, with daily flights to and from Athens, is at Kalamata (about 107km distant).

ARRIVAL BY BUS There is a daily, through bus to Athens, via Sparta. For those disembarking at the northern Peloponnese port of Patras, buses proceed, via Pirgos, to Kalamata. Buses from Kalamata to Githion, route via inland Sparta or coastal Itilo. It may be necessary to change at either town. There is also a daily bus link between Githion and the east coast port of Monemvassia, to connect with the Argo-Saronic hydrofoils.

ARRIVAL BY FERRY A summer months Piraeus ferry-boat docks twice a week and proceeds to Kastelli (Crete), via Kithira (Kapsali) and Antikithira. This craft also calls in on the way back from Kastelli to Piraeus.

ARRIVAL BY HYDROFOIL (Flying Dolphin) None call at Githion but it is possible to connect by bus with the east coast port of Monemvassia, which has a daily hydrofoil service to and from Zea Port (Piraeus).

ARRIVAL BY TRAIN Here again there isn't a direct service but our 'old friend', the circular Peloponnese route has train stops at the branch line port of Kalamata, as well as inland Tripoli. From either of these towns, buses can be used to travel to Githion, the Tripoli bus via Kalamata.

THE ACCOMMODATION & EATING OUT Githion is well endowed with accommodation, as it is with run-of-the-mill restaurant/tavernas.
The Accommodation There is a very satisfying mix of hotels and *Rooms*. Radiating out from the Bus area (*Tmr* 1B/C2) are:

Rooms (*Tmr* 4B/C1)
Directions: Along the side-street, Odhos Herakles, which angles north-east from Leoforos Vassileos Pavlou, and just beyond the OTE (*Tmr* 3B/C1).
A neat, very nice looking, three storey house, part clad with a lovely spread of bougainvillea.

Hotel Laryssion (*Tmr* 5C1/2) (Class C) 7 I Grigoraki   Tel 22021
Directions: Proceed east along the well tree'd park, and at the first side-street, Odhos I Grigoraki, turn left between the National Bank (*Tmr* 6C2) and the Town Hall (*Tmr* 7C2). The hotel is on the left.
A rather swish, C class hotel, all rooms having en suite bathrooms. A single room costs 2500drs & a double 3150drs, respectively, increasing to 3000drs & 3700drs (1st July-31st Aug).

Advancing south, along Leoforos Vassileos Pavlou, and on the right are a row of houses, in amongst which is:-
Rooms (*Tmr* 4B/C2) Leoforos Vassileos Pavlou.
Directions: As above, straddled by a Pharmacy (*Tmr* 8B/C2) and a Cafeteria (*Tmr* 9B/C2), and up a steep, short flight of steps in between the buildings.

Still in a southerly direction, almost immediately beyond the point at which the Esplanade and Vassileos Pavlou merge, on the right is the:
Hotel Aktaeon (*Tmr* 10B/C3/4) (Class D)   Tel 22294
Directions: As above and an old-fashioned, provincial building, almost stretching from the Esplanade to the narrow street behind, which courses along the steep hillside. Some of the front ground floor is occupied by shops and the entrance is up a very sheer flight of steps on the far, south side of the hotel. The ground floor rooms at the back are on the same level as the Esplanade facing first floor bedrooms, the latter having grandiose balconies, from which there are superb harbour views.
Most rooms share bathrooms, from about 2050drs & doubles 2500drs.

Further along the Esplanade is the *Pizzeria Roma* (*Tmr* 11B/C3/4), with a sign in the window for 'Gellys Apartments & Rooms'. Next door is the:
Hotel Githion (*Tmr* 12B/C3/4) (Class A) Vassileos Pavlou   Tel 23523
Directions: As above.
Only quite swish, double rooms, with en suite bathrooms, costing from 3000drs & increasing to 4000drs (1st July-19th Sept).

P.S. Don't miss the rather lovely example of an overhanging balcony, to the south of the *Githion*, prior to the very smart:
Hotel Pantheon (*Tmr* 13B/C4) (Class C) 33 Vassileos Pavlou   Tel 22284
Directions: As above.
All rooms have en suite bathrooms, singles commencing at 2900drs & doubles 3350drs, increasing, respectively, to 3445 & 3740drs (1st April-30th June & 16th Sept-31st Oct) and 4150 & 4400drs (1st July-15th Sept).

Continuing south passes a very wide flight of steps, on the left of which, about half-way up, is *Rooms* (*Tmr* 4B/C4). A metre or so further on is the:
Hotel Kranae (*Tmr* 22B/C4) (Class D) 15 Vassileos Pavlou   Tel 22249
Directions: As above.
'Air Conditioned'. Well it may be, but all rooms have to share the bathrooms, with singles priced at 2000drs & doubles 3000drs.

Next along a few paces is a narrow, stepped alley. This climbs to a 'bit of' a rabbit-warren in which is a **Rooms** (*Tmr* 4B/C4/5).

Back at the Esplanade and close to where the waterfront wall angles sharply towards the Ferry-boat Quay, is the business and office of one of the most important men in town - that of Rozakis Shipping and Travel (*Tmr* 14B/C4/5), of whom more later. The Esplanade parallels the quay wall round to the left (*Town Hall behind one*) to the busy, small Plateia Mavromichalis. Branching off the south of the Square are a number of narrow streets. One of these is Odhos Tzannibi Gregoraki, which gently climbs towards a prominent church, and is bordered by:
Tassos Karlaftis Rooms (& Scooters) (*Tmr* 15C/D5/6) T Gregoraki   Tel 22504
Directions: On the right of the street (*Sbo*).
Traditional 'island' rooms at average prices.

Just around the corner, opposite the church is:-
Rooms (*Tmr* 4C/D6)
Directions: As above and over a Bakers, in a very village area of the town.
Double rooms, sharing the bathroom, start off at about 1400drs.

Following the Esplanade round, past the Ferry-boat Quay, a large Clinic (*Tmr* 16D5), and beyond a Moto Scooter Hire firm (*Tmr* 17D6), are a row of at least five Pensions/Rooms, one of which is the:

Pension Karlaftis (*Tmr* 18D6)   Tel 22719
Directions: As above.
Comes well recommended as a lovingly looked after, spotless, and homely option. Double rooms, sharing the bathrooms, start off at 1550drs.

A last but not least option is to ascend the flight of steps, beyond the Port police office (*Tmr* 19D6) and almost opposite the causeway to Kranai/Marathonisi islet. There are clean, welcoming **Rooms**, to left and right.

Camping The four or five sites are south of Githion, starting at about 3km distant. For those who don't wish to walk, either catch the Areopoli bus, and get off as close to Mavrovouni as possible, or one of the several buses a day which incorporate all the campsites *en route*. That is except the Vathy sites of Kronos and Porto Ageranos, to which it is necessary to walk 3-4km, beyond the last bus stop on the route.

Campsites include: **Meltemi** (Class A, tel 22833); **(Hellenic) Camping Githion Beach** (Class C, tel 23441); **Mani Beach** (Class C, tel 23450); **Kronos** (Class C, tel 24124) & **Porto Ageranos** (Class C, tel 22039). All are 'on the beach', open April to October, and boast varying amenities.

The Eating Out The majority of the fish tavernas are lined up bordering the inland side of the Esplanade, between the Clinic (*Tmr* 16D5) and the Ferry-boat Quay (*Tmr* 2D4). There are plenty of zacharoplasteions and kafeneions, the latter concentrated around Plateia Mavromichalis. Apart from the fish tavernas, fairly centrally located is a:

Restaurant (*Tmr* 20B/C4/5)
Directions: Across the Esplanade from the change of direction in the waterfront Esplanade, from east/west to south/north. The establishment is alongside a narrow, stepped alley, close by Rozakis Shipping & Travel.
Average fare at reasonable prices but no itemised bills. A meal, for two, of briam (good & plentiful), stuffed pepper & tomato (with a 'suggestion' of 3 chips each), a kortaki retsina, and bread, totalled 1400drs.

Another possibility is the **Pizzeria Roma** (*Tmr* 11B/C3/4) but the most reasonable offerings are rumoured to be to the north of the town.
Quite convenient to the Bus office is a Cafeteria (*Tmr* 9B/C2), whilst another (*Tmr* 23D4) handily lurks on the Ferry-boat Quay.

THE A TO Z OF USEFUL INFORMATION
AIRLINE OFFICE There isn't an Olympic office, but our old friend **Rozakis Shipping & Travel** (*Tmr* 14B/C4/5 - *See* **Ferry-boat Ticket Offices, A To Z**), is

a 'hot potato' in this field of activity. The nearest airfield is at Kalamata, whence bus connections, but note this choice of route, coming from Athens, requires an overnight stop at Kalamata.

Aircraft timetable (Mid-season)
Athens to Kalamata (& vice versa)
Daily   1940hrs
Return
Daily   2100hrs
One-way fare 4500drs; duration 35mins.

BANKS The National Bank (*Tmr* 6C2) is to the north of the port, and   cashes Eurocheques. In the same (commercial) area there are some two or three other banks (*Tmr* 21B/C1). If all else fails proceed to **Rozakis** (*Tmr* 14B/C4/5), noting he charges some 2% commission.

BEACHES The main beach, of grey sand but shadeless, with a pebble sea's edge and sea-bed, is almost exactly 1.6km north of town.
   Further on climbs past a very 1930s, circular restaurant topping a headland, to reveal, down below, another stretch of beach, also without shade. The foreshore is, in the main, angled rock. The most noteworthy item is a 'dead', but upright, rust flaked and fire ravaged merchant ship, hove to at the water's edge.
   The best beaches are to the south of Githion, spread along the first four kilometres or so of the coastline.

BICYCLE, SCOOTER & CAR HIRE Centrally located is **Tassos' 'Super Cycle Moto For Rent'** (*Tmr* 15C/D5/6), close by Plateia Mavromichalis, whilst bordering the Esplanade, south of the Ferry-boat Quay, is **Moto Scooter Hire** (*Tmr* 17D6, tel 22853). Average daily scooter hire rates are 1500drs, with a 10drs surcharge per kilometre for those who exceed 100km. Both outfits appear to take a long siesta and a day's hire is between 0900-2000hrs, not 24 hours.

BOOKSELLER There is a Newspaper shop in the front of the *Aktaeon* (*Tmr* 10B/C3/4), but printed matter doesn't get cheaper - a reasonable map costs 1000drs and a quality English paperback some 2680drs.

BREAD SHOPS There is a Baker (*Tmr* 24B1) in the 'northern quarter', close to the junction of Leoforos Vassileos Pavlou and Odhos Kapsali. A small, round loaf costs 60drs. Just to balance matters up, there is a Baker (*Tmr* 4C/D6), to the south of Plateia Mavromichalis.

BUSES The Bus office (*Tmr* 25B/C2) edges Leoforos Vassileos Pavlou, across the road from a park planted with numerous trees.
   A full service allows links with most Peloponnese locations, and Athens.

Bus timetable (Mid-season)
Athens to Githion (Athens Terminal: 100 Kifissou St, tel 512913)
Daily   0945, 1215, 1550, 1815hrs
One-way fare 1750drs; duration 6½hrs.
Note, that Patras port connects with Kalamata, not Githion.

Patras to Kalamata
Daily   0700, 1430hrs
Return journey
Daily   0700, 1430hrs
One-way fare 1400drs; duration 4 hrs.

Githion to Kalamata (via Sparta)
Daily   0730, 1215hrs

Githion to Kalamata (via Areopoli/Itilo)
Daily   0600, 1315hrs
Return journey
Daily   0515, 0730, 1300hrs
Duration 2½hrs.

Githion to Gerolimenas (South Mani) (via Areopoli)
Daily   1315, 1930hrs
Duration 2hrs.

Githion to Monemvassia
Daily   0845, 1430hrs
Return journey
Daily   1115, 1710hrs
Duration 2hrs.

*Note: The Tripoli railway halt allows between two and four bus connections   with
Sparta and Kalamata, both of which link with Githion. There are some five buses a day
from Sparta to Githion.*

COMMERCIAL SHOPPING AREA Plateia Mavromichalis is bordered by
shops, mainly vendors of fish as well as fruit & vegetables. On the left of Odhos
Tzannibi Gregoraki, which climbs from the south side of the Square, is a small,
'swept up' Supermarket (*Tmr* 27C/D5). In stark contrast, and at the other end of
town, on the left of Leoforos Vassileos Pavlou, is a dusty, inexpensive General
Store (*Tmr* 28B1). A Periptero (*Tmr* P) is across the Esplanade from the Petrol
Station (*Tmr* 26D5).
    Although the usual antique or gift shop would not be included in the book, it is
a joy to list the excellent Antique (and junk) emporium (*Tmr* 29B/C4)), next
door to the *Pantheon*. Opening hours are a bit of a mystery!

FERRY-BOATS The very old-fashioned **CF Ionian**, which makes a twice weekly
visit, has second-class, 4 berth cabins in which male and female passengers are
kept segregated. It does at least ensure that the chaps can enjoy the sleep of the
just, whilst the women and (screaming) children are quite rightly kept apart, in
purdah. The time of night that the ship docks results in little or no food or drink
being available at the snackbar.

Ferry-boat timetable (Mid-season)

Day	Departure time	Ferry-boat	Ports/Islands of Call
Mon	2400hrs	Ionian	Kapsali(Kithira), Antikithira, Kastelli(Crete).
Thurs	2300hrs	Ionian	Kapsali(Kithira), Antikithira, Kastelli(Crete).
Fri	1500hrs	Ionian	Ag Pelagia(Kithira), Piraeus(M).
Sat	2230hrs	Ionian	Ag Pelagia(Kithira), Neapoli(M), Monemvassia(M), Piraeus(M).

One-way fares: Githion	to Kapsali (Kithira)	460drs; duration	3hrs
	to Kastelli(Kitira)	1850drs;	7hrs
	to Ag Pelagia (Kithira)	460drs;	2hrs
	to Neapoli	780drs;	4hrs
	to Monemvassia	1130drs;	6hrs
	to Piraeus(M)	2290drs;	13hrs

FERRY-BOAT TICKET OFFICES Only the ubiquitous Mr Big, the splendid Theodore   Rozakis Esq., who runs:

Rozakis Shipping & Travel (*Tmr* 14B/C4/5) 6 Vassileos Pavlou   Tel 22207
Directions: Towards the south end of the Esplanade.
   This old-fashioned, brown painted, wood-panelled office is the lair of the mature (okay, well-advanced in years) Mr Rozakis, who is very helpful, know- ledgeable and speaks excellent English. He not only acts for the **Ionian**, but many other ferry-boat routes throughout Greece, Olympic   Airways, as well as exchanging money. One activity strictly prohibited is the storage of luggage. The office opens daily, between 0830-1300hrs & 1700-2100hrs.

HAIRDRESSERS There is a Ladies Hairdresser (*Tmr* 30C/D5/6) on Odhos Tzannibi Gregoraki, south of Plateia Mavromichalis.

MEDICAL CARE
Chemists & Pharmacies They are plentiful, with a couple spaced either side of the Baker (*Tmr* 24B1) and another (*Tmr* 8B/C2) close to the Bus   office, on Leoforos Vassileos Pavlou.
Clinic (*Tmr* 16D5) A large building bordering the Esplanade, south of the Ferry-boat Quay.

OTE (*Tmr* 3B/C1) At No 8, and close to the junction of Kapsali and Herakles Sts, in the north section of the town. The office is a bit of a muddle and   only opens weekdays, between 0730-2000hrs.

PETROL A Petrol Station (*Tmr* 26D5) is located close to the Ferry-boat Quay.

PLACES OF INTEREST The back road paralleling the north-south Esplanade, but higher up, on the hillside, has some extremely interesting architecture dotted about along its length. To have an overall view of the port and bay, climb the hill side behind the town, Mt Larysiou, on which is an ancient acropolis.
Ancient Theatre At the north end of town, left along Ermou St, west of the Post Office (*Tmr* 31C1), then right along Odhos Archain Theatrou, and round an Army Camp. A lovely but unsung site, with much of the stone seating in place.
Museum A new building is planned but... at the moment the exhibits are stored close by the *Laryssion* (*Tmr* 5C1/2).

POLICE
Port (*Tmr* 19D6) Their office borders the Esplanade, close to the Kranai/ Marathonisi islet causeway.
Town (*Tmr* 33B/C4) The 'cop-shop', which edges Akti Vassileos Pavlou, some 75m north of the 'U' of the harbour, is easily identifiable by a circular, traffic style sign on the edge of the pavement.

POST OFFICE (*Tmr* 31C1) On the far, north side of Ermou St. There is also a Post box let into the facade of the *Aktaeon* (*Tmr* 10B/C3/4).

TOILETS There is a very dead public convenience (*Tmr* 32C1), plonked down in a large 'bomb-site', which has obviously been cleared of old buildings.

TRAINS The circular, single line railway track of the Peloponnese does not come to Githion, but does link to Kalamata and Tripoli. For Bus connections *See* Bus timetables, A To Z.

Train timetable
Kalamata to Athens

Daily	Kalamata	2250, 0640, 0830, 1516hrs
	Tripoli	* 0133, 0934, 1113, 1744hrs
	Argos	0252, 1102, 1235, 1902hrs
	Corinth	0353, 1209, 1341, 1959hrs
	Athens	0542, 1404, 1540, 2140hrs
* Next day.		

Athens (Stathmos No. 2) to Kalamata

Daily	Athens	0707, 1212, 1348, 2255hrs.
	Corinth	0850, 1405, 1540, 0041hrs*
	Argos	0946, 1506, 1645, 0140hrs
	Tripoli	1108, 1637, 1818, 0306hrs
	Kalamata	1341, 1933, 2100, 0550hrs

TRAVEL AGENTS & TOUR OFFICES *See* Rozakis Shipping & Travel, Ferry-boat Ticket Offices, A To Z.

EXCURSION TO THE PELOPONNESE SURROUNDS

Excursion to Kalamata With all the wealth of archaeological sites at one's disposal this may seem a strange first off choice... but all will become plain. Catch the bus via Areopoli/Itilo. Areopoli gives access to the road that runs down the **Sangias peninsula**, the Deep Mani, wherein are the famed Nykhan tower houses. From these the various Mani clans bombarded each other in centuries-long internecine struggles. Villages that still have a fair scattering of these towers include **Kita**, **Vathia**, **Tsikkalia** and **Flomochori** (near Kotronas).

Down the road from Areopoli is **Pirgos Dirou**, close to which is the **Glyfatha Cave** and a subterranean river, an air conditioned, tourist bus target.

The bay of Limeniou, by Itilo is not only lovely, but the village is very spaced out round the edge of the bay - it is a 'bit' of a way-station with the occasional tent and motor caravan. Oh, by the way, the beach edging the bottom of the bay is pebble, as would appear to be the case of most of the beaches spread around the Peloponnese. There are *Rooms* and the *Hotel Itilo*. At the far side is the lovely little fishing hamlet of **Limeni**, with a lot of dressed, cut stone buildings, but no beach. Sadly there is a small, very neat, sympathetically constructed holiday development of stone houses and villas, tasteful but still there, and not yet finished.

Proceeding north along the the western coastline, **Kardamili** really is a little jewel, still with an original milieu to the place. The beach is pebbly, there is the beginnings of a tourist infrastructure, with a few pensions and some *Rooms*, but the single main street remains very Greek. The village is set in lovely countryside, rich in cypress and olive trees.

The large locations along this coast all have campsites. In fact the new highway is bordered by so many that they are not worth listing. The road is very serpentine in places, passing through lovely countryside. What is surprising is the extent of the 'suburban' villa build-up along the steep mountainside, coastal environs south of:

KALAMATA (about 107km from Githion) This is a large, very Greek resort and port, continuing to evince much evidence of the 1986 earthquake, as borne out by the prefabricated housing still littered about the place.

Buses connect with Athens; Tripoli; Argos (for Mycenae & Epidaurus); Corinth; Pirgos (for Olympia); Patras; Sparta (for Ancient Sparta); Pilos (for Nestor's Palace); and Githion.

The train offers a number of interesting possibilities as its circuitous route takes in a number of archaeological sites, or at least has a main town station close enough to offer a local bus connection. Train stations of note include: **Eastwards**: Messini for Ancient Messene; Argos for Epidaurus; and Mikines for Mycenae; **Westwards**: Olympia for Olympia. It has to be pointed out that the following are only the pick of the possible ancient locations that the Peloponnese has to offer but... it is necessary to stop somewhere, as this is a guide book about Crete! Thus it has been essential to omit many archaeological sites, as well as Byzantine, Venetian, Frankish and Turkish constructions.

Ancient Messene A fortified city built about 370 BC and which lies on the same mountainside (Mt Ithomi) as the village of **Mavromati**. Apart from the walls, which were part of a much larger defensive system, there is an extensive Agora, within which is a pretty little theatre.

Olympia The beautifully sited, if rather confusing remains, in a lovely valley is the equal of both Delphi and Mycenae. This site's world-wide fame is based on the legendary Olympiad games. These started in 776 BC, reached their zenith in the 4th century BC, but continued until AD 385, the 291st games, when they were shut down by the Christian Roman Emperor Theodosus I. The site was severely damaged by an earthquake in the 6th century AD, after which the Rivers Alhos and Kladeos burst their banks and covered the remains in sand and silt.

Olympia includes a Museum; Temples to Zeus & Hera; Treasures; a Nymphaion fountain; the Prytaneion administrative hall; a Gymnasion; the Palaistra Wrestling & Boxing School; a Priest's House; Baths; Workshops; the Leonidaion Guest House; Bouleuterion Council Chambers; a Hippodrome; and a Stoa, known as Echo Hall.

Mycenae (Mycene) The Citadel is named after the civilisation (Mycenaean, about 1500-1200 BC) which contributed most to the site.

Homer linked the city with Perseus, who slayed Medusa, the gorgon of many heads. A certain King Atreus fed his brother, with whom he didn't get on, with a meal of his own children, at a banquet. Not unnaturally this miffed the brother, one Thyestes, who laid a curse on the King's family. As a result of this, the King's son, Agamemnon, was murdered by his wife and her lover, after which Agamemnon's son killed his mother and the boyfriend. It makes *Dallas* seem tame, doesn't it.

The Acropolis site includes the oft photographed Lion Gate; a Royal cemetery; Temples; and a Palace. Outside the walls are various Tombs; a Treasury; Merchants' Houses and Grave circles.

Epidaurus Apart from the associated Sanctuary, Asclepeions and Temples, this must be the most amazing ancient Theatre, with, at one time, seating for up to 12,000. It is perfectly situated in an olive tree covered hillside, was constructed in the 3rd century BC, and is still used for modern-day productions.

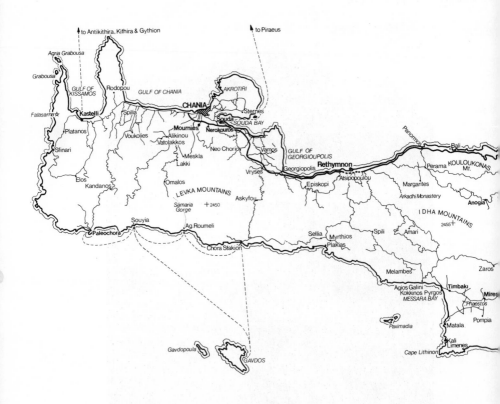

Illustration 7 Crete

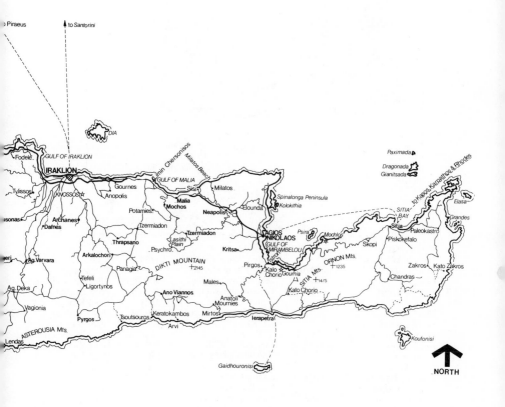

to Piraeus

to Santorini

DIA

GULF OF IRAKLION

Fodele

IRAKLION

Tylissos

KNOSSOS

Gournes

Anopolis

Sisi

Umin Chersonisos

GULF OF MALIA

Malia

Mochos

Potamies

Neapolis

Milatos Beach

Milatos

Spinalonga Peninsula

Kolokithia

Elounda

isonas

Archanes

Dafnes

Tzermiadon

Tzermiadon

Lasithi
Plain

Psychro

Elounda

Thrapsano

Arkalochori

AGIOS
NIKOLAOS
GULF OF
MIRAMBELOU

Psira

Mochlos

Skopi

Paximada

Dragonada

Gianitsada

SITIA
BAY

Sitia

Elasa

Paleokastro

Grandes

to Kasos, Karpathos & Rhodes

Piskokefalo

eri

Ag.Varvara

Kritsa

Panagia

DIKTI MOUNTAIN

+2145

Pirgos

Kalo
Chorio

Gournia

ORNON Mts.

+1235

SITIA Mts.

+14/5

Zakros

Kato Zakros

Chandras

Ag.Deka

Tefeli

Ligortynos

Males

Anatoli
Mournies

Ano Viannos

Kato Chorio

Vagionia

Pyrgos

Tsoutsouras

Keratokambos

Arvi

Mirtos

Ierapetra

ASTEROUSIA Mts.

Lendas

Koufonisi

Gaidhouronisi

NORTH

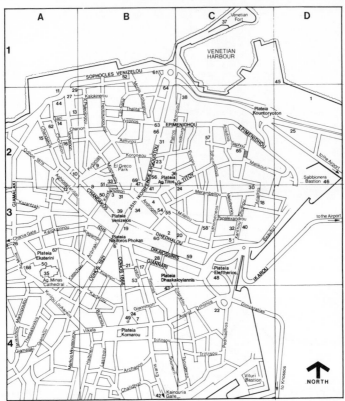

Tmr = Town map reference
Fsw = Facing seawards
Sbo = Sea behind one
Fbqbo = Ferry-boat Quay behind on

Illustration 8 Iraklion

3 PART THREE
IRAKLION (Heraklion, Iraklio, Heracleion)

Crete's largest city, main port & airport; a dusty, bustling, cosmopolitan, urban sprawl; a 'frontier' mix of Cretan & Western European worlds; one-way traffic systems, traffic police, traffic lights & parking meters.

GENERAL (Illustration 8) Tel prefix 081. The population now numbers about 85,000, most of whom seem to be in motor cars.

Iraklion surfaced historically in the Roman era as Herakleium, and was an important port for Knossos. The Arabs took over the town (and island) in AD 824 and named it Khandak, only for the citizens to be liberated by one Phokas, in 961, renaming it Khandax. In 1210 the Venetians made the city their capital, calling it (and the island) Candia. The new overlords heavily fortified the city, over the next 400 years, but the Turks finally wore down the inhabitants, after a 22 year siege, in 1669. This was despite various relief forces being sent from Europe. The Venetian commander at the time of the surrender was Francesco Morosini (honoured and recalled in the same-named fountain on Plateia Venizelos). The Turks followed historical precedents, and re-titled the place Megalo Kastro, the present name being assumed when Turkish rule ended, in 1898.

Perhaps some Italian friends put it best, when they suggested Iraklion resembled Beirut, but they were not sure if that was before the bombing, or not! Which says it all really. This commentary should forewarn visitors that Iraklion can be a disappointing starting point. There is no doubt that the city has all the basic features that should ensure a satisfactory mix. These ingredients include a Venetian harbour, and other fine buildings, a walled city, a lively street market and a cosmopolitan fountain square, in addition to a convenient commercial port and airport. But somehow they have been incorrectly added to the blender. Perhaps it is the lack of any beach and an easily comprehensible layout, but I suspect the problem is rooted in the fact that the Venetian harbour cannot be a hub for the city's day or night time activity. Admittedly, with Iraklion being the administrative and commercial capital of the island, as well as the focal point of the tourist comings and goings, it would probably be asking too much to expect more charm and less frenetic activity. And there can be no doubt that there is plenty of action. Buildings are coming down and going up, all over the place, parking is impossible and the traffic is controlled by traffic lights, policemen and parking meters. Well, well!

The first-time visitor should note that there are a number of central, popular, social, cafe-bar gathering places. The most important, interesting, and expensive is Plateia Venizelos (*Tmr* 39B3), formed by the pedestrian-precinct part of Chandakos St, where it butts on to the High Street of 25th Ikosipende Avgoustou. This irregular-shaped square surrounds the impressive and magnificent Morosini Fountain. Other focal points include Plateia Kallergon/El Greco Park (*Tmr* 47B2/3) and Plateia Eleftherios (*Tmr* 48C3/4). The former tends to be the chosen meeting place for the genus 'space man' (the 'laid back' variety) and drop-outs, whilst the latter is rather too large and spread out to provide a satisfactory venue. A much more attractive, fairly adjacent alternative is Plateia Ag Titos (*Tmr* 36B/ C2/3), a pretty square shielded from almost all the traffic pollution. The more distant Plateia Kornarou (*Tmr* 49B4) is popular with the locals, who languish at the Bembo Fountain cafe-bar while waiting for a bus or taxi.

Confinement of much of the new development, within the old city walls, has given rise to a muddly state of affairs, but where Iraklion has spread outside the constraints of the Venetian fortifications, the resultant suburbs are an absolute mess. To the west, row upon row of ugly,unfinished, pre-stressed concrete, high-rise apartments and hotels are interspaced by poorly asphalted or unmade streets, barren waste areas littered with untidy heaps of rubble, scrap cars, and the inevitable piles of blue plastic wrapped rubbish. To the east, the relatively low-rise, souless 'concrete boxes' evoke recoll-ections of the worst of the Eastern Europe city suburbs. And I would bet, a drachma to a bottle of retsina, that it is only the proximity of the airport that has restricted the builders' towering ambitions, in a heavenly direction!

It would be churlish to end the preamble on this sour note, for many will find Iraklion to be full of interest and fascination: the unexpected and narrow side streets rambling almost drunkenly from one part of the city to another; the sheer pulsating excitement of Plateia Venizelos (*Tmr* 39B3), thronged with a cosmopolitan cafe society; the throbbing street market that fills Odhos 1866 (*Tmr* B3/4) and spills on to Kornarou Sq, as well as its associated side lanes; the Archaeological Museum (*Tmr* 40C3), and its out-standing collection of exhibits; the rebuilt Venetian Arsenals (*Tmr* 38B/ C1/2); the Byzantine and Venetian churches, representative of which is the Church of St Katherine (*Tmr* 67A3) and its outstanding collection of icons; the graceful Plateia Ag Titos, to the east of the recently restored Venetian Loggia (*Tmr* 41B2/3); and finally the night-time bustle of pedestrian-way Odhos Dhedhalou (*Tmr* B3), with rows of restaurant chairs and tables lining one side of the wide passageway. What have I forgotten?

ARRIVAL BY AIR The Airport is fairly close to the City, and can be reached by taxi, a 4km walk or a 10 minute bus ride. Arrivals who can afford a taxi should ascertain the cost before stepping in, and expect a fare of about 450-500drs. You have been warned.

The No 1 Bus halts at the junction of the airport access road and the main, north coast road. The city end of the journey is very conveniently on Plateia Eleftherios, opposite the *Hotel Astoria* (*Tmr* 5C3), at the NTOG and Museum end of the Square. The bus, which gets pretty crowded, should run every 15-20 minutes, between 0600-2300hrs, at a cost of 50drs. Note the 'should' and allow plenty of time. Olympic Airways also operate a coach from their office (*Tmr* 22C4), at the south end of Eleftherios Sq.

ARRIVAL BY BUS Overland buses arrive by ferry, so the information detailed under **Arrival By Ferry** applies.

ARRIVAL BY FERRY The Piraeus boats storm into the port (*Tmr* 1D2), throw out the bow anchor, reverse on to the quay wall and, with a 'squeal of the brakes', the ramps seem to be down and vehicles thundering off, before the ship is finally tied up (In stark contrast to the pussy-footing about of their Italian counterparts).

ARRIVAL BY HYDROFOIL The service is a boon to island-hopping, independent travellers, as it allows speedy transit to a number of the distant, pivotal Cyclades islands. The craft dock at the port (*Tmr* 1D2).

Visitors, wishing to stay on in Iraklion, could consider turning right along the Esplanade, leaving the Venetian Arsenals (*Tmr* 38B/C1/2), on the left, proceed up the rise, passing the small Venetian Harbour, and turn left on to and up the High St, 25th Ikosipende Avgoustou. At the far end, at the crossroads and traffic lights of Plateia Nikiforos Phokas, turn left along Odhos Dikaiossinis, which leads to Plateia Eleftherios (*Tmr* 48C3/4). The point of this roundabout route is that it takes in most of the useful points that a traveller may wish to visit, ending at the NTOG office (*Tmr* 32C3), opposite the Archaeological Museum, both to the left of Eleftherios Sq.

For those arrivals who plan to move-on immediately, one of the main Bus terminals (*Tmr* 25D2) is directly across the dual carriageway, outside the port gates. The information sheet obtainable from this office looks deceptively excellent. What is he on about now? For the answer *See* **Buses, A to Z**. Of the other two main Bus stations, one is at the Xenia Terminal (*Tmr* 27A/B1/2), accessed by keeping straight on along Odhos   Sophocles Venizelou, from the top of the rise west the Venetian Harbour. The third, the Chania Gate Terminal (*Tmr* 26A3), is easiest reached by turning left on to 25th Ikosipende Avgoustou, then right at the top, at Plateia Nikiforos Phokas, to follow Odhos Kalokairinou. If laden-down by baggage, travellers might well be advised to take a taxi, as it is a damned long hike to the Chania Terminal.

THE ACCOMMODATION & EATING OUT

The Accommodation The City is bursting with quarters of every class and type, and there is an excellent organisation called *Filoxenia* (The Association of Rooms to Rent (Pensions) in the Iraklion Prefecture). Phew! Their plaque is stuck on the door of all members and ensures that the accommodation is clean and reasonably priced.

Probably the area containing the widest range of inexpensive and acceptable rooms is to be found to the south of the Xenia Bus terminal (*Tmr* 27A/B1/2), or conversely to the north-west of Plateia Venizelos (*Tmr* 39B3). From the latter, descending Odhos Chandakos leads to:

Hotel Palladion (*Tmr* 8A/B2/3) (Class D) 16 Chandakos   Tel 282563
Directions: Half-way down Chandakos St, on the right.
A truly old-fashioned, Greek, provincial town hotel, rich in mosquitoes, but with a pleasant courtyard and friendly owners. All rooms share the   rather primitive bathrooms, with singles costing 1090drs per night & doubles 1630drs, rising, respectively, to 1270drs & 1905drs (1st July-20th Oct).

Hotel Hania (*Tmr* 9A/B2/3) (Class E) 19 Kydonias   Tel 284282
Directions: Continue on down Chandakos St and turn next right, along Odhos Kydonias. The entrance is slightly set back from the street line, in a recess.
George Thiakakis advertises his establishment 'For hospitality Chania many clear beds'. I think that's supposed to read '...cheap'. In fact the hotel is more a Youth Hostel than most Youth Hostels, and is cheap, cheerful and colourful. To the right of the entrance-way is a short flight of steps, at the top of which are

three black mannequins. Flower pots are scattered about, most with names (like Manfred) and a date! The courtyard is liberally covered in murals and instructions - only disobeyed if guest's wish to incur George's wrath. The reception is at the far end of the quadrangle and is presided over by the patron. Callers should not be put off by his rather 'take it or leave it' attitude. They must also bear in mind that his understanding of English is often directly proportional to his interest in the matter under discussion. Attentive readers will realise that I regard George as an irascible (middle-aged) man, but others have found him to be very pleasant. So take your choice, bearing in mind that I might be adjudged to be an unreasonable so an so! The charge levied is 600drs per head, with between two and four beds per room.

Rooms Christakos (*Tmr* 12A2/3) 15 Psaromiligon/12 Evgenikou Tel 284126
Directions: In the lane across Chandakos St from Odhos Kydonias, and on the right. This quarter is still rich in older properties, with rickety overhanging first floor balconies.
   This 'firm', which is a member of *Filoxenia*, is a nice and clean house. A double room, sharing the bathroom, costs from 2000drs.

Further on down Odhos Chandakos leads to:
The Youth Hostel (*Tmr* 10A/B2/3) 24 Chandakos   Tel 286281
Directions: As above and on the right, but note the establishment is closed daily, between 1000-1330hrs, for cleaning (not that you would think so from a quick, or for that matter a longer gander inside).
   Not very fragrant, but then the average guest looks rather unwholesome. When heaved out of the hostel, the 'inmates' wander into the nearby *Tassos Cafe-Bar*, where the prices are appealing low, as are the standards of hygiene. Back to the YH, a dormitory bunk costs 550drs. Luggage storage is charged 100drs to hostelers, and 200drs to others.

Further down Chandakos St, on the right, is Odhos Kalimerakioff which jinks across Chortaton St to a constricted lane, on the right of which is the:
Hotel Rea (*Tmr* 16A2) (Class D) 4 Kalimeraki   Tel 223638
Directions: As above.
   More accurately could be described as a pension, to which it is more akin. Perhaps that would not suit the self-esteem of the husband and wife team who own the place, and exude a rather smooth, oily ego. The fairly modern building manifests a number of interesting peculiarities. For instance, should it rain (hush my mouth) the balconies do not drain and the lack of a planned third floor has resulted in some interesting architectural features, which are much too difficult to explain. But the Rea is very clean and the shower water is hot, all day. Only double rooms are available, sharing the bathrooms, which cost from 2250drs, despite the official rate being listed at 1675drs.
   Interestingly mine host, Mr Hronakis, also operates a car hire business, Ritz Rent-A-Car. This is no flash-in-the-pan set-up, as he has been around for as many years as I can remember, but note that the printed rates are subject to a 20% surcharge, a fact rather hidden away in the small print.

Rent Rooms Mary (*Tmr* 15A2) 67 Chandakos   Tel 281135
Directions: On the left (*Fsw*) of Odhos Chandakos. The state of the streets, in and around this neck of the woods, is an absolute disgrace. Much of the road surface is badly potholed, if not non-existent. How on earth the residents, hereabouts, put up with this state of affairs, I am unable to conceive. Mind you this is

nothing compared to the disarray in and around the *Hotel Xenia*, where matters are worse, much worse.

A neat, homely, three storey building with friendly owners, who only have some half-a-dozen double rooms for let. They cost from 1800drs, sharing the bathrooms, plus 100drs per head for the use of the shower.

In the parallel street of Odhos Chortaton, across a sea of mud, if it has recently rained, is the:

Rooms Vergina (*Tmr* 14A2) 32 Chortaton   Tel 242739
Directions: As above and close to the junction with Gazi St, which has been renamed Pantelli Pedelaki.

This nice looking accommodation is cool in the summer and is approached across a pocket-handerkerchief sized front garden, overflowing with greenery and, according to the 'management committee', the largest aspidistra in the world. Well, the dear girl is getting very old! Double rooms cost from 2000drs per night, that is when the establishment is open.

Pension Karpathos (*Tmr* 13A/B2) 4 Gazi (Pantelli Pedelaki)
Directions: This lateral street is behind the Xenia Bus terminal.

Continuing on down Chortaton or Chandakos St leads from the sublime to the ridiculous. By turning right at the bottom of either street, on to the incredibly busy thoroughfare of Sophocles Venizelou, advances to the nearby:

Xenia (*Tmr* 11A1/2) (Class A) S Venizelou   Tel 284000
Directions: As above and situated in the shambles of civil engineering 'destruction' that is downtown, west Iraklion.

The setting and the constant stream of traffic that 'exhausts' past the front door belies the hotel's excellence. Despite the undoubted quality, perhaps because of the location, this Xenia is comparatively inexpensive. All rooms have en suite bathrooms, with a single costing 3500drs & a double 5000drs, increasing to 4100drs & 5700drs (15th March-31st Oct). The mandatory breakfast costs 450drs, and lunch or dinner from 1400drs.

Further east along Sophocles Venizelou is the:
Hotel Kronos (*Tmr* 52B1) (Class C) 3 Kalergon Sq   Tel 282240
Directions: As above, sited in a more swept-up section of the Esplanade, and looking out over the sea.

A modern building wherein all rooms have en suite bathrooms. A single room is charged at 3070drs & a double 3885drs, increasing to 3345drs & 4245drs (1st July-30th Sept).

Returning to the top of Odhos Chandakos, immediately prior to Plateia Venizelos (*Tmr* 39B3), and branching off to the left (*Sbo*), is the narrow lane of Kandanoleon St, which harbours a number of accommodation possibilities, including the:

Atlas Guest House (*Tmr* 50A/B2/3) (Class C) 6 Kandanoleon   Tel 288989
Directions: As above, and on the left of this constricted, dark, if not rather canyon-like lane.

A clean, basic choice. All rooms have en suite bathrooms, with a single priced at 2400drs & a double 3000drs. Breakfast is available on the roof garden.

Across the street from *Atlas* is *Georgiadis*, which I am quite convinced is not a member of *Filoxenia*!

Hotel Hellas (*Tmr* 3B2/3) (Class D) 11 Kandanoleon   Tel 225121
Directions: Either east of Chandakos St, or west from Plateia Kallergon. This
end of Kandanoleon St is pretty noisy.
  The proprietor, Mr John, is a strong, engaging, and helpful man. It is more a
pension, or even a hostel, than a hotel, but the Hellas is a relatively inexpensive,
centrally located establishment and useful to have up one's sleeve. It has a pleasant garden patio bar. It is true to say that the longer the stay, the more apparent
is the seediness of the place, with, for example, the hot water being an 'off and
on' commodity, with a lot of 'off'! Almost all the rooms have to share the
bathrooms, with a single charged at 1600drs & a double 2000drs. Additionally
there are a few double rooms with an en suite bathroom (2500drs), and, at the
other end of the price scale, a multi-bed dormitory, where a slot costs 700drs.

Round the corner to the left, in a small cul-de-sac off Odhos Minotavrou (the
OTE street), which edges the west side of El Greco Park, is the 'interestingly
ethnic' looking *Pension Mikonos* (*Tmr* 51B2/3), at No 14 (Tel 242932).

Across 25th Ikosipende Avgoustou, from Plateia Venizelos (*Tmr* 39B3), is the
gently ascending, paved pedestrian street, Odhos Dhedhalou, on the left of which
is the neat looking:
Hotel Daedalos (*Tmr* 2B/C3) (Class C) 15 Dhedhalou   Tel 224391
Directions: As above.
  All rooms have en suite bathrooms, with a single priced at 2800drs & a double
3500drs, which rates increase, respectively, to 3350drs & 4065drs (1st July-31st
Oct). Breakfast may be mandatory, depending on occupancy, and costs 475 drs.

Returning to Plateia Venizelos, continuing up the now slight ascent of 25th
Ikosipende Avgoustou, towards Plateia Nikiforos Phokas, leads to another area
from which fan out a selection of accommodation possibilities.

Hotel Kretan Sun (*Tmr* 6B3) (Class E) 10 Odhos 1866   Tel 243794
Directions: As above, overlooking Nikiforas Phokas Sq. The entrance is immediately to the right on entering the narrow, pedestrian only Odhos 1866. This stall-
lined, part covered lane gets crowded (to say the least) during market hours.
  Every roster of accommodation should list a downbeat, typically ethnic Greek
hotel, in a noisy area (should it not?). The Kretan is clean and basic, and the
owner a humourist. When asked for double room rates he quotes 2000drs, then
quickly adds a further 200drs for 2 showers, which are charged, with or without
use! The pill is sweetened because, as Aliki Tsakiris puts it, guests, having paid,
may have as many 'free' showers as they like! Incidentally, the single room
price is 1800drs.

Around the corner from Odhos 1866, and along Fotiou Lane leads on to Evans
St, the other side of which is the:
Hotel Ionia (*Tmr* 17B3) (Class E) 5 Evans   Tel 281795
Directions: As above.
  Just a little more up-market than the *Kretan*. All rooms share the bathrooms,
with singles starting off at 1300drs & doubles 1400/1600drs. These charges rise,
respectively, to 1500drs & 1600/1800drs (1st June-30th Sept). A shower costs
an extra 100drs, per head.

The oldest hotel in Iraklion, if not the whole of Crete (!), must be the:
Hotel Kritikon (*Tmr* 53B3/4) (Class E) 26 Evans   Tel 220211
Directions: Diagonally across the street from the *Ionia*, some 50m to the south.

Worth visiting, if only to look at the quaint, attractively crumbling, Greek Victorian facade, embellished with rust stained, upper storey, cast iron balconies. Even the mandatory, brown, hallway linoleum is worn through. Double rooms, sharing the bathrooms, cost from 1800drs.

For a total contrast it is only necessary to continue in a southerly direction to the:
Hotel Olympic (*Tmr* 7B4) (Class C) Kornarou Sq   Tel 288861
Directions: On the left (*Sbo*) of the attractive Plateia.
   Pleasantly situated, but no sea views! A single room is charged at 2700drs & a double 3350drs, increasing to 3250drs & 4070drs (1st July-31st Oct). The mandatory breakfast costs 400drs. The hotel notice boards contain a lot of exceedingly useful tourist information.

Returning to Plateia Venizelos (*Tmr* 39B3), but this time descending 25th Ikosipende Avgoustou, the next side street on the right, opposite Plateia Kallergon, is Odhos Androgeo. On the left is:
Pension Lions (*Tmr* 4B/C2/3) (Class C) 9 Androgeo   Tel 225510
Directions: As above.
   The owner was the secretary of the *Filoxenia* organisation and his pension is very clean, if a little dingy, and reasonably furnished. A double room costs from 2250drs, sharing the bathrooms.

Hotel Selena (*Tmr* 54B3) (Class C) 7 Androgeo   Tel 226377
Directions: On the same side but further along Androgeo St from the *Lions*.
   A pleasant hotel, with en suite bathrooms, which, despite its obvious class, still manages to exhibit a few of those endearing little idiosyncratic faults that so captivate the Grecophile. You know, bathrooms with lavatories positioned so that neither the lid nor the seat can be fully raised, requiring males to utilise one extra hand to those that God issued; lavatory flush mechanisms which emerge through holes in the ceiling, but obstruct the window opening mechanisms; and showers where the shower head has a hook, but there is no wall mounted point, or, conversely, there are wall mounted points, but no attachment on the shower head! All rooms have en suite bathrooms. A single room costs 2800drs & a double 3450drs, rising to 3250drs & 4060drs (1st July-30th Sept).

Just around the corner from the *Selena* is the:
Hotel Idaeon Andron (*Tmr* 55B/C2/3) (Class E) 1 Perdikari   Tel 281795
Directions: Probably easiest located from Odhos Androgeo, by turning left along the next side street the far side of the *Selena* (*Kallergon Sq behind one*). This really lovely old building, with an overhanging first storey and a 'sort of' courtyard, is at the next junction of the ways, on the right.
   Owned by an aged little lady, who requests 1700drs for a double room, sharing the bathroom. But there's no extra charge for the use of the shower.

Once again returning to the 'High St', 25th Ikosipende Avgoustou, and descending towards the sea, almost immediately passes the:
Hotel Knossos (*Tmr* 56B2/3) (Class C) 43 I Avgoustou   Tel 283247
Directions: As above, and on the right (*Fsw*), in the area of Ag Titos Sq.
   A fairly modern hotel which only lets double rooms. Those sharing bathrooms cost 2300/3100drs & a double with an en suite bathroom are charged at 3450drs, which prices rise, respectively, to 2500/3300drs & 4065drs (1st July-15th Oct).

By continuing down the 'High St',the last side street to the right is Odhos Epimenidhou. Proceeding along this latter street, the fourth lateral choice off to the right is Odhos Idhomeneos, beside which is the:

Hotel Irini (*Tmr* 57C2) (Class C)   Tel 226561
Directions: As above and on the right (*Sbo*).
All rooms have en suite bathrooms. A single starts off at 3350drs & a double
4525drs, charges that increase to 3875drs & 5035drs (1st July-31st Oct).

By staying on Idhomeneos St, and climbing across Merambellou St, towards
Plateia Eleftherios, the next junction to the right is with Milatou St. Turning
along this and on the left, at No 18, is a neat, interesting, if thin building, in
which is **Rooms** (Tel 228958), close by the corner of Milatou and the small,
paved Ansarantapourou St.

Fairly adjacent is Plateia Eleftherios (*Tmr* 48C3/4), in and around which are a
number of possibilities. These include the:
Hotel Astoria (*Tmr* 5C3) (Class A) 5 Eleftherios Sq   Tel 286462
Directions: The hotel borders this busy, smart, cosmopolitan plateia.
Needless to write,bearing in mind the class of the hotel, the fees are quite
expensive. In fact if you have to ask, you cannot afford to stay. A single room is
priced at 6000drs & a double at 7500drs.

To the west of Plateia Eleftherios, on Dikaiossinis St, is the:
Hotel Petra (*Tmr* 59B/C3) (Class B) 55 Dikaiossinis   Tel 229912
Directions: As above, and on the right.
All rooms have an en suite bathroom, with a single costing 2245drs & a
double 2950drs, prices that increase to 2700drs & 4120drs (1st July-30th Sept).

Back at Plateia Eleftherios, proceeding north on Odhos Xanthou Dhidhou leads
between the NTOG office (*Tmr* 32C3) and the Archaeological Museum (*Tmr*
40C3). At the bottom, turn right along Odhos Merambellou, past the Coin-op
launderette (*Tmr* 30C2/3), where the lane narrows, and the next right is on to
Odhos Ariadnis, on the left of which is the:

Pension Ilias (*Tmr* 18C/D2/3) 43 Ariadnis   Tel 226348
Directions: As above.
Represents a nice, middle-of-the-road possibility, run by a pleasant, alert man.
He charges 2000drs for a double room, sharing one of the bathrooms.

For those travellers arriving at the Chania Gate Bus terminal, who do not wish to
face the slog into the centre of town, there is the disparate choice of either: the
very smart *Hotel Kastello* (Class C, tel 251234), just around the corner from the
Bus station, and where a single costs from 2300drs & a double from 3540drs;
and the 'bit-of-a-sleazo' *Pension Chania Gate*, a 'pace or fifty' through the Gate,
and on the left of Odhos Kalokairinou, the main road into Iraklion.

Camping
Camping Iraklion   Tel 286380/250986
Directions: Take the main coast road west out of Iraklion, for about 5km. The
No 1 Town Bus stops right outside, although, due to the siting of petrol fore-
court petrol pumps, the entrance looks more like a garage.
Camping Irakion is described in glowing terms by the official camping guide,
with every facility including a private, sandy beach (and 'mixed saunas for the
over 60s'?). Charges per night are: adults 400drs and the tent pitch 150drs.
There is one Greek camping essential missing - shade.

The Eating Out Despite there being sufficient establishments, few are are pre-eminent. The cafe and snack bar society are well catered for (sorry), even if expensively, and many of the main square characteristics have been sketched in the preamble.

If ambiance were the only parameter, I would plump for the very pleasant, spacious, stone-paved Plateia Ag Titos (*Tmr* 36B/C2/3). Due to being rather hidden away, it is less of a jungle than, for instance, the nearby Plateia Kallergon. The west flank of Ag Titos Sq is bounded by the rear side of the Venetian Loggia and is most attractively shaded by mature plane trees. These have no doubt inspired the name of the small, basement taverna cafe, set into the foot of a municipal building on the south side of the square. This is 'imaginatively' annotated *Yeros Platanos*, or 'Old Plane Tree', and is a very pleasant spot at which to sip a drink, and tuck into a snack or a meal.

It is axiomatic that the more tourist popular a location becomes, so the indigenous and traditional ways of life, the very attractions that originally attracted the visitors, become more difficult to locate as they disappear under the welter of inevitable despoliation. In the case of kafeneions, the bad news is that they are, in many locations, being ousted by rather nasty substitutes. This is certainly true of Iraklion where, as if to highlight this empirical formula, there is a *Piano Bar Loggia*, and a *Womans Cafe Roof Garden*. This particular pair of delights are to the north of Plateia Venizelos, beside the High St, some three storeys up in the sky. How Greek! Notwithstanding, the cafe and snackbar trade is still well provided for, but perhaps some comparisons will adequately highlight the wide disparity between the possibilities.

A drink at the crowded, cosmopolitan scrum at the Plateia Venizelos piazza (*Tmr* 39B3) costs a minimum of 120drs for a coffee, or an ouzo. It has to be taken into account that this is the smartest location in town. If I had to recommend one of the Venizelos cafe's it would be *Ta Leontaria*. But even here, a post prandial drink and snack of 2 coffees, an ouzo, a raki and a slice of Cretan bougatsa, in which this establishment specialises, costs 680drs. Yes, watch my pen... I have been served a full-blown meal for that price!. One timely warning is that the waiters here have a nasty little habit of serving unordered 'sippers', as well as little bits and pieces of nibbles, with a wink and a nod, AND then charge for them. This regrettable quirk could prove very embarrassing to someone on a tight budget, or who was running short of money. Across the street from Plateia Venizelos is the spacious, large windowed, more genteel *Restaurant Knossos*, wherein clients can settle back, in a milieu rather more redolent of bygone years. There are at least a couple of souvlaki snackbars on the north side of Venizelos Square, where an acceptable 'handful' of souvlaki pita costs 150drs. Incidentally a similar souvlaki counter, on the south side of Plateia Kallergon, offers an excellent example of the 'genus' for the same price.

At the other end of the spectrum to the *Leonteria*, is the more downbeat, local-popular Plateia Kornarou (*Tmr* 49B4), a refreshing change of ambiance and a pleasant alternative to the 'jungle' of Venizelos. At about the centre of this unequal sided square is the tree and hibiscus circled Bembo Fountain. Alongside is a stone, domed and pagoda roofed building, a Turkish addition to the Fountain, now a snackbar. There are some tables and chairs drawn up around the structure, from which a range of drinks and pies are sold. Due to the adjacency to a bus stop and a taxi rank, it is usually quite difficult to bag a seat, but well worth it as a coffee only costs 80drs. Also 'on the menu' are filter (filtro) and cappucino coffee, the latter sprinkled with cinnamon, for only 20drs extra. The snag? Oh, didn't I mention - the snackbar does not open in the evenings.

Around the corner to the left (*Square behind one*), beyond the *Olympic* and bordering Averof Othonos St, is a loukoumades snackbar. The Plateia Nikiforos Phokas crossroads (*Tmr* B3) is straddled by a couple of pie/doughnut snackbars.

The right of the pedestrian way Odhos Dhedhalou, walking up from the Plateia Venizelos end (*Tmr* 39B3), is lined by a row of some five restaurants. It does seem to me that prices and offerings are much of a muchness, except perhaps for *Kostas* (*Tmr* 19B3) at No 6. Surprise, surprise, the owner is named Kostas. He is a pleasant chap, but assumes a permanently worried look, between 8pm and midnight, if his establishment is not well patronised by tourists. Kostas has a theory that any shortfall in clientele is as a direct result of a plot by firms of the United Kingdom and United States of America. He is convinced that they are advising their clients that Greece is full, and even if it isn't, it shouldn't be visited because Greece was not aligned with those 'right-minded', Western European countries who want to rid the world of both Col Gadaffi and Libya! Some way on up the gently ascending street, and once again, on the right, is the small *Cafeteria Dhedhalou* (*Tmr* 60B3), which is popular with the locals. A pace or ten further on along Odhos Dhedhalou, but on the other side of the street, is the *Victoria Pizza Bar* (*Tmr* 20B/C3), which advertises itself as 'The Best Pizza in Town, 22 different kinds'. Certainly their pizzas are enjoyable, varying in price between 550-750drs. However, they do have competition, because at the top, east end of Odhos Dhedhalou is a huge sign pointing around the corner into Eleftherios Sq which reads 'Pizzeria Napoli, the most delicious pizza in the World -20 different kinds'. I can only comment that the *Victoria* used to be the best value.

Stretching the short distance between the Market St of Odhos 1866 and Odhos Evans, is a very narrow, tiny, dark, covered pedestrian alley, Fotiou Lane (*Tmr* 21B3), which is chock-a-block with tavernas crammed into it's short length. A number of these eating houses used to offer cheap food, but are now comparatively expensive, having been 'discovered' by free-spending tourists. 'C'est la vie'. Pushed to recommend one of them, I would name the *Lakis Tavern*.

Around the corner, on Odhos Evans, in the ground floor of the *Ionia* (*Tmr* 17B3), at No 5, is a reasonably priced, traditional town taverna offering a very full menu, including a range of soups.

In the maze of lanes behind the Xenia Bus terminal, is the:
Taverna Roots Rizes (*Tmr* 62A2) 54 Chandakos   Tel 221069
Directions: As above, and actually stretches between the parallel streets of Chortaton and Chandakos, with the main entrance in Odhos Chandakos.

This taverna is lucky enough to enjoy a paved courtyard, and serves an inexpensive, varied list of dishes. These include tzatziki (120drs), Greek salad (180drs), saganaki (150drs), liver on the grill, omelettes (200drs), meatballs (500drs), shrimps (550drs), beer (95drs), retsina (140drs), bread & cover charge (10drs). The doors open between 1900-2400hrs.

Closer to the Venetian Harbour, and edging Akti Sophocles Venizelou is the:
Ouzeria/Taverna Marinakis (*Tmr* 61B1) 3 S Venizelou   Tel 41834453
Directions: Immediately to the west of the main roundabout, at the bottom of 25th Ikosipende Avgoustou. The entrance is either from the Esplanade or the street behind, on the broad pavement of which are spread out the establishment's patio tables and chairs.

Due to this establishment's popularity, it is essential to arrive early in the evening. The choice is excellent, the presentation is imaginative, and the prices are reasonable... no wonder it gets crowded. The open kitchen takes up quite a

lot of the ground floor so the preparation is open for all to see. The menu includes mussels, fish, various salads, aubergines, stuffed tomatoes, snails, prawns,
meatballs, stuffed squid,   liver, dolmades, tzatziki, mashed potatoes, beetroot,
spinach, cabbage,   soups, and more. It's enough to make your mouth water. An
unusual feature is that there is a pre-printed order form which can be filled in,
take-away   style. A meal, for two, of 1 meatballs (400drs), 1 stuffed squid
(490drs), a   plate each of patatas (65drs), spinach (150drs), a plate each of
gigantes (170drs) & cabbage (180drs), 2 carafes of wine (120drs each), nearly
half a loaf of bread & cover charge (40drs each), totalled 1775drs. Another feast,
for two, of meatballs (400drs), prawns (470drs), a plate of beetroot (150drs) &
gigantes (170drs), a carafe of wine (90drs), bread & cover, cost 1360drs.

Next door is the *Taverna Paralia*.

One inexpensive, if rather distant and greasy looking snackbar, at which to pick
up a knife and fork, is alongside the Chania Gate Bus terminal (*Tmr* 26A3). A
couple of souvlaki pita and a bottle of beer costs 380drs. There are also a couple
of nearby kafeneions.
    Before leaving the subject, for those gourmets to whom money is no
impediment to the enjoyment of a meal, it would be churlish not to mention the
Le Parisian Restaurant. This establishment is on the left and almost at the far end
of Ag Titoy St (*Plateia Kallergon behind one*), at No 7. An extensive, French
flavoured, expensive menu.

THE A TO Z OF USEFUL INFORMATION
AIRLINE OFFICE & TERMINUS (*Tmr* 22C4). The Olympic Airways premises
are   located at the south side of Eleftherios Sq, adjacent to Odhos Averof
Othonos. The office opens daily, between 0630-2200hrs, and the airport bus
departs one hour before a particular flight departure, but do check!.

Aircraft timetable
Iraklion to Athens
A minimum of five flights a day 0735, 0840, 1740, 2310, 2330hrs.
From 12th June onwards there is one extra flight a day, at 1910hrs.
Return
A minimum of five flights a day 0545, 0710, 1610, 1720, 1900hrs.
From 12th June onwards there is one extra flight a day, at 1720hrs.
One-way fare: 7300drs; duration 50 mins.

Iraklion to Mykonos island
Wed, Fri, & Sun (1 stop via Santorini)   1040hrs
Tues, Thurs & Sat   1720hrs
Return
Wed, Fri & Sun (1 stop via Santorini)   0840hrs
Tues, Thurs & Sat   1550hrs.
One-way fare: 6710drs; minimum duration 1hr 10mins.

Iraklion to Paros island
From 14th May
Mon, Wed & Fri   1450hrs.
Return
Mon, Wed & Fri   1345hrs.
One-way fare: 7710drs, duration 45 mins.

Iraklion to Rhodes island
Daily   2020hrs
Return
Daily   2150hrs.
One-way fare: 7100drs; duration 40mins

Iraklion to Thessaloniki (M)
Mon, Thurs   1815hrs
Return
Mon, Thurs   2010hrs.
One-way fare: 11700drs; duration 1¼hrs.

Iraklion to Santorini island
Wed, Fri & Sun   1040hrs
Return
Wed, Fri & Sun   0940hrs
One-way fare: 4610drs; duration 40mins.

BANKS There are a number of banks on 25th Ikosipende Avgoustou St, including the **Ionian & Popular** (*Tmr* 63B2) and the **National Bank of Greece** (*Tmr* 23B2), both of which change travellers cheques and accept Eurocheques. *American Express* is represented by **Adamis Tours**, also on 25th Ikosipende Avgoustou, at No 23.

BEACHES None, even within easy walking distance of Iraklion, it being necessary to travel either to the west or east of town.
   To the west is Almiros Lido, about 5km distant, keeping to the Old (coast) Road, not The National Highway. If wishing to travel by bus catch a No 6, at a cost of 50drs, which leaves from the front of the *Astoria* (*Tmr* 5C3), every 20 mins until 2015hrs. Disembark at the sign for *Iraklion* Camping. Alternatively, travel east to **Amnissos** (about 8km), or beyond to **Vathianos Kampos**, both on the Old Road. Those using public transport should catch the No 1 bus from Eleftherios Sq, under the trees opposite the *Astoria*.

BICYCLE, SCOOTER & CAR HIRE Odhos 25th Ikosipende Avgoustou, rising from the waterfront to the centre, is the 'Rent-a-Wheels...' and, incidentally, the 'Travel Agent alley'. But why not try **Ritz Rent-A-Car**, at the *Rea* (*Tmr* 16A2), close by Chandakos St. Here a weeks hire costs about 30000drs, including the various taxes, surcharges and insurances. Another fruitful area for scooter hire is around El Greco Park (**Tmr** 47B2/3), where prices fluctuate around 1500-2000drs a day.

BOOKSELLERS International papers are for sale around the north side of Plateia Eleftherios. An absolutely amazing Bookshop hides away on Odhos Chandakos, a few paces towards the seafront from *Rooms Mary* (*Tmr* 15A2). Their stock of English language books must be unparalleled in Greece, let alone Crete. A narrow shop, selling foreign language books, magazines and newspapers, is boxed in between a couple of souvlaki stalls, north of Plateia Venizelos (Tmr 39B3).

BREAD SHOPS There is a Bread shop (*Tmr* 24B/C2/3) on the right of Odhos Ag Titoy, not far from Ag Titos Sq. Probably the best source is a very large and busy shop (*Tmr* 24B4) to the east of Plateia Kornarou. Those who struggle along Odhos Kalokairinou, on the way to or from the Chania Gate Bus terminal, might like to know that there is a Bread shop on the south side of that street.

BUSES There are three major Bus terminals but, despite the excellent coloured leaflet produced by the authorities, only two are detailed! The three are:

Ferry-Boat, or 'A' Terminal (*Tmr* 25D2). Conveniently situated across the wide Esplanade dual carriageway from the port, in a barn-like building. Apart from a snackbar, edging the large parking area behind the terminal is a Post Office caravan. Incidentally this opens weekdays, between 0800-2000hrs, as well as Saturday and Sunday, between 0900-1800hrs. Their innovation certainly has proved to be a blessing. Back to the matter in hand, Buses using this depot service, amongst other destinations, Malia, Ag Nikolaos, Gournia, Ierapetra, Sitia, Lasithi Plain, Archanes, Ag Pelagia, Sisi and Milatos.

Chania Gate, or 'B' Terminal (*Tmr* 26A3). Inconveniently situated at the far, west end of town. AND do not be fooled by the name (which is that of the nearby Old City wall gateway), this is not the Bus terminal for Chania or Rethymnon, for details of which read on. For example, this is the depot for Phaestos, Ag Galini, Matala, Lendas, Anogia and Fodele. Those travellers who must use this terminal, and are coming up from the port, and do not wish to catch a taxi, should not attempt to walk west along the Esplanade, planning to then cut up, say, Odhos Giamalaki. This choice of route will surely lead to despair, at the best! It is preferable to ascend the 'High St' of 25th Ikosipende Avgoustou, turn right at Plateia Nikiforos Phokas and then follow Odhos Kalokairinou all the way to and through the Chania Gate.

The 'missing' Bus station is the:
Xenia Bus Terminal (*Tmr* 27A/B1/2). It could be that this location remains unheralded because of the appalling state of the area, which really does look like downtown Beirut, after the shelling started! Apart from the importance of the destinations served, Rethymnon and Chania, this small Square has a minimarket-cum-cafe-bar and, at No 29, a General store that sells almost everything.

The **Plateia Eleftherios** (*Tmr* 48C3/4) Bus stops are for the Airport, as well as the local coastline, to the east and west of Iraklion. The couple of stops spaced along the 'up side' of 25th Ikosipende Avgoustou are for buses to Knossos, with the main stop at the Venetian Harbour end of the 'High St' (*Tmr* 64B1/2).

Bus timetables
A. Ferry-boat Bus Terminal (*Tmr* 25D2)
Iraklion to (Limin) Chersonisos, Malia
Daily   0630-2100hrs, every 30mins.
Return journey
Daily   0700-2200hrs, every 30mins.
One-way fare: 260drs; duration 1hr; distance 37km.

Iraklion to Ag. Nikolaos
Daily   0630, 0730, 0800, 0830, 0900, 0915, 0930, 0945, 1000, 1015, 1030,
               1100, 1130, 1200, 1230, 1300, 1330, 1400, 1430, 1530, 1600, 1630,
               1700, 1730, 1800, 1830, 1930, 2100hrs.
Return journey
Daily   0630, 0730, 0800, 0830, 0900, 0930, 1000, 1030, 1045, 1100, 1115,
               1130, 1200, 1230, 1300, 1330, 1400, 1430, 1500, 1530, 1600, 1630,
               1700, 1730, 1800, 1830, 1900, 2000, 2100, 2130hrs.
One-way fare 480drs; duration 1½hrs; distance 69km.

Iraklion to Ierapetra
Daily   0730, 0830, 0930, 1030, 1130, 1330, 1430, 1530, 1630, 1830hrs.
Return journey
Daily   0630, 0830, 1030, 1230, 1400, 1430, 1530, 1700, 2030hrs.
One-way fare: 750drs; duration 1½hrs; distance 105km.

Iraklion to Sitia
Daily   0830, 1030, 1230, 1500, 1730hrs.
Return journey
Daily   0630, 0915, 1115, 1215, 1430, 1445, 1645, 1915hrs
One-way fare: 1000drs; duration 3½hrs; distance 143km.

Iraklion to Lasithi Plain
Daily   0830, 1430hrs
Return journey
Daily   0700, 1400, 1700hrs.
One-way fare 490drs; duration 2 hrs; distance 70km.

Iraklion to Archanes
Daily   0700, 0800, 0900, 1000, 1100, 1200, 1300, 1400, 1500, 1700, 1900, 2030hrs.
Sun & hols 0800, 0900, 1000, 1200, 1400, 1500, 1700, 1900, 2030hrs.
Return journey
Daily   0630, 0730, 0830, 0900, 1000, 1100, 1200, 1300, 1400, 1500, 1600, 1800, 2000hrs.
Sun & hols 0730, 0830, 1000, 1100, 1300, 1400, 1600, 1800, 2000hrs.
One-way fare: 120drs; duration ½hr; distance 17km.

Iraklion to Ag. Pelagia
Daily   0900, 0945, 1430, 1700hrs.
Return journey
Daily   0945, 1030, 1515, 1745hrs.
One-way fare: 220drs; duration ½hr; distance 31km.

Iraklion to Sisi, Milatos
Daily   0845, 1500hrs.
Return journey
Daily   1015, 1645hrs.
One-way fare: 360drs; duration 1½hrs; distance 51km.

Iraklion to Vianos, Myrtos, Ierapetra
Daily   0630hrs
Return journey
Daily   1000, 1630hrs.
One-way fare: 750drs; duration 3hrs; distance 106km.

B. The Chania Gate Bus Terminal (*Tmr* 26C1)   Tel 283073
Iraklion to Ag. Galini
Daily   0630, 0730, 0830, 1000, 1215, 1400, 1600, 1730hrs.
Sun & hols 0730, 0830, 1030, 1215, 1500, 1700hrs.

Return journey
Daily   0800, 0930, 1030, 1215, 1315, 1500, 1630, 1830, 1945hrs.
Sun & hols 0800, 1030, 1230, 1500, 1730, 1930hrs.
One-way fare: 550drs; duration 2½hrs; distance 78km.

Iraklion to Phaestos
Daily   730, 0830, 1000, 1100, 1215, 1400, 1500, 1600, 1730hrs.
Sun & hols 730, 0830, 1030, 1215, 1500, 1700hrs.

Iraklion to Phaestos (Contd.)
Return journey
Daily   830, 1000, 1100, 1230, 1330, 1445, 1530, 1700, 1845hrs.
Sun & hols 830, 1100, 1300, 1530, 1600, 1700, 1800hrs.
One-way fare: 440drs; duration 2hrs; distance 63km.

Iraklion to Matala
Daily   0730, 0830, 1000, 1215, 1300, 1500, 1640hrs.
Sun & hols 0730, 0900, 1000, 1215, 1330, 1500, 1630hrs.
Return journey
Daily   0700, 0930, 1100, 1215, 1430, 1700, 1830hrs.
Sun & hols 0730, 1000, 1200, 1300, 1430, 1600, 1700hrs.
One-way fare: 490drs; duration 2hrs; distance 7km.

Iraklion to Lendas
Daily   0830, 1100, 1330hrs.
Sun & hols 0830, 1100hrs.
Return journey
Daily   0630, 1200, 1445hrs.
Sun & hols 1300, 1430hrs.
One-way fare: 600drs; duration 3hrs; distance 80km.

Iraklion to Anogia
Daily   0630, 0830, 1200, 1315, 1400, 1630hrs.
Sun & hols 0830, 1400hrs.
Return journey
Daily   0730, 0800, 1000, 1330, 1500, 1730hrs.
Sun & hols 1000, 1500hrs.
One-way fare: 240drs; duration 1hr; distance 37km.

Iraklion to Fodele
Daily   0630, 1430hrs.
Return journey
Daily   0700, 1430hrs.
Note that there are no buses on Sundays & holidays, either way.
One-way fare: 240drs; duration 1hr; distance 34km.

C. 'Xenia' Bus Terminal (*Tmr* 27 A/B1/2)   Tel 221765
Note this is not the official designation for the terminal. The Bus office is in the corner
of the square, hedged in by two snackbars.

Iraklion to Chania via Rethymnon
Daily   Some 24 buses a day.
Rethymnon: One-way fare 550drs; duration highway 1½hrs; old road 2hrs.
Chania: One-way fare 1000drs; duration highway 3hrs; old road 5hrs.

D. City Buses (Sky blue in colour)
The information office for City Buses is at the west end of the Ferry-boat Bus terminal
(*Tmr* 25D2), in a kiosk.
The Bus Stop (under the trees of Eleftherios Sq) opposite the *Hotel Astoria* (*Tmr* 5C3)
serves the:
Airport: Bus No. 1 every 10 minutes until 2300hrs, at a one-way fare of 35drs and
Amnissos (beaches to the west): Bus No. 1, every 30 minutes until 2000hrs at a
one-way fare of 45drs.
The Bus Stop (next to the Archaeological Museum) in front of the *Hotel Astoria* serves
the:
Lido (beaches to the east): Bus No. 6, every 20 minutes until 2000 hrs, at a one-way
fare of 40drs.
The Bus Stop on Ikosipende Avgoustou, or on the street next to the fruit market (read
Evans Street), or opposite the Logia (read Plateia Venizelos) serves the:

Knossos Palace and the **Hospital**: Bus No. 2, every 20 minutes from 0630-2300hrs, at a one-way fare of 30drs.

CINEMAS There is a small picture house on the corner of Dikaiossinis St and the pedestrian way of Odhos Byzantiou, almost opposite the Police station (*Tmr* 28B3). The picture house doors open at 1800hrs and, as usual, offerings include American, English, French and German films, with Greek subtitles. A list of film programmes, stuck on billboards, can be found in Dikaiossinis St.

COMMERCIAL SHOPPING AREA The pedestrian-way Odhos 1866 (*Tmr* B3/4), which connects the squares of Nikiforos Phokas and Kornarou, is a Market from end to end. When open (Monday-Saturday mornings until siesta time), it is a throbbing, seething, bustling thoroughfare lined by rows of stalls and shops, where almost everything can be purchased. There are all sorts of goods on sale, except bread, including yoghurt, groceries, meat & vegetables, as well as ironmongery. On the right, at the outset of this lane, from the Nikiforos Sq end, is the noisy proprietor of a cafe-bar/pie stall and his raucous, squawking parrot. Whilst the stall owner screams on about his orange juice, the bird tugs on a clamorous bell-pull. Towards the south end, on the right-hand side, is a good wine shop, whilst still further on, Karterou St snakes off to the right and contains the fish market, followed by a number of cobblers. It is interesting to note, whilst strolling past the fish stalls, that a kilo of prawns cost 1800drs, which helps go some way to explaining their taverna meal price. Whilst on matters piscatorial, there is an informal, from the 'edge of the gutter' fish market, every day that a catch is landed, close to the large roundabout at the Venetian harbour, bottom end of 25th Ikosipende Avgoustou.

The Mini-Market (*Tmr* 29A/B1/2), situated opposite the *Xenia*, alongside the Bus terminal, is an extremely useful store, open seven days a week. It stocks nearly everything a traveller could conceivably require.

Idhomeneos St (*Tmr* C3) contains a concentration of shops selling souvenir lace, embroidery, shawls and Cretan dresses.

DISCOS Usually I do not list them, as they rarely require any advertisement, but to be recommended is the Piper Disco, directly behind the *Astoria* (*Tmr* 5C3).

ELPA (The 'Greek AA') The Iraklion office is in the suburbs, off most maps, but is well signposted from Plateia Eleftherios (*Tmr* 48C3/4). The staff are extremely helpful, their English good, and the wish to help unbounded. But a phrase book is a necessity as the technicalities of automotive engineering is the 'rock' on which many a good translation can founder. A major difficulty for anyone, but a Greek, to understand, is that a particular garage does not carry out a full range of repairs and services. For example, oil is changed by one business, brakes adjusted by another, and engine tuning performed by a third, and so on.

FERRY-BOATS The ships dock at the quay (*Tmr* 1D2), across the waterfront dual carriageway from one of the main Bus terminals.

Fortunately a fairly simple schedule is operated by the two firms, ANEK and Minoan Lines, who slog it out for the eleven hour, overnight journey of the Piraeus to Iraklion voyage. Simple this schedule maybe, but there are a bewildering number of other Iraklion sailing alternatives, listed below. In addition, there are a seemingly endless list of other northern port ferry-boat possibilities, for details of which *See* **Chania, Kastelli, Ag Nikolaos and Sitia**.

In respect of these two major ferry boat companies, I have, over recent years, become a devotee of Minoan Lines. Their whole approach is almost revolutionary. For instance, the average Greek ferry-boat company regards passengers as mindless peasants who must be tolerated, just. Another cause for a good whine is the poor quality of the costly food and drink, often served on board many boats. When open, the snackbars may only be able to offer black coffee, in small plastic cups, to swill down the sole food available, perhaps the contents of a packet of biscuits. Often a ship's alternative source of sustenance, the restaurant, serves disproportionately expensive food, and then only after pre-purchasing a ticket, before sitting down at the table. Not so Minoan who operate their craft with the passengers in mind, actually appearing to have taken the revolutionary step of pandering to the customers! For instance, all that is necessary to enjoy an inexpensive and tasty repast on one of their craft, is to take a seat and order. Whow! On the Piraeus run, the Minoan catering staff conjure up a meal, for two, of 2 lamb & chips, a plate of cabbage, a bottle of retsina, bread & cover charge at a cost of 659drs. Yes, 659drs.

Another ferry that operates out of Iraklion is the **FB Portokalis Ilios**, a smallish passenger boat. The main deck is short on loos, the ladies has 3 'sit downs', the gentlemen's may be locked, and the general shower room full of cleaning materials. A floor down is one ladies' and one mens' toilet, as well as a door marked 'Under No Circumstances Leave This Door Open' - which is nearly always tied wide open with rope! There is the usual mix of television and Greek music and, surprisingly, a money exchange at the Purser's desk, even if the rate of exchange is rather poor. A number of dishes are available from the self-service canteen.

Ferry-boat timetable (Mid-season)

Day	Departure time	Ferry-boat	Ports/Islands of Call
Mon	0730hrs	Mistral II	Santorini (1 day cruise).
	0745hrs	Portokalis Illios	Santorini (1 day cruise).
	0830hrs	Nearchos	Santorini,Ios,Paros.
	1800hrs	Queen M	Kusadasi(Turkey).
	1830hrs	Festos/Knossos (Minoan Line)	Piraeus(M).
	1900hrs	Candia/Rethymnon (ANEK)	Piraeus(M).
Tues	0800hrs	Paros	Santorini,Ios,Paros,Naxos, Piraeus(M).
	1830hrs	Festos/Knossos (Minoan Line)	Piraeus(M).
	1900hrs	Candia/Rethymnon (ANEK)	Piraeus(M).
Tues	2030hrs	Anemos	Santorini,Ios,Naxos,Paros,Tinos, Mykonos,Skiathos,Thessaloniki(M) (Mid-June-Sept).
Wed	0300hrs	QueenM	Ancona(Italy).
	0730hrs	Mistral II	Santorini (1 day cruise).
	0745hrs	Portokalis Illios	Santorini (1 day cruise).
	0800hrs	Skinoussa	Santorini,Ios,Paros,Naxos,Siphnos, Serifos,Mykonos(Mid-June-Sept).
	1830hrs	Festos/Knossos (Minoan Line)	Piraeus(M).

Day	Departure time	Ferry-boat	Ports/Islands of Call
	1900hrs	Candia/Rethymnon (ANEK)	Piraeus(M).
	2400hrs	Hellas Express	Santorini,Ios,Sikinos,Folegandros, Naxos,Paros,Siros (Mid-June-Sept).
Thurs	0730hrs	Mistral II	Santorini (1 day cruise).
	0800hrs	Paros	Santorini,Ios,Paros,Naxos,Piraeus(M).
	1830hrs	Festos/Knossos (Minoan Line)	Piraeus(M).
	1900hrs	Candia/Rethymnon (ANEK)	Piraeus(M).
Fri	0730hrs	Mistral II	Santorini (1 day cruise).
	0745hrs	Portokalis Illios	Santorini (1 day cruise).
	0800hrs	Skinoussa	Santorini,Ios,Paros,Naxos,Siphnos, Serifos,Mykonos(Mid-June-Sept).
	0900hrs	Vergina/S. Paloma	Rhodes,Cyprus,Israel.
	1830hrs	Festos/Knossos (Minoan Line)	Piraeus(M).
	1900hrs	Candia/Rethymnon (ANEK)	Piraeus(M).
Sat	0800hrs	Paros	Santorini,Paros,Naxos,Piraeus(M).
	0800hrs	Portokalis	Santorini.
	1830hrs	Festos/Knossos (Minoan Line)	Piraeus(M).
	1900hrs	Candia/Rethymnon (ANEK)	Piraeus(M).
	2030hrs	Anemos	Santorini,Ios,Naxos,Paros,Tinos, Mykonos,Skiathos,Thessaloniki(M) (Mid-June-Sept).
Sun	0730hrs	Mistral II	Santorini (1day cruise).
	0800hrs	Portokalis	Santorini.
	0800hrs	Skinoussa	Santorini,Ios,Paros,Naxos,Siphnos, Serifos,Mykonos (Mid-June-Sept).
	1830hrs	Festos/Knossos (Minoan Line)	Piraeus(M).
	1900hrs	Candia/Rethymnon (ANEK)	Piraeus(M).
	2200hrs	Hellas Express	Santorini,Ios,Naxos,Paros,Piraeus(M) (Mid-June-Sept).
Every	2100hrs	Espresso Egitto	Venice(Italy).
8 days	2100hrs	EspressoEgitto	Alexandria (Egypt).

One-way fares:	to Piraeus(M)	2600drs: duration 11hrs
	to Santorini	1215drs;
	to Ios	1450drs;
	to Paros	2210drs;
	to Naxos	2210drs;
	to Mykonos	2380drs;
	to Alexandria (Egypt)	15600drs;
	to Kusadasi (Turkey)	6400drs;
	to Venice (Italy)	23300drs;

For another option *See* **Hydrofoils**

FERRY-BOAT TICKET OFFICES Most of the offices, including those of ANEK and Minoan Lines, are ranged along the lower length of 25th Ikosipende Avgoustou St. In amongst these firms are:

Minolines Travel Bureau 37, 25th Ikosipende Avgoustou   Tel 220796
Directions: Next door to and north of the *Knossos* (*Tmr* 56B2/3).
   Staffed by a very helpful team, one at least of whom speaks good English.
They handle the Minoan Line ticket sales, nicely.

ANEK ferry tickets are sold at No 33, 25th Ikosipende Avgoustou, and those of
the **FB Nearchos** by Armillis Tours, at No 9, 25th Ikosipende   Avgoustou.
Consolas Tours (*Tmr* B/C3/4, tel 288847), at Dhaskaloyiannis   Sq, advertise
'student offers' and competitively priced tickets.

HYDROFOIL
The **Nearchos** is a hydrofoil catamaran, running a scheduled service to various of
the Cyclades islands. The journey may be fast but is fairly uncomfortable, even
in calm sea conditions. The craft has one huge cabin into which all the passengers are locked for the duration. Small pre-packed Olympic Airline catering
packs are included in the ticket price but, if it is rough, the majority of the customers will be ill (throwing up). A small export can of Henninger costs 150drs,
but then the same costs 200drs on the Santorini quay.

Hydrofoil Catamaran timetable (Mid-season)

Day	Departure time	Ports/Islands of Call
Mon	0830hrs	Santorini (Arrive 1115hrs; Depart 1130hrs),Ios (A 1230hrs;D1245hrs), Paros (A 1400hrs; D 1415hrs), Ios (A 1530hrs; D 1545hrs), Santorini (A 1645hrs; D 1715hrs), Iraklion (A 2000hrs).
Tues,Thur	0800hrs	Santorini,Ios,Paros,Naxos (A 1430hrs; D 1445hrs), Ios,Santorini, Iraklion.
Wed,Fri	0745hrs	Santorini,Ios,Paros,Mykonos (A 1415hrs; D 1430hrs;), Paros(A 1530hrs; D 1540hrs), Ios, Santorini, Iraklion.

One-way fares: to Santorini   2600drs.
              Ios   3165drs.
              Paros/Naxos   4115drs.
              Mykonos   5815drs.

LAUNDRY There is a haphazardly operated coin-op launderette (*Tmr* 30C2/3),
at No 25 Merambellou St, which is north along Odhos Xanthou Dhidhou from
the NTOG. When open, which should be daily (except Sunday) between 1030-
2000hrs, a wash costs 400drs, a dry 250drs, and a 'helping' of soap powder
50drs. The discs necessary to operate the equipment can be obtained from the
disinterested girl attendant. The better outfit is **Laundry Express** (*Tmr* 65C2) at
No 1 Saphou St. The firm opens daily, between 0900-1430hrs & 1700-2100hrs,
and Saturdays, between 0900-1500hrs, but is closed on Sundays.

LUGGAGE STORE There is a left luggage facility (*Tmr* 66B2) at No 48,
Ikosipende Avgoustou, in a basement opposite the National Bank. Their doors
open daily, between 0700-2400hrs, and they charge 200drs a day, per piece.

MEDICAL CARE
Chemists & Pharmacies Thick on the ground and a rota is in operation to give
round-the-clock cover.
Hospital The Venizelion Hospital is on the left of the Knossos road, some 4km
out of town. For a bus *See* Buses (City).

NTOG (EOT) (*Tmr* 32C3) Conveniently situated in a modern building opposite the Archaeological Museum. The office, the size of which has been severely reduced, now only opens Monday to Friday, between 0730-1430hrs. These hours are rather inadequate, but, worse, the information available is very limited indeed. It is such a shame to see this once superb, if then offhand set-up, now almost totally emasculated. As if to make up for these deficiencies, the manager could not be more helpful.

OTE (*Tmr* 33B2/3) Situated to one side of El Greco Park and open daily, between 0600-2400hrs. Clients are now controlled by entrance and exit turnstiles.

PETROL Plentiful.

PLACES OF INTEREST
Cathedrals & Churches
The Basilica of St Mark (*Tmr* 34B3). Almost opposite Morosini Fountain Sq, but many visitors will only remember the building from having sat on the steps, perhaps whilst consuming a snack. This is a pity, as the oft-restored church now houses frescoes from the 13th to the 15th century, gathered from a wide variety of Cretan churches. It also doubles as a lecture and concert hall. Built in 1240 by the Venetians, it was rebuilt in 1303 and 1508, after earthquakes. The Turks converted it into a mosque and it was finally restored in the late 1950s. The opening hours and admission charges vary. Enough said!
The Cathedral of Ag Minas (*Tmr* 35A3/4) Built in the late 1850s and is beautifully decorated inside, almost every inch being covered by murals. Incidentally, there is a toilet block let into the walled surround of the building. The Cathedral dominates the Plateia Ekaterini, towering above both:
Ag Ekaterini (*Tmr* 67A3) The Church of St Katherine is situated on the edge of the self-named square, was built in the 15th century, altered in the 17th century, and is now a museum of religious art, especially icons. The most renowned of the latter are six painted by one Mikhalis Dhamaskinos, a contemporary of El Greco who, naturally, it is claimed studied here when it was a monastery school and Renaissance centre. It is certain that a number of famous Cretan artists, theologians and dramatists were students. The tiny little church was once associated with the Mt Sinai Monastery and is open Monday-Saturday, morning and afternoon, with a long siesta. Admission costs 200drs.
Church of Ag Minas (*Tmr* 68A3) Of uncertain age and used for the storage of various antiquities.
Ag Titos Church (*Tmr* 36B/C2/3) Originally a Turkish mosque, it was built in 1872, on the site of a Byzantine church which had been destroyed by an earthquake. The building reverted to the Orthodox faith, in the late 19th century.
Koules Castle (*Tmr* 37C1) The Castle was built to in the early 1500s, by the Venetians, possibly on the site of an earlier structure. In fact the name it is known by is the Turkish nomenclature. The structure has been impressively restored and is worth a visit, when do not miss the sculptured Lions of St Mark.
Festival More an event than a place. Iraklion, not to be pushed off the cultural world stage, organises an annual 'Summer Festival'. The jamboree takes place between July and September, during which various worthy, uplifting events take place. For those intending to visit Iraklion, and not wanting to miss some or any of these oases of refined enlightenment, it would judicious to contact the organisers, care of the NTOG or telephone 282221/242977.
Morosini Fountain (*Tmr* 39B3) The lovely Venetian fountain squats on the Plateia Venizelos, more popularly known as Fountain Sq - but no 'Brownie' points for guessing why. It was built by the then Governor, Francesco Morosini,

in the early 1600s, but the lions probably date from the 14th century. The bas-reliefs of the fountain basins have aquatic connections. Over the last few years the structure has been subject to restoration, which is now complete. Unfortunately when the fountains stop gushing, the outer ring of the fountain pool is messy.

Museums

The Archaeological Museum (*Tmr* 40C3) I suggest that any visit is delayed until one or two Minoan sites have been visited, after which the exhibits can be viewed with the archaeological digs in the mind's eye. This museum holds an impressive display, and on the first floor are displayed the Minoan frescoes from Knossos. It is surprising that such exquisite exhibits should be shown off in such an ugly building, added to which the labelling is poor, but the layout is simplicity itself. The water-colour paintings by Piet de Jong, executed to help the partial restoration work at Knossos, are very attractive. The exhibition opens daily, between 0800-1900hrs, except Mondays when admission is between 1230-1900hrs. Entrance costs 500drs and it may be worth noting that there is a most welcome cold drinking water machine, behind the building.

The Historical Museum (*Tmr* 44A2) Opposite the *Xenia*, and contains exhibits from the early Christian period up to and including the Battle of Crete. There are also reconstructions of the studies of Nikos Kazantzakis (1883-1957), author of (amongst a number of renowned books) *Zorba the Greek*, and of Emanuel Tsouderos, the Greek statesman. The Museum opens Monday-Friday, between 0900-1700hrs; Saturday 0900-1400hrs; and is closed Sunday & holidays. Admission costs 300drs.

Venetian Arsenals (*Tmr* 38B/C1/2) Built in the 16th century, those still standing are of a very large size and have been imaginatively restored in two arcaded and vaulted sections.

Venetian Loggia (*Tmr* 41B2/3) The building, fronting on to what was once the Venetian Armoury, has been totally reconstructed and is now the City Hall.

Venetian Walls Built in the 15th century, they are in an impressive state of preservation. A testament to their solidity and effectiveness must be the 22 year siege that raged around them, from 1648, when the Turks attempted to clean up the last outstanding bastion of Venetian rule on the island. After the inhabitants finally surrendered they were allowed to go scot-free, an unusually generous and uncharacteristic act by the Turks. It was their customary practice to make an example of a chap, in those days - you know, burn or skin them alive, or any other similar niceties. Two of the original gateways are well worth a visit, namely Kainouria (*Tmr* 42B4) and Chania (*Tmr* 26A3). A walk around the perimeter, not only proves interesting, but may work off any possible ill-effects of too many ouzos. At the Martinengo Bastion, on the west of the Kainouria Gate, there is a zoo and the grave of the author Nikos Kazantzakis (*See* **The Historical Museum, Places of Interest**. Owing to a difference of opinion with the Orthodox Church, Kazantzakis was not allowed to be buried in any consecrated ground, or even with their blessing. The simple headstone, with an extract from one of his works, is inscribed 'I hope for nothing. I fear nothing I am free'.

POLICE

Port (*Tmr* 45C/D1/2) Where one would expect them to be, I suppose, on the main commercial quayside.

Town/Tourist (*Tmr* 28B3) The tourist police have been absorbed by the Town department, as was inevitable in the light of changes throughout the rest of Greece. They are both housed in the large building beside Dikaiossinis St.

POST OFFICE (*Tmr* 43B/C3/4) Located in a modern building, bordering Dhaskaloyiannis Sq, where the service is rather brusque. In common with most Greek offices, they exchange travellers cheques and carry out Eurocheque transactions. Opening hours for money transactions are between 0730-2000hrs, Monday to Friday inclusive, whilst other business hours are the norm. Apart from the Post Office caravan, behind the Ferry-boat Bus terminal (*Tmr* 25D2), there is another of these most welcome facilities (*Tmr* 69B2/3) at the Kallergon Sq entrance to El Greco Park. It is across the street from a Bank of Crete, and opens daily, between 0800-2000hrs, except Sunday, when the working hours are between 0900-1800hrs. In case I have not stressed the fact, the main function of these caravans is to carry out exchange transactions, including handling Eurocheques, seven days a week.

SPORTS FACILITIES There is a Tennis club (*Tmr* 46D2/3) located alongside Beaufort St, the latter swinging down from Eleftherios Sq. Payment is either by game fees or short-term membership.
There are Horse-riding stables at **Karteros**, about 5km east of the city, on the road to Skalani. They offer day trips on horse-back or by horse-drawn wagon.

TAXIS Ranks are scattered about the City, with include those on: Eleftherios Sq (*Tmr* 48C3/4) - all round the periphery; Dhaskaloyiannis Sq (*Tmr* B/C3/4); alongside the NTOG office (*Tmr* 32C3); around El Greco Park (*Tmr* B2/3), as well as the rank at Plateia Kornarou (*Tmr* 49B4).

TELEPHONE NUMBERS & ADDRESSES

British Vice Consulate	Tel 224012
Hospital	Tel 231930
NTOG (*Tmr* 32C3) 1 Xanthou Dhidhou	Tel 282096
Olympic Office (*Tmr* 22C4) 42 Eleftherios Sq	Tel 229191
Tourist Police (*Tmr* 28B3) Dikaiossinis St	Tel 283190

TOILETS The Ferry-boat Bus terminal (*Tmr* 25D2) 'sports' a pair, as does El Greco Park (*Tmr* B2/3). The latter resembles a small zoo, well more an aviary. The fearsome woman attendant shares her un- pleasant 'hole in the ground' with about 20 bedraggled birds. They are caged, in those typical, unbearably tiny, Greek cages, and deprived of light, despite which the birds sing incessantly. The cream of the collection are two large, miserable, and understandably silent cockatoos. Entrance to the toilet costs 50drs, some of which may help subsidise the aviary...! There is also a public toilet let into the foundations of the wall holding up the north side of Ag Minas Cathedral (*Tmr* 35A3/4).

TRAVEL AGENTS A number of the genre are listed under **Ferry-boat** Ticket Offices, and other firms range along Odhos 25th Ikosipende Avgoustou. One business worth detailing is:
Creta Travel (*Tmr* 31B2) 25th Ikosipende Avgoustou   Tel 227002
Directions: On the left (*Sbo*) of the 'High St', just up from the Bank of Greece. Another Creta office is at 20-22 Epimenidhou, the first side-street to the right, if descending from the 'High St' office towards the sea front, and on the right.
I have chronicled Creta because they probably offer the most comprehensive brochure of Cretan tours and excursions.

WATER Certainly, on some occasions, the town's water is chlorinated. There are drinking water machines at the Archaeological Museum, as has been mentioned, and at the entrance to El Greco Park (*Tmr* 39B3).

ROUTE ONE
To Rethymnon via the National Highway (78m) For many, travel on the National Highway will be interesting enough without venturing on to the byways of countryside Crete. It may seem anomalous to Western Europeans, used to sanitised swathes of concrete that flash hundreds of kilometres to here or there, without sight of the local countryside, that this not-so-new road (or National Highway) often travels through more scenic and dramatic countryside than the Old Road. Not so remarkable is that it is a quicker route, and nowhere is this better exemplified than on the journey between Iraklion and Rethymnon.

The immediate western environs of Iraklion are extremely messy and dusty, trailing past an oil refinery, with tanker buoys in the sea. Once on the adequately signposted Highway, the scenery becomes *au naturel*.

AG PELAGIA (20km from Iraklion) Tel prefix 081. Some 17km from Iraklion, the seaside village is signposted off to the right. The approach, across bare hillsides, is a steeply descending and winding road, allowing splendid aerial views of the lovely bay.

From the Ag Pelagia road, or from a previous branch road off the main route, is a signpost along a side turning to *Angel Village Apartments*. This descends to a long, narrow, sand, fine pebble and biscuit rock foreshore, which undulates in the shape of an 'S'. It is overlooked by a parched hillside, on which are an acceptable number of apartments and villas, as things stand. There is a providential mini-market, to keep the wolf from the door. The Ag Pelagia approach terminates some way above this shore, which makes it necessary to complete the last section on foot.

Returning to the descent to Ag Pelagia, the serpentine road runs out on a car park, at the eastern end of the resort's shore. The rocky, eastern horn of the 'U' shaped bay stretches out to sea, terminating in a rocky bluff. Some dozen boats are moored inshore, half of which are caiques. This narrow end of the very pleasant sweep of beach consists of large pebbles, followed by horizontally angled slabs of concrete, or rock, bedded into the surrounding sand, and then sand and very fine shingle. Without doubt the sea of this somewhat sheltered bay is most tempting and beguiling, to anyone with the slightest inclination to have a dip. It has to be pointed out that the biscuit rock extends well into the sea, at the eastern end, and can be offputting.

The backshore, which is an unofficial thoroughfare, is bordered by the high concrete patios of restaurants, tavernas, bars, shops and accommodation, here and there pierced by access steps. If the menu translations are any guide, the holiday-makers are drawn from a wide range of nationalities including the English, Dutch, German and Scandinavian (Is there such a language?). Businesses at this end include *Rooms Marina Karouzo*, above a supermarket, *Restaurant Alkion*, with 'Greek kitchen, fresh fish', *Rent Apartments*, the *Restaurant Dionissos*, where the speciality of the day is as likely to be the oh, so Greek 'fillet of sole with tartar sauce', the *Restaurant Alexander Steak House*, and a supermarket. Incidentally the beach rubbish bins are regularly emptied.

Halfway along the waterfront is the 'High St', a wide, surfaced road perpendicular to the shoreline, and at the outset of which is a 'portacabin' style OTE. This opens daily, Monday-Saturday, between 0730-2200hrs, Sundays

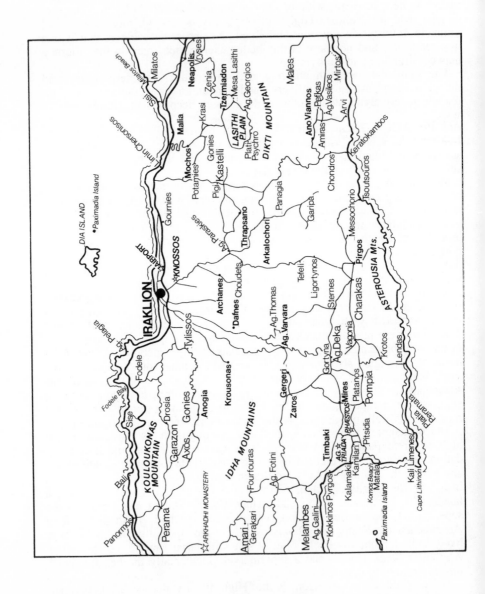

Illustration 9 Crete centred on Iraklion

& Idle days (their wording, not mine, but how apt - and on to which I have latched, with enthusiasm), between 0900-1400hrs & 1600-2100hrs. Gathered along this beach end of the 'High St' are: a Tour office, offering the: Lasithi Plain/Diktaion Cave 2100drs; Ag Nikolaos/Spinalonga 3100drs; Samaria Gorge 'the hard way' (We have ways of making you ...!) 3450drs; a Cretan night in Karazouna 2800drs; as well as Knossos & the museum 2950drs; a large, well run, inexpensive supermarket, on the left (*Sbo*) and selling international newspapers; the *Creto Grill Michael*, where a souvlaki pita cost 120drs, but with patatas 150drs; Auto Tours Express Jeep Safari; a ceramics shop; *Cafeteria Four Star*, *Johnny's Rent A Car*; *Zorba's*; followed by a succession of **Rooms** and a couple of apartment blocks. In effect the 'High St' is a 'sort of' ring   road encircling the outskirts of western Ag Pelagia. I seem to remember, in years gone by, it was nothing more than a summer dry river-bed.

Back at the waterfront and to the left (*Fsw*), the sandy beach is up to 15m wide, even if it is a bit of an assault course due to the massed sun-beds, umbrellas and, needless to say, people. To proceed along this side of the bay, it is necessary to climb up and down the steps of the various concrete patios and terraces. Tucked in between a couple of restaurant/tavernas, is *Rooms Evy*, followed by a few gift shops, a medical officer, above a Car Hire firm, a 'Golden Jewellery', a supermarket, and *Rooms Lady M*. My choice of taverna would be the *To Votsalo*, where the (comparatively) attentive service may be rather precious, but the helpings are good and the dishes are not pre-made. A lunch-time meal, for two, of a tasty tzatziki, an excellent Greek salad (that may have lacked olives but contained greens and had oregano sprinkled on the feta cheese), 2 beers and bread, cost 560drs. A meal, for two, of 1 tzatziki (150drs), a Greek salad (190drs), a pizza for one, which was big enough for two (400drs), 1 spaghetti bolognese (400drs), 1 bottle of kortaki retsina (150drs), bread & cover, cost 1350drs. It has to be reported that the bread was inadequate, but only the bread, as the rest of the meal was excellent.

Towards the far, western end of the beach, where it narrows down once again, is the Kreta Water Sports Centre, more a backshore, deck-chair, folding table and sun umbrella outfit. There is a water-ski run, beyond which sunbathers have to put up with the whine of a swimming pool irrigation pump. This serves the *Capsis Beach Hotel & Bungalows*, a large, luxury complex straddling the headland. I write swimming pool (singular), but there are two and I must report that the *Capsis Beach* appears to be a superb hotel, in an excellent position. Around the headland is a very small, sandy beach cove, only accessible from the hotel grounds. The 'Theatre on the Rocks' is very small, pretty and beautifully sited outdoors, built into the rocks, similar to a miniature, ancient Greek Odeion. This unique theatre, situated along the upward-climbing, seafront road, above the *Capsis*, puts on regular performances throughout the summer.

Those with wheels can approach the *Capsis*, from the New Highway, by picking up the signs for the 'Kapsis Beach', an indicator that suggests this route is only one kilometre in length. Naughty, it must be at least four or five! Beside this bare, wild, mountain tracking road are a number of isolated holiday apartments, including the *Erato*, *Happy Cretan*, a turning off to the *Hotel Peninsula*, the *Taverna Bar George*, the *Pearl Furnished Apartments*, and finally the *Capsis Hotel*.

The Ag Pelagia taverna and restaurant prices are slightly higher than the average, which is not surprising as the resort is almost exclusively, good quality holiday territory.

Back on the New Highway, the route drops to sea level and rushes past:
Fodele Bay (some 24km from Iraklion) Once a nice sweep of shadeless and isolated, if not desolate beach, set in a small, rather inset cove. Once? Well, yes. The authorities have seen fit to allow the middle of the beach to be swamped by land-fill, that has created an unsurfaced car park and split up the original sweep of shore. What is left is a 100m length of pebble and sand to the right (*Fsw*), and a 100m of sand and pebble to the left, both subject to wind-blown rubbish. Tucked into the near or east side are a petrol station, mini-market and a cafe-bar. With all that has been written in respect of this spot, it may seem even more mystifying to have to report that the western bluff of the cove is to be dominated by apartments, now in the course of construction. There's now't so strange as folk, and what has prompted some entrepreneur to build here, I am at a loss to understand.

Off to the inland side of the Highway is a turning to:
FODELE (27km from Iraklion) This beautifully beflowered village, straddling a summer running river, is set in an extremely fertile valley, abundant with orange and lemon trees, and donkeys.
    At the outset to Fodele is a pension/taverna, followed by the *Kafeneion El Greco*, a baker and a 'fast food souvlaki'. The village is famed as the birthplace of Dominikos Theotokopoulos, more popularly known, in art circles, as El Greco. A 16th century artist, he probably studied under Titian in Venice and become a resident of Toledo, Spain. He proclaimed his Cretan nationality, but not where he was born. The selection of Fodele as the location was given the seal of approval, in 1934, when a Spanish university presented the village with a plaque inscribed in both Spanish and Greek. It reads 'The History Faculty of the University of Valadolid gives this plaque made of Toledo rock to Fodele in memory of the immortal glory of Dominikos Theotokopoulos. July 1934.' The village church houses some El Greco momentos.
    A sign directs the inquisitive over the stream and then right again, down the valley, along a spasmodically concrete surfaced track, which leads to a lovely, small, 'wedding cake' church. Close by is a well-indicated, stone flint footpath. This advances through groves of olive trees, past the ruins of an old dwelling, and a donkey-hafted water well, in the bottom of which can be glimpsed some water, amongst the cast-aside Coke and Sprite cans. After about 100m is the extensively restored house, selected as the El Greco family home. I cannot swear that the recently installed concrete, wooden window shutters and electric wiring are anything more than pure 20th Century! On mature reflection the old remains, passed on the way up, are just as likely to be the actual dwelling.

The Highway contours along the low scrub supporting mountainsides, past **Sise**, to dramatic headland views, after which the route plunges down to sea-level, alongside an inlet, opposite which is a petrol station. At this point is a turning off to the left, leading under the road, to double back to:

BALI (50km from Iraklion) The approach road winds up and down, past the *Apartments Bali Mare*, on the left, a *Rooms/Restaurant*, on the right, the *Talia Beach Hotel*, which boasts a swimming pool, a taverna and then a doo-hickey campsite. This latter is one of two that used to be here, the remaining one being very Turkish in style. Continuing on, through progressively scruffier surrounds, are the *Rooms Dolphin*, *Zeedas Garden Rooms*, more *Rooms*, a motorbike rental outfit, and even more accommodation. Hereabouts is a turning down to the small, shadeless, main beach. Situated to the left of a rock enclosed cove, the shore is mainly pebble, with some sand and fine pebble at the sea's edge. There is evidence that the authorities have shipped in sand to cover the middleshore. Bearing in mind the numbers of holiday-makers accommodated in Bali, I am surprised that pedaloes, sun-beds and umbrellas are also allowed beach room. Some small rocks stick up above the water, and the sea-bed is rather weedy, in areas.

The roadsides are now almost swamped by *Rooms*, as well as a supermarket, *Studios Bali*, a hotel, and then the *Bali Beach Hotel*, (Class B, tel 94210) which boasts its own very small, fine, grey shingle beach. In the area of a gift shop, *Rooms*, and *Valentino Apartments*, the presently unsurfaced track curves round to the right, for the final descent past *Villa Gregory Rooms*, down the now con- creted river bed. This approach peters out by a car park, which costs 100drs, if there is anyone around to collect the cash. To the side of the descending slope from the car park, is the hut-cum-shop which houses the 'Racer Travel' office, where they offer a good rate of exchange.

Others confirm my opinion that the natives are considerate and friendly. The heart of their once-fishing boat hamlet is gathered around and up the left-hand (*Fsw*) headland. To the right is the 'town beach', a short stretch of grey sand, pebble and shingle. The backshore is edged by a baker and some five tavernas, one of which has a metered telephone and a wall mounted post box.

A taxi excursion entrepreneur charges 8000drs for a half-day to Arkadhi/Knossos, 15000drs for a day at Festos/Gortyna/Matala/Lasithi Plain, and 16000drs for a day's trip to and from the Samaria Gorge.

Amongst the buildings that scale the left-hand hillside, are a gift shop, selling overseas newspapers, *Rooms/Taverna Panorama*, and the very smart, marble floored *Rooms Elena*. Averagely, the less expensive double rooms in Bali cost from 2000drs a night.

Either by continuing up and over the aforementioned hillside, or by keeping to the road, leads to:
Paradise Beach A very pleasant, small, 'U' shaped, 40m wide cove hemmed in by bare, dusty hillsides. A few pedaloes are drawn up on the gritty sand beach, on which are also planted some sun umbrellas. The sea is startlingly clear, even if, after some 10m, the bottom is weedy and boulderous, but by that time a swimmer is well afloat. Behind and raised above the backshore is a small, neat apartment block-cum-taverna, separated from the backshore by a sloped bank, attractively planted with green, ground covering plants. Alongside the approach track is another compact accommodation building.

Returning to the Highway, it once again climbs up into the mountains, allowing lovely views back over Bali, before descending past a rather large development, on the way to the slip road off to:

PANORMOS (59km from Iraklion) Tel prefix 0834. The Highway skirts Panormos, but consider making the detour as the village has managed to remain traditional and attractive. The rather polite tourism, allowed to intrude, has imbued the settlement with a quiet, prosperous milieu. It has to be admitted that there is no longer likely to be a caique, under construction, on the edge of and dominating the small, main village square. Oh, no. There are now three, very nice, dignified tavernas, including the *Kastelli Taverna*. Their tables and chairs allow a view over a beach, to the right (*Fsw*). But that's not to say the Greece of yesteryear isn't a backyard or two away, with goats a-nibbling and chickens a-pecking.

The road into the village leads past the *Panorma Hotel*, there are quite a few **Rooms** spaced about, including some above a woodworking workshop, and even a 'Ladies Hair Specialist'. To the left (*Fsw*) of the village square is a short, sandy stretch of beach. On the far side, this is bounded by a harbour quay wall, overlooked by the nicely situated, very swept-up *Captains Rooms & Restaurant* (Tel 51352). Here a double room, with en suite bathroom, costs 3000drs a night but much of the time the accommodation is taken up by holiday companies.

Other village facilities, discreetly spread throughout the narrow streets, include: two bakers; an old fashioned general store; a Rent A Car/Travel Agent; a butcher; a shop, where foreign language newspapers are for sale; and a scooter hire firm, where a machine costs an expensive 2800drs a day, and which possesses an international telephone.

From Panormos it is only a few kilometres to:
Lavris Beach This long beach, beyond a pleasant headland, is sandy, with large rocks scattered about. The small plain edging the shore is rather scrubbly, heavily cropped by sheep, and displays signs that 'the unwashed' have camped out amongst the stunted trees. There are many plastic greenhouses, much market gardening and general cultivation, but... development is creeping this way. It is not much further on, at **Skaleta**, that the socking great *Hotel Creta Star* is encountered, bordering a hardly adequate, crowded beach cove. So that the *Star* does not feel lonely, there are a couple of other, adjacent hotels.

To sum up the resorts along this Route, I would plump for Panormos first, Ag Pelagia second, and Bali third. For those who wanted any action, Ag Pelagia would have to move up the charts, as it does have a disco. Certainly Panormos is the most refined, whilst Bali is rather Polpero'ish.

ROUTE TWO
To **Lasithi Plain** via **Potamies** (57km) Proceeding to the east, the turning for the Lasithi Plain, from the Iraklion to Ag Nikolaos Highway, is prior to Limin Chersonisos, after some 22/23km. The road that snakes up to the perimeter of the 'hidden valley' of Lasithi, remains rather narrow, considering the constant stream of tour buses that visit, day in and day out. If for no other reason, this ceaseless invasion of tourists makes it surprising that the villages *en route*, including **Potamies**, **Sfendili** and **Avdou**, have

remained relatively unspoilt and pretty. Petrol is available at **Gonies**, from whence the tree lined route continues to wind though massed olive groves, up the mountainside of the Dikti range, and past the branch turning to:

KRASI (48km from Iraklion) Despite this charming little village being only just off the well-worn main road, it could be a million miles away. It is a popular weekend trip for the locals, for reasons that will become apparent.

There is a triangulated road in and out. The wider of the two, and that is only a comparative term, is the upper or more southerly road. The latter approach decants on a flattened section of ground, immediately beyond a particularly difficult bend into the village proper. A sign announces 'Visit a Cretan House-Freetly (sic) entry'. This indicator points to what looks remarkably like a collection of animal sheds, in a poor state of repair. To those of a jaundiced eye, they may well resemble a pile of stones. Whatever, in amongst this tree surrounded scene of domesticity crouches an apparently demented fellow who, if gestures were enough, would be able to fill his dwelling, night and day.

Just around the corner is the centre of the village, an informal square totally dominated by an enormous plane tree, which might be as big as eleven metres around its bowl. '...there's big'! Spread out around the tree is an irregular, unlovely terrace, the patio of the *Cretan Restaurant Grill Platanos*, which is more a rural BBQ shack. On the nearside is a 'bus shelter' type periptero, whilst to the left, close to the edge of the terrace, are a couple of side-by-side 'telephone box toilets'. Yes, telephone ... I hate to think whence they drain away! If all this were not dramatic enough, the right-hand side of the square is taken up by a wall of catacoomb-like water fountains. On closer inspection these are three arched recesses from which crystal clear water pours. The face of the alcoves are decorated by various ceramic plates and tiles.

The hut alongside the taverna, in which all the cooking is carried out, belches forth great gouts of smoke, like some giant steam train getting up a head of power. The meals are simple, allowing a choice of chops & chips (600drs), salad (200drs), beer (100drs), rusks (15drs per head) and water. Retsina is available, but the service is on the slow side of slow. I have even observed Greeks give up the long wait! A meal for two costs about 1630drs, though this is definitely not one for the gourmets, being more a rendezvous for those who like to see the locals at work and play.

A few paces further on is another taverna, beyond which the road bends round to the left, past several kafeneions and a children's playground, back down to rejoin the main road.

The main route now ascends past the downward plunging path to the **Monastery Kera**, which is also known as the 'Panaghia Kardiotisis'. Next along are the various, cliff-face hanging **Keras villages**, spread throughout which are several tavernas and the singularly named *Coffee Taverna Sincerity*. Beyond the Keras', the road climbs steeply to cross the last ridge along which, to the left, are still ranged a row of some fifteen or sixteen windmills. These are now mostly in ruins, except for one or two, in amongst a small scattering of buildings and a taverna, adjacent to the roadside, and which have been converted into gift shops. The next junction is that with the ring road that circumscribes the:

LASITHI PLAIN The almost kingdom-like plain is remarkable for its hundreds of skeletal water windmills, and their reefing sails. Interestingly, these are not some relic of a Cretan industrial revolution, a flowering of latter-day metal-working, more a Chicago export of the 1920-1930 era. It appears that expatriate Greeks, resident in the USA, realised that the early oil well frames and borers could be adapted to pump water - not oil! The highly cultivated nature of this fertile land, coupled with the massed fruit trees and apple orchards, in amongst which graze many cows and donkeys, results in a very Western European feel to the locality.

In recent years, completion of the circular road has been finished. Due to the original, earlier metalled sections being left as they were, this has resul- ted in a route of widely varying state and condition, ranging from a narrow, moth-eaten and potholed track, to a wide swathe of first-class carriageway.

Proceeding in a clockwise direction, from the Iraklion junction, the first hamlet is **Pinakiano**, in which is a bit-of-a-fruit market. This is followed by rural **Lagou**, wherein are very few hostages to tourism, then a scattering of windmills and **Miadou**, beyond which is a sign carrying on about the demo- cratic citizens welcoming visitors to:

TZERMIADON (60km from Iraklion) Tel prefix 0844. The long High Street is lined with general stores and gift shops, where Cretan crochet is predominant, as well as a 'Popular Art Supermarket'! Many of the facades of the buildings, and their trellises, are prettily covered with vines. The village remains relatively unspoilt, despite the tourists often massing here, during the day. Perhaps the somewhat piratical demeanour of a number of the locals, discourages night-time visits?

Shops and services include: several pharmacies; a bank; a baker; an OTE (open weekdays only, between 0730-1510hrs); a Post Office, close to the 'We speak French taverna'; and a couple of filling stations. Probably in order to con- trol the bursts of human and traffic activity, there are often a number of police cars in evidence. It should be noted that the law officers are usually to be found playing backgammon, in one of the cafe-bars. Perhaps so as to not unduly dis- turb them, in the execution of their duty, a one-way system has been introduced. On the other hand it may be more to do with the fact that the streets become bottle-necked when the tour buses are in full flow.

There are plenty of kafeneions, tavernas and restaurants, as well as a number of hotel/tavernas, which include the:

Hotel/Restaurant Kourites (Class B)   Tel 22194
Actually classified as a pension, and a very pleasant one at that. A double room, with en suite bathroom and balcony overlooking the plain, should cost 2630drs, with singles listed at 2070drs.

The management of the *Kourites* also own an annexe called the:
Hotel Lasithi (Class E)
The telephone number is the same, but the room charges are less expensive, as all rooms share the bathrooms, with singles costing 790drs & doubles 1130drs. Note that the owners have a disturbing habit of raising these official rates, when enquiries are made! A nod is as good as a ...

Hotel Cri-Cri (Class E)   Tel 221700
A less expensive if scruffier alternative to the above, with all bedrooms sharing the bathrooms, a single charged at 900drs & doubles 1200drs, but showers are charged extra, at 50drs a head.

Beyond Tzermiadon is a turning signed to **Kronio Cave**, followed by the spacious, old village of **Marmaketo**, most of which is bypassed, but with a couple of kafeneions straddling the road and a large statue on the outskirts.
    The far side of a petrol station, and alongside a church, is a fork. To the left heads off to Neapolis and Ag Nikolaos, via the agricultural community of tree lined **Mesa Lasithi**, which has a large church, a kafeneion and general store, all set in massed apple orchards. This route continues on through the surprisingly tourist oriented village of **Mesa Potami**. The centre of Potami is almost wholly taken over by tavernas and, at the appropriate season, trestle-tables laden down with fruit for sale. The old ladies who mind the 'shop', hold up and wave pre-packed bags 'in the face' of passers-by. Further on, the fertile landscape becomes almost English country lane in character, around which all manner of deciduous trees grow. The next settlement of **Exo Potami** has a *Little Chef,* close by a couple of fountain heads, but no need to panic, this is not one of the chain, thank God, simply a local name. On the way to the village of **Zenia**, and on a saddle ridge, are three of the nearly unique, 'U' shaped Cretan windmills, one of which has been converted into a dwelling house. From hereon, the mountainsides have suffered from a fairly recent forest fire, which appears to have, in the main, missed much of the hamlets of **Amigdali**, **Kato Amigdali** and **Vryses**.

Back at the Lasithi Plain, at the fork in the road, and continuing in a clockwise direction, advances past **Kroustalenia Monastery**. This was a centre of Cretan resistance to the Turks - more correctly the Turks razed the place to the ground, once or twice. The next settlement *en route,* which lies alongside a dried-up river-bed, is:

AG KONSTANTINOS The dusty village has *Rooms,* the *Dikti Restaurant,* a kafeneion or two, looms, still used to weave carpets for sale, as well as souvenir and gift shops. The natives tend to go a bit OTT, leaping into the road, in front of passers-by, in their attempts to clinch a sale.

Despite the hype in respect of the windmills, their sails and the unique sight of them whirling away, all over the plain, it is sad to report that very few are in operation, hereabouts.

AG GEORGIOS A much more open, widespread and businesslike community than the others encircling the plain. Apart from a large church, a petrol station, a few shops, a cigarette vendor, and a doctor's surgery, there is the *Cafeteria George,* as well as an old kafeneion or three. The accommodation available includes: *Rooms Maria* and a pair of E Class Hotel/Restaurants. The latter are the *Dias* (Tel 31207), with friendly owners, where a single room costs 1000drs & a double 1500drs, plus 100drs per head for the use of the shower, and the *Rea,* across the way from a school, and which has a butchers shop stuck into the corner of the ground floor - convenient for the dining room, if nothing else.

The village's delights embody a doo-hickey Museum of Cretan Folklore.

This side of the plain would be more correctly described as gentle hillsides, if that is not too Irish. **Koudamalia** hamlet is so small that a traveller is in and out of it, without really grasping the fact - a one donkey dropping blip - on the outskirts of the backyard, farming village of **Avrakontes**. Here several kafeneions circle the irregular square, and at the far side is a petrol station. In the middle of the orchards, ranged   alongside the route, is the *Dinos Taverna*, after which is the rural   village of **Kaminaki**, wherein are several *Rooms*, the *Taverna/Cafe Tassos* and some low-key, 'traditional' tourist cottage industry.

The next hamlet of **Magoulas** hosts the *Restaurant Grill Dioyssis*, built in a converted windmill, as well as a gift shop and kafeneion. A petrol station marks the outset of:

PSYCHRO (67km from Iraklion) Tel prefix 0844. I must admit to not hav- ing made up my mind who exactly all this 'popular Cretan Art' is really popular with, but whomsoever it may be, there is a lot of it at Psychro.

One of Greece's saving graces is that, amongst all the doo-hickey glitz, there is just as likely to be a family pressing grapes, in the back of their polythene lined truck. The vehicle may well be parked alongside the ground floor of a skeletal frame, pre-cast concrete building, pressed into service as a animal pen or a store for bales of hay, whilst a goat or two will be found tethered to the 'High St' toilet block.

The main street of this large village is both tree and restaurant/taverna lined, the latter embracing the *Taverna Stavros*, and the *Restaurant Plat- anos*. Apart from two E Class hotels, the *Dictaeon Andron* and the *Heleni*, at the far end of Psychro, close by a branch turning for the **Cave of Dict- aeon**, is the *Hotel Zeus* (Class D, tel 31284), on the right, and the *Res- taurant Grill Girakaki*, on the left.

The settlement's claim to fame is the proximity of the:

Diktaion Cave Supposedly the birthplace of Zeus, the mythological god of gods, but it is sad to advise that the whole enterprise can now turn out to be a bit of a rip-off. Entrance costs 200drs, but visitors   should bring a torch to save having to purchase the rather inadequate, fast burning candles. Nor should they hire one of the guides, who charge 500drs, for very little. One other word to the wise is to avoid the tour coach-popular period, between mid-morning and mid-afternoon. As the cave is open between 0830hrs-1800hrs, that is not so difficult to organise.

Beyond Psychro, the road drop back down on to the plain, in an area where there are many redundant windmills, and acres and acres of apple orchards. In amongst the trees are the *Taverna Antonis*, the *Cafe Restaurant Milos*, and the *Restaurant Manos*, followed by pretty, if squalid **Plati** village. This boasts a couple of kafeneions, a pair of tavernas and a 'dead' school. Here- abouts the apple orchards are interspersed by vineyards, as well as animal corrals and grasslands. **Kato Metochi** is a widespread settlement, the out- lines of which are difficult to define, due to the scattered and intrusive positioning of the farm homesteads.

Travellers who have arrived under their own steam, and do not wish to return by the same route, can consider a couple of choices. There is the already detailed option of turning off at Mesa Lasithi, in the direction of Neapolis/Ag Nikolaos, or the possibility to retrace one's footsteps as far as the fork at which the Mochos road is signposted, beyond Krasi and prior to Gonies. Selecting this alternative advances to:

MOCHOS The Main Square of this unlovely village is bordered by tavernas, with the suggestion of an older settlement lurking up on the left. There is a Post Office and, on the far side, a petrol station.

Once the far ring of hills are breasted, a glorious panorama opens out, taking in tremendous views to sea. The very fast, serpentine and steeply descending road decants onto the National Highway, to the west of **Malia**.

ROUTE THREE
To the east Iraklion Beaches & Ag Nikolaos (69km) The signposting and road east of Iraklion are unclear, to say the least.
Those seeking the nearby beaches should eschew the National Highway and stick to the Esplanade from the east of Iraklion Ferry-boat Harbour, all the way to the sign for the *Hotel Minoa*. The route climbs up from the waterfront, close to where caiques are still being built on the side of the road. These eastern suburbs of Iraklion are a depressing, messy site.
The road skirts the airport, prior to descending and running along the coast. It is interesting that the Armed Forces have an extensive base alongside the runway. Perhaps the authorities have read the insurgent's handbook for revolution - first seize the airport and radio station! Hereabouts the countryside, inland of the juxtaposition of the Old and New roads, is absolutely appalling, if not almost unbelievable. Right in front of one's very own eyes is a sprawling, South American style, cardboard city encampment covered rubbish dump, seemingly home for hundreds of gypsy families.
The road continues along the shore whilst the Highway marches on to the right, forming a long, hotel, pension, restaurant and taverna scattered island of ground, between the two routes. One inescapable drawback is that this stretch of coast, as well as the urban blighted land bordering it, is on the flight path of Iraklion airport. Despite, or perhaps because of this impediment, there are a number of large, modern, package tour hotels, each complete with a swimming pool, cocktail bar and disco nightclub. Super!
The Old Road swings towards and drops down past various abandoned buildings, a smallholding, a two storey kafeneion type cafe-bar, and, on the right, a small chapel, behind which is a 'sort-of-a-grotto' let into the hillside. Beyond the last mentioned religious curio, the road straightens out to run along the nearside of a rather desolate sweep of shore, or:

Beach 1: Supposedly a Municipal beach, and certainly wired off, but the area has little to commend it. A Greek Airforce Club caravan, in to the side of which are let lots of portholes, occupies the middle ground. The beach certainly is sandy, even if the backshore is pebbly. The public or unfenced stretch of sandy shoreline continues on, edged by the road. To the inland side is a not over-wide plain of fields and bamboo groves, hemmed in by low hills, on which are scattered about those telegraph pole-like cactii.

Continuing eastwards, and beyond a dried up river-bed, the plain narrows down. In amongst some hillbilly farm shacks, are the *Blue Dolphin Inn, Rooms*, and a petrol station. The riding school outfit, 'Horse & Waggon Tours', 'up in those there' hills, trek down to this bit of the coastline, the rides emerging alongside *Rooms Stella*. A rather messy area is followed, at the far, east end, by the *Hotel Amnissos*, the *Motel Zenia*, down by the sea's edge, and an outcrop of rock.

Amnisos Or Beach 2 (about 5km from Iraklion) Reputedly the Minoan harbour for Knossos. Offshore is the **Island of Dia**, a haven for the Kri-Kri (Agrimi), a big goat with large curved horns, indigenous to Crete.
   To the nearside is a localised collection of 'Hayling island' shacks, down to which a path cuts, past the smart *Rooms Lakis*, petering out close by the shantyish, seashore bordering *Taverna Amnisos*. The latter may be a not-so-clean-bit-of-a-shambles, wherein toilets and a pay phone, but they know how to charge. Beer is served in half litre glasses, at a price of 130drs, whilst a lemonade costs 70drs, and the menu prices are on the high side. High season competition is supplied by a pair of backshore Cantinas.
   Amnisos is an excellent, some 1km long, broad sweep of gently shelving sand and sea bed, with a tiny inshore islet. There is some pebble broadcast about the duney backshore, and there isn't any shade, but these are trifling cavils. Apart from identifying the make of the undercarriages of the constant stream of incoming aircraft, there is a wealth of water sport activity. This encompasses the hire of: canoes 400drs; water cycles 1000drs; and a jet ski, at a rate of 2500drs for 15 mins. Sun-beds & umbrellas are for hire at 300drs each. Towards the equally praiseworthy, distant end of the beach, where the selfsame shore is named **Tombrouk**... or **Ag Poulka** (Mmmh!), there are some thatched sun umbrellas, the *Minerva Palace Hotel*, a taverna, car hire, and the *Cretan Taverna*.

A short corniche along the rocky coast advances to:
Beach 3 Yet another wide, 300m long sandy beach, with a rather scrubbly backshore and a distinct sea's edge kelp line. Considering the lack of development, I am surprised this particular beach is not more popular, although there are a stack of sun-beds in place. At the west, nearside end is a *Pizzeria Snackbar*, whilst at the far side, coinciding with the commencement of a pleasing curve of rocky coast, there is an outbreak of commercialisation. This takes in a hotel or two, the *Pension Milos*, the large hotel complex *Arena Sand Hotel*, and the *Hotel Armidales*.

VATHIANOS KAMPOS (11km from Iraklion) Vathianos is an uncoordinated and muddled development. Along the length of the 'main drag' are spaced out a number of low-rise businesses, one of which is the intriguingly named 'Megaron Niron Antiquities', as well as several hotels, including the *Knossos Beach*. The narrow shore is 'little to write home about', with some pebble and a smidgin of sand.

KOKKINI CHANIA The shore is much pebble and some sand. In fact Kokkini is really nothing more than an extension of Vathianos, but with a greater concentration of accommodation, restaurants and 'halls of fun'. Hotels include the *Themis Beach*, *Akti* and the *Dani*, in addition to **Rooms**, the *High Laddie Scottish Pub* (about which the mind boggles), more **Rooms**, an OTE shack, and, marking the outskirts, the *Hotel Xenia Ilios*. That is not to say that the construction comes to a complete stop. Oh, no! It is simply spaced in and amongst 'bits' of agriculture.

GOURNES (18km from Iraklion) Tel prefix 0897. Unexpectedly, a well established village, at heart, with an old fashioned, tree lined High Street bordered by an insoluble mix of past and present. The ill-assorted ingredients include the *Pension Fontini*, *Rooms Despina*, a couple of tavernas, **Rooms**, a petrol station, and a mini-market. The east end of Gournes is marked by a Military base.

About the centre of the settlement is a turning down towards the sea, initially pleasantly tree and flower lined. The bundy, across which the road tracks, alongside a bamboo lined river bed, is unfortunately littered by an infliction of skeletal, prestressed concrete constructions. Some of the agriculture is of the worst and messiest type, and includes the dreaded plastic greenhouses. The road stutters to a halt, close to the seafront, alongside a river topped-up swamp, beyond which is a short length of sandy, kelp covered shore. Some enlightened soul has created a little public garden, complete with trees and park benches. The shoreline to the right (*Fsw*) is signed **Critzas Beach**, which heads towards the perimeter fence of the afore-mentioned Military base. Here again this has been thoughtfully tree planted, none of which can conceal the fact that this so-called beach is mainly big pebbles and boulders, over which is spread quite a lot of kelp. Despite all the foregoing, some developer has seen fit to erect the *Critzas Little Beach Bungalows*. My golly gosh! Perhaps it is the same guiding light that inspired the horticultural pursuits?

As the route continues to the east side of Gournes, it skirts the inland edge of the Military base, which is incongruously overlooked by the *Hotel Royal*. Without doubt guests will be able to enjoy a splendid view of the barbed wire of the camp. Perhaps those accommodated in the very top floor might be able to glimpse the sea?

To the east of Gournes the Old and New Highways link, close to the burgeoning resort of:
KATO GOUVES (24km from Iraklion) As things stand, Kato Gouves must now be very much as were Limin Chersonisos and Malia, in years gone by. The hinterland is dominated by a singular cliff face, topped off by a pair of 'Dr No' reflectors. From the New Highway, a lateral road rumbles across the messy cabbage fields in and around which, it goes without saying, new construction is gathering force. There is nothing attractive in the setting, added to which this is the point at which the commercial aircraft flatten out in order to make their final descent to Iraklion Airport.

The approach road junctions with a wide, unsurfaced track that parallels and edges the backshore, alongside the 'smarty-pants', large *Cretan Sun Hotel*. On this seafront the erection of buildings is taking place, at a faster, more frenetic pace. I suppose it would be understandable if there was a glorious swathe of golden sand... But no, the shore is a mix of small and

large pebbles in amongst which are outcrops of rock, and there isn't any
tree cover. I would sue a travel agent who advised me to holiday at this
spot. Turning to the left (*Fsw*), a scattering of old doo-hickey farmsteads,
and their home pastures, are being infilled by a number of kitsch Greek
villa homes, followed by an enormous holiday development. Close to the
latter is a small harbour, within the confines of which is a beach. On this
are drawn up some pedaloes and windsurfers, as well as a few sun-beds and
umbrellas. If this were not enough, there is more tourist inspired expansion
continuing apace, in a westerly direction. Not every bit and parcel of land
has been infilled, yet, but I cannot comprehend why any should take place,
as the unattractive shore is nothing more than rock, backed by pebble. This
soulless, shadeless location is followed by another small harbour, also
enclosing a strip of sand but with the benefit of a beach shower. Next along
passes one really ghastly complex and, at last, a nice if not very wide
stretch of sand. It has to admitted that on the inland side of the now
intermittently concrete surfaced track is a rubbish dump. Oh dear! Of
course the further one proceeds in this direction, the closer one approaches
to the east side of the Gournes Military base, the radio masts of which hove
into view. Many of the to-date, undeveloped plots of land are roughly
divided by wobbly rows of breeze blocks. Almost up against the fence of
the Base is *Camping Creta* (Tel 41400), where the management have
planted a number of trees.

Returning to the the main road, about 2km prior to Limin Chersonisos is
Camping Chersonisos (Tel 22025). Almost on the outskirts of Limin proper, across the Highway from the inland road to Kastelli, is a turning down
to the sea, a beach, an outcrop of development and a model village. This is
certainly more wholesome than the previously described location. Incidentally the Kastelli crossroads have occasioned a rather messy eruption of
buildings.
    The New Highway stands off from the coastline of Limin Chersonisos
and Malia, forming the High Street of both.

LIMIN CHERSONISOS (28km from Iraklion) Tel prefix 0897. The
location has some similarities with an ant-hill. Now that nearly everything
is buried underneath hotels, pensions, restaurants, tavernas, bars and tourist
shops, it is difficult to imagine that this was once the site of the ancient city
of Chersonisos.
    The seafront is edged by a narrow waterfront road which links a series of
small, sandy coves. Towards the western end, an access road to the seafront
emerges near a bulbous if miniature promontory. A small, Cycladean style
chapel is built into the side of this headland, which unequally divides the
sweep of the large bay into two. Tucked into the curve, on the right-hand
side (*Fsw*), is a large fishing-boat quay, in the lee of which is a small,
sandy beach with a few small boats drawn up on the foreshore. It is in this
area that the sunken remains of ancient Roman harbour walls are supposed
to be visible. On the neck of land linking the headland to the Esplanade,
within the confines of a dusty children's playground, are a couple of
'Tardis', or GPO telephone-style toilets.

To the left of the promontory is a crescent-shaped, sandy beach, pleasantly edged by arethemusa trees and which, towards the far, west end, degenerates into large pebble. This shore hosts sun-beds, umbrellas, pedaloes and windsurfers, whilst the backshore is peppered with the concrete patios of the various restaurants and tavernas. The Esplanade runs out, somewhat surprisingly, about half-way round the sweep of the bay.

Proceeding or eastwards for the next two kilometres or so, the rocky waterfront is tightly bordered by an Esplanade, which is edged by literally dozens of hotels, pensions and tavernas, and their awning covered patios. Both beaches are clean and the sea clear, with a gently shelving sea-bed.

Although there is little indigenous Greek surviving in Limin, at least the hotels are low-rise, with a maximum of four storeys. Incidentally most, if not all of the accommodation is very expensive. Throughout the resort are spaced a number of street plans indicating the whereabouts of this or that civic office. Readers should note that the tourist office appears to have disappeared and most of the public services are accessed from the High St. For instance, opposite the two side streets signed down to the 'Port', is a side street leading to the Post Office. About two hundred metres to the east of the latter, opposite a National Bank, is another side street, in the direction of the waterfront, that leads to the OTE, over which is a medical officer. The OTE is only open weekdays, between 0730-1510hrs, and is across the road from a Credit Bank. The Bus stop's and taxi ranks are spaced out along the length of the High St. Just in case anyone is in doubt, there must be more scooters and motorbikes for hire than the Japanese could possibly make.

Proceeding from Limin, in an easterly direction, a glance backwards from the main road allows a glimpse of an isolated chapel, perched on a small rocky headland, at the end of a diminutive causeway.

I suspect the land between Limin and Malia will eventually be completely infilled and a couple of villages *en route* have expanded their 'attractions', in an effort to sidetrack some of the boom trade from Limin and:

MALIA (36km from Iraklion) Tel prefix 0897. A sweeping bay, sandy beach, pleasant vistas, agricultural activity and proximity to Iraklion airport, combined to popularise the once cultivated areas of Malia. These are now criss-crossed by lanes and tracks, and are being developed at an ever-increasing rate. Ploughing, sheep-grazing and cane cutting is still under way, cheek-by-jowl with the rapidly expanding number of hotels, pensions and guest houses. Amongst all the tourist industry blitz, it is reassuring to hear the shrill, tortured bray of a donkey, or two. Haphazard construction erupts skywards out of a panorama still sheltering the occasional, now derelict, skeletal water windmills. The outer ring is marked by a most untidy mess of agricultural plastic greenhouses.

Now the resort spreads along the National Highway, from which branches the down-leg or main beach access street. This latter thoroughfare terminates close by the backshore, on a small, pan-shaped vehicle turn-round point. It is blocked off from the beach by a tiny, caique repair yard, complete with a crude gantry fitted with a double block and tackle. It is flanked by the smart *Hotel Malia Beach*, on the left (*Fsw*), and the *Pension Dramatikakis*, on the right. In the shallows, and slightly to the right of the very sandy beach, is a small chapel interestingly sited on a rocky outcrop. The referred-to, main beach access road is lined with hotels, pensions, *Rooms*, tavernas, beach and cocktail bars, a supermarket, tourist gift shops, discos, Rent-A-Car, scooter and bicycle hire firms.

Some half-way down the beach access road is a crossroads with a street-cum-track which parallels the seafront, some 80/90m back, stretching from the west to east extremities of Malia. To the right (*Fsw*), the lateral road wanders across the fields and from which sundry tracks cut down to various sandy coves. These coves are the result of the bay being broken up by outcrops of larva rock. To date, on this side of Malia, it is about 'even stevens' between the despoilers, sorry developers, and the farmers, with clumps of buildings spotted about. The road narrows down, angling towards the backshore, alongside the *Cactus Beach Bungalows*, which border the edge of yet another golden stretch of sand.

To the left of the centre of Malia, the lateral road runs through a more constricting holiday build-up, only to come to an abrupt end up against the low headland of Stalis Beach, where there is a Post Office caravan, as well as another sandy beach with pedaloes and wind surf boards.

The High St is very long and, as would be expected, there are various services and other goodies radiating off the same. About the middle of its length, on the inland side, is a largish church, the clock tower telling the correct time, on two of its four faces. Behind the church is a bit of the Old Malia, and the Post Office, which opens weekdays, between 0730-2000hrs, Saturdays, between 0730-1415hrs, and Sundays, between 0900-1330hrs. Beyond the Post Office, in an inland direction, and right reveals some small signs for the:

Youth Hostel

Directions: As above and following the indicators, for some 200m, passes the *Mon Mari Apartments*, set in delightfully doo-hickey surrounds.

The buildings are nothing more than single storey, converted chicken sheds which, if I'm not mistaken, still smell of chickens, where a dormitory bunk costs 500/650drs. The usual amount of notices are scattered about intoning on about 'this and that', one giving details of a launderette.

Incidentally, close to the church is the *Restaurante Italiano Al Camino*. How Greek! To the east, along the High St, are a pair of Banks straddling the road. These are followed by the:

Hotel Roussakis (Class D)   Tel 31464
Directions: As above.

Here all the rooms have en suite bathrooms, a single costing 2300drs & a double 2750drs, increasing to 2900drs & 3400drs (16th June-30th Sept).

A little further on is a Souvenir & Gold shop with a sign 'We rent Rooms'. Next along is a side street, alongside a Travel office, on which is a Butcher, a Dentist, both on the left, the *Hotel Apostolos* (Class E, tel 31484) and a Baker.

Back at the High St, opposite a sign pointing down to the beach, is *Pension Mar*, on the corner of a side street, beyond which is the *Pension Socrates*.

Once again returning to the High St and on the left is the *Pension Sophokles* (Class C, tel 31348), above a Supermarket of the same name. Also bordering the

High St are: Malia Scooter Hire, where one day hire of a 2 seater scooter is charged at 2600drs and three days costs 2400drs per day; an English Doctor, one James Hodge, at No 92A (when closed telephone 71265); and the *Bimbo Cafe*. Yes! I did not only draw attention to the latter for the cheap laugh, but in the side street alongside the same is a Baker.

Due to the appalling traffic jams that foul up the High St, in the busy periods of the day, the bus conductors engage in a sort of Russian roulette in which they bawl out the bus's destination as the vehicle crawls along the gutter, repelling all boarders who do not answer correctly!

Going west, towards Iraklion, the first branch street on the left houses the *Pension Verginia*, then the *Pension/Restaurant Hermes*, *Pension/Taverna Emerald*, *Pension Eva* and, across the High St, on the right, the:

Hotel Poppi (Class E)   Tel 31457
Directions: As above.

A double room with en suite bathroom is priced at 2400drs, which increases to 2600drs (15th June-15th Sept).

The *Poppi* is followed by the *Pension Romanos*, above a large store. Any number of package tour hotels line this busy main road but, for the life of me, I cannot imagine what the attraction of this particular strip of tarmacadam is, being some distance from the seashore and quite possibly even out of site of the 'briny'. The ribbon development peters out hereabouts. Just before a petrol station, is the OTE, on the right, which opens weekdays only, between 0730-1500hrs.

Menu signs, so often an excellent bellwether to the general trend of a location, probably say it all. Observed on my last trip were: 'Chile con carne served with chips, rice & salad'; 'Happy hour all night'; 'The Cockney Kid Restaurant', bearing the alluring invitation to "Come on up the apples and pears"; 'Raw Video'(?); 'Roast Beef & Yorkshire pudding'; 'Fish in batter'; 'Bacon butties'; 'Chicken & Chips' (450drs); and 'Original Indian curry, bhrani, madras & vindaloo'. Just 'an everyday Greek village'. Well, not quite!

About 2km east of Malia, on the New Highway, a signpost to the left indicates the olive grove lined side road to the:

Minoan Malia Palace The Palace and the accompanying outlying Minoan remains are perhaps not so striking as those at, say, Phaestos. Nevertheless they are well worth a visit, especially if not dropping in on any of the other excavations. The gates are open daily, between 0830-1500hrs, but are closed on Mondays.

Back on the Highway, a turning to the left leads to the holiday resort of:
SISI (43km from Iraklion) Tel prefix 0841. Last time I dropped in it was possible to refer to this location as a fishing village. Oh dear! Indeed, it was once a look-alike for a Cornish fishing port, but not any more. Development has now almost completely swamped Sisi and its environs.

The pleasant approach still gently winds down through olive groves, but... The necessity for a large notice board, at the outset to the location, bearing the names of all the various holiday businesses, presages the changes that have taken place. New construction is still proceeding headlong and the sound of pneumatic drills is relentless. The few original pensions and tavernas remain, and they haven't managed to alter the intrinsic road layout, yet.

The access road descends gently past *Sophias Pension*, which has been *in situ* for many years, as has the neighbouring *Pension Ireni*, to continue on past various other enterprises, all the way to the main T-junction, in the centre of the village. In fact this is more a staggered crossroads.

The turning to the left (*Fsw*) circles around the back of the harbour, past the attractively positioned *Restaurant Mouragio*. Close to the *Mouragio* is a Baker and round to the right (Fsw), and also looking out over the almost enclosed little port, is the *Harbour Lights Bar*. The *Lights* sets out to attract the United Kingdom element of the tourist hordes, advertising as it does 'Daily English breakfast 650drs. Friendly and cosy atmosphere today and every day'.

The track continues on along the arid, bare, gently sloping hillside. Bare that is apart from any number of holiday apartments and holiday villas - and all this despite the fact that there isn't any beach on this side, only a rocky coastline. Beyond the increasingly scattered development, the track continues on to the middlingly ethnic, very pleasantly tree planted:

Camping Sisi   Tel 71361
Directions: As above, between the track and the rocky seas edge.

Run by a very pleasant, welcoming family, this site has been here for many years. The alert young man who is more than likely to greet visitors, speaks excellent English. To make up for the fact that the 'beach' is rock, with a little sand, they boast a swimming pool. The per person charge is 350/420drs, a tent 300/350drs, and a camper van 400/450drs. It really is a very credible alternative to the 'delights' of Sisi.

Incidentally this rough track continues on, ducking and diving through the bundy, past the *Bella Vista*, in the middle of nowhere, to emerge some 250m prior to the Malia excavations.

Returning to the centre of Sisi, a few metres on down the 'High St', and on the left, is the long established *Taverna Petsalakis*, alongside which is a Supermarket. Diagonally across the High St, on the sea corner of the lateral branch road to the main beach, are the *Petsalakis Rooms*, whilst on the opposite corner is the *Villa Plan Tourist Organisation*. The High St also embraces a car and scooter hire business, a jewellery shop, as well as one or two neon-lit cocktail bars.

The High St descends, now steeply, past the old periptero, overlooking the almost circular sea-wall bordering the right-hand side of the harbour. At the bottom, the nicely positioned, quayside building has had a number of guises, over the years, but is now simply a locals cafe-bar.

The oft referred to main beach road, that branches off to the right (*Fsw*) of the High St, is signed 'Sisi Bay Villas & To Beach'. This track advances through the various 'bits of backyard' of cubic block, after cubic holiday blight, in every conceivable shape, size and style. It must be pointed out that some of these hotel and villas are very smart, if not chic. The road bends round the back of a nice, ever-widening cove, set in low, gorse covered hillsides. This was once a wild, rather swampy river gulch, but now boasts a sandy, man-made backshore, on which is plonked a square, multicoloured beach bar. Most of the seashore is grey shingle and pebble, the water's edge of which is rather kelpy. Beyond this cove, the low, inhospitable hills roll on. Unbelievably, stretching up from close by the rocky coastline is what appears to be a holiday village under construction. I shudder to think that this may be so.

Of all the accommodation possibilities, I can speak for:
Pension Petsalakis
Directions: As previously described.
   The pension has two buildings, one each side of the 'High St'. The accommodation is spotless and pleasantly furnished. The balconies of the rooms of the right-hand unit (*Fsw*) have the better views, those on the left looking out over a backyard. A double room, with bathroom en suite and a balcony, costs from 2500drs. The right-hand building has a pleasant patio area, with tables and chairs, and excellent views over the sea and towards Porto Sisi. The hardworking, very Irish-looking, Greek lady runs the kitchen and serves up a limited menu, whilst her 'hubby' does not appear to overdo things.

Sophia's Pension (Class A Pension)
Directions: As previously described.
   A double room, with bathroom en suite, is charged from 3000drs.

In respect of the eating houses, I can vouchsafe for the:
To Mouragio Taverna
Directions: As described.
   Reasonable food at acceptable prices.

It is no wrench to leave Sisi, but it is not far to one of my old favourites, Milatos Beach. The approach can be made directly via Sisi, or from the direction of Neapolis. From Sisi, breasting a ridge opens up a panoramic view over the large Milatos Plain. In the middle distance is a chapel, standing solitarily on a small hillock. The Neapolis road winds steeply up the mountainside past a ruined village. Nearby are a line of distinctive, but almost entirely disintegrated, stone built Cretan windmills. Sightings of these 'monoliths' always excites me and for those who also enjoy them, there is a fine 'terrace', visible from the Highway, in the area of Neapolis.

MILATOS VILLAGE (about 48km from Iraklion) Tel prefix 0841. Both roads lead through this venerable village, set down on the hillside about 1km above Milatos Beach. There are a number of old and traditional shops, typical of which is the village store, which seems to be part of the family living room. We once purchased some feta cheese here and it had to be dug out of an ancient cylindrical container stored in an antiquated fridge. The purchase caused quite a lot of consternation. There is accommodation available at *Rent a Room* (Tel 32204).
   Close by the village is yet another cave where the villagers, in days of yore, hid, only to be routed out by the Turks and massacred.

The road falls away from the village, past a number of 'villa this and villa that', which includes *Rooms Elena*, down to the seafront and:
Milatos Beach A number of maps simply use the nomenclature Analipsis. This is actually the name of the tiny, now totally rebuilt, dressed stone

chapel, set down to the right of the hamlet's small, sea-bordering, irregular square. Only a dozen or so years ago there was just a few houses, a taverna and the chapel but... At least there aren't any discos or cocktail bars, and fortunately Milatos remains comparatively unspoilt, uncomplicated and pleasant, even if it is no longer undiscovered.

Where the road spills out on to the Square, on the left (*Fsw*) is a reasonably well-stocked village store, then Rooms Elena, followed by the Meraklis Taverna. The latter is at the far, left-hand side, on the corner of the road that tracks along the waterfront to the left (*Fsw*). Ranged beside the rocky, boulderous sea's edge is a periptero, and the awning covered, bamboo sided frames that shelter the patios of the various tavernas circling the inland side of the plateia. Apart from that allocated to the Meraklis, which has been my favourite establishment for some ten years or more, there are, in a clockwise direction, the Restaurant Akrogeli, Restaurant Seashore, and, on the far flank, the Restaurant Mary Ellen. This latter taverna possesses a metered telephone from which international calls can be made. To defeat the effects of the wind most of the shelters now possess roller blinds. On the inland side of the chapel is a tourist shop.

As detailed my choice of eating places would always be the:
Taverna O Meraklis   Tel 81223
Directions: Those readers unable to see the establishment have either finished up in the sea, or that last raki was stronger than was thought!

This is the bar used by the local fishermen. They are often to be found seated here, whiling away any spare time, baiting their fishing baskets, perhaps with an ouzo to hand. Without doubt it is the friendliest of places. Evangeline, a diminutive lady and a gentle soul, runs it with her younger brother, Manoulis, both helped by another brother Georgis. Manoulis trained to be a teacher so speaks some English and is very charming. The prices are comparatively inexpensive, with a lunchtime meal, for two, of pizza and 2 beers costing 780drs. It certainly is a super spot at which to spend an evening eating and drinking the night hours away. A few of the regulars also speak a little English and are delighted to engage visitors in conversation. The family name is Kourdakis and Manoulis will help those seeking accommodation, although they do not have any of their own.

To the right of the square is the settlement's small, grey, large pebble, wall contained beach.

From alongside the *Meraklis*, is a backshore edging concrete track. This runs for about 300m along the pebbly backshore, littered in places with building materials, towards a fairly recently constructed harbour. It leads past a fish restaurant, with **Rooms**, the *Villa Elena*, a cafe-bar, a set back 'villa village', and, close to the harbour, the *Cafeteria Bar No Name*. Also to the left is the *Thalia*, a condominium of three and four bedroomed cabins, with most of the necessary holiday conveniences, including a swimming pool. Continuing round to the right leads past the *Restaurant Panorama*, and the outset of the harbour protection wall. Further on is even more development, and a yard where the sea defence, pre-cast concrete 'five bones' are fabricated.

Bread is delivered daily to the Main Square by a van, at about midday, but it is of the one-hour, brown, round-stone variety. By way of explanation, Greek bread can be quantified by the number of hours in which it must be eaten. One-hour bread is almost beyond redemption, before it is purchased. At the other end of the scale is a white, French look-alike which can last 24 hours or more.

If there is a drawback to Milatos Beach, apart from the lack of an attractive, sandy beach and the overwhelm of new construction, it is the lack of public transport. This omission makes it necessary to use taxis, or hire a car or scooter.

NEAPOLIS (some 54km from Iraklion) Tel prefix 0841. It is worthwhile turning off the New Highway just to visit this busy, bustling, county town. Not actually on the regular tourist track, Neapolis is friendly and colourful, the many shops and stores of which are bursting with their various wares. The expansive, elongated square is bordered by trees, a large church and a petrol station. On the west, petrol-pump side of the plateia are a couple of establishments at which to have a drink. One is a very friendly cafe-bar taverna serving simple fare, such as stick souvlaki, chips and salad. And aren't things cheaper here than in, say, nearby Ag Nikolaos? I know where I would prefer to be. On the opposite corner of the side street, beside the lower (more northerly) of the tavernas, is a National Bank, wherein exchange transactions take place.

From the west side of the Main Square, the High Street runs the length of the town and is lined by most of the town's numerous shops and services. In amongst these are: the Commercial Bank, that changes Eurocheques; a Baker and some General stores, in a side street off to the right of the High St; a super, double-fronted old shop, with metal shutters and a Total yoghurt sign affixed to the fascia, owned by a smiley, bespectacled man who sells lovely, creamy yogurt from the tub, on the left of the High St; a cobbler on the corner of a side street, to the left of the High St, down which are a couple of Bread shops, and a Butcher or two; a Health Studio; and a pharmacy across the High St from the sole source of accommodation, which is the:

Hotel Neapolis (Class D)   Tel 32268/32327
Directions: On the left, and almost at the far west end of the High St.

The hotel has been recently revamped and is a quite surprising sight. It is pure 1930s style - all metal frame windows, external rounded concrete wall corners, as well as a ballroom sized, chintz draped reception lounge.

On a historical note, it may be of interest to note that one Petros Philargos was born, in 1340, in the village of Kares, the site of modern-day Neapolis. Petros was eventually to become Pope Alexander V, but only for about a year, after which he passed away in mysterious circumstances.

From Neapolis, the country route is a pretty, valley road with many old windmills dotted about, passing through the lovely village of **Limnes** and on to Ag Nikolaos. As usual, the presence of any settlement is apparent by the piles of rubbish dumped on the hillsides of the approaches.

ROUTE FOUR
To Knossos & on to Kastelli via Archanes (5km & 38km) The road to the amazing archaeological site of Knossos proceeds south from Iraklion,

through squalid suburbs. The route advances past the town's hospital, on the left, followed by dusty and hilly countryside, but with flowers and vines in abundance. Naturally enough, considering its prime tourist rating, there are an enormous number of tour buses to the location.

Just before reaching the entrance to Knossos, a lane to the right leads up to the Villa Ariadne. This was built by Sir Arthur Evans, the prime mover behind the excavations. Interestingly, the house has experienced a history all of its own that would rate tour visits if it were not overshadowed by the colossus across the road. Dilys Powell wrote a very readable and evocative book entitled *The Villa Ariadne*, ostensibly relating to the history of the building and its occupants, but encompassing much Cretan history. Those who have lived in the Villa include: Sir Arthur Evans, the famous millionaire archaeologist who spent his fortune, and the fortunes of his family, in carrying out the excavations; John Pendlebury, a romantic Byronesque archaeologist-turned guerilla fighter, who perished in the Battle of Crete; the monarch of Greece, King Paul, whilst fleeing the relentless German, Second World War advance; as well as the German commanders of war-time Crete. One of the latter, General Kreipe, was dramatically abducted and spirited off the island during the Axis occupation of the island. This epic act of adventure is well described in the book *Ill Met By Moonlight*, by *William Moss*. Readers interested in this period should also obtain a copy of *The Cretan Runner* by *George Psychoundakis*, which includes much detail of the events, from a partisan's point of view. I am sure there can be no disagreement with my contention that the Villa is a study subject of its own. Whatever, we must now move on, across the road, to:

KNOSSOS (5km from Iraklion) The history of the excavations is well documented, and makes a fascinating thriller story. That is from the luck-of-the-draw in identifying the possibilities, the difficulties Evan's encountered in acquiring the hillside from the Turkish landowner, and the slow realisation that this dig would uncover the jewel in the island's archaeological crown.

As with most Minoan palace sites, the great palace was built around a central court, from which spread a succession of buildings, rooms and cellars connected by staircases, small courtyards, corridors and magazines for pithoi (storage jars and urns).

Evans put into train an imaginative reconstruction. This was based on frescoes found on the site, and the artistic recreations of Piet de Jong, which resulted in a most coherent restoration. It is a pity that his distinctive approach caused so much academic controversy. There can be no doubt that the other island palace remains, that have all been 'faithfully' excavated, are much more enjoyable once Knossos has been visited.

The dig revealed the religious aspect of the complex, with sacred double axes, pillars, shrines, purification or lustral baths, and the mythological Minotaur bull. This is in addition to the outstanding architectural design, coupled to the complicated installation of roadway, drainage and sanitation systems, water hydraulics, as well as what must be the first Greek 'squatty', in the Queen's apartments. It is fascinating to realise that our modern word 'labyrinth' originates from 'labrynthos', a lost Minoan language term!

The site, probably the capital of the Minoan empire, has been continuously excavated from 1900, and remained a 'British dig'. That was due to

Sir Arthur Evans bequeathing the site to the British School of Archaeology, based at Athens, after he could no longer finance the escalating costs.

Habitation of the site occurred as early as 6000 BC. The Minoan period commenced circa 2000 BC, continuing after the great earthquake of about 1700 BC, and the resultant reconstruction. This was followed by another earthquake, circa 1600 BC, after which more rebuilding was necessary, that is until the final apocalypse, in 1400 BC. This disastrous conflagration resulted from a 'big bang', possibly occasioned by the cataclysmic eruption of Santorini's volcano. It was originally considered to have resulted in immediate evacuation and abandonment of all the Minoan sites. More leisurely thought and later excavations suggest that the civilisation did not suffer from a 'here you are, there you go'. There was possibly re-occupation after the disaster, followed by a rapid decline and final desertion. Fortunately, future generations of Cretans were only too aware of the sacred nature of the remains at Knossos, so kept well clear of the locality.

Recent discoveries include the exciting 'Royal Road', lined by the foundations of houses, workshops and, possibly, viewing platforms. For detailed study and enjoyment it is well worthwhile purchasing a 'dedicated' guide book, on the spot. How can one follow Knossos?

Across from the entrance to the site are several cafe-bar/tavernas. One of them is self-service, but rather defeats the object by giving personal attention to the clients! Additionally there is a *Rooms*.

Returning to the route, now badly potholed in places, advances past a rather splendid, Venetian, two-tiered water aqueduct, at a sharp bend in the road. I am sure it was here that a team of British Guerillas and Greek partisans snatched the German General Kreipe, in April 1944. Further on is a turning off to the left, signed for the Nikos Kazantzakis Museum, at **Skalani**. This was the great author's birthplace. The main road proceeds through countryside rich in viniculture, in and out of **Kato Àrchanes** and on to to the dusty, sprawling, old fashioned, drain smelling town of:

PANO ARCHANES (16km from Iraklion) Tel prefix 081. Pano is a centre for grape production and there is an ugly row of industrial buildings at the outset of the 'suburbs'. Beyond these is a counter-clockwise one-way road system, around which are spaced most of the town's notable facilities. Apart from a Post Office, there is an OTE, opposite the Town Police station, across an alleyway from which is the *Mirophiton Cafe-bar*. The latter is an interesting little local joint, almost entirely hidden from view by a bougainvillea and trees. Beyond a petrol station, the street runs on to the sloping Main Square, where the buses pull up. From the bottom, right-hand corner, a road climbs towards **Vathy Petro**. Alongside this, after 1km, and on the right, is the *Hotel Dias* (Class B, tel 751810), an almost look-alike for an English country house.

Throughout the town are plenty of kafeneions, some of them the unique, old fashioned style locations, with large windows, huge interiors and lofty ceilings. There is a bakery, a *mort* cinema, probably another victim of the ubiquitous video, a mini-market, a 'Market' street off to one side of which is a *Rooms*, a dentist, chapels, churches and a zacharoplasteion.

Archanes is a thoroughly worthwhile town to visit, the possessor of a sports ground and even an electrical goods shop. Some of the 'great un-washed' make their way here to join in the grape harvest, possibly when richer pickings are no longer available elsewhere.

Retracing the route into Archanes, as far as the first turning off to the right, leads to **Kounavi.** Here is a pretty little church with four domes and a rather striking bell tower (sorry), and, in the area, a petrol station. The next hamlet is **Kata Largari,** more a distillery really, beyond which the route is attractively lined by youngish gum trees, as far as **Peza.** This community embraces a petrol station, a video club, a busy main street and, nearby, a winery. The profusion of wine factories is not surprising as the fields are covered with trellis supported vines. At the next junction, where it is necessary to turn left, is a further, very large winery. **Ag Paraskies** is another busy High St, with a petrol station, followed by a very pretty route running along a river valley of massed olives, as well as varied deciduous trees, firs and cypress, set in low, gentle hillsides. Beyond a stretch of moorland type scenery, the road runs through a lovely avenue of mature gum trees, which do little to disguise the few industrial buildings, and on into **Apostoli.** The latter irresistibly reminds me of a 1950s, decrepit, French interior town. On the far side is another magnificent avenue of gum trees and, on some low hills to the right, the remains of a row of ruined windmills. The ugly, spread-out village of **Kardoulianos** has a number of 'Lasithi Plain-like' water windmills, and a stooping eagle monument - perhaps something to do with those German parachute chappies.

KASTELLI (44km from Iraklion) A pleasantly Greek, shambolic settlement radiating out from an irregular main square, bordered by a Police station. The buses park here. Accommodation is in the hands of *Rooms Veronique* and *Rooms Kastro,* the latter close to the taxi rank. The inner man is looked after by the *Taverna Hellidoni.* There are lots of General stores, and an OTE, open weekdays only, between 0730-1510hrs.

Apart from the relative freedom from tourists on this route, in and around the surrounds of Kastelli are a number of medieval churches, including those at **Sklaverochori,** a couple of kilometres to the west; **Xidas,** some two kilometres to the east; and **Pigi,** to the side of and two or more kilometres along the route back down to the north coast.

4 RETHYMNON (Rethymno)

Harbour city; seaside tourist resort; cultured & industrious; secretive Old Quarter.

GENERAL (Illustration 10) Tel prefix 0831. The history of this major Cretan city is perhaps not so extensively catalogued as the island's two other major centres, Chania and Iraklion. Rethymnon has some late Minoan traces; the Venetians were responsible for much of the town's development, and, subsequent to a particularly ferocious Turkish pirate raid, the construction of the walls and castle. Despite the fortifications and ramparts, in common with the rest of the island, Rethymnon was overwhelmed by the Turks, in 1645.

The present-day resident population numbers about 15,000 and Rethymnon is possibly the most complete and rounded of all the major Cretan towns. In addition to the 'standard package' of Venetian fortress, City walls, harbour, churches, Turkish Old Quarter, mosques, minarets and fountains, there is a splendidly sandy beach.

As there are no scheduled ferry-boats* or an airport, arrival will be by road. The Highway runs to the south of Rethymnon whilst the Main Road/ High St, Odhos Kountouriotou, skirts the inland edge of the City, with no clearly marked access to the centre. For those with independent transport, from the Main Road it is probably easiest to turn down one of the streets prior to the *Hotel Valari* (*Tmr* 8E6), coming from the east. These lead down to Agnostou Stratiou Sq (*Tmr* F5/6). This may not be the most salubrious area, but it is a convenient point from which to make a sweep along the seafront Esplanade, to the left or right.

To the right (*Fsw*) is a seemingly endless stretch of modern, tourist industry development. This borders a rather sterile waterfront road, even if the beach is more than acceptable and the backshore has been planted with young palm trees. To the left leads along the original town Esplanade, attractively lined with mature palm trees, edging a very generous swathe of sandy beach, and bordered by a variety of old buildings. At the far end it is necessary to jink right and then left to circle the miniature, pretty, inner Venetian Harbour (*Tmr* D/E2/3). Tucked away round the corner, its attractions are rather spoilt by the massed restaurants lining the quay.

One of the problems in establishing a position in the town is that the street layout appears to be based on a grid, but is, in actual fact, a series of slow curves. The most confusing streets are those of Arkadiou and Ethnikis Antistaseos. They both start off in the area of the now 'dead' Museum (*Tmr* 4D3/4), but finish up in completely different quarters, although seeming to run parallel. Know what I mean! Odhos Ethnikis Antistaseos commences its gently curving, uphill sweep alongside the Venetian Arimondi Fountain (*Tmr* 18C/D3) and marks the eastern edge of the original Old Quarter. This street passes the Minaret of Nerantzes (*Tmr* 31C/D3/4), climbing on up to an old Town Gate, outside which is another minaret and a bustling square flanked by the modern Tessaron Martyron Church (*Tmr* 29C/C56).

* *Every so often the possibility of a Rethymnon-Piraeus ferry-boat link pops up, as is the case in 1990.*

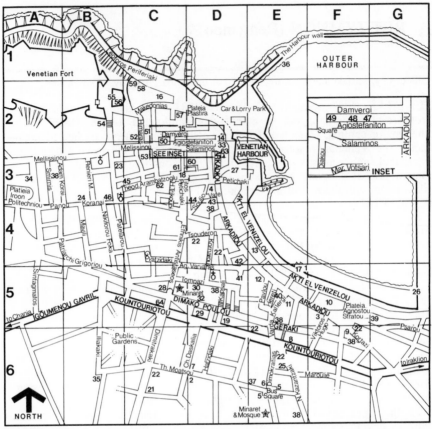

Tmr			
		23B/C3	Bread shop
1E/F4/5	NTOG	24B3/4	Baker
2C/D6	Post Office	25E6	Baker
3E/F5/6	Kara Pasha Mosque	26G5	Beach Bar Delfini
4D3/4	'Dead' Museum	27D/E3	Ladies toilet
5E6	Bus Stations	28C5	Old Town Gate
6D/E6	Hotel Olympic	29C/D5/6	Tessaron Martyron Church
7C/D6	Hotel Brascos	30C/D5	Youth Hostel/'Laundry Mat'
8E6	Hotel Valari	31C/D3/4	Merantzes Minaret
9F5/6	Hotel Acropol	32C/D5	Supermarket
10F5	Pension/Leather Shop	33D2/3	Rent Rooms Helen
11E5	Hotel Minoa	34A3	Police
12D/E5	Hotel Zania	35B6	Hospital
13D/E4/5	Hotel Achillion	36E1	Ferry-boat Quay
14D2/3	Pension Mikonos	37D/E6	Hotel Liberty
15C/D2/3	Dokimaki Rooms	38	Rooms
16C2	Hotel Kastro	39F/G5/6	Hotel Kyma Beach
17E/F4/5	Beach Pavilion	40E5	Rooms Vrisinas
18C/D3	Arimondi Fountain	41D/E4/5	Pension Castello/
19D5/6	OTE		Taverna O Giorgos
20A4	Football Stadium	42D/E4/5	Pension Kallergi
21C6	Airline Office/Hotel Joan	43D3/4	Hotel Leon
22	Banks	44C/D3/4	Olga's Rooms

45B/C3	Rooms Klapaki
46B3/4	Cafe-bar/Rooms
	Ovelistirion
47 Inset	Rooms Irene
48 Inset	Helen Rooms
49 Inset	Rooms Karavasilis
50C2/3	Rooms Corina
51C2/3	Historical & Folk Art
	Museum
52B/C2/3	Rooms Marylee
53B/C2/3	Rooms Pilos
54B2	Pension Anna
55B/C2	Archaeological Museu
56B/C2	Rooms George
57C/D2	Hotel Ideon
58C1/2	Rooms Seeblick
59B/C1/2	Pension Lefteris
60C/D3	Taverna Karia Maria
61C3	Taverna Vattela
62C3	La Creperie
63D2/3	Three Brothers Tavern
64C5	ANEK Office

Tmr = Town map reference
Fsw = Facing seawards
Sbo = Sea behind one
Fbqbo = Ferry-boat Quay behind o

Illustration 10 Rethymnon

Diagonally across the main road are the   Public Gardens. Conversely, Odhos Arkadiou also gently   curves, but   parallel to the seafront, and one block back, spilling out on   to Plateia Agnostou Stratiou, at the east end. Once these two streets are mastered, the rest of the town can be explored, with some confidence.

The western suburbs of Rethymnon are a mishmash of industry, junk and filth, in amongst which are plonked one or two garishly modern hotels. I never cease to wonder!

ARRIVAL BY BUS The dusty, disorganised, somewhat chaotic Bus Square is located to the south of the Main Road. On diagonally opposite corners are a Bus ticket office, apiece (*Tmr* 5E6).

ARRIVAL BY FERRY Once again, the 1990 listings are detailing a Piraeus ferry-boat link, four days a week. If the service does stay in operation, they will dock in the Outer Harbour (*Tmr* 36E1).

THE ACCOMMODATION & EATING OUT Establishments for both are plentiful, but   rather more costly than many other Cretan holiday centres. This is, in the main, due to the explosive discovery and expansion of the Rethymnon package tourist industry.

The Accommodation Generally, the more traditional *Rooms*, Pensions and older hotels lurk in the Old Quarter, whilst the smarter, tourist facilities are ranged along the eastern seafront. Unfortunately, for the independent traveller, many of the small, Old Quarter pensions have been taken over by specialised holiday companies. This, added to the recent dramatic increase in the popularity of Rethymnon, has resulted in it being necessary to arrive early in the day, in order to root out a bed. It has to be admitted that the tout, who loiters at the Venetian Harbour end of Odhos Arkadiou, always seems able to conjure up something in the back alley of Agiostefaniton.

As the vast majority of visitors disembark at the Bus station, I shall commence the description of the accommodation by radiating out from there.

Hotel Olympic (*Tmr* 6D/E6) (Class B) Th Moatsou/Dimokratias   Tel 24761
Directions: It really could not be closer to the Bus offices/terminus, unless it was built over them. For those who do not arrive by bus, turn along Odhos Dimokratias from the Main Road, alongside the square (more a rhomboid actually) formed by the streets of Dimokratias and N Kazantzaki (usually listed as Hortatzi St), with the National Bank (*Tmr* 22E6) in the apex.

An up-market, mainly tour operator booked, expensive hotel. Despite this air of exclusivity, its proximity to the Bus Sq makes for a noisy location, and the first bus slips its 'starting blocks' at 0630hrs. In addition there is a taxi rank across the road. It goes without saying that rooms all have en suite bathrooms, with a single priced from 2500drs & a   double from 3500drs, which rates increase, respectively, to 3200drs &   4600drs (16th May-30th Sept). Breakfast may be mandatory, adding another 500drs or so to the bill. What's money?

South along Odhos Kazantzaki, from the Bus Sq, leads to *Rooms* (*Tmr* 38E/F6) at No 27, whilst west along Th Moatsou St, beyond the *Olympic*, and on the same side of the street, is the *Hotel Liberty* (*Tmr* 37D/E6).

Hotel Brascos (*Tmr* 7C/D6) (Class B) Th Moatsou/Ch Daskalaki   Tel 23721
Directions: This hotel is located in the corner of the third block to the   west of
the Bus Sq.
   Comments as for the *Olympic*, but less bus and taxi noise. All rooms   have en
suite bathrooms, with a single room costing from 2300drs & a double 3550drs,
charges that increase to 3350drs & 4450drs (16th   April-30th Sept). Breakfast
costs a trifling 660drs!

Whilst this side of the Main Road, just around the corner from the *Brascos* is the:
Hotel Joan (*Tmr* 21C6) 6 Dimitrakaki   Tel 24241
Directions: As above and over the Olympic Airline office.
   Single rooms start off at 3500drs & doubles 4400drs, which prices increase to
4000drs & 5400drs (1st June-30th Sept).

Hotel Valari (*Tmr* 8E6) (Class C) 84 Kountouriotou   Tel 22236
Directions: Edging the Main Road and opposite the monument to E Venizelou,
which is adjacent to the National Bank.
   Due to its position, this is a very noisy location. All rooms have en suite bathrooms, with single rooms charged from 2220drs & doubles 2885drs, rising, respectively, to 2820drs & 3600drs (1st June-18th Oct). Note, the   management
may require 'encouragement' to reduce the first (overcharging)   rate quoted.
Nothing like turning, as if to leave...

Before proceeding any further, it might be an idea to call into the NTOG office
(*Tmr* 1E/F4/5), who are still fairly helpful in locating accommodation to suit all
pockets and tastes. I write still, but, naturally, the attitude has changed since the
sad demise of 'Mr Rethymnon', Costas Palierakis.(*See* **NTOG, A To Z**).
   North of and parallel to Kountouriotou is a street named Dimako Poulou (at
the west end) and Geraki (at the east end), along and around which are a
scattering of possibilities, including the:

Youth Hostel (*Tmr* 30C/D5) 41 Tompazi   Tel 22848
Directions: As above and through the bridge span of the Old Town Gate (*Tmr*
28C5), on down Odhos Ethnikis Antistaseos, next right on to Odhos Tompazi
and the hostel is on the right, alongside a launderette.
   Indubitably a popular choice of the young, with hard rock as the background
music. The reception desk opens between 0800-1200hrs & 1700-2000hrs, and a
dormitory bunk costs 500drs per night. Signs indicate that the hot water is turned
on between 0800-0900hrs & 1700-1900hrs, but it is sometimes illusory!

Further east along Tompazi St is *Rooms* (*Tmr* 38D5), close to the junction with
Kapsali St, whilst, at the junction of Geraki and Vardi Kallergi Sts, there is
Rooms Ani (*Tmr* 38E5/6) - 'ask in the souvenir   shop'. Continuing east along
Odhos Geraki leads to Kortazi St, at which   angling down to the left passes
Rooms (*Tmr* 38F5/6). Continuing to descend Odhos Kortazi, towards Plateia
Agnostou Stratiou, leads past the:

Hotel Acropol (*Tmr* 9F5/6) (Class D) Agnostou Stratiou Sq   Tel 23477
Directions: As above, with the spartan hotel on the right, in a not particularly
salubrious situation.
   Despite the location and (lack of) class, the hotel is clean, the bathrooms are
washed down twice a day, and the staff are very friendly... but the supply of hot
water can be erratic. A single room, sharing the bathroom, costs 1200drs & with
en suite facilities 1400drs, whilst a double sharing is priced at 1600drs & en suite

2100drs, which rates increase, respectively, to 1300/1600drs & 2000/2450drs (21st June-30th Sept).

Hotel Kyma Beach (*Tmr* 39F/G5/6) (Class C) Agnostou Stratiou Sq   Tel 21503
Directions: As above and to the right (*Fsw*).
  All rooms have en suite bathrooms, with a single starting off at 3400drs & a double 3900drs, increasing to 3750drs & 4610drs (1st June-25th Oct).

Incidentally the *Kyma* marks the outset of the shadeless, soulless, seemingly endless sweep of the eastern Esplanade, edged by an absolute plethora of hotels. The *raison d'etre* for this 'holiday pox' is the lovely stretch of beach and gently shelving sea-bed, that almost goes on forever.
  From Plateia Agnostou Stratiou there is the choice of proceeding north-east along Arkadiou or the parallel Esplanade, Akti El Venizelou. Most Esplanade edging properties stretch through to the 'back lane' of Arkadiou.

Pension (*Tmr* 10F5) 11 Arkadiou
Directions: To one side of the Esplanade leather shop (of which more, much more later), close to Plateia Agnostou Stratiou, and entered from an external flight of steps. Access can also be effected from Odhos Arkadiou, exactly opposite the *Kara Pasha Mosque* (*Tmr* 3E/F5/6).
  It is difficult to opinion whether the black draped, lady owner is as forbidding as is the very spartan, almost grim but nonetheless clean accommodation. A grotty single room costs from 1200drs, whilst a slightly superior double costs from 1600drs. It goes without saying that the bathrooms are shared.

The first transverse side alley linking the Esplanade and Odhos Arkadiou houses *Katerina's Furnished Studios*.

Hotel Minoa (*Tmr* 11E5) (Class D) 60 Arkadiou   Tel 22508
Directions: From Plateia Agnostou Stratiou, turn long Odhos Arkadiou at the Kara Pasha Mosque (*Tmr* 3E/F5/6), and on the left.
  This Greek provincial hotel, which has undergone a face-lift, is in a super part of town for those who like to be in the 'thick of things'. Furthermore the beach is only a few metres down a short lane and across the Esplanade. The owner is pleasant and the establishment clean and airy. Officially the en suite rooms cost 1300drs for a single and 1500drs for a double, increasing to 2000drs & 2300drs (11th April-15th Oct). Negotiations can be entered into, especially if prospective guests show an inclination to leave!

This area is a rich vein of accommodation, with *Venetia Apartments* at 39 Varda Kallergi St, that is the next side-street leading down to the Esplanade, west from the *Minoa*. The *Venetia's* double room rates start off at 5500drs.

In another side-street, Odhos Hereti, is:
Rooms Vrisinas (*Tmr* 40E5) 12 Hereti   Tel 26092
Directions: As above and on the left (*Sbo*), opposite a baker.
  Comes recommended as some of the best private rooms in town, in a compara- tively quiet street. Double rooms cost from 1800drs.

Pension Zania (Tmr 12D/E5) (Class D) 3 Pavlou Vlasto/Arkadiou   Tel 28169
Directions: The very next lane left off Odhos Arkadiou, to the west of Hereti St, and on the right, almost in the corner of the junction.
  Pleasantly Greek provincial - light, airy, clean, and an excellent choice. Only

double rooms are available, sharing the bathrooms, with charges   starting at 2200drs, which increase to 2500drs (16th June-30th Sept). The landlady is most helpful, offering to place single room aspirants with a friend of hers.

Next door to the *Zania* is *Amica Rooms*. A few metres further west on Arkadiou St, and on the left is an irregular square. Tucked away in a corner, behind the *Taverna O Giorgos*, is the *Pension Castello* (*Tmr* 41D/E4/5). Across the plateia, on the north-west corner of the square and Arkadiou St, above a clothes shop, is the smart looking, three storey *Pension Kallergi* (*Tmr* 42D/E4/5, tel 22433). These are furnished rooms, each with its own balcony (spelt with a 'k') and a fridge, sharing kitchens at 'low prices'. Enquiries must be made in the shop.

On the Esplanade side of Arkadiou St is the:
Hotel Achillion (*Tmr* 13D/E4/5) (Class E) 151 Arkadiou   Tel 22581
Directions: As above, and, as the hotel extends through from the Esplanade, there are entrances at both front and back.
    Somewhat dingy, but what do you expect from a Class E hotel - the Savoy? It does have an air of long-ago, faded elegance. A friendly owner offers double rooms, complete with shower and balcony at the front of the building, for a cost of 3000drs. However, there are less expensive rooms,   at the back sharing a bathroom, costing from 2000drs.

The *Achillion* is flanked by accommodation, with *Rooms Panoramas* on the right (*Fsw*), at No 149. Beyond the lateral side street of Tsouderon is another, Odhos Kornarou, on which are *Rooms* (*Tmr* 38D3/4), on the right (*Sbo*). Further along, and on the corner of Arkadiou and Vafe St, is the classy looking *Hotel Leon* (Class B, tel 26197) (*Tmr* 43D3/4). Vafe St leads to Odhos Soulio, a pedestrian way, where-on to the left, on the other side of this narrow lane, is an excellent second-hand bookshop. A few paces on is:

Olga's Rooms (*Tmr* 44C/D3/4) 57 Soulio   .   Tel 29851
Directions: As above.
    A nice looking establishment run by a pleasant fellow. A single room costs from 1800drs & a double from 2200drs, both including the use of the showers.

Hereabouts Arkadiou St straightens up, in a northerly direction. Beyond the 'dead' Museum (*Tmr* 4D3/4), and off to left is the east-west street of Theod Arambatzoglu. This bounds the southern ambit of the Old Quarter, rabbit-warren of lanes, alleys and streets, in which is any amount of accommodation. Odhos Theod Arambatzoglu leads past Arimondi Fountain (*Tmr* 18C/D3), and Titos Petichaki St, to the left. In the next street to the left, Odhos Haril Trikoupi, is *Marianna's Rooms*, at No 19. Further along Odhos Theod Arambatzoglu is:

Rooms Klapaki (*Tmr* 45B/C3) 61 T Arambatzoglu
Directions: As above and on the right, just past the family's leather shop, where it is 'favourite' to make enquiries.
    This is an elderly building which has been perfunctorily converted to a guest-house. The ground floor entrance is through an amazing wooden door, as old as the house. An enormous double room, with an almost out-of-sight ceiling, and a 'shed-like toilet compartment' bolted into a corner, costs from 2600drs. The family are very nice, if somewhat disinterested.

Not many metres to the west is an attractive square, bounded by a large Church, across from which, at No 18, is the *Cafe-bar/Rooms Ovelistirion* (*Tmr* 46B3/4).

Beyond the last mentioned, and to the right of Odhos Panou Koranai, is Adam Korai St, on the left of which is:
Rooms (*Tmr* 38A/B3)
Directions: As above.
The lady is very nice but does not speak any English. The accommodation is sweet-smelling, with a double room priced at 2000drs.

Back on Arkadiou St, and all on the right are the *Hotel Loggia* (Class E, tel 26269), followed by *Helen's Rooms* (*Tmr* 33D2/3) and, next door, the:
Pension Mikonos (*Tmr* 14D2/3) 303 Arkadiou   Tel 29129
Directions: As above.
A very large building in an excellent position, with a balcony pleasantly overlooking the far end of the Venetian Harbour... but the place is absolutely filthy. These comments also hold good for *Helen's*.

On the pavement hereabouts hangs out a front-man, a tout, who whisks inter-ested punters up the adjacent, canyon-like alley of Agiostefaniton. Herein are a couple of options, including: *Rooms Irene* (*Tmr* 47 Inset), at No 10, where the lady demands 2800drs for an en suite double room; and about 20m further on *Helen Rooms* (*Tmr* 48 Inset), at No 6, where 2000drs is the price for a double room, sharing the bathroom. Both are reported to be clean, although I find the lane rather claustrophobic, and they are asking the same price as owners of other accommodation, in much nicer locations. Still further along Odhos Agiostefan-iton, the alley opens out on to a sunny little square, quite a contrast to the latter street, and bordering which is:
Rooms (*Tmr* 49 Inset) No 3   Tel 26911
Directions:As above.
Not only a most attractive town location, but these are jolly good, clean, plea-santly old fashioned rooms with wooden matchboard ceilings, where a double room, sharing the bathroom, cost 1800drs. The smiley, lady proprietor, Mrs Karavasilis, has a son George who owns de luxe accommodation nearby (*See Rooms Corina, Tmr* 50C2/3).

In the parallel street of Damvergi is **Rooms** at No 27, close to the Arkadiou St end, whilst towards the west end is:
Rooms Corina (*Tmr* 50C2/3) 9 Damvergi   Tel 22574
Directions: As above, and on the left (*Sbo*).
George, the owner, speaks excellent English and is the son of the aforemen-tioned Mrs Karavasilis. George's de luxe double rooms have en suite bathrooms, balconies, but no sea views, and are priced at 2500drs.

Where Damvergi St makes a junction with Messalogiou St, to the right leads past the Historical & Folk Art Museum (*Tmr* 51C2/3), beyond which is **Rooms**, at No 38. To the left of the junction with Messalogiou St, and right on to Melis-sinou St leads to Himaras St (also known as Stef Xanthoudou) on which is:
Rooms Marylee (*Tmr* 52B/C2/3). Himaras
Directions: As above.
This accommodation is overseen by a jolly lady who speaks with an American accent and charges 2800drs for her en suite double rooms. As the pension is above a pool hall-cum-taverna, it may be rather noisy.

To the left of Melissinou St branches off Odhos Stef Xanthoudou, whereon *Rooms Pilos* (*Tmr* 53B/C2/3), at No 37. Further west and on the left of Meliss-inou St, is the extremely smart *Hotel Fortezza*, the sole preserve of the package tourist industry. The other side of the street, to the *Fortezza*, is the *Pension*

Couenis (Tel 29836), which is also solid with package tourists. The gentleman who owns this last mentioned establishment has fair English, and is a smiley, chubby, extremely helpful chap, who is only too delighted to help out by trying to locate accommodation elsewhere, when he is unable to help. Further west on Melissinou St, the road bends left to divert round the foot of the Venetian Castle walls. To the right is a steep slope heading off up towards a flight of steps that climb alongside the fort wall's. This is a very swept-up area. On the left is the:

Pension Anna (*Tmr* 54B2)   Tel 25586
Directions: As above, in a lovely situation.
   This pension is a very neat, Swiss chalet-looking house with a lovely garden. It represents a superb option, with an en suite double room charged at 2800drs. The lady owner is most helpful and welcoming, but her only alternative language is German.

At the top of the rise is the 'under construction', new Archaeological Museum (*Tmr* 55B/C2), prior to which to the right branches off Odhos Makedonias, all the way back down to Plateia Plastira. Almost immediately on the left (*Fsw*) is the nice looking pension *Rooms George* (*Tmr* 56B/C2, tel 27540), where a double room, with en suite bathroom, costs 2800drs. Unfortunately this option is monopolised by a tour operator. Towards the end of Odhos Makedonias, close to Plateia Plastira and on the right, at No 11/12, is *Rooms Eliza*. Plateia Plastira is overlooked by the 5 storey, modern :

Hotel Ideon (*Tmr* 57C/D2) (Class B) 10 Plateia Plastira   Tel 28667
Directions: As above.
   All rooms have en suite bathrooms, with a single costing 2220drs & a double 3130drs, which prices increase to 2720drs & 4300drs (16th May-15th Oct).

A pace or two on towards the Harbour reveals a narrow cul-de-sac, bending round to the right, at the end of which is:
Barbara's Dokimaki (*Tmr* 15C/D2/3) 14 J Dambergi/7A Plastira Sq   Tel 22319
Directions: As above.
   Very nice, if somewhat hostelish accommodation with instructive signs pinned up everywhere, and a flower-drenched courtyard. The very Greek landlady's daughter speaks English well. A single room, sharing the bathroom, costs 1900drs, a double sharing 2300drs, and a double room with an en suite bathroom 2850drs, whilst a room for three costs 3400drs, but prices are set to go up by 20% for 1990!

A stride or ten north-west from Plateia Plastira, along Leoforos Periferiaki, towards the fortress, and in amongst a small row of restaurants, bars and *Rooms*, is the two storey *Hotel Kastro* (*Tmr* 16C2) (Class D, tel 24973), at No 15. In the same terrace is *Rooms Seeblick* (*Tmr* 58C1/2), at No 17/18, and the:

Pension Lefteris (*Tmr* 59B/C1/2) (Class C) 26 Plastira Sq   Tel 23083
Directions: As above.
   Only has double rooms, with en suite bathrooms, which are priced at 2270drs, increasing to 2550drs (16th July-31st Dec).

Camping
The two campsites, *Camping Elizabeth* and *Camping Arkadiou*, are between 3-4km to the east of Rethymnon, along the Old Road (*See* **Route Eight**).

The Eating Out Taken all together, there must be more eating places per metre than anywhere else on Crete, but quantity has not ensured a very good, overall quality. In fact, the sheer weight of tourists has swamped heretofore reliable establishments, with a resultant worsening of the staffs' attitude, a drop in the standards of the food, all accompanied by higher than average prices. Hey-ho!

There are three main localities for diners. One is the stretch of Esplanade, between the Beach Pavilion (*Tmr* 17E/F4/5) all the way round to the outset of the Venetian Harbour (*Tmr* D/E2/3); another is the spread of tavernas around the Venetian Harbour; and the last are those tavernas encircling the Arimondi Fountain (*Tmr* 18C/D3).

The Esplanade eateries have expanded simply by taking over one of the carriageways, which they have appropriated for plush, awning covered terraces. Of this row of choice, which have all smartened up considerably over the years, I can still recommend the *Samaria*, at No 37 El Venizelou. The usual offerings but well cooked and comparatively good value.

The quayside of the Venetian Harbour is jam-packed with the tables and chairs of the tavernas that crowd each other, cheek by jowl, all the way round the small waterside perimeter. Whereas eating in this attractive spot was, in the past, to select the most expensive of the town's options, nowadays prices here are in line with those of the Esplanade listings - and it is possible to order a kortaki retsina. The proprietors are prone to advocate fish dishes, thus causing the meals to appear that bit more costly, but one or two of the tavernas, at the north end, have some typical Greek offerings at 'Rethymnon average' prices.

Any number of tavernas radiate out from around the Arimondi Fountain (*Tmr* 18C/D3), adjacent to Plateia Diog Moshoviti. This 'Fountain Sq' and surrounds are crammed with tavernas and cafe-bars, all well frequented by locals, expatriates and tourists. Of this abundance, I must highlight the:

Taverna Karia Maria (*Tmr* 60C/D3) 20 Diog Moshovoti
Directions: Actually in a narrow alley, parallel to Odhos Paleologou and east of Arimondi Fountain, almost completely hidden away.

In a town where it is so difficult to obtain a decently priced meal, this establishment is indeed an oasis in a desert of 'banqueting' mediocrity. The service is attentive, the cooking excellent, the menu alternatives varied, and the portions ample. Can one say more. A meal, for two, of moussaka (400drs, super), keftedes (400drs, magic), a Greek salad (250drs, as a Greek salad should be, so the price is okay), chips, bread and 2 carafes of very drinkable local red wine (at 150drs a bottle), cost a total of 1380drs.

Of the Fountain Sq alternatives, I suppose the *Cafe-bar/Taverna Vattela* (*Tmr* 61C3) is the pick of the bunch. Across the way, on the corner of Titos Petichaki St, is a traditional Kafeneion which stays open until the early hours. An old lady works her britches off, whilst her '40ish young' son puts in much less, rather bored effort. A Nes meh ghala cost 80drs and an ouzo 90drs. West of 'Fountain Sq', and on the left of Odhos Theod Arambatzoglu is *La Creperie* (*Tmr* 62C3), which is surprisingly busy at nights (that is surprising to me, who considers a creperie as a foreign intrusion). Prices range from 200drs for a jam-job, to 400drs for a Special, with such exotica as Grand Marnier (yes Grand...), chocolate, banana, pineapple, coconut, as well as 400drs for smoked ham, cheese, mushroom, egg and salad creperies.

Other taverna possibilities include the *Cafe-bar Ovelistirion* (*Tmr* 46B3/4), on the corner of the square formed by Panou Koranai and Patelarou Sts. A super meal here, for two, of 2 plates of goulash, a stiffado, a plate of fassolakia freska (green beans), a large 'helping' of apo vareli wine and bread, cost 1450drs.

One 'offering' Rethymnon has not lost is 'the souvlaki' and I can do no more than re-recommend a favourite of many years, namely the:

Snackbar Souvlaki No 70
Directions: Edging Arkadiou St, to the north, or left (*Fsw*), of the *Hotel Minoa* (*Tmr* 11E5), between the side-streets of Kallergi and Hereti. Incidentally this souvlaki house is separated from another, at No 74, by a cosmetics shop.

These two cellar-like snackbars are timely reminders of an inexorably disappearing past. They certainly offer an inexpensive, alternative to the more usual restaurant/tavernas. Of the pair, only No 70 serves giro pita, a very good handful, for 130drs. They also sell a stick souvlaki at 110drs, a bottle of beer 110drs, a bottle of retsina 125drs, a Coca-Cola 60drs, a Sprite 50drs, patatas 70drs... and it doesn't cost any more to squeeze in, to sit down in the cramped interior.

That is not to say there aren't other souvlaki snackbars, far from it. There are two on Odhos Arkadiou, both to the east of the *Hotel Minoa* (*Tmr* 11E5). One is the large *Snackbar Geronimos*, prior to the Kara Pasha Mosque (*Tmr* 3E/F5/6), and the other is the *Ovelesterio*, close to the junction of Viktoros Hugo St with Plateia Agnostou Stratiou. Both appear good value.

At about the middle of Arkadiou St is a small, irregular square in the corner of which is:

Taverna O Giorgios (*Tmr* 41D/E4/5)
Directions: As above.

Apart from the exhausts of the traffic that clog Arkadiou St, this is a pleasant place with a simple, covered pavement area. It has to be admitted that the limited menu dishes are rather galley cooked, and I have a suspicion that the evening meals are on the 'tired side', but they do offer kortaki retsina.

Almost at the north end of Arkadiou St, on the right, is the:

Three Brothers Taverna (*Tmr* 63D2/3)
Directions: As above, and over which is perched the Port police office.

This taverna is a sort of a hole-in-the-wall, with a napkin-sized, pretty, raised 'bit' of garden, to one side. It seems popular with the locals, but only the early, very early evening bird catches a meal here.

Those travellers who don't achieve gourmet happiness, unless tucking into a steak, might consider visiting the *Restaurant Famugusta*, up on Plateia Plastira (*Tmr* D2). Apart from a self-congratulatory hyperbole, stuck in the window, they accept *Diners*, which should give a hefty nudge to those senses registering prices. Enough to say that a steak Diane or pepper steak dents the drachmae pile by some 1150drs. Ouch!

At the Venetian Harbour end of Arkadiou St, is the *Sunny Pub/Pub Why Not*, reputed to serve draught beer and English-style pies. Oh goody!

There are one or two small restaurants alongside the football ground (*Tmr* 20A4), round the corner from Plateia Iroon Politechniou.

THE A TO Z OF USEFUL INFORMATION
AIRLINE OFFICE & TERMINUS (*Tmr* 21C6) The Olympic office is on Odhos Dimitrakaki, just beyond the Bank of Greece.

Aircraft timetable *See* Chania, Iraklion & Sitia.

BANKS They are plentifully scattered throughout the city including: a **Bank of Greece** (*Tmr* 22C6) on Dimitrakaki St; a **Bank of Crete** (*Tmr* 22D/E5/6) on the High St, Odhos Kountouriotou; a nearby **National Bank** (*Tmr* 22E6), close to the junction of Kountouriotou and Dimokratias Sts, opposite the Town Hall, on Plateia E Venizelos; and yet another **National Bank** (*Tmr* 22C/D4), beside Odhos Tsouderon, which changes Eurocheques.

BEACHES Rethymnon is very well endowed (with beaches...), having two, not just one beach.

Main Town Beach: If it were not for the Margate-like crowds this would be one of the best beaches on the island. Mostly excellent sand, the beach extends from the south side of the Venetian Harbour, all the way to the eastern breakwater. The latter juts into the Outer Harbour from close by the *Beach Bar Delfini* (*Tmr* 26G5). I suppose the countless 'straw' umbrellas have to be expected, but I am not sure why the good citizens of Rethymnon allowed the erection of the low, but rather stark Beach Pavilion (*Tmr* 17E/F4/5), smack in the middle of the vista. Certainly some years ago the state of this building was a disgrace, but not now. Perhaps the relocating of the NTOG office here has resulted in a new attitude as the structure has been considerably tidied up. On the credit side, facilities include beach showers and attendant minded, spotless toilets.

The beach is very broad and prettily edged by a mature palm tree lined Esplanade. For some reason the authorities have allowed the backshore couch grass to take quite a grip, especially a swathe in the direction of the Venetian Harbour. The beach is cleaned every morning and it is to be hoped that the locals will be discouraged from allowing their dogs to roam at will, for 'walkies'. The referred to beach showers and attendant minded toilets, as well as the greatest concentration of sun umbrellas and beds, are in the area of the Beach Pavilion (*Tmr* 17E/F4/5). Closer to the foreshore are the massed ranks of pedaloes and stacks of windsurf boards.

The pressures of traffic have resulted in the necessity for vehicle owners, wishing to park along the Esplanade, having to purchase a parking ticket from the NTOG office. Needless to say this piece of petty bureaucracy is ignored by absolutely everyone.

Eastern Esplanade Beach: The *Beach Bar Delfini* (*Tmr* 26G5), and the breakwater, mark the outset of a very long stretch of lovely, gently shelving sand. Quite wide at first, it narrows down and goes on, and on, and on ... for up to 1½km, edged all the way by a low sea wall. Apart from lacking any shade, the inland side of the wide Esplanade is bordered by a seemingly endless row of hotels, which even continue on beyond where the surfaced road comes to an end. There are isolated outcrops of sun-beds and umbrellas. Towards the far end of this eastern suburb, the development becomes scrappier and scrappier, the less frequent occurrence of modern buildings being interspersed with clumps of old houses, agricultural smallholdings and pens of animals, predominantly goats.

BICYCLE, SCOOTER & CAR HIRE The hirers of two-wheeled vehicles are concentrated on Odhos K Paleologou, between the old Museum (*Tmr* 4D3/4) and the Arimondi Fountain (Tmr 18C/D3). One of the firm's is Scooter Hire, where a 50cc moped costs 1200drs for a day, reducing to 1000drs per day, for three days hire, while a larger machine is charged at 1500drs, reducing to 1300drs per day, for a minimum of three days hire. Rethymnon is one of the few places where the easily available scooter hire charges are actually printed.

Cars are rented by a number of travel agents, in addition to which there are car hire firms spaced out around Plateia Agnostou Stratiou (*Tmr* F/G5/6), and along Kortazi St, whereon is a **Hertz** office.

BOOKSELLERS There is a to-be recommended foreign language bookshop on the right (*Fsw*) of Odhos Petichaki, this street running down from the area of the old Museum (*Tmr* 4D3/4) to the seafront. The large shop is almost opposite the Ladies-only WC (*Tmr* 27D/E3).

The *piece de resistance* must be the excellent second hand bookshop located on Odhos Soulio, immediately prior to *Olga's Rooms* (*Tmr* 44C/D3/4). Here prices for English language books start at 200drs, and even popular editions only cost some 300/400drs.

BREAD SHOPS There is a Baker (*Tmr* 25E6) on Odhos N Kazantzaki; one behind the OTE (*Tmr* 19D5/6), close to the junction of Kapsali and Dimako Poulou Sts; another on the left (*Sbo*) of Ethnikis Antistaseos, close to the Old Town Gate (*Tmr* 28C5); a Bread shop (*Tmr* 23B/C3) on Patelarou St; and a Baker (*Tmr* 24B3/4), in the Old Quarter, at No 21 Panou Koronai St.

BUSES The main Bus Square has two offices (*Tmr* 5E6), diagonally opposite each other. The one on the north-east corner deals with buses to Chania and Iraklion, the one on the south-west corner handles the south coast destinations. Another Bus terminus, for transport to some of the inland, south-east villages, lurks in the area of the Plateia Agnostou Stratiou.

Bus timetable (Mid-season)
Rethymnon to Chania
Daily   0615, 0700, 0800, 0900, 0930, 1000, 1030, 1100, 1130, 1215, 1245,
            1315, 1345, 1415, 1445, 1515, 1545, 1615, 1700, 1730, 1800, 1830,
            1900, 1930, 2000, 2045, 2130hrs
Return journey
Daily   0530, 0630, 0730, 0815, 0830, 0900, 0930, 1000, 1030, 1100, 1130,
            1200, 1230, 1300, 1330, 1400, 1430, 1500, 1530, 1600, 1630, 1730,
            1830, 1900, 2100hrs
One-way fare: 480drs; duration 1hr; distance 60km.

Rethymnon to Iraklion
Daily   0630, 0730, 0800, 0845, 0915, 0945, 1015, 1045, 1115, 1145, 1215,
            1245, 1315, 1345, 1415, 1445, 1515, 1545, 1615, 1645, 1715, 1745,
            1845, 2015, 2115hrs
Return journey
Daily   0530, 0730, 0800, 0830, 0900, 0930, 1000, 1045, 1115, 1145, 1215,
            1245, 1315, 1345, 1415, 1445, 1530, 1600, 1630, 1700, 1730, 1800,
            1830, 1915, 2000hrs
One-way fare: 550drs; duration 1½hrs; distance 78km.

Rethymnon to Ag Galini
Daily   0645, 0900, 1030, 1415, 1700hrs
Return journey
Daily   0645, 1030, 1200, 1430, 1600, 1830hrs
One-way fare: 410drs; duration 1½hrs; distance 61km.

Rethymnon to Plakias
Daily   0615, 0830, 0900, 0930, 1115, 1415, 1700hrs
Return journey
Daily   0700, 0930, 1030, 1230, 1500, 1800hrs
One-way fare: 310drs; duration 1 hr; distance 39km.

Rethymnon to Arkadhi Monastery
Daily   0600, 1030, 1200, 1430hrs
Sat, Sun & 1030, 1200, 1430hrs
  holidays
Return journey
Daily   0700, 1115, 1300, 1600hrs
Sat, Sun & 1115, 1300, 1600hrs
  holidays
One-way fare: 160drs; duration ¾ hr; distance 24km.

Rethymnon to Omalos (Samaria Gorge)
Daily   0615, 0700hrs
One-way fare: 1500drs; duration 2¾ hrs; distance 104km.

Return journey
Chora Skafion to Rethymnon
Daily   1830hrs

Rethymnon to Bali (Mpali)
Daily   0645, 1200, 1700hrs
Return journey
Daily   0800, 1245, 1745hrs
One-way fare: 2500drs; duration ¾ hr; distance 32km.

COMMERCIAL SHOPPING AREA Oddly, for a town of this size, there is no central area, which makes shopping a slow business. The nearest approach to a market area is at the Old Town Gate (*Tmr* 28C5) end of Ethnikis Antistaseos. Spread about here are a number of fruit & vegetable shops, grocers, fish and meat stalls, and ironmongers, in amongst which are scattered tailors, dry cleaners and mens' hairdressers.

The Old Quarter area, bounded by the streets of Theod Arambatzoglu (also known as Thessalonikis), its extension Odhos Panou Koranai, Odhos Melissinou and Salaminos St, contains a variety of shops, as does Arkadiou St.

Another fruitful area is in the square and side-streets dominated by Tessaron Martyron Church (*Tmr* 29C/D5/6), including Dimako Poulou St. For instance there is an excellent Supermarket (*Tmr* 32C/D5), immediately alongside the Church. A Supermarket borders Hatzidaki St, south of the Main Road, almost opposite the OTE (*Tmr* 19D5/6). Market stalls are set up, during the week, around the circumference of the Public Gardens (*Tmr* B/C5/6).

The narrow, pedestrian only street of Soulio (*Tmr* C/D3/4) has some classy shops, while nearby Tsouderon St (*Tmr* D4) has a preponderance of tailors, at the sea end, and leather goods, at the far end. With leather shops in mind, I cannot leave the subject without mentioning a father and son duo who dominate this business, at the east end of the Town. (I hasten to add, tourist leather goods...). The father is now only allowed to perform (*sic*) from the Arkadiou St shop, at No 52, whilst his son masterminds the prime site (*Tmr* 10F5) edging the Esplanade, just along from Plateia Agnostou Stratiou. The old boy is bedecked in an 'evening suit' version of the Cretan mountain man's uniform, complete with lace headshawl, waistcoat, horse-riders flared trousers and white boots. Watch out if he offers you a raki or two - it can wipe out an afternoon. The hardened traveller may well not be amused by the old rogue's antics, more especially his habit of handing his girl assistant some of a customers change, as a tip! Certainly do not pay the list price - a gesture of absenting oneself from the shop should result in a 20-25% reduction. The son commands four or five self-taught languages and is prepared to enter into an argument on political philosophy, in English. I must admit that this consists of haranguing on about the UK Prime Minister and the

Government's policies, vis-a-vis the EEC, but there you go! I mean, do you know the name of the Greek Prime Minister, let alone what party he leads? Son follows in father's footsteps by occasionally 'swamping' customers, to whom he takes a liking, with glasses of ouzo or raki. They both have a repetitive habit of referring to Englishmen as "Capitalista - Ah Thatcher". When (!) we experience a change in our government, I am sure they will, within days, substitute the correct name. Almost opposite the Arkadiou St shop, at No. 52, is a local who also runs a leather goods shop, but one cannot but feel the utmost sympathy for him, as he simply does not stand a chance against the competition of his more voluble compatriots.

DISCOS The *Beach Bar Delfini* (*Tmr* 26G5), at the eastern end of the Outer Harbour promenade, has a disco-bar and there are a number of 'offerings' sandwiched between the multitudinous restaurants, tavernas and cafe-bars bordering Leoforos El Venizelou (The Esplanade road).

ELPA The office is on the inland side of the Main road, at the west end of town, immediately prior to the turning down to the Castle.

FERRY-BOATS There wasn't a scheduled ferry-boat service in 1989, but the printed timetables indicate that there are plans for a four to five days a week service, in 1990. The problem is that, over the years, there have been a number of attempts to get a service under way. Perhaps this will be the start of a continuing, year-in, year-out Piraeus connection.

See **Travel Agents & Tour Offices** for details of a catamaran that operates a summer schedule to some of the Cyclades islands.

FERRY-BOAT TICKET OFFICES There is an **ANEK** office (*Tmr* 64C5) to the west of the Tessaron Martyron Church.

HAIRDRESSERS Rethymnon has almost more mens' hairdressers than kafeneions, if such a thing is possible. There are a number of ladies hairdressers to the west of Arkadiou St, in and around the area of Tsouderon St (*Tmr* D4).

LAUNDRY The **Laundry Mat** (*Tmr* 30C/D5), a coin-op launderette, is at 45 Odhos Tompazi. It opens Mon-Sat, between 0900-1500hrs & 1700-2100hrs, and a machine full costs 500drs.

MEDICAL CARE
Chemists & Pharmacies A number in the usual streets of Arkadiou, Ethnikis Antistaseos and Kountouriotou. There is also one on Plateia Agnostou Stratiou, as well as a few spaced out along Th Moatsou St, between the *Olympic* and the *Brascos*. Perhaps the latter are positioned so as to be able to apply soothing balms to clients of these two hotels, suffering from an attack of the vapours after receiving their accounts.
Dentists A dentist's 'chair' (*Tmr* E/F6) is located close to the junction of N Kazantzaki and Marouli E Sts.
Doctors There are two clinics edging N Kazantzaki St, one each side of the junction with the side street Marouli E. A medic also holds sway across the road from the *Mikonos* (*Tmr* 14D2/3). Maybe this chap is strategically placed to revive clients of the aforementioned establishment! I hasten to add, it will be for totally different reasons to those hinted at in the Chemist section comment?
Hospital (*Tmr* 35B6) To the south of the Public Gardens, beside Odhos Iliakaki.

NTOG (*Tmr* 1E/F4/5) The swept-up, smart office is located in the right-hand (*Fsw*) section of the Beach Pavilion. It used to be dominated by the colourful Mr Costas Palierakis, who always went beyond the remit of his office, in order to assist tourists. He was especially kind and helpful to the English, for whom he had a soft spot, no doubt due to old, wartime memories. Sadly Costas has died, - I hope readers will excuse my tribute to his memory. The entrance is from the Esplanade and the doors are open weekdays, between 0900-1630hrs, and week-ends & holidays, between 0900-1400hrs.   Despite there being plenty of information scattered about the place, and the staff being fairly helpful, obtaining specific details is similar to pulling dragons teeth!

Incidentally, in the same building as the NTOG (and the beach bar) is a set-up flogging horse-drawn waggon tours. (I can assure readers, flogging was no more than a pretty wet attempt at ...!).

OTE (*Tmr* 19D5/6) Sited on the 'High St' and open daily, between 0600-2400hrs. There is another office to the east of town, alongside the Old Road.

PETROL There are sufficient petrol stations, including one beside the square to the west of Tessaron Martyron Church (*Tmr* 29C/D5/6), and another on Plateia Agnostou Stratiou (*Tmr* F5/6).

PLACES OF INTEREST
Arimondi Fountain (*Tmr* 18C/D3) Only three heads and a part of the back wall of this pretty fountain survive. It stands alongside the vine, grape and gourd fes-tooned Diog Moshoviti Square.

The Fort (*Tmr* A/B1/2) A large Venetian Castle. The outer walls and one main gate are now in a good state of restoration, but the Turks and Germans, some 300 years apart, ensured that only these, and a domed mosque remained standing. The fort is open Mon-Sat, between 0830-1800hrs. Entrance costs 100drs.

Museums
Archaeological (*Tmr* 55B/C2) Now a new, super-swish facility, high up on the hill, close to the east walls of the Castle. Previously the exhibits were crammed into the rather more romantic, but now 'dead' 16th century Venetian Loggia (*Tmr* 4D3/4), in the Old Town. The entrance fee is 200drs and the museum is open daily, between 0830-1500hrs, but closed on Mondays.

Historical & Folk Art (*Tmr* 51C2/3) The building is on the left of Odhos Messa-logiou (*Facing Plateia Plastira*). The display is open daily, except Sunday, between 0900-1300hrs & 1800-2100hrs. Entrance costs 100drs.

The Old Quarter This area, variously bounded by the streets of Theod Arambat-zoglu/Panou Koranai, Arkadiou, and Makedonias, is extensive and most interesting. Many of the narrow, winding streets and lanes are overhung by Turkish installed, wooden, first storey balconies, which almost blot out the sky, and every so often a building displays a Venetian stone facade.

Public Gardens (*Tmr* B/C5/6) The formally arranged gardens were originally a Turkish cemetery, but now only contain an aviary, wherein the inmates are cooped up in undersized cages. Annually, during the last two weeks of July, a wine festival is held in the grounds. It may have been a serious affair originally, but has now turned out to be a rather fairground, 'razzamatazz' event, with funny hats and false noses not entirely out of place. Entrance costs 400drs, which allows a visitor as much wine as can be drunk, from the various barrels spaced out around the grounds. Don't forget to take a glass, otherwise it will be necessary to beg, borrow or buy one.

Religious Buildings Include the Mosque of Kara Pasha (*Tmr* 3E/F5/6); the Minaret of Nerantzes (*Tmr* 31C/D3/4), not to be ascended by those of a nervous disposition; the newly constructed Church of Tessaron Martyron (Four Martyrs) (*Tmr* 29C/D5/6), which possesses splendid and vast interior murals; and, to the south of the Bus Sq, an extensively restored Mosque and Minaret (*Tmr* E6).

Venetian Harbour Small, very attractive and full of caiques, with its quay crowded out by the chairs and tables of the restaurant/tavernas that line the pavement.

POLICE
Port (*Tmr* 63D2/3) In a narrow building, above the *Three Brothers Taverna*.
Tourist & Town (*Tmr* 34A3) As elsewhere, the tourist police have been drawn into the clutches of the Town force. Their offices are located alongside the 'Municipal Square' of Plateia Iroon Politechniou, well away from the hub of things. Nowadays, the tourist angle is nothing more than an ability to fan out a list of accommodation possibilities.

POST OFFICE The main office is on Th Moatsou St (*Tmr* 2C/D6). In addition, there is now one of those excellent caravan jobs, parked close to the outset of the eastern breakwater, in the proximity of the *Beach Bar Delfini* (*Tmr* 26G5). This opens daily, between 0830-2000hrs, for exchange purposes.

TAXIS There are ranks alongside the Tessaron Martyron Church Sq (*Tmr* 29C/D5/6), as well as in the area of the Bus Square (*Tmr* 5E6).

TELEPHONE NUMBERS & ADDRESSES
Hospital: (*Tmr* 35B6) Iliakaki St.	Tel 22261
NTOG: (*Tmr* 1E/F4/5) Beach Pavilion, El Venizelou	Tel 29148
Olympic Airways: (*Tmr* 21C6) 6 Dimitrakaki St	Tel 22257
Taxis: 24hrs service	Tel 22316
Tourist Police: (*Tmr* 34A3) Plateia Iroon Politechniou	Tel 28156

TOILETS A quaint Ladies' facility (*Tmr* 27D/E3), is on the left (*Fsw*) of Odhos Petichaki. This is a splendidly clean, if somewhat smelly WC, presided over by a lady attendant. She has her other senior-citizen, female friends round for afternoon tea, in the ante-room. Well, why not?

There are 'his and her' toilets, at the Beach Pavilion (*Tmr* 17E/F4/5), as well as some in the north-east corner of the Public Gardens, close to the junction of Kountouriotou and Dimitrakaki Sts.

TRAVEL AGENTS & TOUR OFFICES A 'clutch' are gathered in and around Plateia Agnostou Stratiou.
Nearchos or Thimeaki Travel
Directions: Located at the Venetian Harbour end of Arkadiou St, at No 250, opposite the *Pension Mikonos* (*Tmr* 14D2/3).

The young lady assistant speaks English, and they carry details of the 'Nearchos' catamaran service to various of the Cyclades islands, including Santorini, Ios, Paros, Mykonos, and Naxos. Despite the fact that this is a Rethymnon based company, the craft operates, for the time being, from Iraklion, to which refer for details of the sailings. (*See* **Ferry-boat Timetables, A To Z, Iraklion**).

Creta Travel Bureau Akti El Venizelou   Tel 229155
Directions: Situated on the Esplanade, beyond the eastern breakwater, halfway between Plateia Agnostou Stratiou and the *Xenia Hotel*.

They offer a comprehensive, enterprising list of excursions throughout Crete.

ROUTE FIVE

To Georgioupolis via the north coast Highway (23km) To understand the benefit that the New Highway has been, to the island transport, it is only necessary to compare the new and old route, in respect of this route. The Old Road winds its way inland, via **Atsipopoulou** and **Episkopi**, to close by Georgioupolis, where the two roads cross.

There is little point in using the very pleasant, but winding Old Road, unless for a specific reason. But, for those who must... the road loops via the large, compact village of **Astipopoulou**. **Ag Andreas** squats in a landscape dominated by olive groves, but there are signs of roadside development, despite which the local charcoal burner may be in evidence. The road traverses a lovely, green ravine, very nearly devoid of mechanical traffic, but with plenty of donkeys clip-clopping along, usually laden down with a heavy load, plus the owner.

EPISKOPI (Tel prefix 0831) A pretty, long, snaking, rural village. There is some industry, a Post Office, several tavernas, a petrol station, and one hotel, the *The Minos* (Class D, tel 61208). A side road branches off into the hinterland, and the interesting villages of **Argyroupolis** and **Asigonia**.

Beyond Episkopi, the Old Road crosses the New Highway, with a turning to Georgioupolis and another to the highly overrated, small **Kournas Lake**. I suppose it is Crete's only freshwater lake, but I simply cannot see what all the fuss is about. As the summer wears on the water level falls, exposing various mudflats.

Continuing along the Old Road leads to **Vryses**. (*See* **Route Ten, Chania, Chapter 5**), beyond which the countryside is particularly attractive, being heavily wooded and rich in chapels. **Ag Pantes** is a small, attractive, tree lined settlement, set in farming country, with sheep and chickens everywhere, as are massed vines, followed by very many trees. The landscape is strewn with cypresses, in amongst which is a steep gorge. The road winds down past a chapel, built into a rock on the right, and across the valley, from which is another settlement, sprawling over a lump of rock. Next along is **Neo Chorio**, noticeable for a long, irregular square, a disco (yes a disco), and little else. The route bypasses an almost depopulated, be-flowered village, and after a couple of kilometres, a lovely avenue into the village of **Armeni** village, quiescent in a fertile valley full of olive groves.

Returning to Rethymnon, the Highway speeds past the turning to:
Gerani Bridge & Caves (6km from Rethymnon) The Neolithic cave, discovered when the Highway was bludgeoned through, has not yet been opened to view. A summer dry river-bed divides this very small, boulderous cove, whereon a few metres of sandy shore tucked up against the mole that has been constructed to protect the river mouth. There is a large pebble stretch of foreshore, alongside which is a small chapel. The latter is separated from a couple of tavernas by an orderly grove of trees. The thoughtful provision of a block of two toilets, is rather blemished by their sometimes being in an appalling condition.

From hereon, the splendidly rugged coastline is the subject of extensive civil engineering works. An unsurfaced, coast-hugging track runs parallel to the Highway but (still) seeming to serve little purpose. The occasional

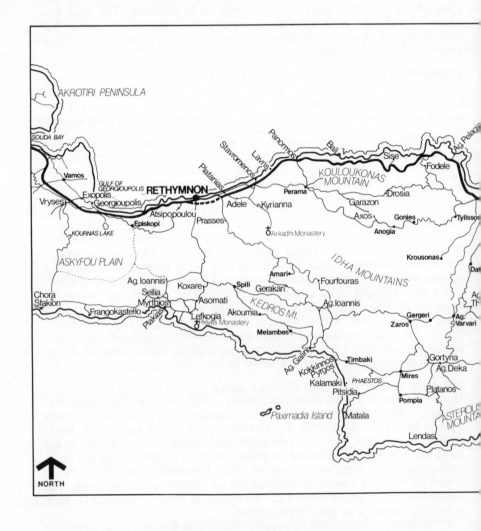

Illustration 11 Crete centred on Rethymnon

inter-connecting accesses are signposted 'Beach Exit'. The entrance 'proper' eventually crops up at:

PETRAS (about 12km from Rethymnon) The name literally means 'stones'. The few buildings, which include the *Petras Taverna* and the Spanish style *Villa Katerina Apartments*, are set down to one side of a rocky shore encircled headland. A cultivated, bamboo-enclosed field is edged by ground vines. On the far side of the headland is a cafe-bar taverna, followed by a rather doo-hickey petrol station and the *Studios Petras*. Beyond another little cove, with some sand but rocks cropping up out of the water, is the Petras River and the start of the:

The Gulf of Georgioupolis This glorious sweep of shoreline, on which white breakers leisurely roll and crash, goes on for several miles. It is edged by a long, empty, 10-20 metres wide, sandy beach, with a pebbly backshore. Almost the only disturbance to the wild, untouched scenery is the backshore track which parallels the sea's edge. The sole shade is that supplied by the trees that border the oleander lined roadway.

As Georgioupolis is approached, the number of taverna and hotel 'inspired' developments steadily increases. The last two of these outcrops include, respectively, a petrol station, the *Asteri Rooms*, as well as the hotels *Akti Manos*, *Happy Days* and *Drefius*, whilst the last takes in the *Paradise Restaurant*, *Poseidon Rooms*, and the hotels *Dorada* and *Mare Monte*. Holidaymakers tempted to 'summer' hereabouts must bear in mind that some form of transport will probably be necessary.

At the far, western end of the gulf is:

GEORGIOUPOLIS (23km from Rethymnon) Tel prefix 0825. A charming location, once one of the finds of Crete, but now a very popular, holiday resort, with accommodation a height of season problem.

The approach roads are most attractively lined with massive eucalyptus trees. The similarly tree shaded, very large Main Square is only a pace or twenty from a bridge over the unexpectedly wide, summer-full River Almyros. Caiques, benzinas and the occasional yacht line both banks of the river. The concrete capped, nearside bank of the watercourse is flanked by a wide, open, flat area, most of which is now used as a civil engineering yard. At the far end, the Almyros is bordered by a narrow, rocky causeway which sallies forth into the sea. The extremity is capped by the solitary chapel of Ag Nikolaos, built on a rocky plinth. From the bridge works, some fifty metres of the pretty, far bank is sheet piled. Beyond this, that side of the river reverts to a somewhat irregular, grassed embankment, edged by a path that leads to a taverna, close by the lovely river mouth. The area to the inland side of the bridge is a delta, a riot of reeds, marsh and sedge. As a correspondent pointed out, where else on the islands would be found, in the height of summer, not one, but three full-flowing rivers - and icy cold water at that?

Around to the right (*Fsw*), from the river, is the delightfully sandy beach, the backshore edged by a stony track hemmed in by tall grass and bamboos. There are a couple of beach Cantinas and the locals have sensibly set down vented 40 gallon drums to be used as rubbish bin/incinerators.

The result is a clean appearance to both the village and its environs. It is unfortunate that the beach showers, close to the village, are 'dead'.

The surrounds of the tree, flower and rose-planted Main Plateia, as well as the streets that branch off the Square, are edged by cafe-bars, tavernas, some small stores, travel and popular Greek art shops, as well as a plethora of hotels, pensions and **Rooms**.

The police station is on the right of the southern approach road; at the outset of the Main Square is a periptero, alongside which opens up a 'from-the-crate' fruit stall; a taxi ranks on the Square; to the right, from the north end of the Square, a street leads to a doo-hickey, open-air cinema (flanked on one side by a chicken run) and which opens at sundown with an entrance fee of 200drs; and the village baker is on the right of the street that angles off from the bottom, south-west corner of the Square.

Of the well-established businesses, there are two side-by-side tavernas, at the north side of the Square. They are on the right of the street down to the river bridge and are owned by the same family, the nearest to the Square being the replacement for the older unit, some way down the slope. Another 'old firm' that I find most interesting is the *Hotel Amfimala*. The ground floor is taken up by the hotel reception and the *Restaurant Peroulaki*, both owned by an old couple. The aged lady is still active and runs the restaurant, really more a kafeneion. Her elderly partner, who is now rather infirm, is more than likely to be found resting in the hotel reception, smoking his hookah pipe complete with hubble-bubble bowl. A Nes meh ghala costs 70drs and the landlady 'knocks' up a number of tasty dishes, including a mouth-watering plate of fried fishes accompanied by a tomato and cucumber salad.

Perhaps some of the names impart the flavour of Georgioupolis: Georgioupolis Club Live Music; Santas Rent A Car & Motorbike; Anatoli Cafe Pub with roof garden; Paradise Taverna Rooms; the White Swan Cafe Pub; Cafe Georgio Polly Pub; Rooms For Rent 'with riverside views'; and Rooms Rent, The Bridge. I must stress that I do not wish to give the wrong impression, as the settlement still hangs on to an air of quiet dignity and has, somehow, managed to retain an allure - possibly the number of mature, graceful trees saves the day!

Accommodation includes: the *Hotel Amfimala* (Class E, tel 61362); the *Penelope* (Class E, tel 61370), where a single room, with an en suite bathroom, costs 2500drs, a double room sharing 2000drs & with an en suite bathroom 2800drs, (both of the afore-mentioned hotels edging the Main Square); the small but very neat looking *Hotel Nikolas*, beside the southern approach road (from the direction of the New Highway), where the en suite rooms are charged at 1800drs for a single & 2200drs for a double, increasing, respectively, to 2300drs & 2700drs (1st May-30th Sept); the *Gorgona Hotel* (Class C, tel 61341), beautifully sited at the far end of the beach, where all rooms have en suite bathrooms, with a single priced at 1805drs & a double 3605drs. Unfortunately the latter hotel is now block booked by a tour company, usually leaving only the balcony-less ground floor available for 'independents'.

Towards the end of the Second World War, Georgioupolis was the eastern extent of the beleaguered German garrison. The old roadway, out towards Rethymnon, marked the boundary, and was gated and barricaded. As the inevitability of their eventual defeat sank in, the Germans continued to hold out. They refused to surrender to the Cretan guerrilla bands, preferring to give themselves up to the British. Probably quite rightly, the Germans feared the retribution the Cretans would be likely to mete out. In an attempt to smooth the path of events to come, prior to surrendering, the Germans were persuaded to exchange prisoners at this gate.

Where the Old Road crosses the Highway, there are bus stops-cum-ticket huts, on both sides of the road.

From Georgioupolis, over the river bridge *en route* to Vamos, the route crosses fields and bamboo groves, prior to starting out on the long, two kilometre, steepening climb, past *Rooms*, to where the mountain side flattens out. The *Taverna Panorama* lives up to its name, looking out over the Bay of Georgioupolis way down below. The *Panorama* is run by a middle-aged, nicely eccentric lady with long hair and a pretty face. The food is unexceptional but the views are amazing. Across the road is the more modern *Georgios Taverna*, which has rooms for rent.

ROUTE SIX
To Plakias & Ag Galini via Spili (60km) The climbing, winding road from the City gives a fine view back over Rethymnon (if attention can be diverted long enough to glance backwards). The journey passes across a very Cretan landscape, being dry, rocky, brown and grey, up and down, with sheep and chapels, everywhere.

To Plakias At 21km, a turning off to the right leads up to **Ag Ioannis** (29km from Rethymnon). The wide road breathtakingly serpentines, via hairpin bends, down the **Kotsifou Gorge**, complete with sea views. The twisting road to Plakias turns off before **Sellia** is reached, towards the village of:

MYRTHIOS (35km from Rethymnon) A large village with a Post Office, several *Rooms*, and a colourful, ethnic *Youth Hostel* (Tel 31202) built over the *Georgios Taverna*. The hostel displays a sign 'If I'm not here, grab a bed and relax, I'll be back soon'. A dormitory bed costs 450drs a night. The taverna is run by a very nice family, who serve excellent, hot food. A meal, for two, of stuffed tomato & pepper, a slab of pistachio pie, zucchini flowers, a fresh, tasty salad, 2 beers and 'more'ish' bread, cost 1097drs.

The road corkscrews another 4km down through olive groves, past *Rooms* and a campsite, to:
PLAKIAS (38km from Rethymnon) Tel prefix 0832. Apart from a few *Rooms* at the outset, the waterfront of this up-and-running seaside resort is now a swathe of holiday businesses. These edge a mainly pebble beach.

The *Alianthos Beach Hotel* dominates the approach, followed by the *Lamon Hotel*. The harbour now has a formal quay wall and there is even a Forum Shopping centre. Oh dear! A caravan Post Office facilitates exchange requirements, but woe is me - the old fashioned caique winch posts have all gone.

A running commentary, moving from east to west, takes in the: *Sophia*

Beach Hotel; *Rooms*; a billiards games hall; the *Pub House*; *Antonio Rooms*; *Rooms*, to the right of the fishing boat harbour; a bakery; *Gio'ma Rooms*; and, alongside the Talisman gold shop, a Launderomat, where a load costs 500drs and a dry 250drs. Continuing westwards there is *Rooms*, the *Sunshine Pub*, and *Julia's Snackbar*, followed by some rocky coves.

The majority of the community lies to the right (*Fsw*), whilst the seashore spreads along to the left, the very long frontage edging the large Plaka Bay. The best sand is at the far, eastern end, reached on a track running parallel to the shore. This is edged by small, spindly trees and scrub, in amongst which tents are pitched and motor caravans park, despite signs forbidding the same. It is a pity that the rubbish bins, so thoughtfully installed, are not emptied (so what's new), an oversight which helps contribute to the rather messy, dirty appearance. On the other hand the swimming is really excellent. At the far end is a *Beach Bar/Restaurant*, where accommodation is available. Despite this being a more than suitable location, strangely enough there isn't any water sports.

Plakias hotels, which all have en suite bathrooms, include the: *Livykon* (Class C, tel 31216), where a single room costs 1730drs & a double 2545drs; *Sophia Beach* (Class C, tel 31251), with a single priced at 2035drs & a double 2500drs, increasing to 2295drs & 3210drs (16th June-15th Sept); and the *Alianthos* (Class C, tel 31280), in which a single is charged at 3100drs & a double 4200drs, rising to 3600drs & 4600drs (1st June-30th Sept).

Back on the main Rethymnon to Spili road, a kilometre further south is a side turning off to the right. This choice advances through **Koxare** and the spectacular, snaking, verdant **Kourtaliotiko Gorge**, set in arid hillsides but down which flows a river. At the far end of the ravine is a fertile valley. The pretty hillside village of **Asomati** has a filling station, and there is a fork in the road, at which turn left (to the right leads back to Plakias).

At the next choice of directions, select the right in order to bump along a metalled, if rough surfaced road towards Plakias, via the nice, pivotal little village of:

LEFKOGIA (32km from Rethymnon) I state pivotal, as this is a good springboard from which to reach the nearby seaside locations of Skinario, Amoudhi and Damouni Beaches. Lefkogia contains *Rooms*, the *Taverna Stalios*, and a supermarket.

From the village, the first left from the Plakias road is along an unmetalled track signed to the *Skinario Beach Hotel*, but it is reported that this is not the best, or shortest choice to select.

It is favourite to take the second track off the Plakias road for the 25 minute walk to:
Amoudhi Beach The approach is along a small valley, through which trickles a sluggish stream, edged by bamboos, and passing, *en route*, *Rooms & Restaurant Amoudhi*. The unsurfaced road spills out on the backshore of a lovely, small, 'U' shaped bay, facing south-west.

The wide shore is gritty sand and angled biscuit rock. The pleasant backshore is speckled with clumps of young arethemusa trees, in amongst which are some tents and the occasional camper-van of the scattered colony of relatively gentle, long-stay, back-to-nature, summer visitants.

Unfortunately, the simple, open fronted concrete block, which contained the beach showers, are deployed as a rubbish dump, as the showers are *mort*. This fact does not auger well for the ad-hoc 'residents', who may well literally become the great unwashed. Incidentally this is a popular spot at which to sunbathe in the nude.

The third turning off the Plakias road is to:
Damouni Beach At the outset of the track, close to a stream, is a quite out of place, smart hotel, as well as a billboard proclaiming the impending arrival of a *Minoan Hotel* complex, sometime in 1990.

This lovely, wide, 'U' shaped, but most developed of the three bays is strung out along a pleasant stretch of coastline. The sharp sand beach is edged by a track that totters along to the left, past various set-back and tree shaded buildings. In amongst the shelter of the branches are spread about a noticeable enclave of greasy looking bikers.

The beach showers do work here, although I am not sure how often some of the 'wild' camping incumbents step beneath the cleansing dribbles (of the showers); nudism is forbidden; and there is an unnecessary amount of rubbish scattered about. 'Support' facilities include the *Taverna Akti*, with more planned...

Returning to the fork in the road, south of Asomati, turn to the right in order to head in the direction of the Preveli Monasteries. The road is badly surfaced in places and frighteningly narrow in others. The route now runs along an extremely fertile river valley, sustaining massed groves of olives, passing a 'perfectly formed' Venetian bridge, which spans a shallow, fast summer running river. Across this river-bed is a track signed to a taverna bordering a pebble beach, from whence yet another sign points around to the right (*Fsw*) to:

Preveli/Limni Beach Limni beach is the point at which the Kourtaliotiko Gorge emerges and supports a grove of palm trees interspaced by olean- ders. It was here that many of the exhausted, fleeing Allied troops waited, after the Battle of Crete, to be taken off by the waiting British Navy ships. Nowadays the location is swamped by sun-seeking holidaymakers. Ironic, isn't it! In fact this spot is more easily and usually accessed across the cliff-top, immediately prior to Piso M Preveli Monastery, so read on.

Back at the Venetian bridge, the roadway climbs up towards the:
K Moni Preveli Monastery (34km from Rethymnon) This now ruined com- plex of interesting buildings was the original monastery and they are worth a look round. A farmer keeps a number of animals penned in the old vaul- ted hall, the walls of which are pierced by cell-like apertures and deep win- dow openings. A 'hermit' camps in another part of the crumbling structure. Various remaining artefacts include circular milling stones, leaning up against the walls, but the most interesting feature is the watch tower-like fireplaces. The roof of the monastery allows a wonderful view back down the valley, with the Venetian bridge prominent. Despite the state of ruin of most of the place, a simple chapel is still in surprisingly good condition.

Continuing on and bearing right, past fire damaged hillsides, crosses a comparatively flat area with, to the sea side, a large, downward sloping field bordering a cliff edge. A well used track wanders over the grass to access the grey pebbles of Preveli Beach.

Straight ahead, lying in a saucer-shaped depression, is the:
Piso M Preveli Monastery (36km from Rethymnon) This attractively sited religious house overlooks the sea. In comparison to its close neighbour and 'parent', Moni Monastery, this is a very large spread of buildings, in an excellent state of preservation and obviously the recipient of continuing refurbishment funds.

The usual admonishments, in respect of visitors' dress, greet the hordes who spew out of the constant stream of coaches clocking in for this particular excursion. Mention of public transport reminds me to warn those travelling under their 'own steam' to be extra careful, as the roads hereabouts are extremely busy.

A particularly pretty if simple fountain gushes forth water, whilst some squatty toilets take care of other bodily functions. A marble, wall-mounted tablet advises '1941. This region after the Battle of Crete became the rallying point for hundreds of British, Australian and New Zealand soldiers. In defiance of ferocious German reprisals suffered by the monks and the native population, they fed, protected and helped these soldiers to avoid capture and guided them to the beachhead Limni where they escaped to the free world by British submarines '.

Once again on the Rethymnon to Ag Galini route, the road passes through straggling **Mixorrouma**, where there is petrol, along the 'rough-in-places' route to:

SPILI (30km from Rethymnon) (Tel prefix 0832) This is a lovely, even beautiful, clean, bustling, 'alpine' village, almost smothered in flowers and set in a green, fertile, cultivated plain snuggling at the foot of the mountain. It is a base for mountain walkers and organised ramblers.

Approaching from the west passes the *Green Hotel* (Tel 22056), where a double room with en suite bathroom costs 2000drs a night. Also at this end of town are: a prominent bust; the school; a pizza restaurant and supermarket; a side street up to the OTE; and a taverna, with yellow chairs and tables, across the High St from which is a zacharoplasteion, where a cream pie costs 70drs and a cheese pie 100drs.

The High St makes a sharp right-hand turn, at the corner alongside which are the fountains. These are around to the left and are a row of lion's heads, which endlessly spew forth cold spring water into a long, rectangular stone trough, set in a tree shaded square.

The buses pull up close to the 'Fountain Square', on either side of which is the core of the town including a *Rooms* above a butcher's, a Bank of Crete, as well as any number of chemists and a Health Centre.

Still at the High St corner, on the left is a petrol station (one of two) alongside a supermarket, followed by a taverna and a souvenir shop, where a few English language newspapers are on sale. Continuing to climb the High St, in a southerly direction, passes *Rooms* on the right, just before a church on the left, followed by a baker and the Post Office, both also on the left. It may well be that it will prove as much a wrench for readers to leave Spili, as it always does for me.

The road east from Spili, as far as **Kissou Kambos**, has been extensively rebuilt, but the next length, as far as the mountainside village of **Akoumia**, has a patchy surface. The next section on to **Nea Krya Vrisi**, and the Melambes turn off, set in very dramatic scenery, is acceptably surfaced.

Next comes a choice. Those of a nervous disposition should stick to the left-hand, northerly route to Ag Galini. Drivers should note that there is quite likely to be at least one or two unheralded, unexplained, and thus un-expectedly nasty stretches of unsurfaced road, which have been inexplic-ably allowed to deteriorate - no disappear. I prefer to turn off to the right to climb to **Melambes**, which hangs off the mountain side. The village square has an incongruously modern monument, the more so as the settle-ment has both feet set firmly in the days of yore, with lots of donkeys, old crones and kafeneions. There are dramatic views to the north-west, out over the **Kedros Mts** and the plain that runs between the two mountain ranges.

The final approach to Ag Galini spirals down past the track to **Ag Giorgis Beach**, and a taverna.

ROUTE SEVEN

To Ag Galini via Amari (about 69km) This is an alternative to the Spili circuit (**Route Six**), skirting the other side of the **Kedros Mt**. The thoroughfare passes through groves of large olive trees, climbing out of Rethymnon to the village of **Prasses**, on the right, and wherein *Rooms* and a big quarry. The road tops a rise to reveal a verdant valley supporting herds of grazing sheep. A deep gorge borders the road, fortunately edged by an old stone wall. Unusually, there are a number of easily visible water points. The highway surface is of 'good character' as the road approaches the attractive, tree lined, mountainside straddling village of **Apostoli**. This is followed by a road junction at muddy **Ag Fotini**, where petrol is available and which serves as a bus change-over point.

The left-hand fork leads to Fourfouras and the right to **Gerakari**. The Fourfouras turning crosses a wide plain and, on a lovely stretch, leaves the Asomati religious school on the left. The route passes through pretty **Vizari**, and not so attractive **Fourfouras**, where petrol is available.

From a distance, many of the old houses in the **Kouroutes** valley, resemble beehives. The next village of **Nithavris** is narrow and scrappy, but houses a petrol station run by a very nice, helpful lady. The route passes on through **Apodoulou**, after which the right-hand turning must be taken for Ag Galini. The islets of **Paximadia** can be seen from hereabouts, prettily set in the 'oh so blue', shimmering Libyan Sea. The olive groves in this area are neatly laid out and off to the left, a track leads down to *Camp-ing Ag Galini*, (*See* **The Accommodation, Ag Galini, Chapter Seven**).

ROUTE EIGHT

To Iraklion via the Old Road (about 80km) The New Highway, which is not so new now, can be picked up on the outskirts of Rethymnon and used as far as the seaside settlement of **Asaniou**. Here the Old Road turning to Perama crosses the Highway.

On the other hand, the Old Road makes off from the eastern suburbs of Rethymnon Town, which now spread through **Perivolia** and on to **Misseria**. Just beyond the latter is *Camping Elizabeth* (Tel 28694), some 3km from Rethymnon, where a pitch cost 350drs and the per person price is 400drs. Another 1km on is *Camping Arkadia* (Tel 28825). At this site, in addition to the to-be-expected shower block, mini-market and self-service cafeteria, there are moped and scooter hire, and money exchange. The per person cost is 500drs, whilst a pitch is charged at 400drs. In years gone by this campsite was in green fields, but not now.

Those travellers who set out fairly early in the morning will find the greatest hazard are the convoys of Safari jeeps that bowl along in packs of up to nine or ten in number.

Soon after crossing a summer dry river-bed, the Old Road drops into:
PLATANIAS (5km from Rethymnon) Despite a few fields still being in evidence, this settlement is a Kosta development, boasting a Chinese Restaurant. Yes, a...! One plus point is the pleasant, wide, gritty sand beach with a fine sand waters edge and sea bed. Some smallish trees give a little shade, and it would be unnatural if there weren't any sun-beds and umbrellas, the occupants of which are catered for by a beach Cantina. It would also be strange not to be able to report that there is a disco or two, as well as the standard 'allowance' of car and scooter hire businesses.

The constricted Old Road winds through olive groves and the villages of **Nea Magnisia**, **Viranepiskopi** and **Alexandrou**. They all lie in low, scrubbly foothills, strong with the smell of wild thyme, but sporadically littered with plastic. The giant cactii to the left of the road are particularly eye-catching. Alexandrou has a petrol station, as has the working town of **Perama** (23km from Rethymnon, tel prefix 0831), which 'owns' a 'proper' supermarket and a market square, but no concessions to tourists.

Perama can be used as the jumping off point for a trip to Melidoni Cave.The route casts off to the left, to the village of **Melidoni**, left again for 3km, followed by a short walk to the entrance to:

Melidonia Cave It has mythological connotations, but achieved comparatively recent historical fame, or more correctly infamy, when, in 1824, a marauding band of Turks fired the entrance, killing a couple of hundred villagers who had taken refuge inside. The Turks seemed to have a predilection for this sort of 'unchappish' behaviour.

From Perama the road runs down a small gorge, lined with white rhododendrons, and through **Ag Silas**, where the road narrows down, with a wall to one side. **Dafnedes**, which boasts a taverna, lies in a lemon grove and charcoal burner inhabited, green valley towered over by **Kouloukonas Mt**, on the left. **Mourtzana** is a pretty, tree lined village, from whence the route bridges a river-bed, amongst the vines, to snake round the foot of the mountain slopes to the very attractive settlement of **Drosia**. From the intensely cultivated, open countryside, heavy with grape vines growing in the red earth, the valley road rises dramatically, via a pinched, serpentine thoroughfare to a mountain ridge at **Marathos**. This small village is set on a boulder-strewn plateau, at the edge of which, beyond the next ridge, is a splendid view out over the   sea and Iraklion. The road now descends, tumbling and zig-zagging to the   outskirts of the City. Halfway down, a turning off to the right leads, after 4km, to the village of **Tylissos**, close by which is an   archaeological site containing the fairly extensive remains of three Minoan villas.

ROUTE NINE

To Arkadhi Monastery (About 22km) The Old Road (coast) must be taken, proceeding eastwards out of Rethymnon, as far as **Platanias**, beyond which the road for the monastery is signed to the right.

The prettier route involves selecting the direct and winding lane, set in olive groves, through the settlement of **Adele**, and on to the narrow streets of **Pigi** village, which are bounded by high walls and whitewashed houses. At the next, small settlement of **Loutra**, petrol is available, as is accommo-dation, at the *Panorama*. The road ascends to large, tree lined **Kyrianna**, which possesses a big square.

Most of the upper end of the journey edges a deep ravine, but close by the Monastery the road vaults a gully, to the right of which is the very narrow bridge built by the monks, as long ago as 1685. The final approach is over a cobbled surfaces, with the monastery to the right, standing rather forlornly in a clinically cleared, wasteground-like area. To the left is a cafe-bar and toilets - but bring your own toilet paper!

Arkadhi Monastery To read the account of this highly revered site, is to understand Cretan history and attitudes, more especially the Greek disposi-tion towards the Turkish nation. Apart from the symbolic importance, the buildings are baroquely attractive and still house a working religious com-munity - an added bonus. The cloistered Monastery, to which entrance is free, is set out in the form of a rectangle which encloses a very pretty church. The placement may well date back to the 5th century AD, but most of the existing buildings were constructed in the 16th and 17th centuries. As with many of the religious establishments of Crete, Arkadhi has, over the millennium, been the centre of resistance for the oppressed natives, a tradition which extended to the guerilla and resistance fighters, during the Second World War.

The fame of the Monastery is soundly and dramatically based on the events of 1866, when Cretan patriots and villagers were besieged by an overwhelming force of Turks. The story goes that, after a number of days heroic resistance, rather than be taken alive by the marauding, bloodthirsty assailants, the Abbot gave instructions for the powder magazine to be blown up. This decision resulted in the death of up to 1000 Cretans and some 2000 Turks. It would be inappropriate, even blasphemous, to suggest that the big bang was the result of a fluke Turkish canon shot hitting the magazine, wouldn't it?

A small museum (entrance 100drs) displays various artifacts, and the story of the Monastery is amply and colourfully set out in an English language guide book.

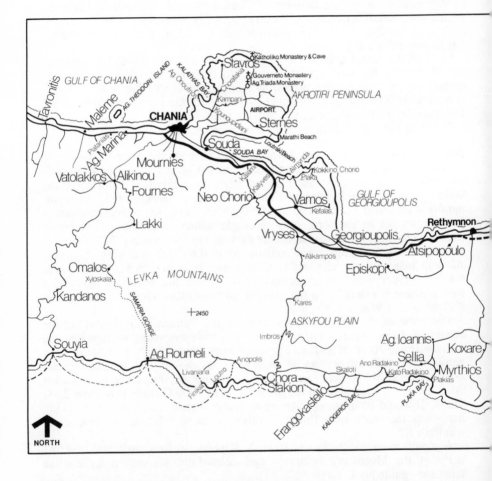

Illustration 12 Crete centred on Chania

5 CHANIA (Hania, Xania, Khania)

Second city, port & airport; Venetian quarter & harbour; old world enterprise; sophisticated, cosmopolitan activity; elegance; friendly people.

GENERAL (Illustration 13) Tel prefix 0821. The population numbers about 55,000 and the city stands on the site of ancient Kydonia. Neolithic and Minoan remains have been found in the Kastelli Quarter and Chania remained important in the post-Minoan period, even up to the Arabian seizure, in AD 824.

The Venetians, after their initial purchase of Crete, circa 1204, named the city *La Canea* but lost it to the Genoese, for a few years, between 1267 and 1290. The Venetians then retook the place, not to let go until 1645, when the Turks overwhelmed the whole island. The Venetians, who built many fine buildings, had to fortify the city after pirate raids, in the 1530s, but the walls were not to prove as impregnable as those of Iraklion.

The Turks converted some of the Venetian buildings, as was their habit, and made Kastelli (as they named Chania) the island's capital, in the 19th century. The Turks were expelled, in 1898, and Prince George became the High Commissioner of Crete, responsible to The Great Powers (Britain, France and Russia).

As Iraklion can disappoint, from the first Chania will surely enchant, and continue to do so with every day that passes. It is not that Chania has any-thing that Iraklion does not - perhaps it is the spacing and harmonisation of the elements. Certainly the Harbour is magnificent, as are the Castle walls; the Venetian Arsenals are noteworthy, being in a comparatively unrestored state; the quayside activity is fascinating; the Topanas, Kastelli, Chiones and Splantzia Old Quarters are aesthetically pleasing; and the Market is in-comparable. Surely these factors have all contributed to the indefinable diff-erence. Whatever the reason, or reasons, Chania is a city that richly re-wards exploration. The areas encompassed by the Old Walls are particularly interesting, with their many winding back streets and lanes yielding up fas-cinating glimpses into the past, at each twist and turn. Some of the streets around Plateia 1866 (*Tmr* 34B3/4) are quaintly commercial, many acts of engineering being carried out on the pavement, and in the gutter. In strict contrast, the area to the south-east is rather palatial, with fashionable 19th century houses and apartments of some grandeur. This latter ambience is probably because Prince George set up home in this district. Naturally, it became the smart thing to reside here, more especially if a person wished to move up the ladder of social success. Eleftherios Venizelos, a Republican Prime Minister and statesman of international repute, after whom seemingly nearly every other Greek avenue, street and square has been named, was born on Crete and also took up residence hereabouts.

The hub of the city is Plateia E Venizelou (*Tmr* B2), situated at the bot-tom of Odhos Chalidon, up against the Outer Harbour. Certainly the Chan-ia I love is the night-time, waterfront Chania. This is best enjoyed by taking a leisurely coffee (at a cost of between 150-200drs), and perhaps a post-prandial drink, at one of the quayside establishments, whilst the constant

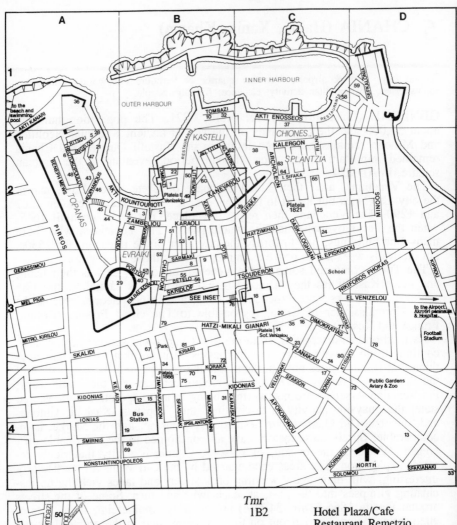

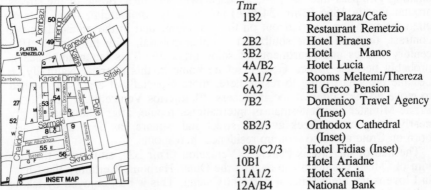

Tmr
1B2 Hotel Plaza/Cafe
      Restaurant Remetzio
2B2 Hotel Piraeus
3B2 Hotel   Manos
4A/B2 Hotel Lucia
5A1/2 Rooms Meltemi/Thereza
6A2 El Greco Pension
7B2 Domenico Travel Agency
        (Inset)
8B2/3 Orthodox Cathedral
        (Inset)
9B/C2/3 Hotel Fidias (Inset)
10B1 Hotel Ariadne
11A1/2 Hotel Xenia
12A/B4 National Bank

Illustration 13 Chania

13D4	Olympic Office	63C2	Pension Mary & Bill
14C3	National Bank	64C2	Rooms Port
15A/B4	Hotels Omalos &	65C2	Rooms Mary
	Samaria	66A/B3/4	Rooms
16C3	Bank of Greece	67A/B3/4	Hotels Arkadi & Canea
17C/D3	Sunny Tours	68A/B4	Chinos Rooms
18B/C3	The Market	69A/B4	Rooms
19A/B4	Bus Terminal	70B3/4	Hotel Anesis
20C3	Souda Port Bus stop	71B/C3/4	Janis Rooms
21A2	Hotel Amphora	72B/C3/4	Rooms Themis & Tasos
22B2	Municipal Tourist Office	73C/D3/4	Hotel Ellinis/Cinema
23C3/4	OTE	74C/D3/4	Hotel Cyprus
24C2/3	Ag Anargyri Church	75B3/4	Local Buses
25C2	St Nicholas Church	76B/C3	Cafe Snack-Bar
26A/B1	The Lighthouse	77C/D3	Bank
27B2/3	Archaeological Museum	78D3/4	Hertz Car Hire
28A/1/2	Naval Museum	79B3	Second Hand Books
29A/B3	Shiavo Bastion	80C/D3/4	All Language Book Store
30C3	Post Office	81B3/4	NTOG
31B/C3/4	Tourist police/Town Hall		
32B/C1/2	Port police	**Chania Inset**	
33D4	Town police	*Tmr*	
34B3/4	Plateia 1866	A2/3B	Rooms
35C3	ANEK Ferry-boat Office	B2/3B	Rooms Neli
36A1	San Salvatore Church	C2B	Fedra Rooms
37C1/2	Venetian Arsenals	D2/3B	Pension Lito
38B/C1/2	St Mark's Arcade	E3B	Rooms Pelraki
39B/C2	Taverna 'No 19'	F3B	Rooms Kostakis
40B3	Guest House Marili	G3B	Rooms Kleopatra
41B2	Rooms George	H3B	Rooms Betelo
42A/B2	Rooms, Pension Teris &	I2B/C	Rooms Stavros
	Restaurant Hamam	J2/3B/C	Rooms Navarino
43A2	Hotel Contessa	K2/3B	Nikos Snackbar
44A/B2	Rooms Archontico	L2B	Cheese Pie Shop
45A2	Guest House Domenico	M2/3B	Apo Vrado Taverna
46A2	Hotel Porto del Colombo	N2B	Taverna To Steki
47A2	Rooms Eleonora	O3B	Car hire
48A2	Guest House Agryro	P3B	Scooter hire firms
49B2	Rooms Stoa (Inset)	Q2B	Moto Sport
50B2	Hotel Amphitriti (Inset)	R2/3B	Auto Moto
51B2/3	Rooms Vassilikos	S2B/C	Motorbike/Scooter hire
52B2/3	Rooms (Inset)	T2B	Bookshop
53B2/3	Kydonia Rooms (Inset)	U2B	Mandakis Travel/
54B2/3	Pension Afroditi/		Minoan Lines
	Laundry (Inset)	V2/3B	Jackie & Bill's Laundromat
55B3	Rooms Korina (Inset)	W3B	Roman Catholic Church
56B3	Hotel Diktynna (Inset)	X2B	Unikreta Tourist
57A/B3	Rooms (Inset)		Co-operative
58C/D1	Hotel Porto Veneziano		
59C/D1	Rooms/Restaurant	*Tmr* = Town map reference	
	Elisabeth	*Fsw* = Facing seawards	
60B2	Anastasia's Apartments	*Sbo* = Sea behind one	
61B/C2	Pension Kasteli	*Fbqbo* = Ferry-boat Quay behind one	
62B/C1/2	Monastiri Pension		

press of people ebb and flow past one's table. The wide pedestrian Esplanade is an explosion of bars, restaurants, hotels and tavernas, and in the evenings is awash with the good citizens of Chania, as well as armed service personnel and tourists. They perpetuate a constant *ramblas* or *volta*, the cacophony of their voices accompanied by an ill-assorted and discordant musical background. Entertainers and pavement artists freelance along the waterfront and may include an amateur 'hooker', a French accordionist, and a fire eater. Added to all this activity, the tavernas employ a *schlepping* technique, potential customers constantly being regaled to see this kitchen or that display of food. It can prove quite exhausting!

From the south, left-hand corner of E Venizelou Sq the view encompasses the square, the rather lovely, domed roofs of the old Turkish mosque (which now houses the NTOG office), the lighthouse and the sweep of the harbour quay.

Parallel to the quayside, Zambeliou Lane twists and climbs up to Theotokopoulou St. On the way, lanes and steps scurry off, hither and thither, and for a glimpse into the past take a look along Beneph Mews which branches off Theotokopoulou St.

Moving westwards, or to the left, around the quayside leads to the turn of the Old Walls at the harbour entrance, just beyond Odhos Angelou (Agelou) and the Naval Museum (*Tmr* 28A1/2).

To the south of E Venizelou Sq, Odhos Chalidon rises past the Archaeological Museum (*Tmr* 27B2/3). This is housed in the once grand Venetian Church of St Francis, built in the 16th century, and converted into a mosque by the Turks - what was not? A few strides further along the ascending street, and almost opposite each other, are the Catholic Church, to the right, and the Square and Orthodox Cathedral of the Three Martyrs (*Tmr* 8B2/3), to the left. The Cathedral was built, in the 1860s, on the instructions of a thankful Turk, whose son had been the subject of a miraculous cure. This was supposedly brought about by the healing powers attributable to an icon belonging to an earlier church that stood on the site. At the top of Chalidon St, and across Leoforos Hatzi-Mikali Gianari, is Plateia 1866 (*Tmr* 34B3/4), notable for its splendid underground toilets.

Left along Leoforos Hatzi-Mikali Gianari, (which is fine if you are on foot, as this is part of a one-way traffic system, going the other way), and beyond the traffic lights, on the left, hoves into sight the very large building housing the Market (*Tmr* 18B/C3). This meets the day-to-day needs of Chania and the surrounding districts, under one roof. Across the avenue, to the right, are a number of streets that radiate out and contain the majority of the city's commercial undertakings.

Left again, on the far side of the Market, leads, with a wiggle, past a solitary minaret, towards the tree-dominated Plateia 1821 (*Tmr* C2). I write 'tree dominated', but that would be to ignore San Rocco Church, on the north side of the square, and St Nicholas Church (*Tmr* 25C2) on the eastern flank. Over the years St Nicholas has experienced the usual changes of 'official' God. Originally built as a Dominican place of worship, it was used by the Turks as a mosque, eventually to become an Orthodox church. This cross-pollination of religions is evident by the building possessing both a campanile and a minaret.

From St Nicholas to the waterfront Arsenals (*Tmr* 37C1 /2), leads past a grid layout of side streets. The Arsenals were arched buildings for ship-building and repairs, elegant Venetian stonework equivalents of Second World War Nissen huts - perhaps not! Immediately behind them, raised up on the hillside of the Splantzia Old Quarter, are the remains of St Mark's Arcade (*Tmr* 38B/C1/2) and to the south of the latter, in the region of Kanevaro St, are the areas of Minoan excavations.

Heading west, back towards Plateia E Venizelou, from the Arsenals, the quayside streets are paved ways cluttered with the paraphernalia of the fish-ing-boat industry.

With all this 'harbour' to hand, it may seem strange that the ferry-boat port is inconveniently situated 6 ½km to the east, at **Souda**. Not so unex-pectedly, the airport is at **Sternes**, some 18km to the east, on the Akrotiri peninsula. Incidentally, despite the City being well equipped with litter bins, the locals around the harbour still appear to use the sea for the disposal of their rubbish, more is the pity.

ARRIVAL BY AIR The airport, known as **Sternes**, is now quite well-organised and arrivals have the choice of the Olympic bus or taxis to get into town. Incidentally alongside the taxi rank is a blank fare indicator board! The bus, which meets the flights, shuttles passengers back and forth to the Chania Olympic office (*Tmr* 13D4), at a cost of 150drs one-way. Just outside the gates is a cafe-bar.

ARRIVAL BY BUS Three times a week a scheduled bus connects with **Thessaloniki**, which, naturally enough, uses the ferry for the sea crossing!

ARRIVAL BY FERRY The port of Chania is across the neck of the Akro-tiri peninsula, at **Souda**, a Naval base and thus a rather souless place. An excellent bus service connects the two, at a cost of 60drs, departing every 15mins, between 0600-2300hrs, from the Bus stop (*Tmr* 20C3), in front of the Market.

THE ACCOMMODATION & EATING OUT Almost all that could be desired within the old City Walls, as circumscribed by the streets of Pireos, Skridlof, Tsouderon, N Episkopou and Minoos.

The Accommodation However much is listed herein, arrivals must bear in mind that, even out of the height of season months, it can prove difficult to locate suitable digs, more so the later in the day the search is made. From Plateia E Venizelou (*Tmr* B2), to the left (*Fsw*), is a mass of accommoda-tion. Much of that which overlooks Akti Kountourioti, and the harbour, have their entrances in Zambeliou St, one back and parallel to the quay. It must be borne in mind that this is a noisy area, especially during the eve-ning hours. Zambeliou St itself is fairly quiet but, despite being very narrow, motorbikes occasionally roar down the alley.

Hotel Piraeus (*Tmr* 2B2) (Class E) 14 Zambeliou   Tel 54154
Directions: In the first block, to the west of E Venizelou Sq.
All rooms share the bathrooms, with doubles costing about 1800drs.

Branching off to the left of Odhos Zambeliou is Kondilaki St, a rich vein of accommodation that includes: *Dias Rooms*, on the left, above a cafeteria; *Rooms & Dogis Rooms*, to the right; *Rooms*, at No 11, & *Artemis Rooms*, both on the left, as are the *Good Heart Restaurants/Rooms & Rooms*. Across Odhos Portou, from the junction with Kondilaki St, is:

Guest House Marili (*Tmr* 40B3) 5 Portou
Directions: As above.
Elegant rooms for rent.

Returning to Odhos Zambeliou, and continuing westwards, offers up:
Hotel Manos (*Tmr* 3B2) (Class C) 17 Kountourioti   Tel 29493
Directions: Further along the Esplanade from the *Piraeus* and above the *Taverna Dionisis*, with the entrance from Odhos Zambeliou. Identification of the premises is made easier by the 'interesting' drinking fountain in the entrance, which resembles a small boy spewing water into a toilet. Very salubrious..! It can prove difficult to raise the management.
     In actual fact this well-regarded accommodation is classified as a pension, with double room rates from 1600drs.

Rooms George (*Tmr* 41B2) (Class C) 30 Zambeliou   Tel 43542
Directions: Close by the *Manos*.

A few metres further west, next door to *Rooms Atlantic*, is the:
Hotel Lucia (*Tmr* 4A/B2) (Class C) Kountourioti/Paleo Limani   Tel 21821
Directions: As above.
     All rooms have en suite bathrooms, with a single room costing 3000drs & a double 3750drs.

The south side of Odhos Zambeliou, between the side streets of Kondilaki and D Douka, are: *Rooms*, at No 47, and *Pension Terris* (Tel 53120), next door to which is the *Restaurant Tamam*.
     Continuing west along the Esplanade passes the *Pension Pasiphae* (Class B), behind which, on the south of Zambeliou St, are *Rooms Archontiko* (*Tmr* 44A/B2) (Class C, tel 59857), and, further on, the:

Guest House Domenico (*Tmr* 45A2) 71 Zambeliou   Tel 55019
Directions: As above.
     Considering the rather shut-in location, the en suite double rooms seem pricey at 3850drs, increasing to 4850drs (1st April-30th Sept). Enquiries should be made at the **Domenico Travel Agency** (*Tmr* 7B2).

Continuing up the flight of steps and right down Odhos Theophanous are a number of up-market possibilities, including:
Hotel Porto del Colombo (*Tmr* 46A2) (Class A) Theophanous   Tel 50975
Directions: As above.
     Actually classified as a pension, all bedrooms have en suite bathrooms, with a single room priced at 4500drs & a double room 5000drs.

Opposite the *Colombo* is *Rooms* (Tel 54729), at No 4, and further down another flight of steps is:
Hotel Contessa (*Tmr* 43A2) (Class A) 15 Theophanous   Tel 23966
Directions: As above. From the waterfront, the Contessa is visible behind a prominent, two storey, wooden, projecting upper floor building, immediately prior to the *Amphora*.

If I was in the mood to splash out (instead of being mean and tight-fisted), then I would plump for this splendid, simply but effectively decorated and furnished, family run, old-world style hotel. The six 'badrooms' (*sic*) all have en suite bathrooms, with a single priced at 4600drs & a double 5200drs.

Round the corner, and up yet more steps, on Parados Theotokopoulou, is *Rooms Eleonora* (Tel 50011), at No 13 (*Tmr* 47A2). Further on is:
Pension Captain Vassilis (Class A) 12 Theotokopoulou   Tel 51122
Directions: As above.
   Not quite so expensive as the aforementioned establishment. All rooms have en suite bathrooms, with a single charged at 3200drs & a double at 4000drs.

Rooms Meltemi (*Tmr* 5A1/2) 2 Angelou   Tel 40192
Directions: Towards the far, north-west side of the Outer Harbour, close to the rampart walls, and alongside the Naval Museum, at the outset of Angelou Lane.
   The house is one of a row of old, narrow fronted, tall buildings that stretch up the tapering alley. The ground floor is a summer-time cafe-bar with a number of tables and chairs 'cramped together' out the front. The lofty, sparse, echoing dormitory rooms are disinterestedly offered from 1000drs for a double, whilst a room for two cost from 1500drs, both sharing the bathrooms. The showers are guaranteed to be hot.

Next door is the:
Pension Theresa (Thereza) 8 Angelou   Tel 40118
Directions: As above.
   This pension occupies a lovely, seven hundred year-old house, and is now owned by a charming computer programmer, Vassili, and his doctor wife. The house is simply but tastefully decorated and the winding, somewhat rickety staircase ascends to the various floors. Do not miss the plain, circular murals on the first floor. The rooms have glorious views of the harbour and are simply furnished with much care. This is evident in the small inset bedroom dressers, complete with a few books and brochures, flowers and individual bedside lamps, with shades. (I used to dream of bedside lamps with shades). There is a 'common room' kitchen on the rooftop, along with a breakfast service. Double rooms cost from 2000drs, with the best, top storey 'penthouse' being charged at 3000drs.

If *Theresa's* is full, *Rooms Stella* is next door, but isn't such a satisfactory alternative. Odhos Angelou winds and climbs up to Theotokopoulou St, close by which junction are the *Pension Palazzo* (Class A, tel 43255), and the:
El Greco Pension (*Tmr* 6A2) (Class B) 47-49 Theotokopoulou   Tel 22411
Directions: As above.
   Smart with pine walled reception and clean-cut, female receptionist, added to which there is a roof garden. Single rooms, sharing the bathrooms, start off at 2350drs & en suite 2500drs, whilst doubles en suite are charged at 3300drs. These rates rise, respectively, to 2750/2900drs & 3800drs (16th June-30th Sept). With Angelou St behind one, and turning left along Theotokopoulou St, advances past the:
Guest House Argyro (*Tmr* 48A2) (Class B) 13 Theotokopoulou   Tel 55019
Directions: As above, and halfway down, on the right-hand side.
   There are a few double rooms available, sharing a bathroom, costing 2900drs, but the hotel is part package tour booked and its forte is furnished apartments. The latter come complete with a fully fitted kitchen, shower, bathroom, and maid service, priced at between 6500-7050drs. There is a roof garden. Enquirers should pop into **Domenico Travel** (*Tmr* 7B2).

There is less expensive, extremely pleasant accommodation next door   (to the *Hotel Argyro)*, at No 9 Theotokopoulou St (Tel 56935), which   is owned by Kiria Irene - thus *Rooms Irini*! Irini is to be found on   the premises, or can be contacted via the General store, across the   street. The very clean double rooms are well equipped, the shared,   spacious kitchens include a fridge and cooker, and there is a roof garden. Charges start from about 2500drs a night.

Back at Plateia E Venizelou (*Tmr* B2) and ranged to the right (*Fsw*), are:

Hotel Plaza (*Tmr* 1B2) (Class C) 1 Tombazi   Tel 22540
Directions: As above, and bordering the quayside. The excellence of the situation is balanced by the fact that this is not the quietest of locations, almost an understatement from a scribbler not known for down-playing a situation. Apart from the Esplanade throbbing with activity, there is a restaurant in the ground floor and, if this were not enough, the alleyway behind the hotel harbour's two of the noisiest, liveliest cocktail bars in town, pulsating with juke-box   music and a clientele who seem to be under the impression that their nearest neighbours are some miles away.

Single rooms, sharing a bathroom, start off at 1400drs & double rooms 2500drs, whilst doubles with an en suite bathroom cost 2700drs.   These rates increase, respectively, to 1600, 2900 & 3100drs (1st April-30th Sept).

Behind and overlooking the *Plaza*, is the nice, 'suburban' Lithenon St, ascending the cliff edge that climbs from Kanevarou St, and bordered by a number of rather 'swept-up' options, all with super   Harbour views. They include: *Rooms Stoa* (*Tmr* 49B2) (Class C, tel   26879), at No 5; followed by *Rooms Bourdaki Despina* (Class A, tel   40135), at No 17; the swish, classical looking *Furnished Apartments Pandora* (Class A, tel 42588), at No 29; and:

Hotel Amphitriti (*Tmr* 50B2) (Class C) Lithenon   Tel 56470
Directions: As above.

As befits the situation, all rooms possess en suite bathrooms, with a single room priced at 5000drs & a double 5500drs.

Once again back at Plateia E Venizelou, but with the sea behind one, walking up Chalidon St leads to a cornucopia of accommodation, radiating out from around the Greek Orthodox Cathedral (*Tmr* 8B2/3), but mainly to the left (*Sbo*). It has to be borne in mind that the Cathedral bells are extremely intrusive, if not bloody annoying, and seem to 'go off' at all or any hour of day and night, more especially early morning - usually after an especially hard evening 'researching' one or three of the local 'halls of pleasure'. Odhos Chalidon has a few *Rooms* on either side of the street, from Zambeliou St all the way to Skridlof St. For instance there are: *Rooms Vassilikos* (*Tmr* 51B2/3, tel 21283), at No 5; *Rooms*, opposite the Archaeological Museum (*Tmr* 27B2/3); and *Rooms* (*Tmr* 52 B2/3), the   proud possessor of 'private bathrooms', at No 34, and opposite an old Hamam, or Turkish Bath, now converted into a row of gold and gift shops. Further south from the latter is the side street of Odhos Sarmaki, which runs along the nearside of the Orthodox Cathedral (*Tmr* 8B2/3). On the left of Odhos Sarmaki is *Rooms* (*Tmr* A2/3B Inset), beyond which is the first of 4 narrow, airless, dark canyons - sorry side-streets - Odhos Isodion. In this are: *Rooms Neli* (*Tmr* B 2/3B Inset) (Class A, tel 55533), at No 21, and:

Kydonia Rooms (*Tmr* 53 B2/3) (Class C) 15 Isodion   Tel 57561
Directions: As above, and on the right.

All rooms have en suite bathrooms, a single costing 2500drs & a double 3300drs, increasing to 2900drs & 3800drs (16th June-30th Sept).

Further along, and on the same side of the street is *Fedra Furnished Rooms & Piano Bar* (*Tmr* C 2B Inset), which building stretches through to the parallel street of Odhos Ag Deka. 'Lurking' on Deka St, on the right, is the:

Pension Afroditi (*Tmr* 54B2/3) (Class C) 18 Ag Deka   Tel 57602
Directions: As detailed. In the ground floor is the family run Laundry.
   Ephdikas is a friendly man who speaks good English. All rooms share the bathrooms, with a single charged at 950drs & a double 1500drs, which rates increase by a few hundred drachmae between July-Sept.

Next east from Ag Deka St, on Odhos Episc Dorotheou is:
Pension Lito (*Tmr* D2/3B Inset) (Class C) 15 E Dorotheou   Tel 53150
Directions: Once again on the right (*Cathedral behind one*), a few metres down from the junction with Sarmaki St.
   Nikos is still the proud, but now elderly owner of the establishment. He sits, propped up downstairs in the old, vaulted, cave-like room which occupies all of the ground floor. Rather than waste the space this is attractively laid out with display cases of jewellery, mainly items of silver. His sons keep an eye on him, more especially well-mannered, middle 30s, and neat Manolis. The whitewash-ed, acceptably clean rooms are quite small but adequately furnished, with a war-drobe, two chairs, a bedside table, wall mirror and hooks. Try to be allocated one of the front bedrooms, which have balconies with a washing line. The rooms at the rear of the premises are airless as the windows are very small. A double room costs from 1800drs, sharing the rather cramped, poorly ventilated bath-rooms. At the time of my last visit, on one of the to-be-expected exhortations not to place toilet paper down the loo, some wag had scrawled "How can we, when you don't give us ANY"!

On the south side of Sarmaki St, behind the Cathedral is:
Pension Fidias (Phedias) (*Tmr* 9B/C2/3) (Class E) 6A Santrivani/Sarmaki
                                                                                Tel 52494
Directions: As above.
   Fidias has a very friendly, if 'dormitory' atmosphere, with the walls covered with posters of Greece, as well as general tourist information. Rooms are avail-able sharing the bathrooms or en suite. Singles kick off at about 1000drs & doubles 1400drs, which prices increase by 200drs for the months between April & September. Singles are also let at the rate of 650drs per bed, in shared rooms. The owners are welcoming and open to negotiation. The main drawback is the proximity to the Cathedral, thus the bells... Looking at the north-west corner of the building, one can only hope the proprietor's decide to replace the decidedly dodgy shoring supporting an upper floor balcony, with something of a more permanent nature. Judging by the plant life that has established itself around the existing prop, this may be a forlorn expectation. Incidentally there is an annex to the *Fidias*, in Odhos E Dorotheou.

South along Odhos Episc Dorotheou, and off to the right (*Sbo*) is Betelo St, which tracks in a westerly direction across to Chalidon St, and is jam-packed with accommodation. Options include: *Rooms Petraki* (*Tmr* E3B Inset); *Rooms Korina* (*Tmr* 55B3) (Class B, tel 53430) at No 41; *Rooms Kostakis* (*Tmr* F3B Inset); *Rooms Kleopatra* (*Tmr* G3B Inset) (Class C) at No 51; and *Rooms Betelo* (*Tmr* H3B Inset, tel 41213) at No 38.
   Back on Odhos E Dorotheou, to the right (*Betelo St behind one*) is the:
Hotel Diktynna (*Tmr* 56B3) (Class C) 1 Betelo   Tel 53737
Directions: As above, and on the right.

As would be expected from the comparatively modern looking exterior, the bedrooms have en suite bathrooms. A single is charged at 2700drs & a double 3340drs, increasing to 3250drs & 4100drs (July-Sept).

Whilst on this (east) side of Chalidon St, and continuing eastwards, in the next, parallel street to Odhos Potie, are *Rooms Stavros* (*Tmr* I2B/C Inset) and *Rooms Navarino* (*Tmr* J2/3B/C).

To the west of Chalidon St is another possibility, **Rooms** (*Tmr* 57A/B3) on the corner of Parados Portou, off Portou St. It is a very nice looking building painted in a pink wash with the stonework picked out.

Once again back to Plateia E Venizelou from whence beyond the NTOG mosque and proceeding along the eastern side Esplanade, Akti Tombazi, is the:

Hotel Ariadne (*Tmr* 10B1) (Class E) 2 Afentoulief
Directions: As above and entered from the street to the rear of the building.

Splendid position but there is a disco in the basement and this harbour situation can get very busy in the summer, at almost any hour.

Much further east along the Esplanade, at the far end of the Inner Harbour are:
Hotel Porto Veneziano (*Tmr* 58C/D1) Akti Enosseos   Tel 29311
Directions: As above.

A very smart, four storey hotel, the luxuriousness being evidenced by the charges of 6200drs for a single room & 8000drs for a double room.

Rooms/Restaurant Elisabeth (*Tmr* 59C/D1) (Class C) Akti Enosseos   Tel 29150
Directions: Next door to the last detailed hotel, on the corner of Enosseos and Defkalonia St.

Quite a contrast to the *Porto Veneziano*, being a pleasantly provincial set-up, in a calm corner of the waterfront.

Another splendid seam of accommodation is to be mined by advancing east along Kanevarou St, from Plateia E Venizelou. For instance, to the left is the side street of Odhos Kantanoleon on which are *Anastasia's Apartments* (*Tmr* 60B2), at No 41, and further up the slope, at No 47, the welcoming and excellently sited *Rooms No 47...* imaginative!

There is a *Pension Kasteli* down the second side street to the right, beyond Odhos Katrie. Confusingly enough, there is another:

Pension Kasteli (*Tmr* 61B/C2) (Class A) 39 Kanevarou   Tel 57057
Directions: On the left of Kanevarou St, beyond Odhos Ag Markou, which climbs steeply up to the left, into the fascinating Kastelli Quarter.

Recommended as comfortable, with friendly owners and the free use of the establishment's washing machine. Can't be bad. A single room, sharing a bathroom, is charged at 1500drs & with an en suite bathroom 1750drs, whilst charges for doubles are, respectively, 2000 & 2750drs.

Mentioning Odhos Ag Markou reminds me that on that street is a fascinating possibility, namely:
Monastiri Pension (*Tmr* 62B/C1/2) (Class E) Ag Markou   Tel 54776
Directions: As above and on the right, about half-way up the street.

Delightfully the building appears to be built in and around an erstwhile monastery (thus the name), as evidenced by the vaulted ceilings and calm, cloistered courtyard. Double rooms are available, with or without en suite bathrooms, those sharing costing 2100drs & en suite 2600drs, which prices increase to 2750drs & 3150drs (April-Sept). I haven't stayed here but would love the to do so, one day.

Kanevarou St makes a junction with Archoleon St, in a rather sterile, downtown area of Chania. Approximately the other side of the road are a couple of possibilities, specifically:

Pension Mary & Bill (*Tmr* 63C2) 68 I Sifaka   Tel 53060
Directions: As above.
A distinctly ethnic option.

Rooms Port (*Tmr* 64C2) (Class A) Archoleon/I Sifaka   Tel 59484
Directions: South a metre or ten towards Plateia 1821 and occupying a large corner site.
Reportedly 'Okay', with an en suite double room priced at 2800drs.

Further down Odhos I Sifaka, and on the right, is *Rent Rooms Mary* (*Tmr* 65C2), whilst to the north, along Archoleon St, in the direction of the Inner Harbour, is a *Rooms/Taverna*. This is tucked away on the left of the corner of the crossroads with Kalergon St. Close to Plateia 1821 is *Nikos Rooms* (Tel 54783), at No 58, on the left (*Sbo*) of Archoleon St. To the west of Plateia 1821, bounded by Archoleon and Hatzimihali Sts, is a fascinating 'Old Quarter' jumble of alleys and lanes, in amongst which is *Rooms Elias*.
In the area of Plateia 1866 (*Tmr* 34B3/4), as well as the more usual run-of-the-mill offerings, there are a number of swish hotels, which include the:

Omalos Hotel (*Tmr* 15A/B4) (Class C) 71 Kidonias   Tel 57171
Directions: South of Plateia 1866 and on the edge of the Bus Terminus.
All rooms have en suite bathrooms, with a single priced at 2845drs & a double 3735drs, which rates increase to 3415drs & 4480drs (July-Oct).

Hotel Samaria (*Tmr* 15A/B4) (Class B) Kidonias/Zimvrakakidon   Tel 51551
Directions: Next door to the *Omalos*.
...and even more expensive. Single rooms start off at 4830drs & a double room 6820drs, boosted to 5600drs & 7950drs (July-Oct).

Across the street, on the north side of Odhos Kidonias, is *Rooms* (*Tmr* 66A/B3/4). South of the Bus Terminus are *Chinos Rooms* (*Tmr* 68A/B4) and, round the corner, a pair of *Rooms* (*Tmr* 69A/B4), but this is a rather grubby, backstreet area. Do not forget that any accommodation in the environs of the Bus Station can prove to be very noisy.

North-west of Plateia 1866 are the:
Hotel Arkadi (*Tmr* 67A/B3/4) (Class B) Plateia 1866   Tel 40181
Directions: As above.
The bedrooms, all with bathrooms attached, cost 3230drs for a single & 3750drs for a double, rising to 3680drs & 4660drs (July-Sept).

Next door to the *Arkadi* is the **Hotel Canea** (Class C, tel 24673). To the east of Plateia 1866 are: the *Hotel Anesis* (*Tmr* 70B3/4) on Koraka St; *Janis Rooms* (*Tmr* 71B/C3/4), around the corner, on Odhos Milonogianni, housed in an older building; and further along Koraka St, on the corner of the busy junction with Karaiskaki St, the very nice looking *Rooms Themis*, above a bookshop, and *Rooms Tasos* (*Tmr* 72B/C3/4). The latter advises 'We rent Rooms by the day, by the week, by the month'. South of the Tourist police office (*Tmr* 31B/C3/4) is a crossroads form- ed by the streets of Karaiskaki and Ipsilanton, around which are a Pension and a *Room* or three.
Close by the Public Gardens & Zoo (*Tmr* C/D3/4) is a little outcrop of accommodation including: *Hotel Ellinis* (*Tmr* 73C/D3/4) (Class C, tel 28070), at

No 68 Tzanakaki St; *Pension Kipos* across the road from the *Ellinis*; and the *Cyprus* (*Tmr* 74C/D3/4), also bordering Tzanakaki St.
Returning to the north-west of the Outer Harbour, in the elbow of the Old Wall, at the outset of Theotokopoulou St is the:
Xenia (*Tmr* 11A1/2) (Class B) Theotokopoulou   Tel 24561
Directions: As above and sited in a superb position.
Mind you it should be an excellent location, with an en suite double room costing 5650drs, breakfast 480drs, and dinner 1380drs.

Another centre of opportunities borders the Beach, to the west of the town (*See* Beaches, A To Z). Inconveniently situated and not enthused about is the:
Youth Hostel 33 Drakonianou St   Tel 53565
Directions: It is necessary to catch a bus from the stop opposite the Market (*Tmr* 18B/C3), or just round the corner on Odhos Apokoronou, for the five or seven minute bus ride in a southerly direction. Passengers should ask the bus driver to indicate the correct spot, but if this fails it is necessary to get off at Dexameni Sq, or the 5th stop.
Rather off-the-beaten-track, and a rather spectacular location... which some maintain are the only plus points! Charges start off at 500drs.

Camping
Camping Hania   Tel 51090
Directions: Follow the westwards coastal road out of Chania, or better still... catch the Kastelli bus from the main Bus terminal (*Tmr* 19A/B4), or a local bus from the Plateia 1866 departure point (*Tmr* 75B3/4). Stipulate the campsite as the destination and or watch out for the more-than-adequate signs off to the right of the main road, after about 3 km. This leads onto a peninsula, a blob of land sub-ject to rather Spanish-like development, at the outset! The area sports a number of not-so-clean beaches, divided by small, tree clad hillocks evincing signs of 'wild' camping. There is a network of roads, complete with street lighting but few apartments and villas. Very Kosta... The street to the site angles sharply backward, after a couple of hundred metres, winding through various holiday buildings and small complexes, prior to arriving at the downbeat entrance to this unprepossessing facility.
There is an octagonal reception shed, marked by a sign 'To Rent Bices' (*sic*). The per person charge is 450drs, but there appears to be an awful lot of long-stay camper vans and tents lurking in amongst the bushes and trees. The site is 'bless-ed' with the usual 'appointments', and is close to one of the beaches hereabouts.

The Eating Out Compared to the profusion of places to lay one's head, there are few good eateries. There are a number of souvlaki snackbars (but a decent fistful now costs 140drs and a bottle of beer 100drs). These estab-lishments include some three on Chalidon St, one across the street from the junction with Sarmaki St, and a pair of side-by-side places, almost opposite the Skridlof St turning. Ambling east along Skridlof and turning right, and then left, leads to the western steps up to the Market. On the right is a worthy and friendly, if cramped, *Cafe Snack-Bar* (*Tmr* 76B/C3) serving souvlakis and bottles of beer.
Whilst adjacent to the Market (*Tmr* 18B/C3), it is worth bearing in mind that inside the hall are a number of intriguing, if 'working-mens' noshing possibilities. On the left of the western aisle is a cafe, with great, simmer-ing pans of fish, meat and vegetable soup. Closer to the centre of the cruci-form is an excellent taverna, on the right, serving a very wide range of

meals, including cauliflower, red cabbage, as well as whole squid dishes.
The eastern aisle has a snackbar, on the left, sporting pans of soup and
meat stews, whilst alongside is a taverna snackbar which specialises in
sausage and meat dishes.

In between the Market and the Outer Harbour, alongside Odhos Sarmaki,
is:

Nikos Snack-Bar (*Tmr* K2/3B Inset)   Tel 23640
Directions: As above and close to the corner of Episc Dorotheou Lane, opposite
the *Fidias*.

Owned by Nikos, who is most friendly and helpful, slight-of-build, in his
middle 30s, smiley but often pre-occupied, if not sometimes worried looking. He
is married to a young English lass and thus speaks excellent English and can be
most informative. The snackbar opens fairly early in the morning, when they
serve anything from a glass of orange juice to a full-blown breakfast, the latter
costing about 500drs. They are open all day through to the late evening/early
morning hours, during which the menu ranges from a Nes meh ghala, costing
70drs, to snacks of all shapes and sizes. Nikos' sometimes fretful look? Well, he
is convinced that 'money is rotting the soul and desire of the islanders to please',
in addition to which he is a partner in a just-out-of-town taverna.

Christos, a very pleasant, retired, near neighbour of Nikos, helps out at the
snackbar, more especially in the evenings. He and his wife, Diamanda, own the
most attractive *Pension Diamanda*, spacious apartments of two rooms for 4
people, with a fully equipped kitchen and use of the lovely garden. These are a
definite possibility at a cost of 3500drs per day. It is probably easiest to go to the
snackbar, but those wishing to strike out regardless must take the main coast
road west out of Chania, for about 2km. If the stooping eagle, commemorating
the German war dead, is passed, then the turning off has been overshot. Back
along the road are some blue promotional flags, followed by two garages, on the
right of the road (*Chania behind one*). Select the side-road off to the left (signed
to Ag Sophia) and almost immediately turn to the right. The pension is on the
left, at No 118 Parigoria (Tel 56060).

Cheese Pie Shop (*Tmr* L2B Inset) Odhos Iris Episkoro
Directions: FOUND IT. This is the definitive location. What is he on about?
Well many years ago I located this then absolutely outstanding shop. Some time
later the situation was queried, then called into doubt, when a follow-up research-
er even denied its existence. Other correspondents claimed to have spotted it, but
in a variety of locations! Readers will understand my determination on this trip to
nail these lies, and settle the matter once and for all. Well, the facts are that the
chap who originally owned the place died in a car crash, thus the shop was sold
and the new owner unrecognisably enlarged the premises into the present-day
Zacharoplasteion AIETHNES. Alas no longer the indelicacy of great slabs of
scrumptious, 'uncontrolled' cheese pie, now more a polite, if tasty portion costing 70drs - but they still open Sunday mornings.

An abundance of restaurants and their outside tables and chairs almost encircle
the Outer Harbour, to the left (*Fsw*) of Plateia E Venizelou, whilst an increasing
number are lining a section east and beyond the NTOG (*Tmr* 22B2). Even the
far Inner Harbour has spawned a row of restaurants, prior to the *Porto Veneziano*
(*Tmr* 58C/D1).

Most of the Outer Harbour establishments have an illuminated glass cabinet
displaying their various offerings. Comparing prices is, in the main, the only lit-
mus test. Despite their proximity and that it would make sense for these closely

packed rivals to be competitive with each other, often prices vary very little. In amongst this 'wealth of knives and forks' I hesitate to recommend any particular outfit, but, in case I might be accused of bottling out, suggest:

Restaurant To Mini Akti Kountourioti
Directions: Situated beneath a lovely, old, wooden, three storey building, close by the *Amphora* and *Contessa* (*Tmr* 43A2).

Friendly service at acceptable prices, and there is a kortaki retsina on the menu. Readers must bear in mind that much depends on the personnel who, at these type of establishments, tend to move on at the end of each season.

Whilst chewing over this waterfront, there are a few more pointers worthy of passing on, namely: probably the least expensive of the cafe-bars is the *Cafe Ilios*, in the ground floor of the *Lucia* (*Tmr* 4A/B2); the least costly eateries are at opposite ends of the quayside, that is the rather sleazy *New Taste*, close by Plateia E Venizelou, and the very last souvlaki joint at the far, west end of the Esplanade. Both of them charge 130drs for a souvlaki and 100drs for an Amstel. For those who simply require to take coffee, there is a marvellous old *Kafeneion* at the extreme, east end of the Harbour area, at No 43 Minoos St, whilst a cafe-bar edging the north-east corner of Plateia 1821 serves two Nes meh ghala, an ouzo and a plate of nuts for 200drs.

Originally the following taverna was the *Numero Uno*, but time takes its toll...

Taverna Apo Vrado (*Tmr* M2/3B Inset) Isodion St
Directions: On the left (*Cathedral behind one*) of the lane, which branches off Sarmaki (or Karaoli) St, and almost opposite *Kydonia Rooms* (*Tmr* 53 B2/3).

During the summer months, the tables and chairs stretch along the narrow street, whilst, in the winter, everything moves indoors. The years have not dealt ever so kindly with the establishment. It has to be reported that the service is still swift, some of the menu listings remain quite interesting and, happily, open wine and a Chania retsina are available. The menus depend on the season. For instance Chania sausages 'rule' until October, when the flavoured Mykonos variety take over. A meal, for two, of 1 lamb stew (not cooked properly, 450drs), 1 special pork (450drs), a plate of gigantes (250drs), an open, pink retsina (150drs), and bread (20drs each), costs a total of 1340drs. The menu may include snails, lamb stew (not fricasse), octopus, rabbit with onions, pork with celery, squid, sausages, meat balls, taramosalata, tzatziki, spinach (cold), salads, saute potatoes, baked beans (Cretan), and good wine from the barrel. The patron is a quiet man aided by a redheaded wife (there are quite a number of redheads on Crete) and one of their two sons.

Whilst in this area, it is worth noting that the locals tend to patronise the *Taverna To Steki* (*Tmr* N2B Inset), which stretches through from Ag Deka to Episc Dorotheou St. Another establishment to bear in mind is:

Restaurant Elisabeth (*Tmr* 59C/D1) Akti Enosseos
Directions: Sited beyond the *Porto Veneziano*, at the very eastern end of the Inner Harbour.

Has managed to retain its 'local' character even if prices have been 'influenced', upwards, by the presence of the swish hotel, bang next door. The menu includes tzatziki 180drs; green beans 195drs; meatballs 340drs; octopus 490drs; lamb chops 550drs; pork chops 615drs; shish-kebabs 550drs; shrimps 900drs; fish 3900drs per kilo; a bottle of beer 90drs; and a retsina 155drs.

Of the tavernas scattered along Odhos Sifaka, the *Taverna* (*Tmr* 39B/C2), at No 19, is interesting, if only because it is built into ruins of the old walls and the kitchen is framed by an ancient archway. An expensive but very good English breakfast is served at:

The Cafe Restaurant Remetzio (*Tmr* 1B2)
Directions: The awning covered tables and chairs edge Venizelou Sq, and the main body of the restaurant occupies the ground floor of the *Plaza*.

A pint of fresh orange juice, coffee, two eggs, some bacon, a slice of tomato, a large toasted bun, butter, jam and cake, for two, costs in excess of 1000drs.

I have to own up to saving the best to last but must report that some thoughtless, mindless tour company representative is advising his or her clients about the existence of this excellent establishment. I must also apologise to the prospective punters concerned, for lurking in the 'night dark' alley and advising enquirers "No, it isn't here", or "It's closed for good, I think!" Oh dear, how low can one sink? After that fulsome panegyric and confession, it might be appropriate to actually introduce the:

Restaurant Hamam (*Tmr* 42A/B2)
Directions: From Plateia E Venizelou (*Tmr* B2), proceed along Odhos Zambeliou. The restaurant is on the left, beyond the Kondilaki St turning. It is rather difficult to locate, before the door opens, at about 2000hrs, being in an anonymous, flat-fronted building butting directly onto the narrow lane and absent of any signs. A pointer is the flower pot placed bang in front of the entrance way.

The restaurant derives its name from the fact that the building was once a Turkish Bath, or *Hamam*. The outer square of seating is on a raised dais, which encircles the sunken central section. The owners have resisted the temptation to go OTT and the decor is simple but effective... whitewash. The waiter service is dramatically dignified, the service is quietly professional, the helpings are large and the food is the 'superb side' of excellent. What more could one ask? This excellent quality results in the seats filling quickly, very quickly. A meal, for two, of a delicious cod or hake fish soup (300drs), a great green salad with avocado, cabbage & lettuce (180drs), a lamb & vegetable dish complete with boiled potatoes, carrots & courgettes (550drs), a liver & mushroom pilaff dish (400drs), a Chania retsina (150drs), water in a jug (and not one of those wretched bottles, inevitably charged extra), and bread (& service 20drs each), cost a grand total of 1620drs. Another sample dinner, for two, included a dreamy vegetable soup (220drs), scrumptious prawns (660drs, you can tell no holds were barred), chicken livers (400drs), a plate of (fatless) veal (500drs, & it was at least ½kilo of meat at the weigh-in), a bottle of that silky Chania retsina (150drs), bread and service, resulted in a 1960drs bill. If I haven't made it plain, this is a 'top-of-the-First Division' establishment.

One slight, but startling intrusion into any daytime, waterfront cafe-bar reverie is the habit of the Greek Air Force to unexpectedly overfly Chania - when fuel coupons allow!

THE A TO Z OF USEFUL INFORMATION
AIRLINE OFFICE & TERMINUS (*Tmr* 13D4) Some official maps still detail the office at the junction of Tzanakaki and Veloudaki Sts, but it is much further

up Odhos Tzanakaki, opposite the far end of the Public   Gardens. The office opens daily, between 0700hrs-2000hrs, and airport   buses depart about 1½hrs prior to a planes take-off.

Aircraft timetable
Chania to Athens
Daily   0720, 1455, 2240
In addition to which are:
Wed   0030hrs
Tues-Sat   1945hrs
Mon & Sun   2015hrs
Return
Daily   0555, 1250, 2115hrs
In addition to which are:
Tues-Sat   1800hrs
Mon & Sun   1830hrs
Tues   1915hrs
One-way fare: 6200drs; duration 45mins.

Chania to Thessaloniki(M)
Tues   2040hrs
Return
Tues   2235hrs
One-way fare: 11700drs; duration 1hr 15mins

BANKS The major bank for exchange purposes, including changing   travellers and Eurocheques cheques, is the **National Bank** (*Tmr* 14C3), opposite the Market. There is another **National Bank** in the   same block as the *Omalos & Samaria* (*Tmr* 15A/B4), conveniently close   to the Bus Terminus. A Bank (*Tmr* 77C/D3) occupies the angle of the   junction of Dimokratias St and Odhos Archontaki. Foreign paper money, acquired whilst on the way to   Greece, say in Yugoslavia or Italy, can only be changed at the **Bank of Greece** (*Tmr* 16C3).

BEACHES There is a sandy, narrow little stretch of   pedestrian-only-Esplanade edged beach, at the east end of town, and   reached along Nikiforos Phokas St, beyond the School. This was once a rather rundown factory area, but in recent years the subject of some cosmetic attention.
   The main beach is a few kilometres to the west. A breach in the fortifications allows Theotokopoulou St to climb   into the Old Quarter, just before the *Xenia Hotel* (*Tmr* 11A1/2). Sharply outlined against the background is an attractive, three storey, Turkish building, the upper two floors of which are   overhanging, clapper board. The tree lined route leads past a private   club, a small caique harbour, the city's Lido and another caique harbour. Beyond the latter hoves into sight the very sandy, gently shelving, some 200m long beach. Offshore are a ring of rocks jutting out of the   water, and beyond them an angled slab of rock, both of which protect   the shore from the more boisterous seas. The beach is edged by an   Esplanade, which terminates up against a building site. This backshore road is bordered   by a row of three to five storey buildings accommodating a few hotels,   some pensions, restaurants, tavernas, mini-markets, a motorbike & car hire business, and a travel office... to name but a few. Most of the   eateries and hotels have shaded patios whereon are served anything   from coffee, breakfasts, pizzas, milkshakes, omelettes, salads, 'long   drings' (*sic*) to ice-creams. A little cupboard-like store sells   foreign newspapers and the original *To Akrogiali Taverna* is   recognizable, because it is one of the only two storey structures. One

of the mini-market's possesses an international, metered telephone. Along the lateral side street of Parados Valestra is *Minos Rooms* and behind the buildings fronting the Esplanade is a grid layout of streets.

The beach is alive with activity. Apart from the more usual and pedestrian sun beds, umbrellas and pedaloes, there are very fast speed boat rides with punters being towed on a circular, tyre-like ring, as well as outboard powered inflatables for hire. Sample prices: canoes 300drs; sun-beds/umbrellas 300drs; pedaloes 600drs; and the speed boat 3000drs, per hour.

Joy, oh joy, there are beach showers at both ends of the beach. Due to the amount of use the shore receives, it is unsurprising that there is a certain amount of litter scattered about.

Keeping on across an outcrop of rocks to the west is an almost unused shore, the nearest of a bay-full of beaches sweeping round to the left (*Fsw*). These are more usually accessed from the main coast road. The first of these turnings is mysteriously signed 'EOT', which route advances down a track to a sandy shore, serviced by a small Cantina and on which are scattered some beach beds and umbrellas. The rest of the bay is reached along the *Camping Hania* detour, which gives access to a series of large coves, either side of a quite prominent, tree covered headland. At some stage it appears that this was destined to be the site of a now long abandoned leisure development, possibly a 'Colonels' folly. Straight ahead is a small, pebbly sand cove with a Cantina. To the left (*Fsw*) is another small but sandy beach backed by a restaurant, as well as a bank of five shower heads. There is a certain amount of water skiing activity buzzing about. To the right is a 150m semi-circular sweep of sandy beach, surrounded by a scrubbly, pampas grass spread of 'Bisley Army range' countryside on the mid-backshore of which are littered about a few buildings. Around to the left is a horn of land projecting into the sea, topped and overhung by a restaurant and terrace.

Incidentally, on the way down to the seafront from the main road, on the left, are the complete remains of a donkey driven, water well mechanism.

BICYCLE, SCOOTER & CAR HIRE The scooter and car hire outfits are fairly evenly spread about, but there is a concentration of businesses at the upper end of Chalidon St (*Tmr* O3B & P3B Inset), one of which is **Olympic Rent A Car.** **Moto Sport** (*Tmr* Q2B Inset) edges Plateia E Venizelou, **Hertz Car Hire** (*Tmr* 78D3/4) is on the left (*Sbo*) of Dimokratias St, and there is an **Avis** office on Tzanakaki St, to the Market side and close by the *Ellinis* (*Tmr* 73C/D3/4). Another outcrop of car hire agencies occur on Odhos Karaiskaki, south of the Tourist police/Town Hall (*Tmr* 31B/C3/4). In addition, there are any number of travel firms that offer Car hire, including **Sunny Tours** (*Tmr* 17C/D3/4). Scooter prices start off at about 1200drs a day, whilst car hire charges are universally expensive, as elsewhere.

BOOKSELLERS On the left (*Fsw*) of E Venizelou Sq is an excellent foreign language Book/Card/Newspaper shop (*Tmr* T2B Inset), with an extensive English section. The 'periptero-like' kiosk at the centre of the Market (*Tmr* 18B/C3) sells a limited number of paperbacks, whilst there is a 'Second Hand Books' shop (*Tmr* 79B3), close by the junction of Hatzi-Mikali Gianari and Chalidon St, as well as the 'All Language Bookstore' (*Tmr* 80C/D3/4) on Odhos Ktisiakti.

BREAD SHOPS As usual, the Bakers tend to be hidden away, no better illus-trated than by the one tucked away on Odhos Zambeliou, between the *Manos* (*Tmr* 3B2) and *Rooms George*. There is another on Odhos Theotokopoulou, south of the *El Greco* (*Tmr* 6A2), in amongst an outcrop of small, good value 'corner' shops. The Market (*Tmr* 18B/C3) has a bread stall which also sells slabs of pizza and various mouth-watering pies.

BUSES The Main terminal (*Tmr* 19A/B4 -tel 23052) is in a rectangle enclosed by Kidonias, Kelaidi, Smirnis, and Zimvrakakidon Sts, alongside the *Omalos & Samaria*. The ticket office complex, in the south-west corner, is a chaotic, all-action office, filled by a bustling mass of humanity, and with a timetable posted inside. There is the usual cafe-bar, in addition to a separate restaurant/bar, toilets, and a number of small shops, selling most requirements, including a garage tool accessory shop. Perhaps this is for the bus drivers?

Some local buses depart from a Bus stop (*Tmr* 75B3/4) on Plateia 1866 (*Tmr* 34B3/4), and a stop (*Tmr* 20C3), close by the Market. The latter, for instance, services Souda. There is another bus stop at the outset of Nikiforos Phokas, close by the School.

Some of the desk clerks speak excellent English and can be very helpful. It is vital to make enquiries here in respect of the various departure points, and at the same time establish whether tickets must be pre-purchased, or if it will be a free-for-all for a bus seat. It must be understood that buying a ticket from the desk does not do away with the joy of fighting for a place, it simple means there is a better chance of getting on the conveyance... and don't forget that constant vigilance is required to ensure at what time and from where a particular bus departs! The bus journeys from Chania are the most beautiful, stunning, breathtaking... and frightening on Crete. Those of a nervous disposition should take some tranquillisers, before commencing on a journey!

Bus timetables
Chania to Thessaloniki (M)
Tues, Thurs 1730hrs
  & Sun
Return journey
Tues, Thurs 0830hrs
  & Sun

Chania to Rethymnon, Iraklion
Daily   0530, 0630, 0730, 0815, 0830, & every 30 mins until 1630, 1730,
            1900, 2000hrs
Return journey
Daily   0530 & every 30mins until 1730, 1815, 1900, 2030hrs
One-way fares: to Rethymnon 480drs
               Iraklion   1000drs
Distance to Iraklion 140km; duration to Iraklion 3 hrs.

Chania to Platanias, Kolimbari, Kastelli
Daily   0600, 0715, 0830, 1000, 1100, 1200, 1300, 1430, 1530, 1630, 1730,
            1830, 2000hrs
Sun & hols 0730, 0830, 1000, 1100, 1200, 1300, 1430, 1530, 1630, 1730, 1830,
            2000hrs
Return journey
Daily   0500, 0600, 0700, 0730, 0800, 0830, 0930, 1030, 1130, 1230, 1400,
            1530, 1615, 1800, 1900hrs
Sun & hols 0500, 0600, 0730, 0830, 0930, 1030, 1130, 1230, 1400, 1530, 1615,
            1800, 1900hrs
One-way fare: 300drs; distance 42km; duration 1½hrs.

Chania to Kastelli, Falasarna
Daily   0830, 1530hrs
Return journey
Daily   1045, 1730hrs

Chania to Kastelli, Platanias
Daily   0830, 1100, 1200, 1300, 1530hrs
Return journey
Daily   0700, 1015, 1245hrs, Oh yes and where's the other two?
Distance 63km; duration 2hrs.

Chania to Vathi, Chrysoskalitissa Nunnery, Elafonisi
Daily   0815hrs
Return journey
Daily   1650hrs
One-way fare: 480drs.

Chania to Paleochora
Daily   0830, 0900, 1030, 1200, 1430, 1700hrs
Return journey
Daily   0700, 1100, 1200, 1330, 1530, 1700hrs
One-way fare: 550drs; distance 77km; duration 2hrs.

Chania to Omalos (for the Samaria Gorge)
Daily   0615, 0730, 0830, 1630hrs
Return journey
Daily   0700, 0900, 1000, 1800hrs
One-way fare: 280drs; distance 42km; duration 1½hrs.

Chania to Souyia
Daily   0830, 1330hrs
Sun & hols   0800hrs
Return journey
Daily   0700, 1430hrs
Sun & hols   1430hrs
One-way fare; 480drs; distance 70km; duration 2 ½hrs.

Chania to Chora Sfakion
Daily   0830, 1100, 1400, 1530hrs
Return journey
Daily   0700, 1100, 1630, 1730, 1830hrs*
* *As the official sheet so charmingly puts it 'The last trip it's depent (sic) from the boat's arrival'.*

Chania to Kolimbari
Daily   0600, 0715, 0800, & every 30mins until 2300hrs
Return journey
Daily   0530, 0630, 0730, 0800, & every 30mins until 2330hrs

Chania to Stalos, Ag Marina, Platanias, Gerani, Maleme, Hotel Chandris
Daily   0600, 0615, 0715, 0800, 0830, & every ¼hr until 1115, 1130, 1200,
               1230, 1300, 1330, 1345, 1400, 1430, 1500, 1530, 1600, 1630, & every
               ¼hr until 1930, 2000, 2030, 2100, 2130, 2200, 2230, 2300hrs.
Return journey
Daily   0535, 0635, 0735, 0805, 0815, 0830, 0845, 0900, & every ¼hr until
               1145, 1215, 1245, 1315, 1345, 1415, 1445, 1515, 1530, 1545, 1615,
               1700, 1715, & every ½ hrs until   2000, 2015, 2045, 2215, 2245,
               2315, 2345hrs

Chania to Anopolis, Frangokastello, Skaloti
Daily   1400hrs
Return journey
Daily   0600hrs
One-way fare: 600drs; distance 82km; duration 2½hrs.

Chania to Kalves, Vryses
Daily   0845, 1145, 1445, 1935hrs
Sun & hols   0800, 1000, 1200, 1300, 1800hrs
Return journey
Daily   0700, 1000, 1300, 1700hrs
Sun & hols   0700, 1000, 1200, 1630, 1800hrs
Distance 33km; duration 1hr.

Chania to Vamos
Daily   0700, 0845, 1145, 1415, 1940hrs
Sun & hols   0800, 1200, 1600, 2000hrs
Return journey
Daily   0700, 0900, 1100, 1300, 1500, 1700hrs.
Sun & hols   0715, 0930, 1300, 1630, 1815hrs
Distance 26km; duration ½hr.

Chania to Chordaki, Ag Triada Monastery (Akrotiri Peninsula)
Daily   0630, 1300hrs
Sun & hols   0730, 1700hrs
Return journey
Daily   0700, 1330hrs
Sun & hols   0800, 1730hrs
One-way fare: 100drs; distance 16km; duration ½hr.

Chania to Kalathas, Chorafakia, Stavros (Akrotiri Peninsula)
Daily   0700, 1000, 1400, 1800hrs
Return journey
Daily   0730, 1030, 1430, 1830hrs
One-way fare: 100drs; distance 16km; duration ½hr.

Chania to Souda
Daily   0600 & every ¼hr until 2300hrs
One-way fare: 60drs.
Please NOTE that these are mid-season timetables, outside of which schedules are severely curtailed.

CINEMAS A quite modern example shares the ground floor of the *Ellinis* (*Tmr* 73C/D3/4), in addition to the open-air cinema, the **Attikon** (*Tmr* D3), to the south of El Venizelou St, on the corner of Iroon Politechniou and Dragoumi.

COMMERCIAL SHOPPING AREA Chania is indeed fortunate to have a central, all-encompassing **Market** (*Tmr* 18B/C3), all under the one roof of a rather unique building. This is constructed in the form of a cross and is reminiscent of, say, Leadenhall market, London, and supposedly modelled on that of Marseilles. (One other, but unwelcome reminder of Western European capitals are the presence of parking meters, yes parking...!) The interior is jam-packed with stalls (from which all and almost everything is for sale) interspersed by the occasional cafe-bars, where simple food is served from tin stoves and steaming charcoal ovens, the smoke piped through the roof or side walls by rickety pipes. The stallholders don't really get going until about 0815hrs and the Market is closed on Sundays, even if in the vicinity there usually is the occasional 'market barrow', open for the sale of vegetables and fruit. The Market west wing is predominantly occupied by fish vendors, one of whom is prone to have a flower in his mouth,

Spanish style. The whole arena is swarming with people and, in amongst the general hubbub, the stall owners shout their wares. Around the periphery of the building are various wholesalers.

In the vicinity of the Market are: Tsouderon St, which has a preponderance of shoe shops; Skridlof St, which is an 'Athens Plaka look-alike', overflowing with leather shops down both sides; and Chalidon St, which is awash with gift & souvenir shops. Distant Odhos Theotokopoulou (*Tmr* A2) houses a number of arts & crafts type establishments, along its length. Angelou Lane, opposite *Rooms Stella*, close to the *Meltemi* (*Tmr* 5A1/2), is an interesting cavern of a shop selling old Cretan blankets, rugs and wall hangings.

DISCO A drawback to listing discos is that they tend to be rather 'fragile', transitory businesses. Furthermore, when in operation they rarely appear to need attention drawn to them, as exemplified by the jukebox-throbbing cocktail bars behind the *Plaza* (*Tmr* 1B2). A little further on is a Disco in the basement of the *Ariadne* (*Tmr* 10B1), whilst the other side of the Outer Harbour, on the right of Angelou Lane, beyond the *Meltemi* and *Thereza* (*Tmr* 5A1/2), is a jazz bar, open early evening to early morning.

ELPA Signposted to the right of Tzanakaki St, or to the left of Apokoronou St, leaving Chania in a south-east direction.

FERRY-BOATS The boats dock six km to the east, at Souda, which is a Navy base and NATO operations centre. Despite the beauty of the Bay, the port is a bit of a dump and it is best to make for Chania as soon as possible.

Ferry-boat timetables

Day	Departure time	Ferry-boat	Ports/Islands of Call
Daily	1900hrs	Kriti/Aptera	Piraeus.

One-way fares: from 2175drs; duration 11hrs.

Piraeus to Chania boats also depart daily, at 1900hrs.

FERRY-BOAT TICKET OFFICES The major ferry-boat owner running into Souda is **ANEK**, which company has a ticket office (*Tmr* 35C3, tel 23636) at Plateia Sof Venizelou, opposite the Market. **Minoan Lines** is represented by **Mandakis** (*Tmr* U2B Inset, tel 23939), at No 8 Chalidon St.

HAIRDRESSERS Okay, they must be there ... I mean to say there is a Bodybuilder (as in gymnasium), close to Sunny Tours (*Tmr* 17C/D3/4), but I own up to not actually pinpointing a Ladies Hairdresser.

HORSE-DRAWN CARRIAGES (Monipos) A number rank alongside the Outer Harbour, on the edge of Plateia E Venizelou. The rather decrepit owners are in stark contrast to their horses and colourfully painted carriages. I worry if the horses are suffering from having to stand around hour on hour, in the extreme heat of the day. As they wear hats and the owners appear to wash down and cool the horses legs, perhaps I should be more sanguine in respect of their welfare. Prospective clients must establish the cost before hiring one of these archaic methods of travel.

LAUNDRY Not one, but two Launderettes in the 'Cathedral' Old Quarter. The **Afroditi Laundry** (*Tmr* 54B2/3, tel 57602) is at No 18, Odhos Ag Deka, whilst

Jackie & Bill's Laundromat (*Tmr* V2/3B Inset) is at No 7, Odhos Episc Dorotheou. Both appear to open daily, between 0800-2000hrs, will do the job for clients, charge 400drs for a machine load, and 400drs for the use of the dryer.

LUGGAGE STORE There is one at the Bus Terminal (*Tmr* 19A/ B4), open daily, between 0600-2000hrs, chargings 50drs an item, per day.

MEDICAL CARE
Chemists & Pharmacies They are fairly numerous, with the majority concentrated in and around Tzanakaki, Dimokratias & Apokoronou Sts, which all radiate out south-east from Plateia Sof Venizelou (*Tmr* C3).
Hospital Reached by proceeding east on El Venizelou St, as far as the main junction with Iroon Politechniou, where turn right. At the second lateral street to the left, turn on to Odhos Dragoumi. The Hospital is on the left, at the junction of Dragoumi and Odhos Kapodistrou. There is a daily outpatients' clinic.

MUNICIPAL TOURIST OFFICE (*Tmr* 22B2) In an imaginary league table of these offices, the Chania one must be one of the country's best. It may well be that the attractive ladies 'on parade' influence one's judgement! Certainly they could not be more helpful and the information available, which is generally first class, includes leaflets in respect of bus and ferry-boat timetables, as well as the Samaria Gorge and other excursion junkets. They open daily, between 0830-1400hrs & 1500-2030hrs, but are closed on Sundays. In addition there is a notice board for messages and a competitive Exchange desk, open between 0915-1315hrs.
The office is most attractively situated in an old, domed mosque alongside and to the right (*Fsw*) of the Outer Harbour. It seems a pity that the elegant lines of the building have been rather spoilt by a very large, flat-roofed extension to the side, which accommodates an extensive cafe-bar. Another part of the structure contains a displayof Cretan arts and crafts.

NTOG (*Tmr* 81B3/4) On the 4th floor of the 'Pantheon' building, bordering the north side of Odhos Kriari, close to Plateia 1866. This is more an administrative office, than one at which to gather any tourist-type information, and is only open foreshortened, weekday hours.

OTE (Tmr 23C3/4) From Plateia Sof Venizelou, the 'Market Sq', proceed up Tzanakaki St, and the building is on the left, beyond the Post Office. Open daily between 0600-2400hrs.

PETROL STATIONS They are plentiful, in the suburbs.

PLACES OF INTEREST Chania's Minoan antecedents are substantiated by the Palace excavated in the Kastelli Quarter, whilst the Medieval Ages are reflected in the Old Quarters of Topanas, Kastelli, Chiones and Splantzia. The Second World War is evidenced by the bomb-site look to much of the Old Quarters!
Churches
The Church of San Salvatore Church (*Tmr* 36A1) The name of this 13/14th century church is derived from the adjacent Bastion of San Salvatore and the building was at one time converted to a mosque.
The Church of Ag Anargyri (*Tmr* 24C2/3) Possesses artistic and venerable icons.
The Church of St Nicholas (*Tmr* 25C2) Situated on the edge of the pleasant, tree shaded Plateia 1821, which it overshadows. It was once a Monastery, then converted into an Imperial Mosque, before being rededicated to the Orthodox faith,

in 1912. Due to this interesting alternation of religious attitudes there is a re-markable coupling of minaret and campanile. In the area of the Market (*Tmr* 18B/C3) is an elegant minaret.

The Roman Catholic Church (*Tmr* W3B Inset) Edges Chalidon St and still active - 'Every Sunday Mass'.

Harbour Area An interesting *tout ensemble*. Viewing the Outer Harbour from the Municipal tourist office (*Tmr* 22B2), housed in the Mosque of the Janissaries (1645), brings Venice powerfully to mind. At the entrance to the Harbour is a distinctive Venetian lighthouse (*Tmr* 26A/B1), the subject of extensive rebuild-ing. Moving eastwards around the waterfront, towards the Inner Harbour, moor-ed craft include yachts, motor boats, commercial fishing boats, of about 50ft to 60ft in length, and some Greek Navy vessels. Beyond St Marks Arcade (*Tmr* 38B/C1/2) and a row of Arsenals (*Tmr* 37C1/2), both built by the Venetians, the boats become much smaller, finally grading down to rowing boats.

Museums

Archaeological Museum (*Tmr* 27B2/3) The interesting exhibits are located in a building, once San Francesco Church, erected in the 14th Century. There is a garden to one side containing a Turkish fountain, a left-over from the Church's days as a mosque. The doors open Monday 1230-1900hrs, Tuesday-Friday 0800-1900hrs, and weekends & holidays 0830-1500hrs.

Historical Museum Proceed south-east along Tzanakaki St, to the junction with Sfakianaki St, which is named Solomou St to the west. Turn left and the Museum is on the right. The exhibits are considered to be outstanding, covering the period from the Byzantine Empire up to and including the German occupation of Crete, between 1941 and 1945.

Naval Museum (*Tmr* 28A1/2) Naturally, a display of maritime exhibits.

Venetian Arsenals & Walls The Arsenals (*Tmr* 37C1/2), despite rapidly crumb-ling, are still inspiring, as is St Marks Arcade (*Tmr* 38B/C1/2). The remains of the Old Walls are best viewed from the west, where there are distinctive outlines of the original, large moats, leading down to the reasonably well preserved Shiavo Bastion (*Tmr* 29A/B3).

Plateia 1866 (*Tmr* 34B3/4) I mention it because of the pleasant, octagonal, panelled water fountain and the old-fashioned, metal shop awnings, on the west flank of the square.

POLICE

Tourist (*Tmr* 31B/C3/4) Their office is buried in the Town Hall complex, a 'hop, skip and a walk' to the east of the Bus terminal. Disinterestedly helpful if deskbound, and only able to proffer a board bearing names and addresses of diverse accommodation. The door opens daily, between 0800-2000hrs.

Port (*Tmr* 32B/C1/2) Close to the *Ariadne*. The Customs authorities are tucked away round the corner, to the east.

Town (*Tmr* 33D4) Rather inconveniently, a long way along Tzanakaki St, just beyond the crossroads with Solomou/Sfakianaki Sts.

POST OFFICE (*Tmr* 30C3) The main office edges Tzanakaki St. The various vans and lorries have a habit of pulling right up to the main steps in order to load and unload, and thus obscure the entrance.

Tourist requirements, especially banking facilities, are supplemented by the provision of a 'Portacabin' Post Office on the Cathedral piazza, between Chali-don St and the Cathedral (*Tmr* 8B2/3). This facility is open daily, between 0800-2000hrs, with Sunday/holiday hours of 0900-1800hrs.

TAXIS They rank in and around the Market (*Tmr* 18B/C3), on Plateia 1866 (*Tmr* 34B3/4), and alongside the Cathedral (*Tmr* 8B2/3).

TELEPHONE NUMBERS & ADDRESSES

Bus office (*Tmr* 19A/B4) Kidonias/Kelaidi	Tel 23052
Hospital, 6-8 Dragoumi	Tel 27231
Municipal Tourist office (*Tmr* 22B2) 6 Akti Tombazi	Tel 26426
Olympic Airways (*Tmr* 13D4) 84 Tzanakaki	Tel 27701
Shipping Offices:	
ANEK (*Tmr* 35C3) Hatzi-Mikali Gianari/Plateia Sof Venizelou	Tel 23636
Minoan (*Tmr* U2B Inset) 8 Chalidon	Tel 23939
Tourist police (*Tmr* 31B/C3/4) 44 Karaiskaki	Tel 24477

TOILETS Almost an abundance including: a fairly clean, underground unit beneath Plateia 1866 (*Tmr* 34B3/4); an ethnic, underground facility, close by the Market (*Tmr* 18B/C3), alongside Leoforos Hatzi-Mikali Gianari; and a disgusting unit on the east side of the Outer Harbour, in the street behind the Port police (*Tmr* 32B/C1/2).

TRAVEL AGENTS & TOUR OFFICES There are any number of firms but a small selection is as follows:

Domenico Tourist & Travel (*Tmr* 7B2) 10 Kanevarou   Tel 53262
Directions: A few metres up the slope, to the east of Plateia E Venizelou, and on the right of the street.

This is a long established, up-market but helpful business run by a Greek, who is more often than not ably assisted by a couple of English people. They can offer various accommodation possibilities, mainly at the upper price end of the market (You know, 'hot and cold running maids'), as well as owning the *Hotel Argyro & Domenico*. They can arrange baby-sitters and do have less expensive accommodation options on their books, if clients can tolerate a hard world with fewer comforts! They also exchange money, hire boats and cars, and no doubt do all sorts of other things...

Nearby, in fact the other side of the street to Domenico, on the way up from the Square, are **Elafonissos Travel** and **InterKreta Travel** (Tel 52142), the latter, coming well recommended, is at No 9 Kanevaro St. Quite close by, in the 'Cathedral Old Quarter' back streets is:

UniKreta (*Tmr* X2B Inset) 18 Isodion   Tel 291338
Directions: Isodion St is the first side street to the right, proceeding along Odhos Karoali from Plateia E Venizelou. The office is on the right (*Sbo*).

The doors open weekdays, between 0900-1400hrs & 1800-2000hrs, and the staff are most helpful, especially Helen, if she is on duty, and will answer any number of wearisome enquiries.

Sunny Tours (*Tmr* 17C/D3/4) 38 Tzanakaki   Tel 54502
Directions: South of the main east-west avenue, Leoforos Hatzi-Mikali Gianari and on the right (*Sbo*) of Tzanakaki St, almost opposite the *Cyprus*.

Yannis, the owner, operates one of the most helpful travel agents in Crete, let alone Chania, his English is very good, and if you want it, he can get it! For instance he acts for ANEK ferries, Olympic airline and rents cars.

EXCURSIONS TO CHANIA CITY SURROUNDS

Excursion to Venizelos' Graves, Akrotiri Peninsula & Souda Bay I must admit that I do not find it a very attractive area of Crete, but it cannot be denied that it is interesting. Apart from the airport, there are the outstanding historical sites of the Hill of Profitis Ilias; the Monastery of Ag Triada; the Gouverneto Monastery; and Katholiko Cave.

The initial stages of the climb, up on to the peninsula, pass through unattractive countryside scattered with outbreaks of modern suburbs, quarrying activity, skeletal, precast concrete structures, and piles of rubbish. Where the road levels out there is a Technical College complex of single storey buildings, across from the gates to:

Venizelos' Graves & Profitis Ilias (6km from Chania) The thin, slab-like tomb stones, of the island's most celebrated statesman, Eleftherios Venizelos, and his son Sophocles, are set down on a raised, crazy-paving surround in a small, calm, nicely vegetated, beautifully maintained park with super views out over distant Chania.

This hilltop is called Profitis Ilias, after the little church that stands on the site, and was the scene of a Cretan uprising against the Turks, in 1897. The rebellion was signalled by running up a flag of Independence. Rumour and legend has it that, the flagstaff being shot away, a resistance fighter grabbed and flew the standard in his hands, whence the land and naval guns battering the Cretan forces stopped firing, to honour his bravery. Yes! Another tradition relates that a shell from one of the attacking ship's made a direct hit on the chapel, whereon the the Almighty intervened, wreaking his vengeance by causing the self-same boat to blow up.

The road layout is nowhere more confusing than on Akrotiri, and nowhere more so than in this particular area. To the right is a 'little bit' of Highway, leading to the Airport, in and around which are spread a couple of filling stations and the metalled road towards:

KOUNOUPIDIANA (8km from Chania) A straggle of a settlement, with not only a BP, but a Mobil petrol station, close to which is a road junction, noticeable by a large red and white sign proclaiming 'To the bakery shop 100m to the right'.

The left fork, signed **Ag Onoufrios**, progresses through a lot of villa development, as well as past *Rooms Titika* and *Hotel Pirgos*. After 2km, the road descends to a bay with a small caique harbour and a refinery. Some wag, probably a retired ship's captain, has set down 'yer actual' merchant ship's bridge, as a dwelling house.

Back at the Kounoupidiana junction, the right-hand choice heads in the direction of Stavros and, almost immediately, on the right is a *Chicken Shack*. This is a 'proper job', with the following prices, per kilo: kotopoulo 1100drs; kokoretsi (lamb) 500drs; and kid (as in billy-goat and literally written as 'little child'!) 550drs. Other prices were: starters 80drs; tzatiki 140drs; Greek salad 150drs; Sprite/Coca-Cola 60drs; bottled beer 90drs; kortaki retsina 145drs; and 'open' wine 200drs. Definitely one to be marked down for an evenings meal.

marked down for an evenings meal.
A couple of kilometres further along the metalled road is a gentle build-up of villas, the occasional Pension and apartment building, and a hillside taverna overlooking:

KALATHAS BAY (10km from Chania) Set in the bay is a small cove of gently shelving, very sandy beach lapped by an extremely inviting looking sea. But one is not alone. Oh, no. There is the *Lina Beach Hotel*, a beach bar, specialising in European cuisine, a little Cantina, some beach umbrellas, and a block of English owned villas, for holiday let. I certainly wouldn't want to be stuck out here, without some form of transport.

Two kilometres on is **Chorafakia**, whereat the *Restaurant Koutras*, a supermarket, petrol station, mini-market restaurant, and *Taverna Irene*.

A further 4km to the north, and the 'till-now', surfaced route runs out at:
STAVROS (16km from Chania) The shanty seaside village, is a 'Canvey-island-in-the-sun', a mishmash of a development, a mix of good quality villas, which include the *Edem Apartments*, and single storey shacks. It certainly is out on a limb, overshadowed, on the right (*Fsw*), by a rather stark mountain range, the lower slopes of which gently slide into the sea.
   The road runs out alongside a small, circular bay, shut off, on the far side, by the barren foothills of the aforementioned mountain, and into which dribbles a fetid streamlet. In the hook of the bay is a caique harbour, as well as a very pleasant sweep of sandy beach, even if it is a shadeless crescent of shore 'sprouting' sunbeds and umbrellas.
   The 'support facilities' encompass the *Stavros Beach Taverna*, a sandwich stall, the *Taverna Dionissis* - a steak-house with 'service in English & Deutch'. Beyond the bay is another tangle of single storey dwellings, and the *Cafeteria Christiana*.
   Incidentally Stavros is yet another location at which a scene or two of the film *Zorba The Greek* was supposedly filmed. Frankly, it would not surprise me if this motion picture legend were not deified, by acceptance into Greek mythology!

On the return journey, at **Chorafakia** turning left, signed 'Ag Triada' (in Greek), leads to the:
Monastery of Ag Triada (Tsagaroliou) (17km from Chania) The last stretch is along an avenue of trees lined track, over the surrounding fields. This celebrated, still working monastery, Venetian in style and founded in the 1630s, has been restored. Notable features are the entrance way and a campanile.

Further north from Ag Triada, some 4km along the initially surfaced track is the:
Gouverneto Monastery (21km from Chania) Built in the 16th century, fortified in appearance and renowned for its domed roof and icons.

Beyond the latter, about half an hour's walk, are the:
Monastery of Katholiko Ruined but close to early Christian rock face caves, a bridged ravine and the:

caves, a bridged ravine and the:

Katholiko Cave A stalactite hung chamber, the one-time residence and death place of John the Hermit. His saint's day is October 7th, when the surrounds are rather busy with the comings and goings of pilgrims.

To explore the rest of the peninsula, proceed past the Airport to the village of **Sternes**, the narrow street of which winds through some very old and crumbly parts of the settlement. Select the right-hand fork, alongside the War Memorial. This passes a military installation, with views of the fortified islet in Souda Bay, and proceeds to a simple bay on which lies:

Marathi Beach (18km from Chania) A tree lined, and thus shaded, narrow but sandy shoreline is bordered by a peculiarly Greek seaside resort - of 'brown paper and wooden shacks'. Apart from a scattering of fishing boats drawn up on the shore, there are a few pedaloes resting on the main portion of the beach, a pocket-handkerchief sized triangle formed by the caique harbour. Offshore is **Palaiosouda islet**.

At the outset, where the approach road 'junctions' with the backshore, is the *Albatross*, a self-service taverna. On a nearby gum tree, a sign proclaims 'For rent motorboats, waterscooters, water skiing, ski lessons reasonably priced, come ski boat with somebody at Marathi Beach, ride on a banana boat. For rent umbrellas...'. Continuing to the left (*Fsw*) shambles past a *Rooms*, a fishing boat harbour, and the very simple, hut edged patio of a doo-hickey taverna. Despite it's evident unpretentiousness, the prices do not reflect this modesty, with a beer costing 100drs and a Greek salad 250drs. In addition to the location's naive charm, one of the real attractions must be that it is the chosen weekend venue at which an amateur dance band trio, and their spouses, from nearby Chania, often relax. They are of retirement age, but enormously talented (if that isn't being too patronising) and marvellous to listen to, when they stop playing the fool and settle down to the serious business of making music. The one-time industrial chemist is the accordianist, and his English is absolutely brilliant, whilst the 'Jack Benny' of the group is the guitarist, who maintains they don't practice much, just six hours a day! The mature lady-wives are a very lively accompaniment and their weekends are spent playing 1930s dance tunes, laughing, joking, swimming, and enjoying themselves. There are times when I dearly wish I could stay on, and on, and on...

Just around the corner, to the right (*Fsw*), and signed from the Marathi road, is an unmetalled track down to:
Loutraki Beach A small, almost circular cove in a gorgeous little bay, with the narrow entrance seemingly blocked off by a close-too islet. Some tamarisk trees shade the backshore, the middleshore is pebbly, but the sea's edge and the first 1½m of the seabed are sand.

In the field behind the cove is a sweetwater well and the surrounding slopes sport the remains of once substantial walls. This would be a splendid spot at which to camp, as long as victuals were packed.

To exit the peninsula an option is to select the southern road and follow the signs to Souda. This route passes by plenty of petrol stations and through a urban Souda build-up, in what appears to be strenous efforts to cover each and every parcel of undeveloped land, if the cement lasts out! From this direction it is a left turning to the:

Souda Bay Cemetery An official United Kingdom and Commonwealth burial ground, there being some one thousand five hundred and twenty-seven servicemen interred here. A reverential calm lays over the beautifully laid out site, which is attractively located close to the waters of Souda Bay. Those of an emotional nature may well be best advised to steer clear of the place, as it would be an iron-willed person who failed to be moved, not only by the simple, carved headstone tributes, but also by the personal messages left by grieving relatives who have visited the graves. Many are heartbreaking, harrowing testaments to the fallen. I think I expressed the following sentiment when mulling over the Commonwealth cemetery on Leros, in the Dodecanese, but it is still appropriate to comment that 'There's no sand, souvlaki, sun or s... for these chaps'. A plaque close to the entrance records the brief details of the Battle of Crete.

SOUDA (9km from Chania) Tel prefix 0821. Apart from the important Greek and NATO Naval base, Souda is the ferry-boat port for Chania. In common with many sea-going ports, throughout the world, the location has its detractions, and very few attractions! Most visitors sally forth to more attractive pastures, as quickly as possible.

Buses for Chania depart every quarter of an hour, between 0600-2300hrs.
For those who arrive by ferry-boat it is a 100m or less, gentle ascent up a dual carriageway to the Main road/High St. For details of the sailings See **Ferry-boat timetable, A To Z, Chania**.
A taxi rank edges the Square, at the junction of the Main road and the ferry-boat quay road.
For those who must stay, there a couple of hotels, the:

Knossos (Class D) 31 Plateia Pringipos Georgiou   Tel 89282
Directions: Close to the Main Sq, and on the right (*Sbo*), as are various ticket offices and cafe-bars.
All rooms share the bathrooms, with a single priced at 1500drs & a double at 1800drs

and the:
Parthenon (Class D) Pringipos Georgiou Sq/29 El Venizelou   Tel 89245
Directions: Sited on the far side of the Main road, at the junction with the ferry-boat quay dual carriageway.
Prices as for the *Knossos*.

The rates of both hosteleries benefit from a little bargaining, especially if more than a few days stay is contemplated, but why?

From the Main Sq, to the left (*Sbo*) along the High St is a petrol station, a ferry-boat ticket office and another garage, all on the inland side of the road, whilst on the bay side is the austere wall of the Naval base. Back at the Main Sq, straight ahead is a National Bank, which cashes Eurocheques, in addition to the more mundane currency exchange. To the right beside the High St are: a sprinkling of tavernas; cafe-bars; a few shops, including a baker; a chemist; an OTE, on the right; a large supermarket, the Creta Market, also on the right, as is a socking big oil storage depot; the local cop shop, up a lane to the left; a Post Office, also on the left, as is a dentist... beyond which Souda peters out.

The 'Rue National' to Chania is most pleasantly lined by a row of mature gum trees. For those approaching Souda from the direction of Chania, the cemetery is signposted to the left, initially along the Airport road.

Excursion To Vamos Peninsula The atmosphere engendered on this headland   is rather unique, and decidedly very pleasant. From Souda the road   follows the coastline to join the National Highway, after a few kilometres, and prior to the turning off towards:

KALAMI (12km from Chania) The hamlet is only a few buildings gathered on the hillside, one of which is a sleepy kafeneion and another a taverna. The settlement is overlooked by the Turkish fort of Izzedine.

From hereon the road, set halfway up the mountainside, skirts the edge of the very lovely, large and azure Souda Bay, much of which is taken up by the Greek and NATO Navy forces, thus restricting access. The British and Commonwealth cemetery is clearly visible on the distant water's edge of the Akrotiri peninsula. The route then drops down to sea-level, at the very west end of a long, flat coastline, close to the entrance to Souda Bay, and by which stands **Kalyves**. Hereabouts an unmade track, signed to two tavernas, angles off behind on olive oil factory, paralleling the seashore, prior to running out on the backshore of a lovely stretch of beach. A rivulet from an inland lagoon trails across the shore. As indicated, there are a pair of (beach backshore) tavernas, the *Kiani Akti* and the *Amalia*, the nearest boasting a couple of shower heads and toilets, in working condition.

Back at the Main road, and continuing in an easterly direction, advances past land under the plough, separated from the Highway by a band of bamboos, a grove of olives, some *Rooms*, and a 'summer-wet', bamboo edged river-bed. Beyond the latter are some holiday apartments, close to a very pleasant, if not very wide, length of beach.

KALYVES (some 16km from Chania) The large, straggling, seaside village, with an untidy but pleasantly tree lined layout of streets, is almost a town. Kalyves stretches along a flat coastline set in a well-cultivated area. Over the recent years quite a lot of holiday related development has taken place, without, as yet, spoiling the intrinsic charm of the place. But others might maintain that Kalyves has expanded and changed, that little too much.
   The Main Square is agreeably shaded by the spreading branches of a plane tree, around which are spaced a number of welcoming tavernas. Also

in the immediate vicinity are a baker, Kalyves Travel office, and a kafen-eion or three. Edging the High St, to the west, is the Post Office, a couple of mini-markets, another baker, a chemist, a fruit & vegetable shop, and a general store. The street is separated from the sandy shore by an almost continuous row of buildings, in amongst which are *Rent Studios*, *Studios Flisvos*, and *Rooms Nosios*. This beach continues on westwards in a most acceptable sweep. To the east, the High St passes by several small shops, one of which is a 'chicken butcher', *Thameris Suites*, and, above a store, *Rooms* (Tel 31219), prior to bridging a river. The other side of the stream is a turning down to a backshore and caique harbour, followed by a barrel-maker, a petrol station, a Motorbike rental business, and more *Rooms*. Where the road starts to climb away from Kalyves, there is a *Rooms*, on the right, and a view over the caique harbour, close by which is a dimin-utive, sandy cove with beach showers. Down on the waterfront, near the point at which the beach curves round towards the harbour, are a couple of cafes, the *Cafeteria/Music Bar Roula* and the *Cafe Maistrali*. The rest of this foreshore is very rocky and edged by a concrete surfaced track parallel-ing the High Street. Crowning the headland, overlooking the eastern side of Kalyves, are the *Amelia Studio Apartments* and the *Pension Twins*.

The only classified hotel, not dedicated to the package tourist industry, is the small, neat *Koralli* (Class E, tel 31356). This is peacefully situated in a screen of bamboo and olive groves, built on the backshore of the lovely, sandy bay and green peninsula, to the west of Kalyves.

Continuing to the east, *en route* to Almyrida, reveals a lovely seascape with a barren islet offshore. A small bridge and an archaeological site, rich in mosaics, to the left, marks the outset of:

ALMYRIDA (some 19km from Chania) Once a quaint, little fishing ham-let. Almyrida has now rather outgrown itself on a 'diet' of holidaymakers, and is at about the stage of development that nearby Kalyves was, a few years ago. From a purists point of view, it has to be reported that any visit now, is probably a year or three too late.

Once over the bridge there is a 30m row of *Rooms*, on both sides of the street, and Rent A Bike Almryida, followed by the 'High St/Esplanade' (Oh,ho-ho!) which parallels the curve of the bay, prior to running away from the shoreline. Establishments present include the *Dimitrias Taverna*, *Snack Bar Elicos*, *Zorba's*, *Almyrida's*, the *Thelame Taverna*, and the *Cafe Nikitas Beach*. Close by a mini-market, an unmade track, as distinct from the 'High St', continues to shadow the backshore. This crosses a quite wide, summer-dry river-bed, prior to becoming surfaced, alongside a two storey *Rooms/Restaurant*, which possesses a bamboo shaded patio and a darts board!

Before the bay runs out, on the lower slopes of the far headland, beyond the pebbly shore, there is a nice, sandy stretch of beach with a small caique harbour at the far side. The actual shoreline is only about 150m long but this is an attractive location, with an offshore islet to the left (*Fsw*), as well as a rocky bluff capped by a 1m high chapel. A few pedaloes and caiques are pulled up on the foreshore and a water sport business operates, at the outset of the sand.

PLAKA (some 20km from Chania) A few metres of the old settlement still remains, but is overshadowed by the overwhelm of new building in hand, despite the fact that Plaka is some several hundred metres above sea-level. All around the tree shaded Main Square are *Rooms,* including *Studios Kokouros,* some of them advertising 'Rooms with kitchen'.

In the distance, across a moorland terrain of stone, is a lighthouse.

Beyond Plaka are a number of old-world Cretan hamlets and villages, nestling on a predominately granite landscape supporting some olive groves, but mainly prickly scrub, and criss-crossed by dry stone walls. Amongst these settlements are **Kokkino Chorio, Drapanos,** on a surfaced road, despite most map indications, and **Paleloni,** which has some lovely roadside gum trees, a ruined Martello tower and a substantial, Santorini-like, domed roof church. Next along the country-lane route is:

KEFALAS (some 28km From Chania) A super 'villagy village' through which the street winds. Apart from a lot of kafeneios, there is a largish church and campanile, and yet another church, edging the Main Square, across the way from which is a cafe-bar/taverna.

The road from the far side is also gum tree lined and passes by a threshing circle.

VAMOS (24km from Chania) The village is encircled by agricultural countryside, with the vines fighting the olives for space. Despite the attractiveness of Vamos, part of the surrounds appear to have been chosen as the rubbish dump of Crete. The settlement is very Greek, not at all touristy, with a 'bit-of-a-High Street', a Post Office, a number of shops, the to-be-expected tavernas, and a petrol station on the Kalyves side, in which direction are some lovely views.

ROUTE TEN
To Chora Sfakion via Vryses & on to Loutro & Frangokastello (73km)
Every day hundreds and hundreds of buses and coaches rumble along this route, most of them involved in the 'Gorge excursion' junket. Proceed east on the Rethymnon road, as far as the signposts for Vryses.

There is a turning to the latter from the Highway, through **Neo Chorio,** as well as a minor, rather badly indicated exit, almost adjacent to:

VRYSES (Vrises) (33km from Chania) A very leafy, pretty village, with a tree lined main street, situated in a fertile lowland. Much of Vryses lies to the south of a substantial river, the deep bed of which crosses the High St, at right angles. The village is a major change-over point for switching from the Chora Sfakion/Chania bus to the Rethymnon or Iraklion bus.

On the northern side of the river are *Rooms,* the *Hotel Orpheus,* and a number of tavernas. To both sides of the watercourse are fountains, whilst to the south is the Main Square, alongside which is the settlement's largest statue and a taxi rank. The other side of the High St, to the left (*Facing south*), is the branch road to Rethymnon. On the corner is a pharmacy and a few metres along the Rethymnon road is a baker, across the street from *Rooms.* Further south along the High St is a Post Office and a Restaurant cafe-bar, trebling up as a ferry-boat ticket-cum-exchange-office, with furnished apartments for rent. Petrol is available.

South of Vryses, the road slowly ascends through pretty countryside planted with olive groves and vineyards. Between Vryses and **Alikampos** the Turks suffered two massacres at the hands of Cretans, probably Sfakiots. At about 50km, the flat **Askyfou Plain**, hedged in by encircling mountain peaks, startlingly opens up below and in front of the road, which skirts the sunken plain, on its western perimeter. Where the road swings over the crest, a Venetian fort, built on a large, but isolated hill, dominates the lovely, cultivated valley. Another nearby, extinct volcanic core is also capped by some castle remains. The first of the rural villages and hamlets, through which the poorly surfaced, encircling route passes, is **Kares**. This village not only has a general store, a baker, several kafeneions, and a petrol station, but at least three houses offering *Rooms*. Other settlements include **Ammoudari** and **Petres**. Churches are scattered about, as are the occasional petrol station.

At the tiny, nice, wayside halt of **Imbros**, wherein a couple of cafe-bars and a mini-market, traditional costume is still unselfconsciously worn. The road finally tops the rise out of the plain, to plunge through a gorge named after the hamlet. It then takes a turn, as it were, to the terrifyingly dramatic outset of the hairpin descent, through in excess of one hundred bends, to Chora Sfakion. The latter small port is hidden from sight, way, way down below, and the Mediterranean Sea appears to stretch away in the distance, forever, with rugged southern coastline to either side. Those of a nervous disposition should have already taken some pills, and if not driving might consider closing their eyes. Bus passengers, of a religious persuasion, could turn to prayer, whilst others must cling to the possibly comforting thought that the drivers have covered the ground, thousands of times... and must not dwell on the fact that maybe his, and thus the client's number might be up, this time!

With some 4km to go to Chora Sfakion (to which we will return in a few paragraphs), a surfaced turning to the left runs parallel to the coast, leading through **Komitades** and **Vraskas** to **Patsianos**. Whatever the maps indicate, the road is metalled, even if the surface can be of a very indeterminate nature through the actual villages. Incidentally there are *Rooms*, a few shops and a petrol station in Komitades. Prior to Patsianos, a fast road angles off across a very flat, almost totally featureless plain, past initially rather untamed coastline. This is followed by a gentle but inexorable build-up of random development including *Rooms Taverna Vranos, Cafe X Rooms, Rent Rooms Oasis*, a beach, the *Blue Sky Disco, Rent Rooms Taverna*, a mini-market with accommodation, a doo-hickey taverna, and the extremely smart *Castello Apartments*, 200m beyond which is:

Frangokastello Castle (some 16km from Chora Sfakion) The still impressive, if squat Venetian fortress dominates the unattractive, large, level plateau, hemmed in, to the north, by an uncompromising mountain range. It was built in the 14th century, in a vain attempt to dominate the eternally troublesome locals. All that survives are the castellated walls and corner towers, laid out on a square ground plan. In 1828 the Turks slaughtered

each and every one of those defending the fort and it is alleged that annually, in May, their ghosts appear and dance around the walls.
The Castle overlooks a marvellous, large spit of sandy beach. A distant semicircle of rounded, wave-worn rocks projecting through the water's surface indicates that, in the distant past, the sea must have broken through an earlier outer ring of coastline. This impression is reinforced by the fact that the shallow sandy sea-bed extends on for hundreds of metres. It truly is a lovely place at which to have a swim. The backshore is tree covered and between the south fort walls and the sea's edge is one of the original tavernas. Close to the east walls, leaving enough room for a wide car park, is the rather fanciful, 'Swiss chalet' style *Drousoulette Bar*, complete with a spacious, rustic, covered, paving stone laid patio. To the right (*Fsw*), beyond the spit of beach, is a line of houses, mostly offering **Rooms**. These dwellings sweep down to a lone Martello tower, standing sentinel on a low promontory, and close to which is the *Coral Restaurant Rooms*, where a double bedroom costs, on average, 2000drs a night.

To save retracing one's steps, via the Askyfou Plain, on the return journey, continue in an easterly direction along the in-part unmetalled road, via the hamlets of **Skaloti** and **Argoules**. The main streets of both the latter are in a poor state. Beyond Skaloti it is possible to turn off to descend some 2km, on a surfaced road, to the peaceful, unspoilt, sandy grey beach of **Kalogeros**, edging a small bay. The gently shelving shore is spattered with pebbles and stone. At the large rock-bordered eastern end, up against the backshore, is a dilapidated hovel and a house. At the western side is a sign indicating a taverna, located around the bluff. Sure enough, following the wide, unmade track leads past a series of pretty, small, sand and rock coves to a couple of *Rent Rooms/tavernas*. They battle it out in this comparatively deserted spot, bordering a rock beach with some sand to the left (*Fsw*). I can never understand this Greek predilection to spoil each other's trade by immediately throwing up competition, wherever and whenever one business seems to be pulling in a few drachmae. The simple taverna nearest the sea allows visitors to soak in the luxury of usually being quite alone in this isolated location, that is apart from the possibility of a few, distant scuba divers.

Returning to the Main route, the mountain track winds through the old, pleasant village of **Ano Rodakino**, which has at least one house with accommodation. The next settlement of **Kato Rodakino** (28km from Chora Sfakion) has a petrol station, two pensions and a track down to a beach. Both the Rodakino settlements hang on to the mountainside. The next and last village is **Sellia**, with a very large church sitting on a mountain top and where a link is made with the Rethymnon to Plakias road (*See* **Route Six, Chapter 4**).

Back on the main Chania route, the road descends to:
**CHORA SFAKION (Chora Sphakion, Khora Sfakion, Hora Sfakion,
                                                                    Sfakia)**
A harbour village & bus assembly point.

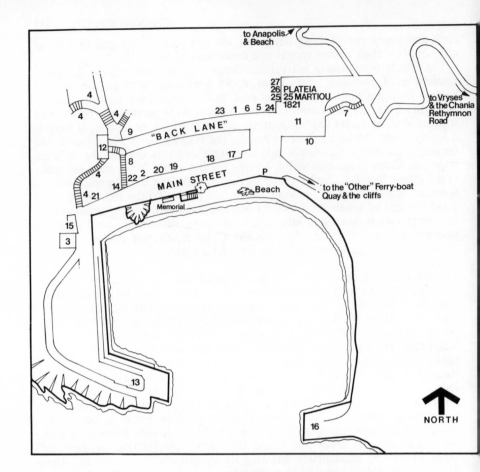

Tmr

1 Pension Sofia
2 Sofia Souvenirs
3 Hotel Xenia
4 Rooms
5 Bakery
6 Supermarket
7 Clinic
8 OTE
9 Post Office & Box
10 Police
11 Main Sq/Bus & coach park
12 Hotel Stavris/Cafe-bar/Bank Agent
13 Passenger Ferry-boat Quay
14 Ferry-boat ticket hut
15 Taverna Psaro - The Harbour
16 Vehicle Ferry-boat Quay
17 Hotel/Restaurant Samaria

18 Hotel/Restaurant Livikon
19 Supermarket/Rooms
20 'Travellers Centre'
21 Restaurant Lefka Ori
22 Periptero/store
23 General Store Sofia
24 Taverna O Bros Gialos
25 Cobra Disco Bar
26 Cafeteria
27 Pharmacy
P Periptero

Tmr = Town map reference
Fsw = Facing seawards
Sbo = Sea behind one
Fbqbo = Ferry-boat Quay behind one

Illustration 14 Chora Sfakion

GENERAL (Illustration 14) Tel prefix 0825. Most people touch base at Chora Sfakion as the disembarkation port on the Samaria Gorge under-taking. There are few other reasons to pass through or stop over, unless catching a local ferry to one of the small, south-west coast port villages of Loutro, Ag Roumeli, Souyia or Paleochora. In fact the harbour has devel-oped, in the main, because it is necessary to catch a boat from Ag Roumeli, the village at the bottom of the Samaria Gorge, that is unless travellers are prepared to retrace their steps. From Ag Roumeli, the small boats ply to Paleochora, in the west, and to Chora Sfakion, to the east. Due to the shorter distance involved, the tourist organisations prefer the Chora Sfakion route, thus the ferry-boats plough their watery course to a timetable that fits in with the daily descent of the Gorge. The visitors trudge their weary way round from one of the Ferry-boat Quays (*Tmr* 13 & 16) to the Main Square (*Tmr* 11). This Plateia, at the east end of the village, is where the buses, tour coaches and cars line up in terraced ranks to await the endless, serried but ragged columns of the hordes of Gorge walkers who stream round, day in and day out, all summer long.

Smaller than Ag Galini, Chora Sfakion has a certain fascination, despite the somewhat beleaguered and or bemused air of the residents. Not that the 'Sfakiots' are downtrodden or servile. Oh no! They represent a rugged breed of Cretans who have lived on the southern foothills of the Levka Mountain range, which stretches all the way from Paleochora to beyond Chora Sfakion. Over the centuries the Sfakiots fought and battled, evading submitting even to the usually all-powerful, all-conquering Venetians and Turks. In so doing they established a deserved reputation for being extremely tough, individualistic characters.

It is perhaps a conundrum that nowadays the majority of visitors to Crete and Chora Sfakion, are Germans, despite the plaque recording that this was the port from whence the majority of the British, Australian and New Zea-land troops were evacuated to North Africa, after the Second World War Battle of Crete. This was in 1941, when the Germans finally succeeded in overrunning the island. Perhaps they have returned to complete the job!

ARRIVAL BY BUS Buses from the various northern towns, as well as an inexhaustible number of excursion coaches, park on the Main Square (*Tmr* 11) during the day, only to depart at night, once all the Gorge walkers have finally staggered off the boats.

ARRIVAL BY FERRY From Ag Roumeli, the local ferries motor round, often calling at Loutro, to moor to one of the two quays (*Tmr* 13 & 16). Those jettisoned on the left-hand quay (*Sbo*) must trudge round, following the gently curving and ascending quayside wall. This leads to the Main Square, via a 100m or so of awning covered, table and chair strewn 'fore-courts', belonging to the row of hotels/restaurants that border the 'Main St/Esplanade' and overlook the narrow beach. The other passengers, who disembark at the west quay, have a less interesting, if more direct perambulation along the dusty swathe of track to the Plateia.

THE ACCOMMODATION & EATING OUT Generally it is true to say that the hoteliers, restaurateurs, and their staff, tend to be rather blase, operating on a 'take it or leave it' basis. This is probably as much to do with the 'Sfakiots' character as disinterest or boredom.

The Accommodation Considering the comparatively small size of 'Chora', there is a remarkable amount of accommodation available (but it should be noted that there are very few single rooms for rent). Mind you this abundance does not go amiss as the location is one that has attracted a steadily growing number of devotees and care must be taken to acquire a bed, as quickly as possible. Devotees? Yes, this location, and its surrounds, attracts certain Cretan aficionados, the type who wishes to be close to the heart of the action, but not actually in the hurly-burly; who wants to be in amongst the Crete of yesteryear, but not without a handful of modern-day conveniences; who yearns for the simple, unaffected life, without loosing a life-line to those (few) more pleasant facets of the 1990s. Here, at 'Chora', it is merely necessary to sneak away for the afternoon/early evening hours to escape the only intrusion from the outside world, namely the arrival, and subsequent loading, of the transport necessary to whisk away the Gorge walkers. After this regrettable, intrusive, daily reminder of organised package tourism, the ambiance reverts to a slower, more traditional pace - the leisurely breaking of bread or gentle contemplation of life over a backgammon board, with a coffee and Metaxa at one's elbow. Tough! Moreover Chora Sfakion is ideally situated to allow trips, of a day or three, to other, equally attractive locations. For example, within easy reach is the mountain village of Anopolis, as well as the coastal sites of Frangokastello, Loutro, Ag Roumeli, Souyia and Paleochora. And don't let's forget the possibility of a trip to Gavdos island, but the latter will possibly require a spare week. For details of the various aforementioned destinations, refer to the relevant Chapter entries.

From Plateia 25th March 1821 (*Tmr* 11), the 'Main St' boasts the:
Hotel Samaria (*Tmr* 17)
Directions: The first establishment on the right from the Main Sq, at the outset of the covered Esplanade.
Echoing double rooms, with a small en suite bathroom, cost 2000drs, in mid-season. Incidentally most Sfakion rooms are of the 'echoing' variety!

Next door but one, is the *Hotel Livikon* (*Tmr* 18), for comments about which *See* the *Samaria*. A few metres yet further along, is a Supermarket (*Tmr* 19) with accommodation, as has the *Restaurant Lefka Ori* (*Tmr* 21), both charging the 'village average'.

Hotel Xenia (*Tmr* 3) (Class B)   Tel 91206
Directions: At the far, west end of the 'Main St Esplanade' and the pension, for that is how the establishment is categorised, is on the right.
A single room, sharing the bathrooms, is charged at 3500drs, a double room sharing costs 3900drs, whilst a double room, with an en suite bathroom, is priced at 4200drs.

Back at the Main Sq, the other village street is the 'Back Lane', which parallels the Esplanade. On the right, beyond the Baker and a Supermarket, is:

Pension Sofia (*Tmr* 1)   Tel 91259
Directions: As above and side-by-side with the General store Sofia. (I think we should be told if they are related?)
   Since the absence of the very helpful English girl, in residence for some years, the attention is rather disinterested. The rooms are somewhat cell-like and the en suite bathrooms tend to be smelly. They have a single room for 1000drs, with doubles costing 2000drs.

Continuing along 'Back Lane', at the far end, the other side of an informal, tree shaded square, is the:
Hotel Stavris (*Tmr* 12)   Tel 91220
Directions: As above.
   This behind-the-scenes location, a beehive of activity, is owned by Stavros, Georgio and Aristotles, the three, smiling, efficient brothers Perrakis. Their English is excellent and their manner most helpful. When enquiries are made about accommodation a prospective client is as likely to be advised that prices are "All negotiable, (it is) a free market". But don't be misled, the Brothers are nobody's fool... and business is business, even if it is served with a pleasant countenance. Their double rooms, with en suite bathroom, cost between 2000-2500drs a night. Apart from the accommodation, they have a kafeneion-cum-cafe-bar, with tables and chairs pleasantly arrayed under the spreading branches of a mature tree or two, on an informal square across the street. In addition they also operate a money exchange, possess a metered international telephone and have a small rack of foreign language paper backs.

   In the lane, to the left of the *Stavris* (*Hotel behind one*), are a number of other *Rooms* (*Tmr* 4), scattered about.
   Beside the Anopolis road are the *Hotel Restaurant Panorama* and *Apartments To Rent*, for details of which apply to the *Restaurant Livikon* (*Tmr* 18).

The Eating Out The Esplanade hotels have tavernas in their ground floors. The staff's main function is to *schlepp* the passengers who disembark from the Ag Roumeli boats. But this source of 'captive' punter has seriously diminished since the construction of the 'other' vehicle Ferry-boat Quay (*Tmr* 16), with the consequence that many passengers proceed directly to the Main Sq, without having to run the gauntlet of the 'Main St' Esplanade.

From the port's available options my choice is the:
Restaurant Lefka Ori (*Tmr* 21)
Directions: At the west end of the Esplanade, adjacent to the steps up to the Hotel Stavris.
   The establishment has a row of tables and chairs spaced out along the sea wall edge of the street, overlooking the beach. Apart from fairly prompt and attentive service, the dishes are reasonably interesting and include: briam 250drs; cheese pie 300drs; kalamares 350drs; spanokopita 400drs; patatas 70drs; and kortaki retsina 150drs. A meal, for two, of briam (250drs), a moussaka (400drs), a chicken (300drs), a plate of peas (250drs), a Greek salad (200drs), a bottle of retsina(150drs), bread & service (20drs each), cost a not inexpensive 1590drs.

A more kafeneion-like, but certainly engaging alternative is the :
Perrakis Taverna (*Tmr* 12)
Directions: As for the Hotel Stavris, which is under the same management.
   They serve a good looking breakfast, with humour, and are open until early

in the wee hours. A Nes meh ghala costs 70drs, a bottle of retsina 150drs, and an ouzo 70drs. For both accommodation and dining this is my first port of call.

Incidentally the literal translation of the *Taverna O MPROS GIALOS* (*Tmr* 24), on the edge of the Main Sq, is the 'Taverna In Front of the Seashore'.

THE A TO Z OF USEFUL INFORMATION

BANKS None, but there is a Post Office (*Tmr* 9), and don't forget our friends the 'Brothers Perrakis' at the *Stavris* (*Tmr* 12), who not only exchange money but Eurocheques.

BEACHES The narrow, shingly, grey sand, not-so-clean beach, on which are scattered some 'Act of God' boulder outcrops, is 'trapped' between the high sea wall edging the Esplanade and the sea of the pleasant, if small bay.

For a satisfactory, if somewhat distant alternative *See* **Excursions To Chora Skafion Surrounds.**

BREAD SHOPS There is one (*Tmr* 5), conveniently on the corner of the Main Square, diagonally opposite the Police station (*Tmr* 10), whilst another is alongside the Anopolis road out of town.

BUSES The buses park on the Main Sq (*Tmr* 11) and their schedules are tied into the Gorge walk.
Bus timetable (Mid-season)
Chora Sfakion to Chania
Daily   0700, 100, 1530, 1830hrs.

Chora Sfakion to Plakias & Ag Galini
Daily   1630hrs
One-way fare: 700drs; duration 3½hrs.

See Chania & Rethymnon City Bus timetables.

COMMERCIAL SHOPPING AREA It would be a surprise if there were any, but there are a few shops, including a couple of Supermarkets (*Tmr* 6 &19), the General store Sofia (*Tmr* 23), and a Periptero/store (*Tmr* 22). Opening hours are the usual siesta routine, but the souvenir shops open seven days a week, during the season.

DISCOS There is one (*Tmr* 25) edging the Main Sq.

FERRY-BOATS On occasions, the information regarding these local, south coast excursion sized ferry-boats differs from port to port. This system connects Chora Sfakion to the south-western ports of Loutro, Ag Roumeli, Souyia and Paleochora. The confusion is sometimes increased by the northern city NTOG offices issuing timetables that disagree, in detail. Oh dear me! Certainly, either side of the height of season months, the schedules are foreshortened.

Day	Departure time	Ports/Islands of Call
Daily	1030, 1130, 1645, 1830hrs	Loutro, Ag Roumeli.

Ferry-boat timetables (Mid-season)
One-way fare: to Ag Roumeli 680drs; duration 1hr.

Day	Departure time	Ports/Islands of Call
Sat, Sun (June-Aug)	0900hrs	Gavdos island.*

One-way fare: 1100drs; duration 4½hrs.
* For further details *See* Excursions to Paleochora surrounds, Paleochora, Chapter Six.

FERRY-BOAT TICKET OFFICE (*Tmr* 14) More a hut, edging the Esplanade.

MEDICAL CARE
Chemists & Pharmacies One (*Tmr* 27) adjacent to the Main Plateia.
Clinic (*Tmr* 7) A small building to the east side of the Main Sq.

OTE (*Tmr* 8) At the west end of 'Back Lane', opposite the Post Office. Open weekdays, between 0730-1510hrs.

PLACES OF INTEREST
Boat Trips Close to the *Stavris* is a sign 'Geros Strakos Boat Trips to Sweetwater Beach. Depat (*sic*) 1000 & 1600hrs; Return 1030 & 1630hrs' . For more details of this attraction *See* Excursions To Chora Sfakion Surrounds. The 'Two Brothers' advertise boat trips to Filaki Beach, departing at 1030 & 1700hrs, returning at 1100 & 1730hrs.
Cave of Daskalogiannis To the west of Chora, prior to Ilegas Beach, and one of several caves in the area. Daskalogiannis was a Cretan revolutionary who led an uprising against the Turks, in 1770. Unfortunately he agreed to attend a peace conference, was snatched, tortured and skinned whilst alive. His heroic, if 'possibly' involuntary death was celebrated in The Song of Daskalogiannis.

POLICE (*Tmr* 10) There is a 'Cop shop' on the south side of the Main Square.

POST OFFICE (*Tmr* 9) Opposite the OTE, at the west end of 'Back Lane'. Conducts exchange transactions.

TAXIS Rank on the Main Square, where else?

TRAVEL AGENTS & TOUR OFFICES An Esplanade business (*Tmr* 20) advertises 'Travellers Centre'.

EXCURSIONS TO CHORA SFAKION SURROUNDS
Excursion to Ilingas Beach There is a sign at the far end of the village to 'Nice Beaches'. During the height of the summer sun this can prove to be a long, hot, shadeless walk, there and back, so do not forget to pack a picnic bag as there are no supplies or services *en route*, or at the beach. The path leads out on to the Anopolis road, which skirts the coastline for a kilometre or so until a path branches off to:

Ilingas Beach The steep track descends to the pebbly cove, now overlooked by the two storey *Hotel Cafe-Bar Restaurant Ilingas*, accessed down a separate path from the Anopolis road. Around to the right (*Fsw*) are a number of caves, only visible from the sea.

Excursion (by foot) to Loutro It is from the Anopolis road/Ilingas Beach path that the some 10km/2½hr switchback walk makes off to Loutro. A couple of sections of this scramble are not for the fainthearted. For instance, there is one particularly difficult stretch of 'goat path' that inches over the bare, steep-sided mountain rock face that plunges quite steeply and inexorably into the sea, some way down below. About 1½hrs from Chora Sfakion, the path drops down to the shore of:

Sweetwater Beach This is a magnificent sweep of sand and very fine shingle, shut in by a sheer cliff face, the foot of which provides the only shade. The beach derives its name from the drinkable, fresh water that 'wells' to the surface at a number of spots, mainly towards the west end of the shoreline. This occurrence, combined with the caves set into the base of the rock wall, has resulted in the location proving ideal for the back-to-nature brigade. Thus, over the years, the beach has supported a small, loose-knit, gradually revolving commune of drop-outs. The arrival of one particular individual appears to have coincided with an upgrading of the 'type' of cave dweller, who nowadays more closely resemble the clean-limbed, flower power hippies of the 1960s. This newcomer, the neat, clean-shaven, 'Rasputinish' fellow, 'aka' Patrick Goddard amongst possible other *nom de plumes*, has established himself at the extreme west end of the shore. Here he manages an *ad-hoc*, rustic, taverna-like establishment. Admonishing signs abound, more especially those 'proclaiming' that he, Patrick, is only the general dogsbody and others are actually responsible for the ownership. Yes, well, I suppose anything is possible! This disclaimer is necessary to ensure that he does not fall foul of the Greek employment laws, more especially in respect of work-permits. But I'm sure all is in order! In the meantime, and I am absolutely convinced nothing to do with Patrick, an outcrop of rock rearing out of the shallows, in front of the aforementioned taverna, is being modified. Possibly this is to become a landing stage... or perhaps a revolving taverna or...?

Those Loutro bound package holidaymakers, brave enough to venture this far, may be regaled with mine host's reminiscences about his being a victim, a refugee from the '87 stock-market crash, that he is of Belgium/ Luxembourg/.... nationality, has a 'Sweetwater wife', a library, and more, much more...! Whatever, I think it is a pity to observe yet another, to-date unspoilt, once natural location being subjected to 'improvement', however rustic that amelioration might be.

Nudism rules and to save on the foot-slog, a small fishing boat runs a daily water taxi service to and from Loutro.

Excursion To Anopolis (12km) From Chora Sfakion, the road runs out past Ilingas Beach, from whence the serpentine, steep ascent commences all the way up to:

ANOPOLIS (12km from Chora Sfakion) The village of this pleasant, spaced out, agricultural community is built on a flattish, mountain plain between the precipitous drop to the sea and the looming bulk of the White Mountains. It is spread out in and amongst gnarled olive trees, old stone walls, aged ruins, boulderous fields, pine trees and a cemetery. Many of the locals dress daily in traditional costume.

From the outset of the settlement, all the way to the Main Square, are scattered various establishments offering meals and accommodation. These

include the *Taverna/Rooms Panorama*; **Rooms**, opposite which is the delightful, if ethnic *Taverna El Vicha*, run by a 'nothing-is-too-much-trouble' couple, the wife of the 'team' making and selling traditional Cretan headscarves, at a cost of some 850drs; the *Restaurant/Rooms Tria Adelphia*, and **Rooms**, alongside the almost circular Main Square, as is a cafe-bar.
    It is not necessary to walk - a Chora bus journeys backwards and forth, but the perambulation does allow magnificent views out over the surrounding countryside and coastal strip.

From the village, it is possible to follow a track down a steep, tricky mountain side descent to Loutro, but why not take the ferry-boat? The last chap I met who braved the scramble incurred blistered feet, but it has to be admitted that his footwear was not very suitable. * *See* Page 277 for an omission.

LOUTRO (Lutron, Loutron)
Harbour hamlet.

Tel prefix and number 0825 91227. Yes, as in the days of yore, there is only one telephone, situated in the *Pension Phoinis*. When it is ascertained who the call is for, it is simply a matter of bellowing across the bay for the intended recipient! I can't but be pleased to find at least one of the old necessities still in place. Furthermore donkeys are the norm.
    Loutro lies inset at the far end of a mountain enclosed bay and the small settlement spreads thinly around the seashore. The Venetians used Loutro as a medieval spa, or watering hole, and alongside the small church, in the centre of the village, are two small Arsenals.
    Until only a few years ago this fishing hamlet was the preserve of the more adventurous traveller, but no more, not since the erection of the *Hotel Porto Loutro*, which has enabled a limited number of package tourists to holiday here. Naturally, to accommodate this upgrading of Loutro to that of a resort, however low key, the location has experienced a metamorphosis. Nowadays the ferries run to a timetable that can almost always be relied upon, the ambiance is almost glitzy, as evidenced by the presence of the *Maistrali*, a cocktail/cafe-bar, and there is a general air of quiet wellbeing. Oh dear! Christina of the *Maistrali* probably put it best, 'My heart mourns the changes, but my senses (pocket) welcomes them!' This particular storm-cloud does have a silver lining, and that is the generally good standard of the taverna offerings. In fact two of the establishments have achieved an outstanding quality, so much so that even the Greeks rate the Loutro eateries as some of the best on Crete, if not on a par with some of the finest that Greece has to offer, including those of Thessaloniki - praise indeed. It has to be admitted that menu price lists are rare to non-existent, and the drinking water is slightly brackish. Before leaving the subject of Loutro's late move into the 20th Century, it is a conundrum that the villagers loudly protest that they do not want 'the road' to include their settlement. This is an allusion to a swathe of track invitingly wandering about, way up on the mountainside, but that oddly enough 'threatens' **Finikia**, over the hill, more than Loutro. Methinks the protestations are to enable the inhabitants to keep some pride in their hardiness and individuality. Somehow I think they feel that a road would finally emasculate them.

Loutro still has a village school, even if there are only five pupils. It is said that the 'Supply' teachers cope with the rigours of the summer months, but as winter sets in, have a tendency to disappear, before Christmas.

The Cretan people of the south-west coast, usually typified by the Chora Sfakiots, exhibit many characteristics in common with the more infamous Sicilians. They were once a hostile, warrior community, unconquerable and prone to blood feuds, marriage by abduction (with the subsequent vendettas), and sheep stealing. Modern-day folk of the area reveal some of the traits of their ancestors, especially a dislike of all or any authority. There were many manifestations of this individualism, probably mainly rumours, of course, but with the steady and inexorable advance of modern day commerce much of the eccentricity has withered on the vine. Certainly the illustrious citizens no longer wish to be reminded of their 'goings-on' of years gone by. Why not read earlier editions for some of the tales?

The passenger boats still dock at the small quay to the extreme left (*Sbo*) of the village, whilst the bow-door opening vehicle ferries run up the beach, in front of the *Hotel Porto Loutro*. Loutro cannot be reached by road although it is possible to struggle down the mountain face goat track, from Anopolis village, or along the coastal rock face, from as far away as Paleochora, via Souyia and Ag Roumeli, in the west, or Chora Sfakion, in the east.

Generally speaking the first, left-hand (*Sbo*) half of the bay, encircled by the hamlet, consists of lodging houses and tavernas. These are linked by a series of concrete paths and terraces. About a third of the way round is a narrow, stony beach which occupies the middle ground. The initial stretch of backshore is dominated by a smart, low-rise hotel. From two-thirds of the way round, as far as the right-hand extent of the settlement, is another series of pensions and tavernas, inter-connected by of steps and patios.

Returning to the quay, at the left (*Sbo*) of the development is the splendidly situated *Katerina's Rooms/Cocktail/Cafe-Bar Maistrali*. The family lived much of their life in America and Katerina's vivacious, married daughter, Christina, she of the lovely smile, speaks excellent English. Mother, who nowadays takes rather more of a 'back seat', and daughter are both very pleasant and helpful. Once only *Rooms*, they have 'bolted on' a tasteful cocktail cafe-bar, the tables and chairs of which are bunched up on the chic patio bordering the water's edge. To run the bar, Christina is helped out by her brother and husband. This is the only one of its type in Loutro and is popular by day and extremely busy by night. The bar prices are understandably higher than most other outlets. A coffee costs 100drs, an Amstel 100drs, a large brandy and a very big ouzo 350drs. A nice thought is the provision of sets of chess, draughts and backgammon. Apart from a full range of drinks, ice-creams and a variety of tasty 'tosts' are served. The double room accommodation, charged from 2000drs a night, is still rather basic and the shared bathrooms 'homely'. Those who must have a long night's sleep should try to obtain a room at the rear of the building.

Proceeding in a clockwise direction, alongside *Katerina's* are the steps leading to the path that rises up, over and down to **Finikia Bay**. The next house has two large, ancient arethemusa trees in front and is a reminder of the Loutro of yesteryear. The elderly widow has stuck out and her house is one of the few that does not offer accommodation, or harbour a taverna. Her daily sluice has to take place in a bowl, as she does not have running water. The ferry-boat ticket desk, with a current schedule pinned to the surface, is still plonked down on the patio close to this building, between the trees and the original ferry-boat quay.

The schedules are as follows:
Ferry-boat timetables (Mid-season)

Day	Departure time	Ports/Islands of Call
Daily	1000hrs	Chora Sfakion.
	1100hrs	Ag Roumeli.
	1200hrs	Ag Roumeli.
	1445hrs	Chora Sfakion.
	1615hrs	Chora Sfakion.
	1715hrs	Ag Roumeli.
	1730hrs	Chora Sfakion.
	1830hrs	Chora Sfakion.
	1900hrs	Ag Roumeli.

One-way fare: to Ag Roumeli/Chora Sfakion 680drs; duration to Ag Roumeli 1hr.
Chora Sfakion ½hr.

The next building contains the *Restaurant/Rooms Maderes*, traditionally painted in brown, alongside which is a *Rooms/Mini-Market/Exchange*, where a double bedroom costs 2500drs per night.

The above are followed by the *Taverna To Loutro/Rooms* - 'Rooms, Restaurant and Breakfast'- which is still owned by one-handed, furrow-browed, and now not so smiley Yanni. Frankly whether he smiles or not is of no consequence, while his daughter occupies the kitchen. The food served here is absolutely outstanding and includes some dishes rarely seen, anywhere in Greece. A glance in the window of the taverna reveals the culinary delights on offer, any particular evening, and the food is absolutely fresh - no lunch-time left-overs served at this diner. Furthermore the meals are always dished up hot. Several items were firsts, such as meat & courgette pie and a potato, as well as a cheese & ham quiche, both priced between 330-380drs. A meal, for two, of one plate (each) of the aforementioned, with servings of green beans and gigantes, in addition to a bottle of retsina and bread, cost 1430drs. Also observed were stuffed pancakes and stuffed squid. A lunch, for two, of an exquisite spinach & rice 'mess', aubergine pancakes, fassolakia freska, retsina and bread, was charged at 1070drs. An evening meal, consisting of a vegetable & zucchini pie, aubergine pancakes (well 'her outdoors' liked them), a Greek salad, a bottle of retsina and bread, cost 950drs. Without wishing to appear to be some sort of Egon Ronay PR firm, employed by Yanni's establishment, one other meal for two of a meatloaf with egg (super, 400drs), a meat pie (very tasty,   400drs), a plate of green beans (200drs), 2 bottles of retsina (150drs each) and bread, cost 1340drs. If within a few hundred miles, why not pop in and gourmandise. And I promise, I have no reason to go overboard about this, or a number of other Loutro establishments. Oh no!

Due to gently humorous, if penetrating comments (!), in previous editions, I was identified by an expatriate fellow country person and left in no doubt that some of the residents of Loutro would greatly enjoy having my neck between their hands, as they closed! I suppose being of Celtic origins, which 'Master Race' has a surprising affinity to the Cretans, I should be far more understanding about the possibility of hurt feelings, added to an awareness about some races having a tendency to lack any sense of humour, when the nonsense is at their expense, shouldn't I? Back to the origins - who ever heard of a chap having a Welsh mother and an Irish father (I hasten to add both from the south of their respective countries)? Enough of this bandinage, this foolish chatter. Incidentally the patio tables are painted blue and the chairs are yellow. Before passing on I must not forget that Yanni runs a daily water taxi service to and from Sweetwater Beach. He departs about 1000hrs, returning at around 1700hrs for the homeward trip, but it is best to check these times the day previous.

A few steps up lead to a building block, the first business in which is *Restaurant/Rooms*, with blue painted window shutters and a verandah. Alongside is the *Restaurant/Rooms Phoinis*, the terrace being shaded from the heat of the midday sun by a couple of large, gracefully spreading tamarisk trees. This taverna houses the village phone and inside is an old photoograph of a traditionally posed Sfakiot man. There is also a postbox, but I am not sure if and when it is emptied. The food is 'galleyish' and the service lackadaisical, with a frappe coffee and Amstel beer costing 200drs.

Reputedly the next Pension has the best accommodation in the village, with en suite bathrooms, but naturally the price reflects this excellence. It is closely followed by a small office where currency can be exchanged, and run by yet another of the old stalwarts, a lady who wields a fly-swat and resembles a latter-day Queen Victoria. Next along is a single storey block in which is a shop with a limited amount of goods, new and second hand books, posters, as well as postcards.

The patio of the last place drops down on to the outset of the large pebble beach, alongside a well established tree. The first building bordering the backshore is a delightful, end on, green 'garden shed', the home of Nikos, a lovely old boy, aged 89, who owns the Seagull outboard powered, green hulled dinghy, moored in the adjacent shallows.

A few metres on is the reason for Loutro's lost innocence, the edifice that resulted, once and for all, in the reluctant but bewitched inhabitants being dragged into the flight-path of present day tourism, namely the *Hotel Porto Loutro*. This was built, and is owned and managed by Stavros Androulakis and his English wife, Alisson. Don't misunderstand me, the hotel is most tastefully constructed, in a 1930s, Habitat style, and is a low, three storey, white with blue trimmings building - almost 'dignified Moorish', if you get the picture. It requires quite a stretch of imagination to realise that all and every bit of material required in the construction had to brought in by donkey or by boat. I believe it took two winters and a summer to complete, or 18 months, and there is no doubt that one has to take off one's hat to Stavros and Alisson, if only to acknowledge their resolve. Furthermore by any Greek standards, the finished article is excellent, but that does not nullify the enormous changes to the all-but lost ecosystem of this once almost forgotten fishing boat hamlet (ecosystem, there's smart). Despite first impressions, Stavros did not knock down the original buildings. In fact he is planning to rebuild the old chapel and the accompanying cells. Nice that.

It would be understandable if readers were to construe that I was related to the family, after this panegyric. But nothing could be further from the truth. In fact on my last visit, Alisson, she of a rather forthright '... and I told him' disposition, was the blunt, vocal instrument chosen to read me my horoscope, as spokeswoman for her husband, and one or two of the other inhabitants... and some would think none too soon! Be that as it may, the hotel is, in the main, the preserve of one or two refined travel com- panies, with some freelance guests taken on board... if Alisson likes the look of enquirers! The super en suite double rooms cost about 3500drs a night. For the moment Stavros hires the blue coloured canoes, from an arched window in a building next door to the hotel, but I'm certain that a man of his undoubted energy and talents will seek more demanding channels for his vitality, sometime in the future.

Whilst touching on water sport matters, there are also some red coloured canoes for hire and a chap with a speed boat trolls about, here and there, offering the delights of water skiing. In the region of the *Porto Loutro* is a beach sign intoning 'No topless bathing on this beach please', a polite re- quest that is speedily reinforced if ignored. One drawback to the location, for sun worshippers, is that the sun puts 'it's hat on', about mid-afternoon. The sea is pleasantly clean, and even in the shallows bordering the infor- mal row of patios, is clear enough to be able to easily read the label of the the occasional olive oil can or yoghurt carton. A metre or so further along the beach is an old house, alongside which is the village periptero. The owners of the periptero hire sun chairs (100drs) and sun umbrellas (150drs), both by the hour. A crudely painted, white sign points the way along the path that cuts round the backyards of the buildings to the east and is the outset of the Anopolis/Chora Sfakion walk. This passes by two other **Rooms**, then some ruins, before shaking off the outskirts of Loutro.

The landing craft ferry-boat crunches ashore hereabouts, a point that swimmers should bear in mind. Beyond the Anopolis/Chora path is an old house, set back a little, followed by the *Restaurant/Rooms Ilios*, once owned by Stella and now run by her son. The *Ilios* has a pleasant, nicely mature, tree shaded patio, and makes for a very acceptable spot at which to down a coffee (80drs) or a bottle of retsina (120drs). As they own the only coloured television in Loutro, the inhabitants gather here in order to watch important events, such as momentous football matches or, as was the case when we last visited, the news-flash in respect of the assassination of the son of the leader of the political party *Nea Dhimokratia*. The *Ilios* was one of the establishments which I was retrospectively advised was 'out-of- bounds'. When questioned it became apparent that this was due, in part, to some previous observations I had put into print regarding the (I thought) most amusing saga concerning a near-neighbour. He was accused, by all and sundry, of 'stealing the sea', in order to build an extensive patio. This and the ensuing Keystone Cop histrionics did make for most amusing copy. Oh well, one man's belly-laugh must be another Greeks poison, to thoroughly misquote the adage.

Beyond yet another old house is the *Restaurant/Rooms To Limani* owned by Manousos, Yanni's brother, who is '...now much nicer'. I have placed the comment in parenthesises to stress the point that, as in the past, I am only reporting the more innocent observations made to me, by a most erudite informant! I think I'm correct in saying that Manousos is not too enamoured with me, due to previous unsolicited remarks. He should realise that at least half my readers ensure they do something to gainsay my more controversial utterances. You can just imagine the scene - "Come on darling, if that self-opinionated O'Connell reckons it's no good, it must be great! (I think that's enough blood-letting and general self-justification, don't you?). Certainly the *To Limani* comes very highly recommended, some of the plaudits being received from readers. Additionally the establishment is very popular with Greeks as Manousos owns his own goats, makes a special Sfakiot pie, and specialises in fish dishes.

The steps climb across yet another patio, that of a seemingly deserted building. This belongs to the expatriate who originally pushed his patio frontage too far into the sea, an action no longer resented or the subject of litigation, as the other owners in the row have sensibly joined in, and extended their own terraces! If you can't beat them, then...

Next on is the newly established (1989) *Restaurant Kri-Kri*, run by a pair of helpful chaps, where a bottle of beer and a Greek lemonade costs 150drs. A couple staying at the *Porto Loutro* advised that they enjoyed a superb meal of kid here.

Beyond the *Kri-Kri* is yet another old house, after which the path drops on to a short section of backshore, prior to stepping up to an irregularly shaped forecourt, edged by three side-by-side buildings. In front of the first is a 'bit of a derrick'. The last is *Keramos   Rooms*, owned by Manolis Patrou- sakis who lets out single, double and 'three-bedrooms'. A double cost be- tween 2200-3000drs - the price " ...all depending"! The small *Santa Rosa* boat operates from this quayside patio, between Loutro & Marble Beach, departing at 1000hrs, returning at 1700hrs, for a cost of 200drs, each way.

EXCURSIONS TO LOUTRO SURROUNDS

Excursion to Finikia Bay Close to the bottom of the ferry-boat finger pier, between *Katerinas* and the old lady's house, are the rough hewn steps that give way to the footpath looping up the western hillside to the headland top. Hereon is a very small, ruined Venetian fort, whose walls are almost intact, as well as an adjacent, interesting, sunken Arsenal, inside which is a well. The latter is now used as an animal coop. The thirty minute walk continues down the other side, still in a westerly direction, descending to:

Finikia Cove A small, pleasant cove set in a picturesque, if rocky bay, at the foot of a gently sloping, if massive mountainface. Apart from one huddle of buildings, hunched up close to the shore, the location is devoid of any development. The lack of any other easily visible traces of man is rather surprising as this was the site of *Ancient Finix*, a thriving settlement in Roman and Byzantine ages, as well as an important port, down the ages. Well, you could strike me down with a 'willy-warmer'. In historical times it was significant enough to have been the harbour for which the ship carrying St Paul, when a prisoner of the Romans, was attempting to head. Despite the suggestion that he did land here, a more substantial account reports that the boat was swept on to Kali Limenes, to the east, round Lithion Cape, *en route* to Lendas.

Nowadays Finikia espouses more the atmosphere engendered by the Loutro of old, even though due allowance has to be made for the fact that there is only one family, not a hamlet, and they own the *Rooms/Taverna Finix* (Tel 0825 91257). The head of the clan is the very pleasant, helpful Joseph Athitakis, who is aided and abetted by his wife and a number of children. Joseph speaks 'Street English', certainly enough to answer the telephone and take bookings for his accommodation. This leads me to advise that a double room, sharing the bathroom, costs 1500drs, whilst a double, with an en suite facility, is charged at 2000drs. Food and drink cost a few drachmae more, but supplies do have that little further to travel.

For those who find Loutro too commercial, this location must rate serious consideration. An ominous sign is the tell-tale, bulldozed swathe of track scaring the mountain side heights. Joseph is only to happy to explain, in full detail, the combined stupidity and duplicity of the contractors. It appears they were supposed to have aimed for the now deserted village of **Livaniana**, but took an incorrect turning, and started on the way down towards Finikia Cove. Somewhere in the narration is buried the tale of some double-dealing in respect of their packing-in the job, when they were unable to locate a supply of drinking water. But where that came into the original calculations, I was never able to fully understand! Whatever, the nub of the matter is that the track finished up some 1000m short of Livaniana and 25/30 minutes stiff walk from the Cove. *C'est la vie.*

To the west, over a boulderous coastal outcrop, is another Rooms/Taverna, close to a stretch of pebble beach, as well as a sea cave, often inhabited during the summer months.

Yet further on leads to **Marble Beach**, which is at the bottom of the previously described gorge, some forty minutes from Livaniana, via Anopolis village. *See* Page 277 for an omission.

ROUTE ELEVEN

To Ag Roumeli via Omalos and The Samaria Gorge (60km) Follow the Kastelli road, for a few kilometres, after which take the turning to the left, signposted Omalos.

For the amount of traffic this route has to endure, the road's surface, and general engineering, is of a rather poor standard. Be that as it may, it ascends through verdant orange groves, passing the branch road to **Alikianou** (12km). The latter village has a memorial to Cretan partisans killed by the Germans, during the Second World War.

FOURNES (14km from Chania) A quite a large village, with a couple of mini-markets, a taverna and a petrol station.

The road, still in 'orange grove' countryside, starts to climb in a series of loops, passing through the picturesque mountain village of:

LAKKI (24km from Chania) This settlement served as the military headquarters of the Cretan guerillas, during their internecine struggles with the Turks. Apart from a couple of tavernas, there are **Rooms**.

The orange groves recede, as the altitude rises, giving way to olive trees, which in their turn yield to mountainous hillsides and a vista of granite rocks, speckled with conifers. Finally the road tops a rise and opens out on to the fairly fertile plain and straggling hamlet of:

OMALOS (37km) Straggling it may be, but now a rather 'swept-up', sanitised way-station for the Gorge excursion coaches, with some fairly new flatlets, some sophisticated restaurants, and the 'Charles Forte' smart *Hotel Restaurant Nea Omalos*. The latter serves cafe-style meals, of strictly measured quantity and strictly calculated prices, inevitably reminding one of the UK motorway offerings. There are *Rooms*.

The large open plain supports crops, as well as grazing for goats and sheep, and is enclosed by gaunt, granite mountains, bringing to mind 'The Hidden Valley'. The poorly surfaced road climbs again, at the far side, towards:

Xyloskalo (42km from Chania) The *raison d'etre* for this Alpine-like grouping of buildings is that this is the head of the Gorge. There are dramatic views through the mountains, as well as a corralled car and coach park, which enclosure contains a 'tastefull' snack-bar. A notice board declares that the entrance fee is 200drs, unless a person is '...an old age pensioner, under 15 years of age or deceased (*sic*)'. I think this should read 'diseased'! Whichever, I'm not sure any one of the three categories should be contemplating the adventure. By the by, tickets should be kept as they are collected at the exit of the National Park. This is not the end of the walk, so those walkers counting the kilometre marks will be disappointed, as there is another mile to go. A wooden fence edges the rim of the almost vertical face of the Gorge and the xyloskalo (or wooden steps), which descend to the floor of the Gorge. To the right, up a sharp, short, steep drive is the *Xenia Pavilion* (Class B, tel 93237), but to get a room it is necessary to make a booking through the Chania Town NTOG office.
     The Gorge opens from 1st April to 31st October, with due allowance for any exceptionally inclement weather, at either end of the season. For instance, torrential rain, over a prolonged period, may well cause the river, that flows down the Gorge, to rise to dangerous heights. It must be pointed out that there have been flash floods, or a 'fresh' as they are known in North Yorkshire, which, as recently as October 1988, killed several walkers. To obtain information, and particular advice in respect of weather conditions, telephone the Forest Service office at Chania (Tel 22287).

Samaria Gorge Before discussing the walk, it might well be germane to enlighten the waverers and the doubters as to why they should disturb the happy holiday rhythm of late-rising, flesh-toasting during the day, with breaks for 'drinkies', and joyous rioting all night. Why not put aside these hedonistic delights, for just one day, and satisfy the twin emotions of curiosity and self-satisfaction. The Gorge is possibly the longest and largest in Europe, and is extremely beautiful. In addition it includes: a number of ancient buildings and hamlets; engenders interest in the flora, fauna and wildlife thriving therein; and possibly occasions amazement, if not thankfulness, when the jaunt is finished. Readers should now be persuaded. By catching an early bus (0615, 0730 or 0830hrs), it is possible to make the round trip in a busy, hard day. That is get from Chania to the top of the Gorge, effect the descent, walk the 18km Gorge to Ag Roumeli, catch a ferry to Chora Sfakion, then a bus back to Chania, in the evening. But why burst a blood vessel? Why not stop-over at Ag Roumeli or Chora Sfakion, for a night or two? Incidentally there are some amongst us who cheat, yes there is no other word for it, cheat. This refers to those who walk up the Gorge, from Ag Roumeli, the two hour climb as far as the *Iron Gates*, and then toddle back as if they had completed the job properly. Cads!

Without the modern-day advantage of the wooden staircase, access must have been a bit of a bind, a fact that was exploited through the ages, by both bandits and guerilla fighters alike. This was no more so than during the Turkish occupation, and up to and including the Second World War. It is reported that even the partisans fighting the Germans were at risk from small bands of Gorge based brigands. I wonder if the latter were related to the predominant family finally relocated when the majority of the Gorge was designated a National Park, in 1962. They were reputed to have had a direct ancestral link to a prominent Byzantine stock.

The walk should take between four and six hours, depending on the participant's state of health, his or her partner's condition, and whether or not children are included in the expedition. Members of guided tours tend to be regulated by the pace of the weakest member of the party. The perambulation is mainly a matter of picking a way over, round and through the boulderous river-bed. As anything up to two thousand people a day pass down the length of the Gorge, there are unlikely to be any unexpected hazards. Wear sensible shoes, not flip-flops, and consider packing a small holdall containing a snack and something to drink. There is no need to get too fussed about beverages or victuals as there are the occasional water points, the river water can be drunk, and private enterprise has reared its ugly head at the Gorge hamlet of Old Ag Roumeli, close to the end of the walk. There, for instance, by the pathside is an untidy bar where an elderly lady twiddles cans of expensive soft drinks in a bucket of water.

The walk commences by descending the wooden staircase/path for some 2km, after which, on the right, is the small chapel of Ag Nikolaos set in a copse of firs. At about half distance is the now uninhabited village of **Samaria**, with a restored house, picnic tables and benches. A little way on is another church, the 14th century Ossia Maria. Interestingly enough this Maria may not be the omnipresent Virgin Mary, but a Middle East prostitute, who 'saw the light'. The next major attraction has to be the narrowest part of the Gorge, known as the 'Iron Gates' or **Sidherportes**, where the towering walls slim down to a mere two metres in width. Further on the path threads its way through the stone walled pathways of the village of **Old Ag Roumeli**, where a few houses have been restored, there is a kafeneion, bar and from which a donkey service runs (or clip clops) down to Ag Roumeli. Beyond Old Ag Roumeli, the mountain walls are pushed back and the Gorge widens out on to a narrow river valley. The last kilometre or two does drag a little, more especially as walkers will now be in the full glare of the sun's rays. The path winds seawards down the unmade, dusty and dirty surface that doubles for a road, with the stony, wide river bed to the left. The latter is still spanned by a rather forlorn Venetian bridge, structures so distinctive due to their angular arch and high curved parapet. The track finally links with another, rough surfaced thoroughfare that runs parallel to the seashore of:

AG ROUMELI (60km from Chania) Tel prefix 0821. There was an ancient settlement here, as long ago as the 5th century BC, as evidenced by archaeological excavations to the left (*Fsw*) of the Gorge. In an attempt to hold down the locals the Turks built a fort (surprise, surprise).

Ag Roumeli continues to resemble a hot, Alaskan shanty town, the only 'establishments' missing being John Wayne and a bordello! The rustic, doo-hickey ambiance is accentuated by the wandering, foraging chickens, goats and sheep. Other animal life *in situ* include mosquitoes, and the dawn chorus of the village's stray dogs will doubtless wake the heaviest sleeper.

The inhabitants ('Sfakiots') have had a pretty hard life for the last 1000 years or so, what with tending and skinning goats, and sheep, in order to earn a crust. But now they are engaged in tending and skinning the tourists, so as to be able to afford holiday apartments in Chania, Rethymnon or Iraklion. On a serious note, it is worth bearing in mind that Ag Roumeli has the dubiously unique distinction of being one of the only gathering of Greeks where I have been, have observed, and have heard of tourists being 'ripped off', and not by fellow tourists. All goods and supplies arrive by boat and are trucked about the settlement, as required. Incidentally most of the eating places conduct currency exchange.

The description of Ag Roumeli naturally depends from which direction a traveller arrives, be that by ferry or on foot. I cannot possibly get it right for both, so have chosen to describe the approach from the Gorge end. Incidentally most of the buildings are 2-3 storeys high, but that is all they have in common. There is a great variety of styles, quite a few displaying the distinctive 'Ag Roumeli unfinished' look, which has been in vogue for a number of years.

The track has to cross from the right (*Fsw*), leaving the river-bed to run on into the sea, at the left of the bay. That contractors have chosen the bed of the creek, in which to manufacture the enormous 'fives-bone-like' sea defence structures, certainly doesn't help improve the look of the place. Where the track straightens up, to head down towards the sea, there is *Rooms Livikon*, with hot showers, on the right, *Rooms* on the left, and *Rooms Stratos* on the right. Next is the Supermarket Yannis, on the right, followed by some waste ground and the tawdry *Hotel Kri-Kri*, apparently aspiring to a Spanish style, with balconies and decorative lights. Mmmh!

To the right stretches an inland cliff-face, on the top of which is a ruined Turkish fort constructed of local stone. The Castle must have been the inspiration behind the naming of *Rooms Kastro*, which appropriately lies beneath the ruins, in the irregular grid layout of tracks behind the lateral 'High Street' to the right. This latter road lies back and parallels the beach backshore. It is crossed at right angles by the Gorge path, close to the *Rooms Restaurant Lefkahori*.

The High St is nothing more than a short cul-de-sac to the left (*Still facing seawards*) with, close to the crossroads and on the far, sea side, our old friend the:

Restaurant Rooms Tara   Tel 29391
The brothers Stavrondakis run the show and both speak English. A double room, with an en suite bathroom, costs from 2000drs. Be careful climbing the external, precast concrete steps up to the first storey. There is an irregularity in the rise which causes the unwary to trip, and that is without taking into account any intake of retsina. A meal at the Tara, on the excellently positioned, covered, if rather dark terrace, is good value.

Next door to the *Tara* is the *Restaurant Rooms Zorbas.*

To the right, the High St stretches out westwards, towards the far headland cliff. On the right is the:
Rooms Restaurant Samaria
Run by a smiling, helpful, likeable bandit - no, hush my mouth, a Sfakiot. He has double bedrooms, with en suite bathrooms, for between 2000-2800drs, "...depending and negotiable". He can also offer rooms sharing a bathroom, if necessary. Apart from accommodation, the patron runs a very good kitchen, and sample menu prices include: tzatziki 200drs; yoghurt 150drs; Greek salad 200drs; stuffed vegetables 300drs; moussaka 430drs; spaghetti 360drs; chicken 380drs;   squid 450drs; lamb 580drs; pizza 650drs; pork chops 650drs; souvlaki 600drs; and fish 850drs. A meal, for two, of tzatziki (singular & plentiful), a Greek salad (distinctive with plenty of cabbage, if only one olive), an unimaginative but worthy pizza, 2 beers and a small amount of bread, cost 1400drs.

Continuing along the High St passes, all on the right, the: *Gorge Rooms Restaurant*; another Rooms/Restaurant; a number of near completed buildings; *Rooms Gigilos*, with 'zaparate bathroom'; and, at this far end of the development (to date), the *Hotel Restaurant Ag Roumeli* (Class B, tel 25657). At the latter, all rooms have en suite bathrooms with a single costing 3200drs and a double 4000drs. On the other, beach side of the track, sorry, 'High St', border- ing the backshore, is a snackbar/cafeteria alongside which are some beach showers. Those wishing to use them must pay 50drs, whilst clients get the use of them free. Well, that's subject to interpretation as a large lemonade and a small bottle of beer costs 325drs. Whow!
   Back at the crossroads, the ever-widening path progresses in the direction of the Ferry-boat Quay. Almost immediately on the right is the Ferry-boat ticket office shed. The boat timetables are posted on the external walls.

Ferry-boat timetable (Mid-season)

Day	Departure time	Ports/Islands of Call
Daily	0930, 1415, 1545, 1700, 1800hrs	Loutro, Chora Sfakion.
Tues,Wed,Fri Sat,Sun	1630hrs	Souyia, Paleochora.
Mon,Thurs	1030hrs	Souyia, Paleochora.

One-way fare: to Chora Sfakion 680drs; duration 1hr.
              to Souyia   440drs; duration 1hr.

Opposite the ticket office is a post box mounted on the wall of a Souvenir shop, as well as a gravelled path between a Self-service shop and the *Rooms Restaurant Peralia.*

The surprisingly large, very wide, fine pebble, black beach extends away to the right, edging clean seas beneath which the sea-bed shelves extremely steeply. Unfortunately there is a fair amount of rubbish strewn about the shore, most of it left by 'overnighters'. The backshore has a row of about a dozen sun umbrellas and sun-beds. To Gorge walkers the beach may well look like paradise and it tends to fill up and empty, contemporaneously with the arrival and departure of the ferry-boats. Don't forget black pebbles really soak up the heat and can easily burn bare feet. The far end of the beach is bordered by the aforementioned cliffs, which bend round towards the western headland and over and around which goats often perform a miraculous balancing act.

ROUTE TWELVE

To Rethymnon, via the Old Road (some 70km) From Chania, initially the main road is used, but after some 18km, follow the signposted branch road to **Armeni**. This village lies in a fertile valley full of olive groves with a lovely avenue out of the village. The route bypasses a dying, be-flowered village and proceeds to **Neo Chorio**, which has a long irregular square, a disco (yes a disco), and little else.

The route winds up and out of Neo Chorio, past a chapel built into the rock, on the left, whilst across the valley another settlement sprawls over a lump of rock. The landscape is strewn with cypresses, in amongst which is a steep gorge and very many trees followed by massed grape vines. **Ag Pantes** is a small, pretty, tree lined settlement set in farming country with sheep and chickens everywhere, and charcoal burners in evidence. This section of the route is particularly attractive, being heavily wooded and rich with chapels.

From Vryses (*See* **Route Ten**) sorties can be made to Georgioupolis (*See* **Route Five, Chapter 4**) and the overrated, freshwater lake at **Kournas**.

Back on course, **Episkopi** (Tel prefix 0831) is a large, long, winding settlement with some industry, a Post Office, tavernas, a petrol station, as well as one hotel, *The Minos* (Class D, tel 61208).

The road traverses a lovely, green ravine very nearly devoid of mechanical traffic but with plenty of donkeys clip-clopping along, usually laden down with a heavy load, plus the owner. **Ag Andreas** squats in a landscape of olives, but there are signs of development at the roadside, despite which the local charcoal burner is still in evidence. From here the road loops via the large, compact village of **Astipopoulo** to Rethymnon (*See* **Chapter 4**).

ROUTE THIRTEEN

To Ag Marina & Platanias (9km) The very first section of this route to the west, along the north coast, is detailed under **Camping & Beaches, A To Z, Chania**. The other side of the road to the most westerly of the 'peninsula' beaches is a Mobil petrol station run by Mr Konstantinou, who is only too happy to help travellers. The thirsty might like to know there is an iced drinking water machine on the forecourt. The road passes along or near the coast, through a stretch of haphazard, urban, seaside development. After some 3km, on the left-hand side, opposite a BP petrol station and the some 3km, on the left-hand side, opposite a BP petrol station and the *Chania Fedra Hotel*, is the rather bellicose statue of a stooping eagle. This was erected to commemorate, or more truly mourn, the heavy losses of the crack 7th German Parachute Regiment that spearheaded the German inva-sion, in May 1941. The main assault took place on this stretch of coast, but the attrition was so heavy that Hitler is supposed to have ordered that no more attacks of this type were to be undertaken. Now that there are a blocks of apartments to one side and to the front, the monument is not so easy to see when approaching from the west.

The next coastal spot lies on a nice little bay, with a caique harbour to the west. On rounding a bluff the bold looking, offshore islet of **Ag Theodori** hoves into view. This is reputedly a refuge for the legendary Agrimi or Kri-Kri, (the Cretan wild goat or chamois), an object of venera-tion in Minoan times. On the inland side of the road is the *Hotel Restaurant Bar Dolphin*. Across the thoroughfare is a small, tree shaded, little head-land that marks the very east end of a pleasant sweep of beach. Unfortu-nately, if inevitably, this has been disfigured by clumps of sun-beds and umbrellas, as well as the messy backyards of the various apartment and villa constructions that border the backshore. The *Dolphin* is followed by a ribbon development, amongst which are the *Hotel Gallini*, the *Santa Marina Hotel* and a small brickworks. A correspondent has recommended 'Rent A Car & Motorbikes. Duke of Crete', on the inland side of the road, opposite the *Taverna Meltemi* and about 1km east of the brickworks. The owner is Yannis who speaks excellent English, which is not so surprising as he is married to an English girl.

The *Ag Marina Campsite* (Tel 68555) is also hereabouts, in the strip of land trapped between the main road and the shoreline. The per person charge is 500drs, the cost of a tent 300drs. There are the to-be-expected facilities of a taverna, mini-market, and a shower/toilets block. Visitors can catch the Chania/Ag Marina/Maleme/Chandris bus.

The campsite is about opposite the west end of Ag Theodori islet, close to a spot on the beach where an outcrop of rock divides the beach and the *Cantina Florinta* is located. Apart from dispensing pizzas, tost, bottles of beer and soft drinks, this unimposing little shack emits waves of gushy Italian melodies.

All this has been a prelude to:

AG MARINA (5km from Chania) Tel prefix 0821. A sprawling urban development, an excellent example of a particular genre, namely the middle-of-the-road Kosta growth encouraged by the burgeoning package holiday industry. The once lovely strip of beach is now submerged in a welter of water sports activities, cafe-bars, tourist shops and hotels. This to-be-regretted evolution includes a ghastly little outcrop of accommodation cubes; the *Odysseus Suites*; *Studio Katerina*; expensive, tour operator booked *Santa Marina* (Class B, tel 68570), with en suite single rooms priced from 3300drs & doubles from 4800drs, plus a nice garden down to the beach; *Rooms Antonis*; tourist offices; *Rooms & Apartments Georgina*; the *Ta Thodorou* (Class C, tel 68510), as well as a number of pensions and **Rooms**, both in and around Ag Marina.

Perhaps the best that Ag Marina has to offer is in the old village, about 2km up and inland from the main road. One of the signs to follow, to find this desirable outpost of sanity, is that for *Rooms Despina* (Tel 68559). These lead to a Main Square, where turn right to beyond the church, and then left. The interesting *Despina* house, full of knick-knacks, is not quite the highest in the settlement, but damn nearly. The owners are Pandelis & Despina Maragoudakis who, it is reported, spent a number of years running a 'hamburger joint', in Harlem, New York. They offer rooms, sharing or with en suite bathrooms, and the views are amazing. Both Pandelis and Despina, as well as their daughter, speak good English. Also in this upper settlement, is the *Taverna Falcon Kostas*, the owner of which has accommodation at *Rooms Danai*.

PLATANIAS (some 9km from Chania) Tel prefix 0821. Due to the almost out-of-control, uncurbed building taking place along this length of coast, Platanias is almost a continuation of Ag Marina, or vice-versa. The original village has spread down off its small, flat-topped hill into a sprawl of Kosta development, with the reinforced concrete skeletons of buildings randomly sprouting out of cultivated fields and bamboo groves. Apart from a small factory, there are **Rooms** of all sorts and sizes, *Marika Rooms*, Car hire, a bank, *Montreal Rooms*, a supermarket, the *Mill Taverna*, *Blue Sea Apartments*, the *Hotel Ideal Beach* (which it isn't), and *Rooms George*. Two Class B hotels, are the *Filoxenia* (Tel 68502), where a single room with an en suite bathroom costs from 2000drs & double from 2500drs, and the *Villa Platanias* (Tel 48333). The beach is low, flat and sandy.

The coastline to the west of Platanias, beyond **Gerani**, where there is an 'alligator swamp' of a river-bed, is the subject of the most haphazard building and random construction. This blight edges a dirty dune backshore and a beach of small to fine pebble. Yet further on, the road narrows down to corridor through tall bamboo-fencing wind breaks, pierced by poorly made doors of tin and plastic.

6 KASTELLI (Kastellio, Kissamos, Kisamou)

An (English) market town & ferry-boat port

GENERAL (Illustration 15) Tel prefix 0822. A rapidly expanding and thriving town which radiates out from a busy little square, above and some 200/300m from the seafront. Connecting them are two roads. One routes around the Castle walls, before spilling on to a small waterfront quay square, at the west end of the waterfront. The other is a wide, dirt track that bumps down to the centre of the beach backshore. Sadly the land between the two, once cultivated fields and smallholdings, is now 'dedicated' to rather disjointed package holiday development. Left (*Fsw*) of the quay is a messy wasteland, the shoreline edged by a rough track. Along this rumble lorries on their way to dump rubbish, as well as rocks and soil, cleared from various developments and civil engineering works in the area. To the right, a dirt Esplanade edges the long seafront facing up the very large Bay (or Gulf) of Kissamos. Beyond the aforementioned swathe of apartments, a hotel, a couple of restaurants, and a cocktail bar, the track edges an ever-widening pebble beach, on one side, and, on the other, an unattractive, bamboo scattered scrubland.

The main road bypasses Kastelli to the south, to all intents and purposes delineating the development in this direction.

After a slow, lazy morning start, the town becomes very busy with local citizenry, a lot of vehicles, and youngster propelled scooters. Apart from the indigenous population, holiday-makers are now very much in evidence, but neat and tidy Kastelli is not yet inundated, or overwhelmed. Having come late to tourism, it remains an agricultural town at heart, adapting, possibly reluctantly, to modern-day requirements and demands. Incidentally, in 1989, a new main drainage system was being installed with the result that many side-streets were in a frightful mess. In Odhos Papagianniki these excavations revealed remains of the old city walls, thus the residents could be in for a long wait for the work to be completed, whilst the archaeologists and civil engineers fight out the issues involved.

ARRIVAL BY BUS Buses pull up on an elongated square (*Tmr* 1C/D3/4), to the north of the Main Road.

ARRIVAL BY FERRY The ambitious harbour quay, at which the Peloponnese ferry-boats dock, is about 2km west of the town. The pier has a Customs office and bar. About 150m west of the harbour is an embryonic infrastructure of development, with some villas and the *Hotel/Restaurant Via*, set in rather scratchy agriculture surrounds. Away to the right (*Fbqbo*), beyond scrubbly foothills, is the massive peninsula of Grabousa.

Beside the curving walk round to the town, after about 1km there is a little chapel, set into a cave on the inland side, followed by the *Villa Apartments Chryssani* (See **The Accommodation**). Further along, on the left, is a picturesque caique fishing boat anchorage, a huddle of houses, a couple of

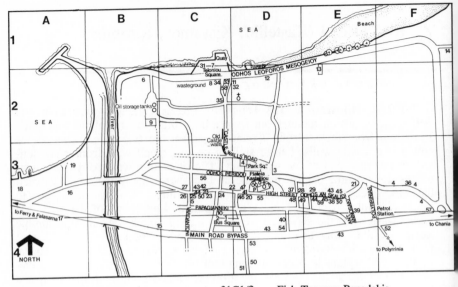

Tmr		
1C/D3/4	Bus Square	
2C3/4	Bus ticket office/ Cafeteria Santana	
3D3	Hotel/Restaurant Castelli	
4	Rooms	
5C3/4	Zimmer Rooms	
6B/C1/2	Sunshine Rooms	
7C1/2	Quay Square	
8C1/2	Argos Rooms/Bar/Cafeteria	
9B/C2	Agricultural Co-op Supermarket	
10C/D3/4	Andoni's house/shop	
11C/D1/2	Hotel Bay Guest House	
12D1/2	Mandy Suites	
13E1/2	Taverna Rooms	
14F1/2	Galini Beach	
15B/C3/4	Hotel Kissamos	
16A3	Hotel Peli	
17A3/4	Hotel Eri	
18A3	Hotel Elena Beach	
19A3	Rooms Kastanaki Maria	
20C/D3	'Main Sq' Cafeteria	
21E3	National Bank	
22C/D3	Taverna	
23C3	Kafeneions	
24C/D3/4	Cafe-Bar	
25C3/4	Restaurant	
26C3/4	Pan Vik Cafeteria	
27B/C3	To Agrimi Restaurant	
28D/E3	Restaurant Papadaki	
29D/E3/4	Restaurant Galaxias	
30E3/4	Restaurant Stimadorakis	

31C1/2	Fish Taverna Papadakis	
32C/D1/2	Restaurant O Makedonas	
33C/D1/2	Mini Restaurant	
34CD1/2	Mikes Place Pub	
35C2	Taverna Piccadilli(sic)	
36F3	Restaurant Angelika	
37D/E3/4	General Tourist Agency/ Rent A Car/Olympic Office	
38E3/4	Commercial Bank	
39E3/4	Anthony's Bikes	
40D3/4	Scooter & Car Hire	
41C/D3	Bread Shop	
42C3	Baker	
43	Supermarkets	
44	Butchers	
45	Fish Shops	
46C/D3/4	Fruti & Veg Shop	
47C/D3	Ferry-boat Ticket Office	
48D/E3	International Paper shop	
49D/E3/4	ANEK Office	
50	Pharmacies	
51C/D4	Hospital	
52E/F3/4	OTE	
53D4	Petrol station	
54D4	Post Office	
55D3/4	Taxi office	
56C3	Leather workshop	
57F3/4	Dentist	
58C/D1/2	Barrel factory	
59D/E3/4	Travel office	

Tmr = Town map reference
Fsw = Facing seawards
Sbo = Sea behind one
Fbqbo = Ferry-boat Quay behind one

Illustration 15 Kastelli

tavernas and a small cove with pleasant swimming. For Kastelli keep left where the road forks.

THE ACCOMMODATION & EATING OUT

The Accommodation There has been a marked increase in the availability of beds with a number of new **Rooms,** pensions and hotels. Out of the height of season months, when there are less tourists than rooms, owners will 'negotiate'!

Castelli (Castle, Kastron) Hotel (*Tmr* 3D3) (Class C) Kastelliou Sq   Tel 22140
Directions: On the right (*Fsw*), or east of the Main Square. Incorporated with the hotel is a large restaurant (*See* **The Eating Out**).
    The hotel is clean, very convenient and reasonably priced. A single room, en suite, costs from 2800drs, a double, with shared bathroom, 3000drs, whilst an en suite double room starts off at 3500drs. Outside the height of season the owner may 'lower his sights'... and prices. During the months of July-September breakfast might be a mandatory option (!), at a cost of 300drs per person.

Close by, in fact across the Square and a small park bordering the 'Castle Walls' street, down to the waterfront, are some very smart **Rooms** (*Tmr* 4C/D3) above a wholesale builders merchant.

Adjacent to the centre of the town, on the left (*Sbo*) of Odhos Vardantoni, is:
Zimmer Rooms (*Tmr* 5C3/4) Odhos Vardantoni
Directions: As above.
    Females, who make enquiries about accommodation, will quite probably know where every portion of their anatomy is situated, and so will the proprietors. The box-like rooms are rather dark but adequately clean, costing from 1500drs, sharing the bathrooms.

In the 'eastern suburbs', beyond the last Bank (*Tmr* 21E3) edging the High St, and continuing on in that direction, there are **Rooms** (*Tmr* 4F3, tel 22105), **Rooms** (*Tmr* 4F3, tel 22927), both on the left, and more **Rooms** (*Tmr* 4F3/4), on the right. Where the High Street merges with the Main road bypass, alongside a water fountain in the form of dolphins, is the signposted turning down to the:

The Galini Beach Hotel (*Tmr* 14F1/2)   Tel 23288
Directions: As above, and about 500m towards the beach. Alongside a football field turn right (*Fsw*) for the three storey hotel, beyond which is a possibly dead disco. This road continues on through 'bamboo', agricultural countryside, roughly parallel to the foreshore.
    A package holiday hotel.

The other two focal points for accommodation are on the waterfront and bordering the Main road to the west of the town. In the area of the waterfront are:

Sunshine Rooms (*Tmr* 6B/C1/2)   Tel 22452/22073
Directions: From the small quay square (*Tmr* 7C1/2), turn left (*Fsw*) along the dusty, unmade, stony track, past *Mikes Place Pub* and *Argos Rooms* (*Tmr* 8C1/2), some wasteland, a couple of dwellings, and on the far side of a narrow side-street is the single storey building.
    Bearing in mind the price, this is my favourite lodgings, even if they are rather doo-hickey. Furthermore, since the decision was made to reshape the surroundings and sea wall, by the extensive dumping of boulderous oversite, the

surrounds are comparatively unattractive. There never was much of a beach hereabouts, and that which does poke through the rubble is covered in kelp. The only traffic is the contractors' lorries, which rumble past on their way to the tipping grounds.

Andoni, the landlady is very smiley and helpful and her daughter, Chrisoula, reluctantly speaks English. Mother is a 'real caution' and might be encountered anywhere between the digs, the informal common grazing land, north of the Agricultural Co-op Supermarket (*Tmr* 9B/C2), where she hobbles the family goats and sheep, or her home (*Tmr* 10C/D3/4), over 'the shop' - in this case a grain business. Incidentally, Andoni reckons her animals are the best looked after in town, because they enjoy an ample supply of food and water, as well as being well-sheltered. Favoured guests might well be treated to some freshly milked goats milk - straight from the teats, as it were. The average double room rate, sharing a bathroom, is 1500drs a night. It has to be admitted that repairs and renewals to the property would appear to be low in the order of priorities, as evinced by the peeling paintwork, but she is the kindest soul. The front rooms, edging the 'Esplanade', benefit from a narrow, concrete verandah with a table and a couple of chairs. Plus points include bedside-lights, but the shower head does not have a point on which to hang it, and despite the dear woman's rotestations, the water is not solar heated.

The other accommodation hereabouts is ranged either side of the Main Square/ 'Castle Walls' road down to the waterfront and includes:
Argos Rooms (*Tmr* 8C1/2)
Directions: As above and on the left (*Fsw*) of the road junction with the 'Esplanade', Leoforos Mesogeiou.
A very smart, four storey package tourist hotel.

Similar to the *Argos*, is the: *Hotel Bay Guest House* (*Tmr* 11C/D1/2), on the right of the T-junction.

Mandy Suites (*Tmr* 12D1/2)   Tel 22830
Directions: Further east from the T-junction.
Advertises 'Apartments - Rooms for Rent', but once again, a holiday company location.

Taverna Rooms (*Tmr* 13E1/2)
Directions: Even further to the east, about 100m from the quay, about opposite where the beach starts to widen out and a short line of backshore trees commences.
Standing on its own and noticeable because of the wooden first storey, topped off with a ridge roof. The 'lady of the house' is rather surly, if not guilty of dumb insolence. A double room starts off at about 1500drs.

Along the noisy Main road bypass, to the west of the town, are, in strict order of progression, the:
Hotel Kissamos (*Tmr* 15B/C3/4) (Class C)   Tel 22086
Directions: On the right, with the bus office 100m behind one.
The proprietor is pleasant, helpful, friendly, and serves good wine from the barrel. All rooms have en suite bathrooms and most have balconies, with a single priced at 3000drs & a double 3800drs.

Hotel Peli (*Tmr* 16A3) (Class C)   Tel 22343
Directions: Next on, from the *Kissamos*.
Built in 1987 by the very friendly Costas, and named after his mother and

daughter (Penelope). A reader advises it is a super hotel, with endless hot water and huge white towels. The en suite rooms cost 3200drs for a single & 4000drs for a double.

Rooms Kastanaki Maria (*Tmr* 19A3)   Tel 22610/22120
Directions: Close by the *Peli*, but on the beach.
   All rooms have en suite bathrooms and a number of them open on to a verandah. Doubles cost from 2500drs a night.

The *Hotel Eri* (*Tmr* 17A3/4) is further along, and on the inland side of the Main road. Last, but not least, in this direction is the:
Elena Beach Hotel (Class B)   Tel 23300
Directions: As above, and close to a side road junction with the bypass.
   Newish, block booked by a German holiday company, and expensive. All rooms have en suite bathrooms, with a single priced at 3140drs & a double 4560drs, increasing, respectively, to 4155drs & 5200drs (16th June-30th Sept). Breakfast is listed at a staggering 715drs, rising to 935drs - for which price it would have to be a full-blooded, English 'executioners', complete with bacon, kidneys, sliced liver, sausages, fried bread, eggs, tomatoes, and creamed mushrooms, with orange juice, tea and coffee... I did write, 'would have to be', not is! One item of note is that the beach, to the fore of and to the east side of the hotel, is the best in town with fine sand stretching into the sea. Despite being crowded right in front of the hotel, it is less so 'towards the edges'.

Apartments Chryssani (Class C)   Tel 23390
Directions: Situated about 2km out of Kastelli, overlooking the fishing boat anchorage.
   A fairly new apartment complex, run by Dimitris Chryssani, who is also involved in the Ferry-boat ticket office. The suites are 'equipped' with a full bathroom, sitting room, kitchen complete with fridge, sea-view balconies and a telephone. There are also entertainment rooms and a children's playground, all of which has to be paid for, at a cost of 6500drs per night for a double room, rising to 7500drs (1st July-30th Sept). Golly gosh!

Camping There is a location, even if it is to the west, some 6km distant, close to the village of Drapanias.

Camping Mithimna 73400 Drapanias   Tel (0822) 31444
Directions: There are signs pointing along tracks, on the Kastelli side of and in the village of Drapanias. These lead down to a wide backshore path edging the far, east end of Kissamos Bay.
   The nicely positioned, if somehow rather unattractive site is well tree'd, but close by some fairly extensive greenhouses. The office can give details of nearby *Rooms Leonardis*, and there is a taverna a couple of hundred metres further east. The daily per person rate is 450drs, pitching a tent costs 300drs, and cabin rooms cost 2500drs. A very useful facility is a metered phone. The wide, more than acceptable beach has a sandy sea-bed, the sea's edge pebbles are very small, and the middle shore has its fair share of larger pebbles. A mini-bus departs for Kastelli at 0930hrs, returning at 1230hrs, but those campers prepared to wander the 1km up to Drapanias can catch one of the regular Kastelli/Chania buses.

The Eating Out There are many more establishments now, as there would have to be in order to cope with the increase in the number of holiday-makers, but there aren't any souvlaki kiosks. It has to be admitted that a number of the restaurants serve take-away souvlaki pitas at a cost of about 120drs. Genuine kafeneions are in short supply, although there are a couple (*Tmr* 23C3) on the left of the High St, west of the Main Sq. Cafeterias are in the ascendency.

Working out from the town's Main Square, Plateia Kastelliou, the most central establishment is *The Castelli Restaurant* (*Tmr* 3D3), located in the ground floor of the hotel of the same name.

Diagonally across the Square, on the south-west corner, is the:
Main Sq Cafeteria (*Tmr* 20C/D3)
Directions: As above. The cafeteria edges the pavement, with chairs and tables across the street, on the terrace beside the church. It is a shame that this small, pleasant area has been created by knocking down a charming old clock tower that used to butt on to the church.

A splendid location from which to watch the comings and goings of the town. These include the policemen issuing parking tickets to those motorists that 'transgress', and a 30 'year young' man (your age is showing GROC) and his motorbike. The fellow in question is inordinately large and he has owned the most expensive, fastest, black motorbike in Kastelli, for some years. His idea of a night on the town is to mount the machine, time after time, and propel it down the one-way High St, only to reappear *Clouseau-like* (*a la the Peter Sellars character*) from this or that side-street. The pretty daughter of the house must have been suffering from an unspeakably painful medical ailment during our last visit - she served, but 'in grimace'. A Nes meh ghala costs a reasonable 80drs, and an ouzo, with nuts, 100drs.

Incidentally, the proprietor of the shop next door would love a visit from any Scottish people. He has obviously visited Edinburgh, and if under the impression that a 'Brit' hails from north of the border, is more than likely to sneak an ouzo across. On the right of Odhos An Skalidi, to the west of the Main Square, are stretched out the night-time tables and chairs of the adjacent:

Taverna (*Tmr* 22C/D3)
Directions: As above.
This establishment specialises in hors d'oeuvres type mixed dishes. A very nice, tasty meal, for two, of tzatziki (200drs), keftedes and a few bits & pieces (350drs), a mixed grill (giro meat, a meatball, a sausage, a black sausage, a few chips, yoghurt, a bit of this & a bit of that - 470drs), bread (40drs), and a bottle of kortaki retsina (140drs), cost 1100drs - I know, it should have totalled 1200drs! This family owned establishment is run by the youngsters, waitress Eleni and her 'mad' brother Yianni.

Further along the street are a popular *Cafe-bar* (*Tmr* 24C/D3/4), the aforementioned *Kafeneions* (*Tmr* 23C3), a Restaurant (*Tmr* 25C3/4), the *Pan Vik Cafeteria* (*Tmr* 26C3/4), and the *To Agrimi Restaurant* (*Tmr* 27B/C3). In the main, the latter three diners serve souvlaki style meals, and associated offerings, as do most establishments in Kastelli.

To the east of the Main Sq are a few possibilities. The first two, on the left of the High St, the *Restaurant Papadaki* (*Tmr* 28D/E3) and *Restaurant Galaxias* (*Tmr* 29D/E3/4), appear to only open whilst the going's good, that is during the height of season months.

As a matter of interest, *Papadaki* is probably owned by the same gentleman who had the now defunct *Hotel Morpheus*, a building to the rear of the restaurant. The ground floor, once the hotel lobby, is now a smoke-filled, *ad hoc* kafeneion, frequented by locals. Mr Papadaki now 'proprietors' the *Hotel Kissamos*. Further along the High St, on the right, is the:

Restaurant Stimadorakis (*Tmr* 30E3/4)
Directions: As above, with a Pool Hall to the right (*Sbo*).
Specialise in fish dishes, and a meal, for two, of a couple of huge bowls of fish soup, a kilo of very palatable open retsina, and bread, cost some 1350drs.

The brother of the lady in the last mentioned fish restaurant runs:
George Stimadorakis Fish Restaurant
Directions: Bordering the road out to the port, alongside the caique harbour (and not the fish taverna 'in amongst' the caiques, of which more later!).
A blow-out meal, for two, of grilled octopus & 2 ouzos, 2 excellent fish soups, a feta-less Greek salad (!), 2 bottles of kortaki retsina, and 2 coffees, cost 2000drs (which included a couple of drinks on the house).

Referring to the taverna in the harbour, it may have been an off day but I have received an adverse report of an offhand, surly response to a well-travelled couple's attempts to eat there.
On, or close to the waterfront is (another) *Fish Taverna Papadaki* (*Tmr* 31C1/2). This is on the site of the old fishing boat quay, which has been tarted up and is now a concrete expanse, formally planted with shrubs and bushes. Also hereabouts is the:
Restaurant O Makedonas (*Tmr* 32C/D1/2)
Directions: As above, behind and below the *Holiday Bay Guest House*, to the right (*Fsw*) of the 'Castle Walls' road down to the seafront.
It would be unrealistic not to expect the BPTs to dine here - and they do. Apart from the location, this is made doubly more likely by the generally good quality and plentiful size of the portions of the lunchtime food. If one had a cavil it would be in respect of the rather lackadaisical, long-winded process in taking clients' orders. It has to be admitted that the homely, smiley, middle-aged couple, who run the place, are under some strain, at times. Their son (?), a hip, John Travolta type, aged about 30, does not contribute to the general effort. Another whine is that the evening meals tend to be lunchtime left-overs, or grilled dishes. It has to be admitted that the reasonably varied menu is weighted towards the latter, in any case. It also has to be noted that small bottles of retsina are not available, but a bottle of beer is not too expensive at 90drs. A meal, for two, of stuffed tomatoes (370drs), an enormous pizza (very nice, if salty - 700drs), a super Greek salad (150drs), bread (30drs each), 2 lemonades (Greek which is unusual - 50drs each) & 2 beers (100drs each), cost 1560drs. It was noticeable that the patron rounded up his official menu prices, by some 10drs each, for a number of items, only to reduce the bill by 30drs!

Close to the restaurant is a large cocktail bar, with a terrace, about which no more need be said. Further east along the waterfront Esplanade is a *Taverna Rooms* (*Tmr* 13E1/2), conveniently situated to the nearside of the main beach. Unfortunately the service is 'dumb out of insolent' and the few canned drinks available are expensive - a tin of Sprite costs 80drs.

Just around the corner from the *Restaurant O Makedonas* is the:
Mini Restaurant (*Tmr* 33C/D1/2)
Directions: As above.
Potential clients should not be put off by the clean, bistro-look to the place as

the meals are very tasty, and individually prepared. Certainly evening diners should arrive early, especially if a table is required out the back. Those who have to sit down inside might well find it gets quite warm, but it is diverting to watch the dishes being prepared at the long, glass fronted counter. Specimen prices include: tomato salad 100drs; roe or Russian salad 120drs; tzatziki 100drs; rice 200drs; patatas 50drs; spaghetti 300drs (this is one of the only places in town which actually serves this dish, as distinct from making a menu listing); moussaka 350drs; fried chicken 300drs; pork 350drs; a plate of sliced giro meat 400drs; and pizzas 700drs. The marketing thrust is to attract the BPTs, but as that results in fast, friendly service, so be it. The ½ litre mugs of beer, costing 130drs, are to be regretted, but they do serve a kortaki retsina, even if it is pricey at 150drs a bottle.

Across the street is *Mikes Place Pub* (*Tmr* 34C/D1/2), which appears to be under the same ownership, and knocks out night hours hard rock music. Just up the road, heading towards the Main Sq, is the *Taverna Piccadilli* (*sic*) (*Tmr* 35C2, tel 22054), with 'Rooms For Rent', written on the side of the building, a promotional hustle which, I'm fairly certain, dates back to a now ceased activity. Almost as far east along the High St as the junction with the bypass, is the *Restaurant Angelika* (*Tmr* 36F3).

THE A TO Z OF USEFUL INFORMATION
AIRLINE OFFICE More the **General Tourist Agency** ('Hermes Rent A Car') (*Tmr* 37D/E3/4), which is also an Olympic Airways agent (*See* **Travel Agents & Tour Offices, A To Z**), on the Chania side of the High Street Main Sq.

BANKS There are a couple along the east High St, the **Commercial Bank** (*Tmr* 38E3/4), on the right, and the **National Bank** (*Tmr* 21E3), which deals in Eurocheques, on the left.

BEACH Apart from the section adjacent to the *Hotel Elena Beach* (*Tmr* 18A3) (*See* **The Accommodation**), the main beach commences just about opposite *Mandy Suites* (*Tmr* 12D1/2). From here this shore widens out in an easterly direction. That sand which is visible is rather grey and 'sharp' but, unfortunately, most of the surface is sweeping crescents of large pebbles, with small pebbles at the sea's edge. There is quite a lot of sea blown rubbish mixed in with the cigarette ends, apple cores and tins, despite there being a few tidy bins. A plus point is that the gently shelving sea-bed is very sandy, and the sea-water is quite clear. About 100m from the outset of the beach is a set of backshore trees in amongst which the occasional tent is pitched, and camper-van parked. About 200m along is a beach shower, whilst at the far, right-hand (*Fsw*) end of the bay there appears to be a couple of factory chimneys.

BICYCLE, SCOOTER & CAR HIRE
Rent from Anthony (*Tmr* 39E3/4)Tel 22909
Directions: On the left of Odhos Ant Annosaki, which angles off from the eastern end of the High St.
　　Anthony is a bearded, 35 year old Greek, 'wearing 50', who sometimes smiles and often looks as if he hasn't been to bed since the last time I was here! He speaks adequate English, is an old 'adversary' and hires a variety of two-wheeled velopeds. A Vespa costs 1500drs for one day & 4800drs for three days. Larger engined bikes work out at about 6000drs for the same 3 day period.

Other firms include:-
Fotis Daratsianos (*Tmr* 40D3/4)   Tel 22965
Directions: In a narrow side-street which branches off the Main road bypass, alongside the Post Office.

One day scooter hire costs 1700drs and 3 days 4500drs. They certainly represent a friendlier, keener, better alternative to bored old Anthony.

Motors (*Tmr* D3)
Directions: The office edges the east side of the Main Sq, Plateia Kastelliou.

They actually advertise 'Enjoy your holidays, we rent every kind of motors'.

BOOKSELLERS There is an International Papershop (*Tmr* 48D/E3), on the right
(*Main Sq behind one*) of the High St.

BREAD SHOPS A Bread Shop (*Tmr* 41C/D3) borders the south-west of the Main Sq, with the sign over the door 'Melissianos - 1898'. 'The' Baker (*Tmr* 42C3), who has been there for as many years as I can remember and bakes in a massive oven or three, also sells a 'mean' slab of cheese pie for 80drs. He opens in the evenings as well, even on the town's closing night of Wednesday.

BUSES The buses park on the Square (*Tmr* 1C/D3/4) adjacent to the Main road. On the corner is the Bus ticket office-cum-*Cafeteria Santana* (*Tmr* 2C3/4).

Bus timetable (Mid-season)
Kastelli to **Chania**
Daily   0500, 0600, 0700, 0730, 0800, 0930, 1030, 1130, 1230, 1400, 1530,
            1615, 1800, 1900hrs.
Return journey
Daily   0545, 0715, 0830, 1000, 1100, 1200, 1230, 1530, 1630, 1730, 1830,
            2000hrs

Kastelli to **Chora Sfakion**
Daily   0700, 0830, 0930, 1230, 1400hrs

Kastelli to **Paleochora**
Daily   0800, 0830, 0930, 1130, 1400, 1630hrs.

Kastelli to **Rethymnon, Iraklion, Plakias, Ag Galini, Arkadhi Monastery, Anogia**
                                    (close by Gonies, Iraklion)
Daily   Between 0500-1800hrs (but no specific times).

Kastelli to **Samaria Gorge**
Daily   0500, 0600hrs
Kastelli to **Chrysoskalitissa Nunnery, Elafonisi Beach**
Daily   0930hrs

Kastelli to **Falasarna (via Platanos)**
Daily   1000, 1700hrs

There is also listed a daily bus to Thessaloniki, via Chania (1730hrs), leaving Kastelli at 1615hrs.

COMMERCIAL SHOPPING AREA It is tempting to write 'None', but Kastelli has a fascinating facility, not an old-fashioned market building, more an:
Agricultural Co-op Supermarket (*Tmr* 9B/C2)
Directions: From the Main Sq, turn down 'Castle Walls' road and, at the outset of the Old Castle Walls, keep straight on to the first crossroads. Here turn right and follow the road round to the side of the large building, which houses the supermarket, up on the left. To the right are some large storage tanks.

Don't be shy. Go in, climbing the inclined ramp on the nearside of the square, concrete edifice. Inside is an absolute Aladdin's cave of a supermarket - not quite Harrods, more the equivalent of a French out-of-town-shopping-centre. For Greece, this establishment sells an amazingly wide variety of goods at exceptionally reasonable prices. It opens mornings and evenings, and is even used by the old, black-clothed crones, who are to be observed wheeling about their trolleys with the best of them.

In fact, there are a number of establishments acclaiming their supermarket status but, more often than not, they are nothing more than glorified stores. These embrace a number spaced out along the High St, including a Supermarket (*Tmr* 43C3), the Mare Market (*Tmr* 43E3/4), as well as a couple of Butchers (*Tmr* 44C3 & 44D/E3/4), a number of Fish Shops (*Tmr* 45C3) and a Fruit & Veg Shop (*Tmr* 46C/D3/4), of which there are plenty of others in the High St. Edging the Main road bypass are a couple of more 'serious' Supermarkets (*Tmr* 43E4 & 43D4), the one furthest from the Bus Sq labelled the Agora Market.

Admittedly not unique, but of interest must be Kastelli's cottage industry of leather manufacturing. At the western end of the back street, Odhos Peridou, is a shop-cum-workshop (*Tmr* 56C3). A pair of men's sandals cost 1400-1500drs, whilst a pair of ladies sandals is priced at some 1200drs.

FERRY-BOATS The boats dock at the 2km distant Ferry-boat Quay. Schedules tend to be regarded, even by the Greeks, as highly unreliable, so they must be! Locals talk of at least two hours leeway, either side of the listed/quoted arrival and departure times. The major problem is that the ferry-boats have motored all the way round from Piraeus, via various Peloponnese mainland ports of call, as well as the islands of Kithira (Kythira) and Antikithira.

Ferry-boat timetable (Mid-season)

Day	Departure time	Ferry-boat	Ports/Islands of Call
Mon	2400hrs	Ionian	Kapsali(Kithira), Antikithira, Kastelli(Crete).
Thurs	2300hrs	Ionian	Kapsali(Kithira), Antikithira, Kastelli(Crete).
Fri	1500hrs	Ionian	Ag Pelagia(Kithira), Piraeus(M).
Sat	2230hrs	Ionian	Ag Pelagia(Kithira), Neapoli(M), Monemvassia(M), Piraeus(M).

One-way fares: Githion	to Kapsali (Kithira)	460drs;	duration	3hrs
	to Kastelli(Crete)	1850drs;		7hrs
	to Ag Pelagia (Kithira)	460drs;		2hrs
	to Neapoli(M)	780drs;		4hrs
	to Monemvassia(M)	1130drs;		6hrs
	to Piraeus(M)	290drs;		13hrs

FERRY-BOAT TICKET OFFICES
E Xyrouhakis (*Tmr* 47C/D3) Plateia Kastelliou   Tel 22655
Directions: On the west side of the Main Sq, in the same block as a Pharmacy.

The office represents the *CF Ionian*, and the excellent Minoan Lines' craft. The latter not only operate boats between Crete and the Greek mainland, but international ferries to Italy. The office doors open mornings and early evenings, even on Kastelli's night off (Wednesday), between circa 2030-2100hrs.

There is also an ANEK shipping line office (*Tmr* 49D/E3/4) on the right of the High St (*Main Sq behind one*).

HAIRDRESSERS A ladies hairdressers is situated on the right (*Main Rd behind one*) of the 'Hospital' St (*Tmr* D4), whilst there is a Unisex job, just to the east of Mare Market (*Tmr* 43E3/4), on the left of the High St.

MEDICAL CARE

Chemists & Pharmacies Apart from a pharmacy next door to the Main Sq ferry-boat ticket office (*Tmr* 47C/D3), there are a number spread about the town, including a couple (*Tmr* 50C3) on the left of the High St (*Main Sq behind one*), and another (*Tmr* 50D4) across the street from the Hospital.

Dentist (*Tmr* 57F3/4) Close by the junction of the main Chania road and the eastern end of the High St.

Hospital (*Tmr* 51C/D4) The inland side of the Main road bypass.

OTE (*Tmr* 52E/F3/4) The office is on the right of the main Chania road, and only opens weekdays, between 0730-1510hrs.

PETROL There are seven petrol stations on the Main road bypass, including a BP garage (*Tmr* 53D4).

PLACES OF INTEREST

Castle More the remains of the Venetian fortress walls, than a full-blooded fort. Unfortunately, what is left standing has, in recent years, been further invaded by the building of new apartments and an 'alley of scrap'. The Venetians secured their stronghold as the town was an important bishop's seat.

There were earlier Roman fortifications, Kastelli being the harbour for the hilltop settlement of:

Polyrinia The historic site is some 6km south of Kastelli, close by the modern-day hamlet of Polyrinia. There is a rumour of 'every other day' buses from Kastelli but... The most direct route is up the narrow lane alongside the OTE (*Tmr* 52E/F3/4), which passes through a couple of hamlets. The road terminates close to the *Polirinia Taverna*, whence splendid views and probably much needed refreshment. From the village it is about a twenty-minute hike to the widespread remains. Ancient Polyrinia dates back to the 8th century BC, and was in constant occupation over the centuries, being a fairly important Roman, Byzantine and Venetian encampment. The Church of the Ninety Nine Martyrs stands amidst the various archaeological fragments, and was probably constructed from bits and pieces of temples and fortifications of much earlier periods.

Another interesting way to reach the site, suitable for committed hikers, is to catch a bus from Kastelli to the end of the line, at Sirakari. This allows a 'Gorge' walk, from alongside a solitary church, which requires care in following the route of the path, and, in addition to the bus journey, takes about 2½ hours.

Museum The facility used to occupy a room of the Main Sq church-cum-clock tower and accompanying steps. Since the to-be-regretted removal of the clock tower and steps, the exhibits have been removed, I know not where. Apart from the small leather workshop, another industry of some interest (well to me, anyway) is the making of barrels, which takes place in a tall, decrepit building (*Tmr* 58C/D1/2) alongside 'Castle Walls' road, close to the waterfront.

POLICE Not so much a Police station, more a Customs house sited, on the Ferry-boat Quay.

POST OFFICE (*Tmr* 54D4) On the left-hand side of the main Chania road, east from the Bus Sq.

SPORTS FACILITIES Not a lot, but readers could try their hand at the Greek equivalent of snooker, in the two-table hall, just beyond the Commercial Bank (*Tmr* 38E3/4). Thinking about it, this is probably 'pool' - yet another American corruption of a worthy, 'why-not-leave-it-alone', British game. Incidentally, what was wrong with rounders?

TAXIS A taxi office (*Tmr* 55D3/4) borders the High Street side of Plateia Kastelliou, alongside which rank the cabs - until moved on by the police.

TRAVEL AGENTS & TOUR OFFICES Apart from E Xyrouhakis (*Tmr* 47C/D3 - *See* **Ferry-boat Ticket Offices, A To Z**), and a High St Travel Agent (*Tmr* 59D/E3/4), there is the:
General Tourist Agency (*Tmr* 37D/E3/4)   Tel 22980
Directions: The office is on the left-hand side of the High St (*Main Square behind one*).
     This business opened its doors in 1986 and is symptomatic of the increasing ground-swell of tourism that is, now, thundering towards the west of the island. The very helpful proprietor, Stefanos Rimantonakis, who speaks good English, is assisted by his 'American speaking' daughter, 'when I can afford to pay her'. They have connections with Sunny Tours of Chania. Although a travel agency, they also act as an unofficial information office and gladly supply details of accommodation, local events and timetables.

EXCURSIONS TO KASTELLI SURROUNDS
Excursion to Tigani Bay, Agria & Imeri Grabousa Islets Although there appears to be a bulldozed swathe to the northern end of the Grabousa (Grambousa) Peninsula, be assured the journey has to be completed on foot - and it is a shadeless hike. Why not catch a caique from the Ferry-boat Quay, at a cost of 1500drs per head.
     For those who must 'go walkies', it might well be best to obtain a lift to Kalyviani village located at the root of the finger of land. The path starts out by the village kafeneions, leads past a statue and church to advance up the east side of the peninsula's spiny range, prior to crossing over to the west side. Hereabouts allows views over a superb, narrow neck of almost white sand stopped off, at the far side, by an upstanding blob of rock. Beyond this can be seen the offshore islets of **Imeri** and **Agria**, and to the right of which is a startlingly turquoise blue lagoon - Tigani Bay. This is a walk of some 3½ hours there, and 3½ back! In common with Falasarna Beach, visitors must watch out for the blobs of tar scattered about the beach.

ROUTE FOURTEEN
To Falasarna (18km) The road proceeds west from Kastelli, across flat, threadbare countryside, planted with olive groves, past the turning off to **Kalyviani** and on to **Ag Georgios**. Here is another signpost to 'Ag Grabousa'. The next village, almost abutting Ag Georgios, is **Zerviana**, both through which the road climbs, in a southerly direction. Where Zerviana runs into Kamartses, it is possible to glance away to the right and catch a glimpse of a shore-driven shipwreck, in the angle of Kissamos Bay and

Grabousa Peninsula. Kamartses is little more than an extension of the previous settlements, and itself almost merges with **Lardas** (circa 9 ½km).

Away to the right is a double-roofed chapel, with a large number of startlingly white headstones in the form of a cross.

PLATANOS (circa 11½km from Kastelli) The outset of this large, spread out village is indicated by a petrol station, and a fork in the road. Coincidentally, Falasarna is signed along both routes! To the left are indicated a mini-market, *Rooms*, and the *Cafe Souvlaki*. Almost immediately there is a T-junction, with Falasarna indicated to the right, beyond which, after a few metres, is yet another fork with Sfinari to the left and Falasarna, once again, to the right. Alongside this junction is the *Cafeteria Disi*.

The Falasarna turning passes by *Rooms/Restaurant Zacharias* and, at the almost indistinguishable hamlet of **Kavousi**, a small chapel, on which is rather incongruously affixed a TV aerial. Almost immediately beyond the latter is the most impressive panorama over a long, narrowing plain edging a gentle bay, rimmed by a glorious sweep of sand. The lowland sustains massed olive groves, in amongst which are areas of intensive agriculture, with a concentration of plastic greenhouses at the broader, south end. To 'balance' the latter, the north sector supports an outcrop of buildings. The mellifluous tinkle of sheep and goat bells drifts across the countryside, as do the bees busily winging their way to and from the brightly coloured hives, all overlaid by the familiar smells of Greece - wild thyme, broom and oleander. In the sea's shallows are speckled the tiny, low islands, more rocky outcrops of **Petalia**, to the north, and **Koursapes**, to the south.

A serpentine, still metalled road snakes down the mountainside to a fork in the route, in amongst the heather. To the left is rather grandly signed 'Port' and to the right 'Falasarna'. It is noticeable from here that the great sweep of beach is, in actual fact, two sections, divided by a rocky outcrop. The 'Port' turning runs out at the south of the bay, close by a small chapel - a spot decidedly lacking in harbour facilities! The road to the right runs north, parallel to the sea-shore, and off which is the branch track to a flattened, unsurfaced car park area, from whence access to the beach is gained. The narrow plateau is about 30m directly above the wide expanse of sweeping sand and blue, blue sea. A steep goat track weaves down through huge, litter-covered, fallen rocks to the backshore. The raised plain was probably once the sea bottom, which explains the 'aggregate' look to the rocks. Apart from lacking any shade, or a Cantina for that matter, closer inspection reveals that the main beach is littered with blobs of tar, thus great care is needed when laying down clothes or a beach towel.

Continuing along the still metalled 'main' road passes by: a slip turning, up to the right, to *Ret* (Sic) *Rooms Stafis* (Tel 41480), where nice, en suite, double rooms are charged from about 2500drs and breakfast 300drs; another path to *Rooms To Let Golden Sun* (Tel 41485), where rather dormitory style double rooms cost from 2000drs; and, on the left, *Cafeteria/Rooms For Rent Kalami*.

Very close to the bluff, at the top end of this stretch, in amongst plastic greenhouses are: on the right, the *Aqua-Marine Rooms For Rent* (Tel 22003); to the left, the small, two storey *Falasarna Rooms*; and then a

Illustration 16 Crete centred on Kastelli

taverna, followed by another **Rooms** block. The last-mentioned is closer to the cliff-edge, so referred to as it is still necessary to climb down to what is now a wide, scrubbly backshore. Hereabouts are a series of small, grotty, sandy coves. Beyond this outcrop of development is a sign to an archaeological area, where the road finally becomes a track.

By following one's nose, through the customary olive tree groved Cretan countryside, on the left is an 'absolutely thrilling' pile of stones - the '25th Department of Antiquities, Falasarna Site'. The dig appears to be moribund. The unmade track continues on, through the equally commonplace, wild countryside of rocks, more olive trees, plastic agriculture and the occasional hillbilly homestead, to end up alongside the site. Even at second glance, this still fails to impress. But those who persevere and continue on into the shadow of a huge outcrop of rock, forming a stony bay with the peninsula, will locate quite a length of easily distinguishable walling. A small chapel has been forlornly sighted on this untamed moorland.

To the north, at the top of the peninsula, beneath the islet of Agria Grabousa, is **Imeri Grabousa islet**, once an almost impregnable pirates' lair, the raiders using an abandoned Venetian fort as their base (*See* **Excursions...**, **Kastelli**).

Out of the height of season months, very few daily visitors make the trek. Incidentally, the Falasarna tomato festival is a movable feast, usually held in July, but only celebrated when the tomatoes are ripe and harvested. Wild life hereabouts includes glorious, soaring eagles, and the more lowly, unwelcome mosquitoes.

ROUTE FIFTEEN
To Stomio, Chrysoskalitissa Nunnery, Elafonisi Beach & islets, to return via Elos (about 98km) Take **Route Fourteen** as far as **Platanos**, where fork left in the direction of Sfinari, through 'modern' Platanos. Hereabouts are a petrol filling station, a mini-market, and to the south of the settlement a water tap.

The moth-eaten, metalled road, the edges of which are scattered with oleander bushes, circuitously winds across a barren, wild mountainside, whence breathtakingly dramatic views down to the sea, deserted beaches and rocky outcrops. There are lovely prospects of serried, terraced hillsides to the north, as well as glimpses of still distant Falasarna Bay. At the outset, the dramatic coastline must be some ½km down below, but at about 4½km from Platanos the road descends towards the far side of the very long, flat, irregular bay of:

SFINARI (about 18km from Kastelli) The onset of the village is marked by the *Cafeteria/Rooms Theodorackis* (Tel 22153), built on a slight rise, on the left. The feeling that this is an area popular with German youth can only be heightened by the sign advertising 'Rooms 650DM', which 'translates' to a per head, basic room rate of 600drs, increasing to about 900drs. The patron, Antonio, and his wife are equally friendly, middle-aged and spherical. The patio is very attractively trellised with grape bearing vines but the remoteness has not depressed prices as 2 large coffees and a big slug of brandy cost 300drs.

From the cafeteria, the road narrows down past a taverna, a kafeneion, and the *Fidias Taverna* (Tel 22589), with signs in German and where a cell-like bed is priced at about 500drs per head.

Alongside the latter establishment is a backwards angled, unmade track, signed 'Restaurant/Bar Dilina. Fresh fishes in wonderful land near the beach. Camping this way 200m'. The lane initially threads its way through the backyards of various homesteads, clad in bougainvillea and surrounded by a scattering of amphoria. After about 200m there is a pleasantly ethnic *Rooms*, whilst close to a chapel is a concreted section, beyond which the going gets pretty rough and stony. The other side of a bridge over a summer-dry river-bed (alongside which was a wrecked, GB camper-van), keep to the left, away from the shore, and then swing right. The track finally emerges, alongside a fresh water trickle of a stream around which flutter dragonflies and butterflies, at the south end of:

Sfinari Beach The shoreline is an unprepossessing length of grey pebble in which is some similarly coloured sand. To the right (*Fsw*) is a bumpy back-shore track edged by rows of large plastic greenhouses. To the left is a single storey, 'prefabricated' taverna/cafe-bar, surrounded by an almost lawn-like swathe used as informal campsite, in the height of summer months. The mature trees that circle the 'green' make for a nicely shaded location. On the periphery is a fairly squalid toilet block. It appears that campers are allowed to pitch a tent free, as long as they patronise the taverna. (Immediately prior to the campsite, on the left, is a small chapel let into the hillside). The lady who runs the place can be most informative (in Greek) and narrates with gusto the scenes in Sfinari when the first motor car arrived, in 1964, on the then new road. 'Great excitement, we were all in the streets waving', she exclaims whilst taking off her apron and flapping it about as a demonstration. Her taverna used to be a fish weighing station for boats from North Africa. She explains that the villagers realise the lack of a really sandy shore 'is a bad thing for tourism', so they are considering building their own beach!

Sfinari might be considered a find, a place with 'a miles from anywhere' ambience, even if there is rather a lot of rubbish. Certainly it is more than likely to be popular with German bikers, than Thomson BPTs, and 'nudies' sunbathe at the left-hand end of the bay. This is without doubt quite a wild spot, about a twenty minute walk from the village. For visitors lucky enough to visit Crete in the grape picking season (September to October), Sfinari is one of the countless villages where the 'pressing' will be observed, taking place in the back of vans, trenches - in fact in any indent that can be lined with plastic.

Beyond Sfinari the road climbs past an outcrop of chestnut trees towards **Ano Sfinari**, a one donkey-dropping settlement wherein a baker. The route continues to ascend into the mountains, overlooking a beautiful, green flowering valley. Hereabouts the road switchbacks at the head of a ravine, continuing to climb (at least some 3½km from Sfinari) across an unmade section on the other side of the mountain. This section is subject to rock falls and varies in width, being quite broad in places. About 5½ km from Sfinari, the route cuts inland up on the side of a highly cultivated hillside.

Another kilometre on, the road starts to   descend, past *Tavern/Rooms Lefterias*, on the outskirts of:

KAMPOS (about 28km from Kastelli) The rather spread-out village straddles the hills, the road passing two simple bar/restaurants, in amongst the olive trees, a small kafeneion, and the *Restaurant Lefterias* in the small hilltop hamlet, as well as another kafeneion and a store.

Beyond Kampos the road continues to drop quite steeply through a water-rich area, before ascending again, beyond a bridge. In the middle of absolutely nowhere, on the left-hand side of the road, is a little cafe-bar, after which the metalled surface of the road runs out, there are captivating views, and into sight hoves a massive, cultivated plain, edging the sea. At a division of the ways, an acutely backwards angled turning is subject to a modern-day version of the 18th century Cornish wreckers craft (what is he on about?). Modern-day version...? Yes, instead of a lantern mounted reef, there is a sign pointing down the flinty track to 'The Monastery 15km. The Elafonisi Restaurant - fresh fish. Free Camping 2km'. A seascape spreads out to the right, well down below this point, as the track is still high on the mountainside. Frankly, it is best to ignore the siren calls of the signpost as there is no beach, and the whereabouts of the campsite is a mystery. There is a spaced out settlement and the *Cafe Uzeri* owned by Andrea, an old fellow who almost drags clients into his simple building. For those who are sidetracked, he serves most reasonably priced, if simple fare. Two beers, a Chania bottled lemonade, a nice little Greek salad (less the feta!), a very small plate of fish, and some fruit (a cross between apricots & peaches), cost 450drs... yes, 450drs. He advised us that an en suite double room in the   village cost (an expensive) 2000drs. Needless to say this is not the region of the Monastery, or Elafonisi!

Back at the main route, perhaps the only way to describe the scenery is as a layered cake, gently sloping to the sea's edge. The road surface becomes surfaced for the passage through **Keramoti**. This lofty section of the route allows stunning and attractive snapshot panoramas of the surrounding countryside and coastline, with the switchback, roller coasting road's surface alternating between surfaced and unmade, without rhyme or reason.

Amygdalokefali (36km from Kastelli) This part-deserted hamlet, possessing a kafeneion, is to one side and below the road. Hereabouts the route cuts inland over massively rolling mountains, sparsely covered with sage type brush. The next sign indicates **Simantiriana**, where the road starts a long descent but, being well inland, there are no sea views. The next hamlet of **Oavadiana** is quite large and set in chalky soil environs, after which the now metalled route progresses to:

KEFALI (43km from Kastelli) The village has a number of **Rooms**, including *Kefali Rooms*. Despite its remoteness, this is hardly an idyllic, away from it all little spot - as evidenced by the number of tourists present and the tally of signs (in German). For the delectation of the punters the *Taverna/Snackbar Panorama* cajoles 'Come and enjoy yourselves, out backsite of our shop with beautiful scenery while eating'. Well they would, wouldn't they? Opposite is a cafe bar/taverna and another catering giant is confusingly named the *Coffee Bar Elefnosis* - there goes that old wreckers lantern again.

Beyond Kefali, at last, in a densely wooded section, is the junction - straight on for Elos, whilst to the right is officially signed 'Chrysoskalitissa 11km', and informally indicated to 'Elafonisos' (Elafonisi). The road surface remains metalled, but only for a short stretch, and the route continues to steeply and windingly descend towards:

VATHI A tiny but swept-up, attractive village with a tree centre-stage of the almost circular square (How very Irish), surrounded by verdant, water-rich countryside. The settlement boasts a rather smart kafeneion, a Post Office and a shop sporting an old Singer Sewing Machine Company sign.

The next location, and larger than Vathi, through which the ever-falling, presently surfaced route gently winds, is **Plokamiana**. Further on the road, alternating between being surfaced and unmetalled, sweeps down to a summer-day, stony river bed, with a dusty roadway on both banks and a concrete block, way-station of a cafe-bar on the far side. The all-invasive, white dust present is due to a nearby stone crushing works, away to the right, on the edge of a wild, boulderous cove, with a large pebble shoreline - where isn't it rocky in this region? So much for supposedly sandy Stomio Bay! This gulf is followed by an equally boulderous, desolate, sharply in-letted coastline, prior to an 'outbreak' of civilisation in a rather God for-saken setting (I hope the nun will forgive this blasphemy). It is rather reminiscent of the wilder sections of the West coast of Ireland, on a very, very hot day. To the left is an ugly, white, concrete cubic village, whilst bordering the right of the track is an intrusive huddle of buildings. These include the *Cafe-bar Restaurant Golden Step* (Oh dear!). A sign to the right indicates 'Beach', passing the *Zima Restaurant,* and in which direction is the clearly visible:

Chrysoskalitissa Nunnery (53km from Kastelli) The current view of the magnificently located, dazzlingly white nunnery, built some 50m above and part overhanging a small, rocky inlet, has been rather spoilt by the tacky, haphazard, encircling constructions. The present-day building is not very old, but the site is purported to have been a religious location for centuries.
      The priory is supposed to have a golden stair-tread on one of the ninety steps that zig-zag past a wall mounted post box (I wonder how often collec-tions are made from this?), and a very welcome drinking water tap. This particular step is rumoured to only be visible to those who have not comm-itted a sin. I don't suppose it has been seen by many. A solitary, middle-aged, smiley nun oversees the nunnery, showing interested guests round the pretty chapel. It would be nice to think everyone left a *pourboire.*
      From the main terrace, a path leads up to a small room containing a wooden seated, one-person loo which appears to 'waste' into the sea below...! Whilst here the 'bathroom' allows lovely sea views with a rocky headland stretching away in the distance. To one side of the main structure

are a number of low buildings, including a quadrangle, some of which were obviously animal compounds in the more populated days of yore. It has to be admitted that the outbuildings are not nearly so out of place as they appear, when looking towards the nunnery.

To continue it is necessary to return to the main route and follow the sign-post 'Elafonisi 5km'. Only a few metres beyond the junction is a *Cafe-bar/ Ouzerie/Rooms*, beyond which the dusty, unmetalled road gently climbs and snakes between low scrub, some cultivated bits of land and a number of fairly large olive groves. Where the countryside becomes a moorland of granite and shrubs, there is a not-too distant mountainside, on the left, prior to descending through an incongruous pair of gates, past a taverna, on the left, prior to running out on:

Elafonisi Beach (60km from Kastelli) More a beautiful, idyllic, gorgeous sweep of sandy lagoon, than a beach enclosed, shallow turquoise blue seas, hemmed in by an offshore reef. Parts of the shore are lovely, if pale golden sand fringed by pink coral at the waters edge. Other sections are covered in a dense, coarse, short sea-grass.

Unfortunately this paradise of sand and sea has been well and truly discovered. As a result the backshore is scattered with a few camper-vans, one or two buses, and some 'wild' campers, in addition to the daily onrush of excursion coach visitors. The Chania bus advertises 'Still Deserted Beach'! It has to be admitted that the sheer size of the location can easily swallow up the present numbers. Two bamboo wind-break surrounded Can-tinas cope with the 'inner person' and one of them rents pedaloes (400drs per hour), sun-beds (200drs), and sun umbrellas (200drs). Fortunately, to date, there isn't any water-skiing. Despite the press of people, there is little rubbish, even if the bins provided do not appear to be regularly emptied. At about 1500hrs, the tour buses start their homeward trek.

It is interesting to note that a trip boat connects with Paleochora (on the nearby, south-west coast). Departures from Elafonisi take place at 1500 and 1700hrs, at a cost of 580drs. Incidentally, for those who feel energetic, it is possible to trek round to Paleochora, which perambulation allows spec-tacular views, as well as encompassing a couple of genuinely deserted bea-ches. It should be noted that it is difficult, in places, to search out the correct path, and a day should be allowed for the adventure.

Not far offshore is the stunning:
Elafonisi Islet A paradise of beach, on beach, on beach reached by wading across the warm, shallow, aquamarine waters of the lagoon. There is supposed to be a monument to Australian merchant men, drowned here when their ship foundered in 1907 - but I haven't seen it.

To save making the return journey back along the outward route, why not turn right at Kefali, along the metalled but dusty road that climbs towards Elos? Those who do should bear in mind that even the Greeks regard the amount of summer traffic as dangerous. Where a minor road branches off down a steep valley, to the village of **Perivolia**, there is a drinking water fountain. The winding, ascending route passes through the hill-hugging village of **Louhi** (some 18km from Elafonisi Beach), wherein lemon and chestnut trees, and beyond which is a totally incomprehensibly signed junction. Enough to write that it is necessary to keep to the right, for:

ELOS (27km from Kastelli) This very pretty village is the centre of the local chestnut industry, thus a chestnut festival is held every year, on the third Sunday of October. The main street winds down through Elos, past a cafe-bar, some kafeneions, a bakery, a small square, brimful of little tavernas, some cafe-bars, as well as 'Souvenirs - hand made' (Oh, goody), a petrol station, on the right, and a clinic.

The route continues to descend, past a stream, through massed chestnuts and deciduous trees, set in heather-clad hills, followed by low bush and scrub covered moorland. About 3km beyond Elos, the hillsides evince evidence of past fire damage, after which is a side turning, to the right, to **Strovles**. This is followed by the main road village of **Mili**. To the left is a track signed **Vlatos** and **Rogdia**, which settlements are on the almost parallel road that bypasses Elos. Hereabouts olive trees, with black nets draped around their base, shoulder aside the chestnut trees. A roadside taverna marks the onset of oleanders spaced along the 'kerbside', and the angle of descent lessens, to flatten out temporarily at **Koutsomatados** (about 15km from Kastelli).
  Beyond the latter village, the road dives into a gorge. Almost immediately, on the left, is Ag Sophia's Cave, noticeable by the chapel set high up on the mountainside and topped off with a man-made star. Steps ascend to the religious site, once inhabited by early man. The road hugs the rock face of the gorge, which is narrow in places. Prior to a small but awkward tunnel, with a left-hand dog-leg, there is a sensibly sited lay-by. Once through this hazard, the route ascends out of the gorge, allowing a glimpse of the distant sea, prior to:

TOPOLIA (12km from Kastelli) A very beautiful, busy, mountain village, the houses of which are hung with bougainvillea. The extremely winding High Street is bordered by a Post Office, on the right, and a baker, on the left, about where the thoroughfare widens out. There are various little shops and businesses, including a taxi firm and a fish/souvlaki taverna, on the left. Towards the northern outskirts there is a lovely fountain, followed by a couple of spectacular twists and turns in the road, beyond which is a rather pleasant church campanile clock tower.

The reasonably wide road, now very pleasantly chicanes down through olive groves to:-
VOULGAROU Not so much a village, more a dormitory 'town'. On the left is a newish petrol station, then a taxi service, a kafeneion, incredibly yet another garage, a large church and one more kafeneion.

POTAMIDA Within the village are 'clutched' four kafeneions, a very smartly signed *Strathakis Jujus and Restaurant*(!), and a modern church.

The now bumpy valley road runs alongside a river-bed, through groves of oranges and lemons, as well as olives, as far as **Kaloudiana**. This has a number of shops and stands close to the junction with the main Chania-Kastelli road.

ROUTE SIXTEEN
To Paleochora via Kandanos (82km) Proceed west out of Kastelli, along the main Chania road as far as Tavronitis. The immediate outskirts of Kastelli are the usual mishmash, with a fuel station on the right. Beyond the Sirikari turning is *Rooms*, on the left, and, about 1½km out, an 'Antika' Museum. This section of the road is rather winding. At some 5km, where the route is approximately one kilometre from the coast, a side road to the left leads to a *Restaurant/Rooms*. Beyond Kaloudiana, and the route to Elos, signposted Topolia, the road bridges a rather unsightly river-bed.

DRAPANIAS (5km from Kastelli) Apart from the signs to *Camping Mithimna* (*See* **The Accommodation, Kastelli Town**) and 'Private Parking near the beach'(!), there are a baker, a petrol station, another baker, and a kafeneion/taverna.

The next settlement is **Koleni,** wherein two petrol stations, a river-bed, and a kafeneion, after which the road starts the climb off the Kastelli plain. The old road is very windy and narrow, and crests the col at **Plakanola.** There are great views back over Kastelli and the Gulf of Kissamos. A new road is in the course of construction, 'most seriously' in the area of **Kalydonia** village (16km from Kastelli).

Back on the old road, from Plakanola, the road gradually descends to the inland turning for **Nochia,** from whence it commences to climb, again, past Kalydonia - a couple of kafeneions and a taverna - and badly fire-damaged hillsides to the main route crossroads of:

KOLIMBARI (18km from Kastelli) (Tel prefix 0824). Around this busy, messy junction are scattered a petrol station, taxi rank, a couple of cafe-bar/tavernas, a chemist, dentist and the *Hotel Rosemarie* (Class D, tel 22220). The latter certainly was run by a wartime resistance fighter, as testified by the faded newspaper clippings. All rooms are en suite, with a single starting at 1800drs and a double 2200drs.

The inland turning is confusingly signed to the distant hamlet of **Deliana,** rather than the more appropriate **Spilia.** In the area of the latter are: a 14th century church, with super frescoes; a large cave, in which is an amphitheatre; and further south, at **Episkopi,** one of the island's oldest churches.

The left-hand turning, signposted for the Orthodox Academy of Greece and the Monastery of Ghonia, leads to the main village. Some 30m from the Main road is *Rooms Restaurant Lefka*, on the right, followed by a sign for *Rooms*, to the left, *Furnished Rooms*, on the right, and *Peace & Friendship Furnish Studios*. These accommodation opportunities border the road, as does a large, messy 'grape factory', which parallels the sea-shore, prior to the main settlement.

The almost endless, shadeless, clean, entirely pebble beach, which stretches away to the right (*Fsw*) for some miles, is separated from Kolimbari High St by a single row of buildings. In fact all the way along are beguiling glimpses of the sea-shore. The village is well worth considering as an away-from-it-all base, as there are few, if any, concessions to tourism. The majority of visitors are Greeks visiting Ghonia Monastery, a short distance north of Kolimbari. This monastery was originally founded in the early 1600s, submitting to alterations in about 1880, despite which Turkish canon balls remain lodged in the outer walls.

Most facilities edge the High St, including: a Post Office; the *Aeolos Apartments* (Class C, tel 22203); the *Hotel Dimitra* (Class E, tel 22244), with en suite doubles from 2800drs; an OTE, over which is *Rooms* (Tel 22596); a baker, almost opposite the OTE; a taverna; a restaurant; and a small caique harbour. A few gift shops are scattered about the village, a result of the 'monastery trade'.

Rodopou Peninsula Those of an ambulatory frame of mind might well consider the 5½/6 hour, shadeless, round-hike from **Rodopou** village to Ag Ioannis Gionis Church, and back again.

The Chania road east of the Kolimbari crossroads, crosses a flat plain. The village of **Minothiana** (some 21km from Kastelli) marks the onset of some scattered hotels, fleshing out the seaward side of the route, with thick river-bed bamboos to the right. The once simple hamlets hereabouts are 'spreading out' a little and **Skotelonas** almost immediately follows the last settlement. The coast is a rather barren vista of allotments and smallholdings, as yet unbuilt on! The messy village of **Rapina** is in a state of development flux, with the strip between the backshore and the road still dominated by agriculture. But there is an *Olympic Hotel*, a couple of petrol stations and a cafe/pizzeria. Beyond the side turning inland to **Vouves**, the ribbon development runs into **Kamisiana**, proud possessor of a BP petrol station, a mini-market, taverna, the awfully smart holiday apartments *Okastallia Suites*, the signposted *Rita Studios*, and a supermarket. As a matter of interest, the atypical *Studios*, plonked down on the scrubbly, unattractive coastal strip, is close to a smallholding, specialising in geese, and a very large scrapyard. The unappealing, pebble shore is steep and kelpy. Need one say more?

TAVRONITIS (22½km from Kastelli) A busy little place with shops, a 'Video Club Original', a petrol station and a clinic. The sea-shore is still some 200m away, across a bamboo scrubland littered with a collection of smallholdings. The Travel Club of Upminster is present, a villa set-up is signed down a track in the direction of the sea, and there is the *Pension Ireni*. At Tavronitis is the cross-island road for Paleochora.

Initially, on the left is a broad, summer-dry river-bed being quarried for gravel. The route ascends slowly, weaving through fields of olives, oranges, lemons and vines, past the small village of **Neriana** (29km from Kastelli). From this area, the road, the surface of which deteriorates to its former poor condition, advances up a very green valley past bamboos, a petrol station and several war memorials.

VOUKOLIES (31km from Kastelli) This extensive village has a large Main Square and a busy High St, shaded in places by chestnut trees. The Square spawns an expansive Saturday market and 'possesses' some rather dirty and smelly public lavatories. There are all sorts of shops and businesses, a baker, kafeneions, bars, a petrol station, Post Office, chemist and a school.

The road winds steeply upwards, the vegetation becoming less dense *en route* to **Dromonero**, where the bus drivers often pop out, drop down a few steps and refresh themselves at the village fountain. Despite the road's surface being rather suspect, the civil engineers are obviously 'girding their loins' to resurface and realign the route. The pretty, tree lined, kafeneion-or-two village of **Kakopetros** clings to the side of a towering, bare granite mountain, fissured with deep valleys. Between Kakopetros and **Mesavlia** (48km from Kastelli), the road slowly descends through more cultivated surrounds, which alternate with sandy gorse, heather and wild thyme, spread in amongst which are haphazardly dotted about clusters of coloured beehives. Towards the south of this section, the highway rims a ravine.

This is an area where the older men still sport the traditional Cretan costume, as every day apparel. Despite the evidence of fire-damaged hillsides, on the left, chestnut trees continue to proliferate. The thoroughfare winds along the old road, through two-donkey dropping **Floria**, wherein a couple of cafe-bars, to the long descent in the direction of:

KANDANOS (61km from Kastelli) The large village, which makes no concessions to tourism, lies in a bowl of land surrounded by mountains. It is an uneasy mix of agriculture and industry, with a large wine factory prominent. The High St is tree lined and edged by a number of kafeneions, a Post Office, an OTE and, at the far side, a clinic. The modernity of Kandanos is due to the unchappish Germans destroying the town, during the Second World War. Their excuse is that they found the local populace difficult to control and reluctant to give up their 'unsporting', resistance activities. A monument commemorates the valiant citizens efforts.

The next village is pretty **Plemeniana**, surrounded by lovely, mature olive groves and having a restaurant, followed by **Kallithea** and **Kakodiki**. Despite a sign indicating **Vlithias**, there don't seem to be any houses - perhaps it was also razed to the ground by our German friends. Next along is **Kalamos**, then a sign for invisible **Lygia** and a turning off towards Souyia. Towns and villages on either side of this area of the route are famed for their various Byzantine churches, frescoes and paintings.

The road now makes a craggy, ravine descent over a river-bed bridge, around which the route is under reconstruction. Thus, for the time being, the old, olive tree lined road is still in use, all the way to the mature gum tree edged outskirts of:

PALEOCHORA (Palaiokhora, Kastelli Selinou)
A seaside holiday village & port.

GENERAL (Illustration 17) Tel prefix 0823. Paleochora is one of those few locations that can be said to have benefited from the advantages of tourism. What! Shock, horror! Well, the holiday-makers have, without doubt, inexorably squeezed out the 'great unwashed', who until a few years ago dominated this resort. That is not to say that some dross doesn't occasionally turn up, mainly British and Italian. When they do, cafe-bar owners tend to ask for money 'up-front'. Perhaps the undesirables of ten years ago are now returning as respectable visitors? In actual fact the bulk of the tourists are now Austrian singles and Swedish family groups. The season does not end until mid-October. Incidentally the weekends bring a flood of Greeks, mainly Chanians.

Paleochora was a fishing village, as evidenced by the disproportionately large harbour installation at the lighthouse end of the peninsula. Here the small fleet rides out the worst weather, but many fishermen now content themselves as proprietors of apartments and pensions.

The eastern Esplanade borders a neat, but initially rocky sea's edge. At the south end is the Ferry-boat Quay (*Tmr* 1E5), at the north end an extremely pebbly beach. The western Esplanade edges probably one of the finest beaches on Crete, with a huge, gently curving, large, tree fringed, sandy shore, bordering the impressive, distantly cliff edged bay. Nowadays only a comparatively small number tent in the backshore grove, in some dozen or so plastic-covered shelters, of every size and description.

Keep an eye open for the handless, sightless villager, probably an ex-fisherman, who still walks his pelican around the village. The reason for the loss of limbs? It is more than likely he was injured when 'tempting' the fish out of the water, with sticks of dynamite!

Rather conveniently, and pleasantly, there are old-fashioned, cast-iron drinking water fountains spaced about throughout the town.

ARRIVAL BY BUS The bus thunders along the High St, which runs down the middle of the village, through rows of cement faced buildings. These whitewashed rectangles, arranged on a grid layout, are progressively squeezed in between the two seashores. At the south end, the peninsula narrows down to the bulbous, lighthouse-mounted headland that encompasses the harbour proper, some way beyond the main town. The buses pull up (*Tmr* 2D4/5) on the High St, towards the lower part of Paleochora, in amongst a welter of bars, restaurants, tavernas and souvenir shops.

Left (*Chania behind one*) is the eastern shore and Ferry-boat Quay, right is the western beach, and back along the High St is the centre (if it can be called that) of the village.

ARRIVAL BY FERRY The small, south coast ferries, which link Souyia, Ag Roumeli, Loutro and Chora Sfakion, dock at the equally small, eastern Esplanade Ferry-boat Quay (*Tmr* 1E5). *See* **Excursions To Paleochora Surrounds** for the Gavdos island connection.

THE ACCOMMODATION & EATING OUT

The Accommodation There is a plethora of *Rooms*, as there are hotels, but most of the latter are 'dedicated' to the package tourists. In general terms, accommodation to the east of the High St is more characterful, that to the west is more expensive, being biased towards organised holidays. The local populace do not hesitate to offer their Rooms, as soon as travellers disembark from bus or ferry, but it can be difficult to locate a bed. When one is found, the average price for a double room with an en suite

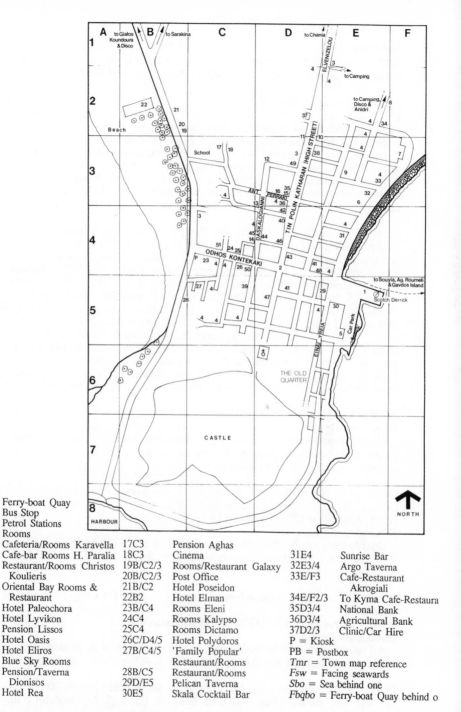

E5	Ferry-boat Quay		
D4/5	Bus Stop		
	Petrol Stations		
	Rooms		
E5/6	Cafeteria/Rooms Karavella	17C3	Pension Aghas
E3/4	Cafe-bar Rooms H. Paralia	18C3	Cinema
F3	Restaurant/Rooms Christos	19B/C2/3	Rooms/Restaurant Galaxy
	Koulieris	20B/C2/3	Post Office
E/F2	Oriental Bay Rooms &	21B/C2	Hotel Poseidon
	Restaurant	22B2	Hotel Elman
E3	Hotel Paleochora	23B/C4	Rooms Eleni
D/E2/3	Hotel Lyvikon	24C4	Rooms Kalypso
D2/3	Pension Lissos	25C4	Rooms Dictamo
C/D3	Hotel Oasis	26C/D4/5	Hotel Polydoros
C/D3/4	Hotel Eliros	27B/C4/5	'Family Popular'
C/D4	Blue Sky Rooms		Restaurant/Rooms
D3/4	Pension/Taverna	28B/C5	Restaurant/Rooms
	Dionisos	29D/E5	Pelican Taverna
D3/4	Hotel Rea	30E5	Skala Cocktail Bar

31E4	Sunrise Bar
32E3/4	Argo Taverna
33E/F3	Cafe-Restaurant
	Akrogiali
34E/F2/3	To Kyma Cafe-Restaura
35D3/4	National Bank
36D3/4	Agricultural Bank
37D2/3	Clinic/Car Hire
P = Kiosk	
PB = Postbox	
Tmr = Town map reference	
Fsw = Facing seawards	
Sbo = Sea behind one	
Fbqbo = Ferry-boat Quay behind o	

Illustration 17 Paleochora

bathroom is about 2500drs. The 'convenient and good' goes quickly, the further out, and not so modern, may stay available for some time. There are quite a lot of opportunities in the Old Quarter, one of the best of which is:

Pension Spamados (*Tmr* D/E6/7)   Tel 41197
Directions: Hug the Old Quarter waterfront, keeping an eye open for a small boat, dry-land stored in an alley. Or follow the signs along Einai Yreia St, in the direction of the *Hotel Aris*, to beyond a possibly 'dead' leather sandal workshop.
    The building, noticeable for the very neat exterior stonework, over looks the sea. Friendly John Lougiakis, from Paleochora, and his lovely wife, from Corfu, own this extremely 'swept-up', very nicely located Pension. Ground-floor double rooms, sharing the bathroom, are charged at 2200drs, whilst first-floor doubles cost 2500drs, with en suite bathrooms.

Other accommodation, close to the Ferry-boat Quay, is available at *Cafeteria/ Rooms Karavella* (*Tmr* 5E5/6) and *Rooms* (*Tmr* 4D/E5). Various alternatives are spaced out along the eastern Esplanade, which include: *Rooms* (*Tmr* 4D/E4/ 5); *Rooms* (*Tmr* 4E4); *Cafe-bar H Paralia* (*Tmr* 6E3/4, tel 41495); *Rooms* (*Tmr* 4E/F3); *Restaurant/Rooms Christos Koulieris* (*Tmr* 7F3); and *Oriental Bay Rooms* (*& Restaurant*) (*Tmr* 8E/F2). One street back and parallel to the eastern Esplanade (more or less) (*Ferry-boat Quay behind one*) are: the Class E *Hotel Paleochora* (*Tmr* 9E3, tel 41023), where a single room, sharing a bathroom, costs 1000drs, a double, sharing, costs 2000drs, and a double en suite 3000drs; and a row of *Rooms* (*Tmr* 4E3, 4E2/3 & 4E2). The *Lyvikon* (*Tmr* 10D/E 2/3), a lovely, old style hotel, edging the right-hand side (*Harbour behind one*) of the High St, was established in 1935 but is now thoroughly 'dead', the ground floor being occupied by a wholesaler of plumbers' fittings. Across the road is the:

Pension Lissos (*Tmr* 11D2/3) (Class C) 12 E Venizelou   Tel 42166
Directions: As above.
    Double rooms only, those sharing a bathroom costing 1550drs, & those with an en suite bathroom 2260drs, prices increasing, respectively, to 1810drs & 2620drs (1st July-30th September).

On the same side of the road, further south, are *Rooms* (*Tmr* 3D3) above a Fina Garage. Down the side-street next along, and on the right, is the:
Hotel Oasis (*Tmr* 12C/D3) (Class E) Daskalogianni   Tel 41328
Directions: As above.
    Double rooms only, those sharing a bathroom cost 1710drs & those with an en suite bathroom 2510drs, increasing, respectively, to 1810drs & 2710drs (1st July-31st Aug).

Continuing round the acute left-hand corner of Odhos Daskalogianni, and on the right is the:
Pension Eliros (*Tmr* 13C/D3/4) (Class B) Daskalogianni   Tel 41348
Directions: As above.
    All rooms have en suite bathrooms, with a single priced at 2000drs & a double 3325drs, increasing, respectively, to 2330drs & 4000drs (1st April-30th Sept).

Further south, still on Odhos Daskalogianni, are *Rooms* (*Tmr* 4C/D4), followed by *Blue Sky Rooms* (*Tmr* 14C/D4). Back on the High St, probably the best accommodation-cum-eating house value in town is the:

Pension/Taverna Dionisos (*Tmr* 15D3/4) (Class D) Tin Polin Katharan Tel 41243
Directions: As above and on the right (*Facing the harbour*).
   Always popular and offering good, clean, reasonably priced rooms.

Hotel Rea (*Tmr* 16D3/4) (Class C) Ant Perraki   Tel 41307
Directions: Down the side-street from *Dionisos,* and on the right.
   All rooms have en suite bathrooms, with a single room charged at 2800drs &
a double 3500drs.

Across the street are **Rooms** (*Tmr* 4D3/4).

Continuing west along Odhos Ant Perraki, advances to a T-junction. To the left,
across the street, is **Rooms** (*Tmr* 4C3/4), whilst to the right, and keeping straight
on (not following the street round to the left), leads to the:
Pension Aghas (*Tmr* 17C3) (Class B)   Tel 41525
Directions: As above, on the left across the way from the Cinema.
   All rooms have en suite bathrooms, with singles costing 2500drs & doubles
3500drs, increasing, respectively, to 3500drs & 4540drs (1st June-30th Sept).

Back at the last junction, and turning towards the western sea-shore passes a
large school and playground. At the Esplanade, turning right (*Fsw*) leads past
Rooms/Restaurant Galaxy (*Tmr* 19B/C2/3), next door to which is the Post Office
and, further on, the:
Hotel Poseidon (*Tmr* 21B/C2) (Class E)   Tel 41374
Directions: As above.
   Double rooms only, with those sharing bathrooms priced at 2300drs, & those
with an en suite bathroom costing 2800drs.

Diagonally across the Esplanade is the *Hotel Elman* (*Tmr* 22B2), more furnished
apartments. Turning back and proceeding south along the western Esplanade
progresses to the turning up the main east-west street, Odhos Kontekaki, which
forms a crossroad with the High St, where the buses 'terminus'. Selecting this
street gently climbs past *Rooms Eleni* (*Tmr* 23B/C4) on the right (*Sbo*); a couple
of **Rooms** (*Tmr* 4C4/5), straddling a lane, and on the right; *Rooms Kalypso*
(*Tmr* 24C4) on the left; *Rooms Dictamo* (*Tmr* 25C4), also on the left; and the:

Hotel Polydoros (*Tmr* 26C/D4/5) (Class C)   Tel 41068
Directions: As above, and on the right.
   All rooms have en suite bathrooms, a single charged at 2000drs, a double
3100drs, which prices increase to 3100drs & 4100drs (26th June-5th Sept).
A pair of lanes to the south of Odhos Kontekaki sally forth into a warren of
streets and accommodation, including **Rooms** (*Tmr* 4C5, 4C5, 4C5 & 4C4/5), as
well as the 'Family Popular' *Restaurant/Rooms* (*Tmr* 27B/C4/5) and, back on the
Esplanade, *Restaurant/Rooms* (*Tmr* 28B/C5), just beyond the *Seagull Bar.*

Camping
Paleochora Camping   Tel 41068
Directions: Bordering the eastern beach, and accessible from the beach
backshore, the Anidri road, or from the north end of the Chania road.
   The site offers a toilet and shower block, with hot water, a snackbar,
mini-market, and restaurant.

The Eating Out There are numerous establishments, some already
mentioned under **The Accommodation**. Convenient for the Ferry-boat Quay
is the:

Pelican Cafe-Restaurant (*Tmr* 29D/E5)

Directions: At the outset of the eastern Esplanade, almost directly opposite the Ferry-boat Quay.

Convenient the Pelican may be, but it is expensive, with a bottle of water charged at 120drs, bread 20drs and most of the dishes being that 10-50drs more expensive than the 'norm'. For instance, a bottle of beer is charged at 100drs, a Greek salad 220drs, and a 'special' salad 350drs. This 'special' is a very annoying habit and the Greeks should never have been introduced to the word. It must be admitted that nowhere in town is inexpensive, now that package tourists rule - with some restaurants accepting credit cards. Back to the *Pelican*, from this general musing, despite the waiter running on occasions, service borders around about a state of quietly controlled chaos. Mind you, the establishment does get busy. The best bet is an unlisted potato omelette, cooked with ham and cheese, costing a reasonable 250drs. Other prices include: tzatziki 160drs; cucumber/tomato salad 190drs; green beans 220drs; chicken 350drs; lamb 480drs; moussaka 400drs; meat balls 370drs; pork or lamb chops 700drs; and swordfish 750drs. Only 'superior' retsinas are available. Building work in progress in 1986, was still the order of the day in 1989, if now around the car park corner, and tends to make the situation noisy, and dusty.

Whilst in the area, I shall make a plug for the:

Skala Cocktail Bar (*Tmr* 30E5)

Directions: Across from the *Pelican* and to the right (*Fsw*) of the square.

Don't be put off by the smart appearance and 'Cocktail' portion of the title, this is more a pleasant, clean, well-run cafe-bar, with a relaxing attitude. A Nes meh ghala costs a reasonable 80drs. Plug? Well, I have to own up that English Donna (once from Winchester and the young lady of the house, being married to Dimitri the owner) is the sister of a girlfriend (in the old-fashioned sense) of my stepson! For those who want a complete genealogical chart, please apply to...

My own choice of eateries would settle on either:

Taverna Dionisos (*Tmr* 15D3/4)

Directions: Half-way up the High St, on the left (*Harbour behind one*).

A family run concern which, over the years, has offered friendly service, coupled with acceptably priced meals. As a result, the taverna fills up quite quickly in the evening - so arrive early in order to guarantee a table. All the daily cooked dishes are 'on view', in the large kitchen. *Bon appetite,*
or the:

Restaurant Galaxy (*Tmr* 19B/C2/3)

Directions: Borders the north end of the western Esplanade.

This extremely reasonably priced establishment has a large and varied menu: Nescafe and milk 53drs; bread & cover charge 15drs; various soups 150drs; tomato salad 120drs; Greek salad 220drs; a 3 egg omelette 150drs; spaghetti 200drs; stuffed tomatoes 370drs; French chicken 250drs; moussaka 400drs; meatballs in lemon sauce 370drs; ragout of rabbit 450drs; pork & celery in lemon sauce 295drs; pork fillet 480drs; string beans 200drs; briam 220drs; and an Amstel beer 94drs, but no kortaki retsina.

The eastern Esplanade hosts, from the Ferry-boat Quay end, the *Sunrise Bar* (*Tmr* 31E4), the *Cafe-bar H Paralia* (*Tmr* 6E3/4), the *Argo Taverna* (*Tmr* 32E3/4), the *Cafe Restaurant Akrogiali* (*Tmr* 33E/F3), and the *To Kyma Cafe Restaurant* (*Tmr* 34E/F2/3).

THE A TO Z OF USEFUL INFORMATION

BANKS The National Bank of Greece (*Tmr* 35D3/4), which accepts credit cards and Eurocheques, and the Agricultural Bank (*Tmr* 36D3/4), which effects exchange facilities, are located, close by each other, on the left of the High St (*Harbour behind one*). Naturally the Travel Agents offer exchange facilities.

BEACHES Most relevant information has been disseminated in the Introduction and various preambles. It only needs to be added that the western Beach sports sun-beds/umbrellas (300drs each), and surfboards are for hire, close by the *Hotel Elman*. Both beaches benefit from the provision of showers. *See* **Ferry-boats, A To Z** for the Elafonisi Beach connection.

BICYCLE, SCOOTER & CAR HIRE There are (at least) three outfits, which include a Car Hire business alongside the High St Clinic (*Tmr* 37D2/3), **Kydon Rent A Car** (*Tmr* 38D/E2/3), a few metres to the south and the other side of the road, as well as **Paleochora Moto-Rent** (*Tmr* 39C/D4/5) in a side-street towards the Castle. The latter outfit rents scooters at a daily rate of 1500drs, whilst a sample of the charges for cars is as follows: one day from 1600/3535drs to 2200/4440drs, plus per kilometre costs of between 22/27drs; three days 18500/23500drs to 30000/42000drs. And do not forget the iniquitous deposit charges! This drain on the wallet is 'once removed' if payment is made with a credit card.

BOOKSELLERS The High St spawns a Kiosk (*Tmr* 40D4) which sells overseas newspapers and paperbacks. There is also the rumour of a second-hand bookshop, somewhere.

BREAD SHOPS There are two Bakers (*Tmr* 41D5 & 41D/E4/5), both east of the High St, quite close to the Bus stop.

BUSES The present arrangement retains that chaotic charm of yesteryear, with the buses still pulling up to 'terminus' on the crossroads of the High St, Odhos Tin Polin Katharan and Kontekaki St.

Bus timetable
The timetable is screwed to the wall of a convenient taverna wall edging Kontekaki St, on the Ferry-boat Quay side.

Paleochora to Chania
Daily   0700, 1100, 1200, 1330, 1530, 1700hrs
Return journey
Daily   0830, 0900, 1030, 1200, 1430, 1700hrs
One-way fare 550drs; duration 2½ hours.

CINEMA (*Tmr* 18C3) The management puts on a daily, open-air show in the summer months. There really isn't any need to give directions as signboards are displayed on the pavements - but it is opposite the *Pension Aghas*, towards the western Esplanade. Most of the expatriates appear to troop off to watch.

COMMERCIAL SHOPPING AREA None, but the wide diversity of tourists has ensured that there are sufficient shops and general stores, which keep the usual hours. Supplies in the supermarket type shops are reasonably priced, even if those of the western Esplanade Periptero (*Tmr* P4B/C) are not, with a can of Sprite lemonade costing 80drs.

DISCOS One on each of the beach backshores, both at the northern end.

FERRY-BOATS The port hosts the Paleochora to Souyia and Ag Roumeli passenger ferry-boat connection, as well as the Gavdos (Gavdhos) island link, and the Elafonisi daily excursion, on the *Captain Monossos*. On Thursdays the Ag Roumeli craft is the *Samaria*, a small but 'perfectly formed' car ferry. The schedule is posted on the 'Bus timetable taverna wall' and is available from the Municipal Tourist office (*Tmr* 42D3/4).

Ferry-boat timetable (Mid-season)

Day	Departure time	Ports/Islands of Call
Daily	0900hrs	Elafonisi.
	1100hrs	Elafonisi.
	1600hrs	Elafonisi.
Mon, Thurs	0730hrs	Souyia, Gavdos island.+
	1230hrs	Souyia, Ag Roumeli.*
Tues, Wed, Fri, Sat, & Sun	0830hrs	Souyia, Ag Roumeli.

One-way fares: Paleochora			
to Souyia	440drs;	duration	1hr
to Ag Roumeli	440drs;	"	2hrs
to Elafonisi	580drs;	"	1hr
to Gavdos	1100drs;	"	6hrs

* *See* **Ag Roumeli** for the link-up between Ag Roumeli, Loutro & Chora Sfakion.
+ This voyage is dependent upon the weather and sea state being calm!
Note: Schedules approximately halve outside of the mid-May - mid-September months.

MEDICAL CARE
Chemists & Pharmacies (*Tmr* 43D4) Borders the High St, close to the Bus Stop.
Clinic (*Tmr* 37D2/3) At the north end of the High St, on the right.
Dentists (*Tmr* 44C/D4) On Daskalogianni St.
Doctors (*Tmr* 45C/D4) Across the road from the Dentist. Surgery hours are weekdays, between 0830-1400hrs & 1730-2030hrs.

MUNICIPAL TOURIST OFFICE (*Tmr* 42D3/4) This is truly a shining example to all such similar offices. For a start it opens daily, not weekdays only, between 0900-1400hrs & 1600-2100hrs. Secondly the young German lady, Gabriella, is most helpful, has been in office for eight years and, fortunately for all visitors to Paleochora, intends to continue in the job. Thirdly the quality of the information available, including a map, as well as boat & bus timetables, does credit to what is only a small town facility.

OTE (*Tmr* 46D4) Perhaps surprisingly, there is one open weekdays, between 0730-1510hrs.
The *Restaurant/Rooms* (*Tmr* 28B/C5), next door to the *Seagull Bar*, has a sign nailed to tree advising 'Public Telephone International Calls All Day, All Hours'.

PETROL There are at least three filling stations (*Tmr* 3D/E1/2, 3D3 & 3B/C3/4) spaced throughout the town.

PLACES OF INTEREST
Castle (*Tmr* C7) Named Kastelli Selinou by the Venetians, who built the fort about 1280, and after which title the port was alternatively known. The Turks

(who else?) destroyed the castle and it was never rebuilt. See **Excursions to Paleochora Surrounds.**

POLICE
Port (*Tmr* 47C/D5) To the south of the 'bus terminus' crossroads, rather out of site of the quayside, and straddled by cafes.
Town (*Tmr* 48D/E4/5) A rather poky office bordering Odhos Kontekaki.

POST OFFICE (*Tmr* 20B/C2/3) Rather out-of-the-way, towards the north end of the western Esplanade.

TELEPHONE NUMBERS & ADDRESSES
Interkreta Travel(*Tmr* 50C/D4/5) 4, Kontekaki	Tel.41393
Police (*Tmr* 48D/E4/5)	Tel 41111
Syvia Travel (*Tmr* 51C4) 40 Kontekaki	Tel 41198

TOILETS A flat-roofed building on the eastern shore Esplanade, a few blocks north of the *Pelican Taverna* (*Tmr* 29D/E5). Only for use in dire emergencies, as it is usually left in an 'eye-watering' state.

TRAVEL AGENTS & TOUR OFFICES There are at least three travel agents, all of which seem pretty swept-up and include **Paleochora Travel** (*Tmr* 49D3), on the High St, **Interkreta** (*Tmr* 50C/D4/5), and **Syvia Travel** (*Tmr* 51C4), the latter two on Odhos Kontekaki. The last mentioned, for instance, offers 'boat booking & ticketing, organised excursions, accommodation in Rooms, hotels & studio apartments, money exchange, sea sports, rent-a-car & bicycle, student fares & youth reductions', and opens daily, between 0800-1330 & 1700-2100hrs.

EXCURSIONS TO PALEOCHORA SURROUNDS Paleochora must be
one of the finest Cretan centres for excursions and trips. Possibilities include: Elafonisi, Souyia and Ag Roumeli by boat; coastal walks to the west (Gialos & Elafonisi) and the east (Lissos - about 3hrs; Souyia - about 4½hrs), as well as to inland hamlets and villages. A popular venue is **Azogires** which has a monastery museum.

Excursion to Gavdos (Gavdhos) island The south coast ferry-boats voyage to the island of Gavdos, some 50km south of the 'mainland', and about a six hour journey, weather permitting. The island has some simple *Rooms* and beach shelters, as well as about forty or so inhabitants, but it is back to the 'roots'. Those wishing to get away from it all certainly should consider this as a most attractive option.

Boats dock at the very small port of **Karabe**, which has a couple of kafeneion/tavernas and a few *Rooms*. The capital, if that is not too grand a word for the falling-down huddle of **Kastri**, is about an hour's trudge from the port. There is the island's Post Office-cum-OTE-cum-shop-cum-cafe-bar, and one or two *Rooms*. Close to Kastri is a now defunct prison, once used to house political undesirables - rather reminiscent of Psara island. There are beaches at **Potamos**, **Sarakinikos**, **Korfos** and **Tripiti**, as well as hamlets at **Ambelos** and **Vatsiana**. It would indeed be strange if Gavdos were not food and water short. Most supplies have to be shipped in, except for locally killed meat (on a when-and-if basis) and some vegetables. Visitors should ensure they bring along any necessities, must note it is pretty quiet, that if landed on a Monday it will be impossible to get off until Thursday (and so on), and inclement weather stops all and any sailings!

ROUTE SEVENTEEN

To Souyia via Maleme (90km) Take the north coast Chania road to Tavronitis, and then continue on towards:

MALEME (26km from Kastelli) Tel prefix 0821. Almost immediately beyond Tavronitis is the Maleme airstrip. It was from here that the German crack parachutists made their breakout, at the outset of the Battle of Crete, in May 1941. The supreme irony was that the Commanding Officer of the defendin Allied forces knew where the Germans were going to concentrate their attack - due to the Enigma code breaking machine. But this vital intelligence could not be used in case the Germans realised their security had been infiltrated! Nowadays the occasional, rather desultory Greek soldier mans the fences, whilst German tourists now invade the *Hotel Chandris*, and the encircling, extensive holiday development.

The resultant Second World War carnage is memorialised by a:
German Cemetery The turning up to the site is alongside the chic *Sunny Suites Hotel*, which is 'as awfully nice', as it's name suggests, and possesses a cubic-shaped swimming pool.
    The narrow road winds the 1½km to the beautifully kept, if rather stark, hillside location. The road pulls up alongside a number of low buildings, which include spotlessly clean toilets, a *Cafe-bar 107* (that's probably Hill 107...), and an information board. The latter tell's it from the other side's point of view, which is natural enough, I suppose. The chilling facts are that the Germans lost some 6,580 men, of which number 4,465 are buried in the cemetery. Perhaps it might be worth recalling that a total of 15,700 of our chaps 'called it a day'. The marble headstone slabs are set down flat in a sea of ice-daisies, with a few, low flowering bushes and trees breaking up the rather bleak outlook. By a strange quirk of fate, until recently the caretaker was one George Psychoundakis, who, incongruously, during the Second World War, was one of the major island 'players' in the Allied guerilla warfare waged against the occupying German forces. With the guidance of his mentor, Patrick Leigh Fermor, George Psychoundakis wrote the *The Cretan Runner*. This book is the moving story of Crete's involvement in the struggle, written from a partisan's point of view - a must for anyone interested in the period. George has now retired, living quietly in nearby Tavronitis.
    Maleme village offers the *Pension Electra*, a cafeteria, a petrol station-cum-*Hotel Mike*, the *Hotel Kastro Pool Bar*, a police station, a clinic, Rent-A-Car & Motorbike, a tourist office/scooter hire outfit, followed by *Rooms*, the *Hotel Albatross*, butting on to the Main road, a newspaper shop, the side turning up to **Xamoudochori** (and on to Souyia), another petrol station, *Rooms*, the *Pension Stamatis*, *Rooms*, and *Rooms Pirgos*.

By taking the Xamoudochori turning it is possible to proceed, via the hamlets and villages of **Zounaki**, **Nea Roumata**, **Prases**, where the church has a couple of imposing husband and wife busts, **Epanochori**, which has a cafe-bar, and is set down in massive mountainsides, thinly covered with olive trees, **Kampanos**, wherein a comparatively large number of donkeys, followed by the junction-of-the-ways. The turning to the right is for Paleochora and left is for Souyia. At **Monio** there is running water, *Rooms* and a taverna. The track then edges a wide, boulderous, summer-dry river-bed, some 3km from:

SOUYIA (Sougia, Soughia)
A seaside way-station port.

Tel prefix 0823. There are two daily buses from Chania, at 0700 & 1430hrs. Sundays there are three, at 0700, 1430 & 0730hrs.

The Ferry-boat Quay is some 250m away to the right (*Fsw*), beyond the end of the beach. Being linked in to the south coast ferry-boat carousel, Souyia enjoys daily links with Paleochora, Ag Roumeli, and thus on to Loutro and Chora Sfakion, as well as a twice weekly connection with Gavdos island (*See* **Excursions To Paleochora Surrounds**).

Ferry-boat timetable (Mid-season)

Day	Departure time	Ports/Islands of Call
Mon, Thurs	0830hrs	Souyia, Gavdos island. +
	1110hrs	Paleochora.
	1320hrs	Ag Roumeli.*
	1900hrs	Paleochora.
	2100hrs	Paleochora.
Tues, Wed, Fri	0930hrs	Ag Roumeli.*
Sat & Sun	1730hrs	Paleochora.

One-way fares: Souyia			
	to Ag Roumeli	440drs; duration 1hr.
	to Paleochora	440drs;	1hr.
	to Gavdos	1100drs;	5hrs.

* See **Ag Roumeli** for the link-up between Ag Roumeli, Loutro & Chora Sfakion.
+ This voyage is dependent upon the weather and sea state being calm!
Note: Schedules approximately halve outside of the mid-May - mid-September months.

The spaced out, disjointed scattering of Souyia edges a rather lifeless, great sweep of pebble beach rimming a shadeless bay. Shadeless that is apart from a tamarisk tree lined, metalled track which edges the backshore to the right (*Fsw*). In amongst the trees are some comparatively long-stay tenters and camper-vans, whose sojourn is made the more comfortable by the provision of a couple of beach showers, where the trees peter out.
    From the junction of the approach road with the backshore, to the right leads past the *Lotos Cafe-bar*, where prices are probably 5drs more expensive than other Souyia establishments. Incidentally sample charges are: bacon & eggs 150drs; special omelettes 190drs; tzatziki 130drs; Greek coffee 50drs; Nes meh ghala 65drs. Up against the backshore is a Periptero, whilst next along from the *Lotos* is the rather down-at-the-heel *Nikos Restaurant*, with tables and chairs shaded by the backshore tamarisk trees. The next building has a *Rooms & Cafe-bar*, beyond which the trees run out.

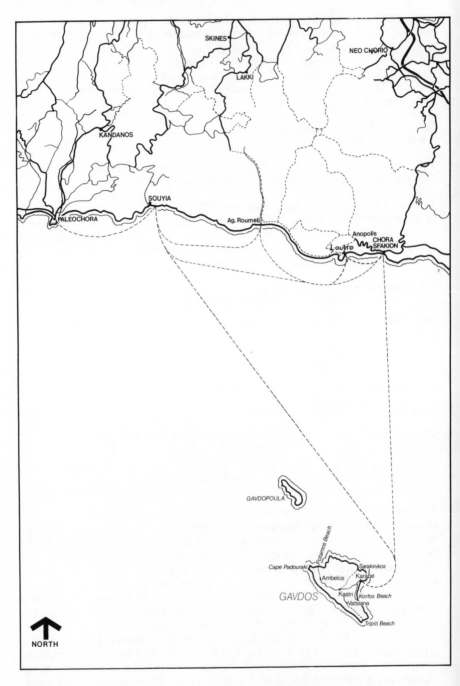

Illustration 18 South-west coast & Gavdos island

A small church is followed by a factory of sorts, and then the nice, tidy *Zorba's Rooms*, where an en suite double room costs 2500drs a night, rising to 3000drs for the height of season months. To the left of the junction, and also tree shaded, are two side-by-side tavernas, with **Rooms**, and *Rooms Cafe-bar Maria* (Tel 51358), beyond which is yet another building in the course of construction, followed by a summer-dry river-bed. This side of Souyia has quite an infrastructure, with a mix of old and new buildings, some even fitted with sun-blinds, stretching back for two or three blocks, and in amongst which is *Filoxenia Rooms*. With the backshore behind one, and proceeding up the 'High St', there is the usual litter of 'dead' deep-freezers lying about, as well as a Mini-market, quite possibly run by a bit-of-a-bandit, on the right, as there is a track. This latter is signed 'To the Tourist office', parallels the backshore and wanders in amongst various buildings, which include the *Restaurant Bar Platanos*, *Rooms for Rent Lissos*, *Rooms Vagelis* and *Cafe Pizzeria Breakfast Paradissos*, *Rooms for Rent* (Tel 51359). Turning left (*High St behind one*), along the referred to river-bed, advances to the Tourist office. The staff are warily helpful, hand out timetables, as well as transacting exchange and Eurocheque dealings, and are open daily, between 0930-1300hrs & 1700-2030hrs. Continuing north along the High St passes by the *Restaurant Anchorage*, a small cafe-bar, **Rooms**, the *Hotel/Restaurant-bar Pikilassos* (Tel 51242), and a village store. Towards the outskirts are the *Rooms Elenakis*, the *Stekkie Cafe-bar*, which has all the appearance of being a rock music joint, the *Hotel Irtakina*, and *Rooms Ilias Tzatzimakis*.

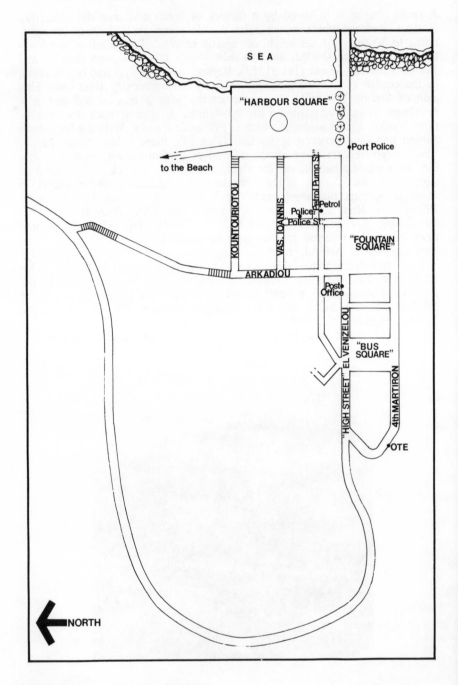

Illustration 19 Ag Galini

7 AGIA GALINI (Ayia Galini)

Look-alike for a Cornish fishing village; masses of villa tourists

GENERAL (Illustration 19) Tel prefix 0832. The years of constant development and exploitation have been good for the pockets of the locals. The reverse side of the coin is that the inexorable growth in tourism has despoiled the native charm, squeezing out any residual Cretan characteristics and thoroughly desanitising the place of the unique, uncapturable 'essence of Greece'. Just as guests at a Hilton Hotel could be anywhere in the world, well almost, so with Ag Galini. In fact if one was transported here blindfolded, and asked to make a snap decision as to the location, a snap response might well be one of the Spanish Costa's, and all this without even a presentable beach!

The village is sandwiched in a narrow, constricted defile. This has resulted in most development being either alteration of existing buildings or their replacement by new structures. These are now stacked up either side of the one and only road (in or out). Very little of the original, old-world, fishing village charm of Ag Galini has been retained. There are no 'Places of Interest' to view, anywhere, not even a Venetian or Turkish fountain. No, I forgot, on the path round to the beach are some caves, now sealed off, which were used by the Germans during the Second World War as machine gun nests.

The Main road snakes steeply down the 'canyon' along which the village is layered, prior to spilling out on to the very large Harbour Square. In the middle of this concrete plateia are railings surrounding a small fountain, which is not a Venetian, or a Turkish relic, more a modern, rather pathetic dribble. As advised, the whole village borders the Main road/High St, which is almost entirely true, but there are a few lanes and streets that both branch off and run parallel to this thoroughfare.

From the top, the High St winds and zig-zags down to the Harbour Square, passing on the way down: a turning off to the right, which bends back to parallel the Main road, forming the far side of the 'Bus' and the 'Fountain' Squares; the Bus Sq, on the right, across the way from which are two lanes, on the left, one angling acutely back up the hillside, the other, half-left, which also parallels the High St and runs all the way down to the Harbour Sq; a narrow lane to the right; Fountain Sq, to the right, across the road from which is a lateral side-street that tracks across the previously referred to left-hand, parallel lane, then past the top end of two more lanes, that also drop down to the Harbour Sq, before breaking into steps and clambering the hill, to rejoin the Main road, some half-way up its length; and off the bottom nearside of the Fountain Sq, another lateral street off to the left, which cuts across the first two of the left-hand parallel lanes; after which the High St descends to the emerge at the right-hand side of the Harbour Sq.

To give a snapshot view of the village, all that is necessary, is to proceed to the Harbour Sq. Standing there, with one's back to the sea, and swivelling around in an anti-clockwise direction, reveals the following: on the right, edging the far corner of the Plateia and raised up on stilts, is a red fuel tank for the fishing boats; the smart, new path round to the Beach; *Zorba's Roof Garden*, with a jazz club in the basement, the *Hotel Aktaeon* above, and the *Hotel Acropole* to the right; the steep steps down from Odhos Kountouriotou, on the left of which is the *Restaurant Barbosos*, above which is the *Hotel Selena*, and alongside which, and still swinging left, is the *Paradiso Bar*, then the steps down from Odhos Vas Ionnis; a 'pack' of *Bo Bar/Whispers Bar/Restaurant Onar Roof Garden*, alongside the *Restaurant Fivos*, followed, at   ground level, by a Souvenir Gift shop; 'Petrol Pump' St - well that's my pet name for it, as I know no other, and there is a pair of petrol pumps rather incongruously edging the lane; a block incorporating the *Restaurant Pizzeria*, with the *Hotel Soulia* above, both on the corner of the High St, Odhos El Venizelou. On the left-hand side (*Sbo*) of the High St is the Port police office above a Clinic, with the left-hand side of the Square bordered by the fairly massive 'ramparts' of the fishing boat quay wall, on which are a some Public toilets. Phew!

ARRIVAL BY BUS The Bus Sq is on the outskirts of the 'core of the village', alongside Odhos El Venizelou. On the south, far side of the Bus Sq is the *Hotel Ikaros*.

THE ACCOMMODATION & EATING OUT
The Accommodation Apartments, hotels, pensions and **Rooms** line the Main road, all the way down to the Harbour Sq. I do not think I have seen as much accommodation in any one village, but most of the beds are block-booked by package holiday firms. The charges made by the hotels in Ag Galini are sensitive to tourist fluctuations and a shortage of visitors results in prices plummeting, even in the height of season. Most establishments are uninterested in 'one-night' stands. **Rooms** are not much cheaper than the less expensive hotels and, due to the almost inexhaustible number of places, I have only listed a few of the possibilities.

Hotel Ikaros (Class D) 23, 4 Martiron   Tel 91270
Directions: On the far, south side of the Bus Sq.
   The small number of buses that arrive and depart do not cause an unsociable amount of noise, and the first bus of the day does not start-up until 0645hrs! Not the most modern of hotels but nice and clean, with a pleasant owner and, possibly, a resident priest! All rooms have to share the bathrooms, with a single charged at 1200drs & a double 1500drs, which prices increase, respectively, to 1400drs & 1700drs (1st July-15th Sept).

Hotel Creta Sun (Class D) 4th Martiron   Tel 91123
Directions: The right-hand street that parallels the High St, continues on from the far side of the Bus Sq towards the waterfront. The hotel is on the right.
   All rooms have en suite bathrooms, with a single priced at 1535drs & a double 1810drs, increasing to 1810drs & 2435drs (1st July-30th Sept).

Opposite the *Creta* is *Pela's Rooms*, whilst back on the High St/Bus Sq, on the other side of the High St is the:
Hotel Moderno (Class E)   Tel 91387
Directions: As above, but not as modern as the title would suggest!
   Single rooms from 1600drs & doubles 2000drs.

The *Restaurant Megalonissos*, a few paces down the High St from the Bus Sq and on the right, has some interesting if not particularly inexpensive accommodation, for which *See* **The Eating Out**. For those prepared to climb back out of the village there are any amount of pickings, one of the nicest of which is the:

Knossos Rooms (Class A)   Tel 91302
Directions: On the left (*Sbo*), about half-way up the hill and towered over by a smart block of apartments, the *Hotel Erofill*, and *Rockas Restaurant*, all to the rear of the *Knossos*.
A very nice, modern pension owned and run by a surprisingly homely, most polite, middle-aged couple, who could as well be imagined running a hilltop smallholding. The best rooms are the upper storey bedrooms and an almost luxurious double room, with en suite bathroom, costs from 2500drs.

Across the road is *Manolis Rooms*, whilst a little further up the road, on the right, is the pleasantly clean *Rooms Michael* (Tel 91315). Here singles are charged from 1500drs & doubles 2000drs.

Aktaeon Hotel (Class E) 4 Kountouriotou   Tel 91208
Directions: From the Bus Sq proceed down the High St, towards the seafront, past: *Rooms Manos*, on the right; *Rooms*, on the right and next door to a Bakery; the Post Office, and *Hotel Festos*, both on the left. Then turn left along Odhos Arkadiou past: the *Hotel Korali*, on the left; *Rooms Ariadne*, on the right; *Rooms Maria*, on the right, beyond the first side street; then the second side street; and on the left the hotels *Candia* and *Daedulus*, opposite which is the third of the side streets. Turn along this and the Aktaeon is on the right, close to the steps down to the Harbour Sq.
Run by a very pleasant landlady, who is prone to massaging the official rates, in an upwards direction, by some 100/200drs per night! Single rooms, with an en suite bathroom, are charged at 2000drs, a double room sharing the bathroom 2100drs, and a double, with en suite bathroom, 2300drs.

The description of the route to the *Aktaeon* has drawn attention to a number of the countless accommodation opportunities. For instance, opposite the Baker, on the Main road, is the house of an old lady who charges 1500drs for an acceptable double room with a balcony, which price increases to 1975drs, at the height of the season. Around on Odhos Arkadiou, *Rooms Maria* is a good choice where a double room, sharing the bathroom, is charged at 1900drs, with guaranteed hot water, all day. On the outskirts of Ag Galini, at the top of the hill, beside the Main road and with magnificent views over the sea, are a choice of hotels including the:

Hotel Adonis (Class C)   Tel 91333
Directions: As above.
All bedrooms have en suite bathrooms. A single room costs 2650drs & a double room is priced at 3700drs.

Hotel Minos (Class D)   Tel 91292
Directions: As above.
A single room, sharing, costs 1500drs & a double room, en suite 2000drs.

and the:
Hotel Idi (Class D)   Tel 91152
Directions: As above.

Only en suite double rooms, costing 2000drs, and increasing to 2500drs (1st July-31st Oct).

Camping
Camping Ag Galini   Tel 91386
Directions: The site is some 2km north-east along the coast and is signed with a board from the beach.
A well facilitated site. The per person charge is 400drs with 250drs for a tent.

The Eating Out The majority of restaurants edge the town side of the Harbour Square or line both sides of the pedestrian way Odhos Vas Ionnis, the second street to the left (*Fsw*) of and parallel to the High St. Between the High St and Vas Ionnis is the 'Petrol Pump' St, along which are scattered one or two eateries and souvlaki pita snackbars.

Kafeneion Sinantisis
Directions: On the left-hand side of the 'crossroads' along 'Police St', with the High St behind one.
It is very pleasing to be able to report that, amongst all this glitz, there is a traditional kafeneion - such a refreshing change to the 'cocktail bar-this' and 'rock bar-that'. Two Nes meh ghala and an ouzo, with a plate of nuts, cost 190drs. - "Dear girl, that's less than a cocktail at the 'Club Adultery'"!

Of the selection of dining opportunities edging Odhos Vas Ionnis, the most highly recommended is *Cafe Restaurant Greenwich Village*, across the way from a Butcher. Perhaps the proximity of one of the primary sources of supply has something to with the plaudits. Generally, the press of tourist clients has, had the predictable effect on the various eateries, where above average prices are charged, for below average offerings.
An unexpected, unusual possibility is the:

Restaurant Horiatis
Directions: Across the other side of the High St from the upper end of the Bus Sq, close to Biggi's Bikes.
It has to be admitted that the owner, the establishment, and the staff exude an expensive, self-satisfied, rather precious air, but when the alternatives are, in the main, purveyors of 'galley food', I know where I will park my seat. It is nice to be able to advise that the service and attention matches the auguries - it is slick, swift and attentive. The owner is a smooth, middle-aged, well set-up, rather lecherous chap who insists on showing each and every client the evenings goodies. This is not such a bad thing as there aren't any menus! The attractive looking dishes are pre-prepared and finished off in the microwave. Yes, the microwave... A meal, for two, of 2 plates of smoked ham, baked potato & tomato (750drs each), open wine (apo varelli, or from the barrel, and an interesting little number, with a rather urinal look about it, 300drs), and hunks of toasted bread (no charge), cost 1800drs.

Also in this area, just down from the Bus Sq, moving towards the sea and on the right, is the:
Restaurant Megalinissos
Directions: As above.
A popular breakfast spot where a Nes costs 70drs and an Amstel 120drs. They also offer accommodation and a double room, with en suite bathroom and the use of a kitchen, is charged at 2800drs.

The *Cafe Stelios*, edging Fountain Sq, offers loukoumades. Amongst other Ag Galini delights, I suppose it would be remiss of me not to mention *Georges Pub*, which has a 'Happy Hour' and serves cocktails of the evening, such as 'Football Fan', at a cost of 250drs. This hang-out edges the High St, up from the Bus Sq.

THE A TO Z OF USEFUL INFORMATION

BANKS Despite the amount of tourist money swilling about the resort, there is only a **National Bank** change office, in Police St. This opens daily, in the summer months, between 0900-1400hrs &1700-2200hrs. The innumerable Tour offices effect exchange, and don't forget the Post Office.

BEACHES The concrete path, that tracks along the cliff face for the five to ten minute walk round to the beach, starts out from the north-east of the Harbour Sq. It has been tidied up and straightened out. Despite this, it is still necessary to drop down on to and cross a small stretch of pebble shoreline, prior to climbing up, round and down to the nearside of the beach. In all the realignment, it is good to see that the old, wartime machine gun nests have been left *in situ*. Without doubt they are probably the most interesting thing about Ag Galini.(You bitch you).

The first eighty metres or so of the already narrow beach is reduced, even further, by the intrusion of various backshore businesses. These include the *Restaurant Bar Dionyssos*, *Katies Place*, a beach bar, and the *Sirocco* discotheque. During the day the disco doubles as a beach bar, opening up the loud pedal at 2200hrs. Another 50m on is the *Restaurant Bar Costas*.

The messy shore is sand interspersed with slate grey shingle and a mix of various size pebbles, some large, which extend beneath the water's surface. The foreshore serpentines on past a bridge spanning a river trickling into the sea. It is thereabouts that access can be made to the Campsite.

Sunbathers tend to pile up the pebbles in semicircular walls to form sun-traps/ wind breaks. Sun-beds, pedaloes and windsurfers spice up the attractions of the beach, further complemented by 'sea taxis' plying for hire. These ferry clients to more far-flung alternatives,   such as Preveli Beach, to the west, and Matala, to the the east. In fact a series of long bays curves all the way round to Kokkinos Pyrgos and scenically the distant view is magnificent, with the Gulf of Messara edged by an eastern landmass.

BICYCLE, SCOOTER & CAR HIRE Most of the Tour offices offer car hire. In addition there are one or two 'specialist' firms, such as *Galini Rent A Car*, across the street from the Post Office. Of the scooter hire businesses, prominent is **Biggi's Bikes** opposite the Bus Sq.

BOOKSELLERS On Odhos Vas Ionnis, opposite the *Restaurant Libyan Sea*, is a foreign language newspaper shop selling popular English books and newspapers, as well as guides and maps.

BREAD SHOPS A Bakery edges the High St, across from the Post Office.

BUSES As detailed previously, the Bus office and terminus is on a square, to one side of the High St.

Bus timetable (Mid-season)
Ag Galini to Iraklion
Daily   0800, 0930, 1030, 1215, 1315, 1500, 1630, 1830, 1945hrs.

Return journey
Daily   0630, 0730, 0830, 1000, 1100, 1215, 1400, 1600, 1730hrs.
One-way fare: 550drs; duration 2½hrs; distance 78km.

Ag Galini to Rethymnon
Daily   0645, 1030, 1200, 1430, 1600, 1830hrs.
Return journey
Daily   0645, 0900, 1030, 1415, 1700hrs.
One-way fare: 410drs; duration 1½hrs; distance 61km.

COMMERCIAL SHOPPING AREA None, which is not surprising in a village of this size, but a number of shops serve most needs and   requirements. These include Butchers, a few Mini-markets, one rather   tatty Fruit & Vegetable shop, on the High St, 'up' the road from the Post Office, and another more 'swept-up' Fruit,Vegetable & Drinks store, opposite the petrol pumps, as well as many gift and souvenir shops. Adjacent to the Police station is a Periptero.

DISCO/COCKTAIL BARS Yes. 'Petrol Pump' boasts the *Blue Bar*, a cocktail haunt, and the beach sports a couple of discos, which at least keeps the thumping, ear splitting sounds to a muffled and   distant echo. Incidentally the cliff walk round to the beach is illuminated at night, possibly to save losing, with any sort of regularity, the occasional client, now and then!

HAIRDRESSERS Soula's Hairdressing is located in a basement, on the far side of Bus Sq.

MEDICAL CARE A Pharmacy lurks close to the Harbour Sq end of the High St, and there is a Clinic on the right-hand side of the Harbour Sq, beneath the office of the Port police.

OTE The building is on Odhos 4 Martiron. This is accessed either up the High St from the Bus Sq, and round to the left at the first turning to the left, or up the lane from the south-west corner of Bus Sq, which loops round to rejoin the High St. Open weekdays only, between 0730-1510hrs.

PETROL In the next street parallel to the High St, at the top end.

POLICE
Port On the right (*Fsw*) of the Harbour Sq.
Town On the side lane off the High St, at about the Harbour side of Fountain Sq, that laterally crosses to make a junction with Odhos Vas Ionnis.

POST OFFICE On the left of the High St, close to Fountain Sq.

TAXIS When available, they rank beneath the spreading trees on the right of the Harbour Square, as well as opposite the Bus Sq.

TOILETS There is a public lavatory block, up the flight of steps that leads to the curving, rather massive sea wall, just along from the Police station. Modern they may be, but the facilities are very primitive and smelly. The gentlemens is open-air, with the urinals fixed at a toe-stretching height, whilst the ladies, only just separated from the men's, are 'squatties'.

TRAVEL AGENTS Simply lots and lots of them, in fact nearly as many as there are restaurants, offering any number of 'goodies'.

ROUTE EIGHTEEN
To Lendas & on to Kali Limenes via Phaestos, Ag Triada, Matala and
Gortyna (a minimum of 65km) After rounding the mountains to the east
of Ag Galini, the very large Messara Plain unfolds below. The nearside of
the landscape looks, to all intents, as if it were a flood plain, an illusion
created by the massed, shiny plastic greenhouses glinting in the sunlight.
Closer inspection reveals an appallingly squalid situation, with the greenhouses and their surrounds resembling a polythene shanty town. The pity is
that the authorities do not make the farmers clear up the old, windblown,
dirty brown sheets of shredded plastic that flap in the breeze and lay
scattered all over the countryside.

From the Timbaki road a backward angled turning, alongside the *Disco
Space*, traverses disgustingly messy scenery on the way to:
KOKKINOS PYRGOS (13km from Ag Galini) Tel prefix 0892. A sprawling, threadbare seaside village, with a few spindly trees, some bamboos
and the occasional, obligatory (also threadbare) donkey. It has been extensively cleaned up over recent years, but is still subject to defacement from
waste polythene sheeting blown in from the Messara Plain.
   The road fringes the waterfront, from one end to the other. An insigni-
ficant caique mole divides the seafront into shingly sand to the right (*Fsw*),
and rocks to the left. Behind the mole is a small repair boatyard. The road
runs out alongside a fishing boat quay at the top of the settlement, to the
right of which is another stretch of beach. The shorelines, to either flank of
the fishing boat quay, possess backshore showers.
   Progressing through the village passes: *Restaurant Rooms Umbrella*;
Apartments Akti Stella; a fish taverna; *VIPS Music Pub*; *Hotel Libyian Sea*
(Class B, tel 51621), where all rooms have en suite bathrooms, a single room
costing 2200drs & a double 2600drs; *Hotel El Greco* (Class E, tel 51182), with
singles sharing priced at 1500drs, a double sharing 1800drs & a double room,
with en suite bathroom, 2200drs; and the *Hotel Filipos* (Class B, tel 52002),
where rates are about the same as the *Libyian*.

Beyond the junction of Kokkinos Pyrgos and the main road, is a Greek Air
Force base, followed by mountain-to-mountain olive groves *en route* to:
TIMBAKI (14km from Ag Galini) Tel prefix 0892. A very busy, agricultural town, with no concessions to tourism. There are a few hotels, including the *Ag Georgios* (Class C, tel 51678), and the *Pension Stella*, as well as
such delights as Disco Magic and Video Club The Champ As befits a place
of this size, also present are a bank, an OTE and a petrol station. The dusty
sprawl is augmented by an Army camp and concrete works.

From Timbaki, the Mires road plunges back into a countryside of plastic
greenhouses and olives. Most of the peasants are donkey-borne (a phrase
that is acceptable as long as the typesetter gets it right!). Some 4km on is a
sign for the *Pension Margit*, beyond which is a turning off to Vori, the
proud possessor of the Cretan Ethnology Museum. A side road from the
Mires road advances across a much prettier landscape, devoid of plastic, to:

Phaestos (21km from Ag Galini) A splendidly situated Minoan site, well-placed on a shadeless hillside overlooking part of the Messara Plain. It was largely excavated by the Italians. Serious digging commenced in 1900, and has continued, on and off, to the present-day. To the layman the ruins might prove to be confusing, there being little 'imaginative', above ground reconstruction - in direct contrast to Knossos. Purists regard Phaestos as classical restoration and Knossos as having experienced the equivalent of archaeological rape.

The excavations are open daily, between 0800-1900hrs, and on Sundays, between 0800-1700hrs. It is possible to purchase inadequate guides (550drs) from the ticket booth staff, and entrance costs 300drs. The car and coach park may well 'sport' a few natives, dressed in Cretan costume, selling various goodies, and begging.

For a small treat, and to avoid the stream of Phaestos excursion coaches, from the parking space take the Matala road and, after some 200m, the first right-hand fork for the 2km drive to:

Agia Triada The road terminates at a cul-de-sac of an irregular vehicle park. This is on the side of a hill, at the foot of which spreads the small, tree shaded Minoan site, named after an adjacent Byzantine church. The excavations revealed a royal palace, believed to have been closely linked with Phaestos. The gates open daily, between 0845- 1500hrs, except on Sundays, when the hours are 0900-1300hrs. Admission costs 200drs.

It is impracticable to continue on as the plain to the west is taken up by an airfield.

Back on the road between Phaestos and the Mires/Matala junction, an attractive roadside chapel is passed, whereabouts there is the option to turn off to the right, along a chalky, unmade road to the agricultural village of:

KAMILARI (25km from Ag Galini) Archaeologically famous for the Minoan tomb of Tholos, there is a surprising amount of accommodation. For instance, in addition to the *Pension Psiloritis*, *Pension Anna* (Tel 51876) and *Pension Phaestias*, there is the unlikely *Hotel Oasis* (Class E, tel 42217). Here all the rooms have en suite bathrooms, with singles starting off at 1070drs & doubles 1980drs, increasing to 1130drs & 2020drs (16th May-30 June) and 1200drs & 2100drs (1st July-10th Oct).

At the far side of the settlement is *Rooms Ovgora* and Rent Bikes Kamilari - 'Special Price'. Travellers should note that the signposting, in and around this area, is poor and confusing, so be warned and make frequent enquiries, as even some of the locals are not sure! From Kamilari, a rough track makes off towards the west and the small, hillbilly settlement of:

KALAMAKI (29km from Ag Galini) It is rather a surprise to come across this resort in the almost deserted, out-of-the-way location. The raw simplicity of the past has been replaced by a more worldly-wise, if still rather wild-west ambiance. Despite Kalamaki growing and filling out considerably, it still can only boast a beaten earth 'Square' and 'High St'. But now that selected package tourists have arrived, it will only be a matter of time before tarmacadam also arrives!

The regularly spaced buildings, in amongst which are some unlovely concrete-box homes, as well as a few sophisticated, Spanish Costa-like apartments and hotels, are set in low, almost saucer-shaped hillsides radiating out from the backshore sand dunes. The long, gently curving bay, that still hints of wildness, is edged by shelving biscuit rock along its length, but there is a pleasant, sandy midshore section with a fine, sharp sand-cum-tiny pebble foreshore. A beach sign declares 'Keep the Clearness' and a few rather tired arethemusa trees have been planted along the edge of the dunes, to the left (*Fsw*).

The approach is bordered by: the neo Spanish-villa style *Hotel Phillar-homenie*, **Rooms**, *Rooms Nossos*, *Rooms Galakios*, the *Hotel Ilios* and *Hotel Maria*. Around the Square are several vehicle hire firms, the *Taverna Kreti* and *Rooms Market*. Bordering the short 'High St', linking the Square with the backshore, are the *Restaurant Pub Skorfios/Rooms Galaxy*, and, on the right, *Rooms Psiloritis* in a rather smart, three storey building, to the side of the original *Cafe-Bar Vangelis*. A 'Main Sq' double room, sharing a bathroom, costs from 1200drs, whilst one of the smarter establishments, with an en suite bathroom, charges from 2200drs. A two seater, automatic Honda is priced at about 1400drs a day.

Returning to Kamilari allows a turning to the right in the direction of the Mires to Matala road. Once again to the right at that junction, close to a water fountain, heads towards the coast. The road passes through **Pitsidia**, where the accommodation includes *Rooms Agari*, *Rooms Maranta*, and *Kalenteridis*, where rooms have the use of a kitchen.

Half-way to Matala is a track off to the right, the first of two, this one running out on the reverse side of the dunes that back:

Komos Beach A lovely, wide sweep of sand, backed by an upward sweep of sand on which are planted arethemusa trees. At the far, left-hand end of the beach is a beach-bar overlooked by a chapel up on a cliff. The foreshore has quite a lot of angled biscuit rock and, to the right, the dunes give way to very low cliffs.

Apart from the beach, the really outstanding thing about the location is the substantial, interesting looking archaeological site. Due to the general lack of regard and bezazz, this must be Roman remains. I cannot leave that snide insinuation on the record without the rider that Komos may well have been the Minoan port for Phaestos.

The next track off the Main road, almost amongst the onset of the Matala glitz, is signed for the *Taverna/Restaurant Mystical View*, which is perched on the top edge of a high cliff. The location allows superb views out over the bay, all the way from Matala, in the south, via the offshore **Paximadia island**, past the headland of Kokkinos Pyrgos, round to the north, as far as Ag Galini, the latter with the distant Kedros Mountains as a perfect backdrop.

A multitude of hoardings at some considerable distance heralds the approach to:

MATALA (31km from Ag Galini) Tel prefix 0892. The road narrows down and descends on to a low, mountain edged, tapering plain to roll along to the holiday resort. The approach passes by a superabundance of apartments, hotels, villas, guest houses and *Rooms*, prior to the short right-hand turning up to *Matala Camping*, as well as signs for the beach and the OTE. Opposite this junction is a launderette and hereabouts the High St starts to take shape. On the right is the 'out-of-town' car parking.

Progressing towards the hub of the place leaves a motorbike hire firm on the right, as is the *Bambou Sands Hotel*, opposite which is the large, three storey *Hotel Zafira*, with a *Rooms* annexe, and a taverna on the right. To the left is a 'suburban' street, the 'accommodation alley' of the village, being absolutely packed with guest-houses - similar to Torquay! Well, not really. On the corner of the side street is a Rent Bikes firm and a well stocked Bookshop selling international newspapers. Next along are some timely reminders of the Greece of old - several little chapels, in between which are spaced some not so evocative cafe-bars and the Festos Rent A Car Tourist office. Alongside the latter is a short lane to the right, allowing a glimpse of the sea and the beach, across the terraces of the *Panoramic Restaurant* and the *Lions Pub*. There is a giro souvlaki counter, close by the *Lion*, and a periptero on the corner of the lane.

Hereabouts the dark confines of the High St open out and spill on to the glaring daylight of the large Main Square, in the middle of which is plonked down a building. The perimeter of this Square is chock-a-block with services and supplies, including two Tourist offices, opening seven days a week, and offering book swap, currency exchange, excursions, tours, wheels hire, boat trips and useful information. The right-hand edge of the Main Sq parallels the backshore of the narrow shore that runs along from the beach. Between the Square and the backshore is a lane, on which is a Post Office caravan, and the village 'souk', a covered market lined with stalls. At the entrance is a drink and souvenir shop, then the stalls, from which are sold leather goods, fruit and pharmaceuticals, followed by a Mini-market store.

Bordering the Main Sq, in an anti-clockwise direction, are, for instance, a jewellery shop, a small Mini-market, a boutique, one or three more Mini-markets, and, at the far right-hand corner, the *Narcissus Bar*. Alongside the latter is a path down to the waterfront Esplanade. To return to the Square, on the distant edge, backed by the face of a vertical hill, is a T-shirt shop, over which is *Rooms* (Tel 42251), *Rent Bikes & Motoblaze*, and, in the far left-hand corner, a toilet block. Here a lane leads to several *Rooms* and the *Pension Fantastique*. Coming down the left flank of the Square, that is the side furthest from the sea, is a Rent A Car firm, which sells Olympic Airways tickets, and, in the fourth alley to the left, the Police station.

Returning to the *Narcissus*, this bar overlooks the sea and is followed by the *Taverna Plaka*, the *Restaurant Bar Olympia*, and an indigenous house where a village lady has a display of crochet work. The lane then opens out on to a wide street or Esplanade bordering the waterfront in a very attractive and pleasant area of Matala, rather reminiscent of *Alefkandra*, the Venice Quarter of Mykonos. This walkway curves round past *Georgios Pub*, *Georgios Place*, *Taverna Plaka*, the *Kahlua Pub* (the what!), *Marinero Pub* and, on the tip of the rocky projection, the *Odyssey Bar*. Many of these establishments, one of which advises 'We speak native English', have patios that extend out over the scant, pebbly shore and clear sea. Despite the confined nature of the water's edge, there are a few sun-beds and umbrellas. Sample restaurant prices hereabouts are: an Amstel beer

95drs; a very small Greek salad 280drs; tzatziki/taramosalata 200drs; moussaka 400drs; spaghetti 350drs; chicken 400drs; and veal 700drs'ish.

Back at the centre of things, the comparatively small, shadeless main beach, at the bottom of the indented bay, consists of sharp sand mixed with fine, grey shingle and pebble, edging a smooth, rock foreshore. The high cliffs, forming the right, or north horn of the bay, contain serried caves, used by Christians in the 5th century AD. Nowadays an official patrols the chambers and insists that 'bottomless' sunbathers dress. To the left of the bay are lower hillsides into which the old village was built.

In the lee of the right-hand cliffs is a beach taverna, around which flourish some arethemusa trees that appear to have spread out and down from the adjacent campsite. Otherwise the lack of tree cover, added to the enclosed nature of the bay, ensures that the beach gets extremely hot in the middle of the day. The referred-to taverna is a possible lunchtime venue but, as elsewhere in Matala, the menu prices are expensive. A meal, for two, of 2 plates of stuffed tomatoes (450 drs each), 2 beers (120drs each), and bread, cost 1150drs. The salads here follow a to-be-regretted trend, increasingly prevalent in the more tourist ravaged areas, being piddlingly insubstantial servings. Other dishes available include keftedes and potatoes, stiffado, moussaka, and stuffed aubergines.

Oh yes, unless I forget, it is possible to hire sun-beds (200drs) or chairs (300drs), and umbrellas (400drs). The OTE hut is to the rear of the beach.

Matala's fame was based on a departed culture - hippies and flower-power children of the 1960s - some of whom lived in the cliff-face caves overlooking the neat little bay. They were followed by the smart, 'inter-national' set, who made way for a more egalitarian clientele. A present-day, stereotype male holiday-maker (Matala man?) is a middle-aged 'youngster', his paunch ill-disguised by a necklace hung, rectangular bar dangling over a greying, hirsute chest, with long sideburns and a thinning head of hair frizzed and frantically combed to cover the balding patches.

I am of the opinion that Matala has the discernable sound of money grabbing and the odour of 'rip off', but that is a personal point of view.

THE ACCOMMODATION & EATING OUT
The Accommodation Generally a bed is rather more expensive here, than in the surrounding area. On the other hand, the disparity is not as great as it used to be, mainly because the other locations have increased their prices, even more than Matala. It is worth bearing in mind that **Rooms** in nearby Pitsidia village, some 6km back along the Main road, are up to 500drs less costly. The previously referred to side street off the High St, on the corner of which is the *Hotel Zafira* and a bookshop, has a wealth of choice including the:

Hotel Scorpios (Class E)   Tel 42102
Directions: As above, and on the right.

Only double rooms are available, those sharing a bathroom priced at 2600drs & those with an en suite bathroom 2800drs, which charges increase to 2900drs & 3100drs (1st June-15th Oct).

It may be worth noting that most of the signs in this row are in German! Next along is an Accommodation Information Centre, followed by the *Hotel Sophia*

(Class E, tel 42134), where single rooms with a bathroom are also available at a cost of 2300drs, rising to 2600drs, and double rooms are a similar price to the *Scorpios*. Other options in this street are the *Pension Nikos* at least three *Rooms* and the:

Hotel Fantastic (Class E)   Tel 42362
Directions: As above, and on the right.
    All rooms have to share the bathrooms. A single is charged at 1200drs & a double at 1450drs, increasing to 1350drs & 1600drs (1st July-30th Sept).

Beyond the *Fantastic* are *Rooms Sylvia*, the *Hotel Eva Marina* (Class C, tel 42125), and *Rooms Antonios*.
    Any amount of the accommodation throughout Matala is charged at about the aforementioned prices. A stay of three days or more can be used to negotiate a reduction from, say, the double room average of 2900/3000drs to 2500/2600drs.

On the left and right of the High St are the:
Hotel Zafira (Class D)   Tel 42366
Directions: As above.
    All rooms have en suite bathrooms. A single rooms costs 2500drs & a double 3000drs, rising to 3000drs & 3500drs (16th May-30th Sept). Rates quoted by the management tend to be at least 300drs in excess of the official prices,
and the:

Hotel Bambou Sands (Class C)   Tel 42370
Directions: As described, across the street from the *Zafira*.
    All rooms have en suite bathrooms, with a single charged at 2000drs & a double at 2600drs, increasing to 2500drs & 3200drs (1st June-30th Sept).

Camping Those tempted to 'wild' camp in the caves or on the beach, might reconsider. The police are vigilant and the fines very expensive.

Matala Camping
Directions: Signposted from and immediately to one side of the access road into the village. It is attractively located just beyond the beach backshore, in a tree shaded location.
    Perversely, bearing in mind that most other Matala goods, services and supplies are more expensive, the campsite charges of 200drs per head and 200drs for a tent, are inexpensive, even if the showers are cold.

The Eating Out Many of the establishments and sample prices have been described in the previous text.

THE A TO Z OF USEFUL INFORMATION
BANKS No official Bank but the Travel offices service most exchange requirements, and don't forget the Post Office.

BEACHES Apart from the town facility, and nearby Komas Beach (already detailed *en route*), to the south of Matala is another beach. This 2km hill walk leads past more caves, in which reside the old-hand, long-stay squatters whom the authorities appear to leave in peace.

BICYCLE, SCOOTER & CAR HIRE There are a number of firms, with several spaced out around the Main Sq. A Honda automatic costs 1500drs a day, with no reduction for three days hire, and a large Vespa sized bike costs 3000drs. Car hire rates are the usual expensive overcharge.

BREAD SHOPS One hides in the left-hand lane that emerges on the Main Sq.

BUSES The buses pull up close to the beach backshore.

Bus timetable (Mid-season)
Matala to Iraklion
Daily   0700, 0930, 1100, 1215, 1430, 1700, 1830hrs.
Sun & hols 0730, 1000, 1200, 1300, 1430, 1600, 1700hrs.
Return journey
Daily   0730, 0830, 1000, 1215, 1300, 1500, 1630hrs.
One-way fare: 490drs, duration 2hrs.

Matala to Festos
Daily   0930, 1100, 1215, 1430, 1700, 1830hrs.
Sun & hols 0730, 1000, 1200, 1300, 1430, 1600, 1700hrs.

Matala to Ag Galini
Daily   0700, 0930, 1100, 1215, 1430, 1700, 1830hrs.
Sun & hols 0730, 1000, 1200, 1300, 1430, 1600, 1700hrs.

COMMERCIAL SHOPPING AREA None, but apart from the various shops there is the 'souk' alongside the sea flank of the Main Sq. Most supplies are that little bit more expensive than elsewhere on the island.

LAUNDERETTE As detailed in the introduction, the Launderette is across the Main road from the campsite. Opens daily, between 0900-1300hrs & 1500-1900hrs, and on Sundays, between 0900-1300hrs. A wash costs 300drs and a dry 200drs, per machine load.

MEDICAL CARE For all matters medical it is necessary to go to Mires, some 16km distant.

OTE To the rear of the beach backshore, in a portacabin type hut. Opens daily, between 0730-2200hrs, and on Sundays & 'Idle' Days, between 0900-1400hrs & 1600-2100hrs.

POLICE The chaps have an office near the Bakery, on the left of the Main Sq.

POST OFFICE The Post Office caravan is sited on the lane edging the shore to the side of the Main Sq. Open for business daily, between 0830-1900hrs, and on Sundays, between 0930-1700hrs.

TOILETS The public loos are in the south-east corner of the Main Sq.

TRAVEL AGENTS & TOUR OFFICES There are sufficient, with two on the Main Sq. Incidentally boat trip destinations include Ag Galini and Paximadia island, the latter offshore from Matala.

To reach Lendas and Ag Deka (for Gortyna), the choice lays between returning to the main Timbaki to Ag Deka road, or selecting the often poorly signposted, rough, cross-country route via Petrokefali and Platanos. It just depends on a traveller's sensibilities. The road from Platanos and Pompia is bad, and Peri has many bumpy bi-ways. There can be no doubt that there are some very pretty villages and hamlets in this 'neck of the woods', some of them detailed in the following descriptions.

The pretty, agricultural village of **Petrokefali**, wherein petrol is available, has a white chapel and unusual campanile, a central square, beflowered gardens and plenty of trees, and charcoal burners in the area.

A traveller may divert through **Pompia**, which is almost a town. There is a clinic alongside the Main Square, as well as a pharmacy, stores, cafe-bars, a petrol station and a monumental church, with noticeable, stained glass windows. The Post Office exchanges foreign currency and cheques, but there are no other concessions to tourism.

Pigaidakia is apparently prosperous and some of the older buildings having interesting looking chimneys. There are a couple of kafeneions, a store and, on the Pompia side, on the left, a low, open fronted shed with a wine or olive press inside... and sometimes a donkey. Very few tourists make it as far as Pigaidakia.

Choustouliana village can offer petrol. Beyond **Plora**, the road climbs, after the right-hand turning to Lendas, in a series of hairpin curves with, to the rear, magnificent views back across the lovely Messara Plain. The route passes a spectacular, sheer rock face, disused ruins and, before going through the pass to Miamou, a massive building simply miles from any-where. Goodness only knows what its purpose is, and for whom? Once through the mountain hanging village of **Miamou**, the road crosses brown moorland hills prior to eventually gaining the top of the steep, extremely long, cliff edge descent to Lendas. The views extend all the way along the coast to distant Cape Lithinon. Eagles may well be observed soaring back and forth - that is as long as the locals haven't shot them all!

LENDAS (60km from Ag Galini) It is questionable if the journey is worth the effort. The place really is a flyblown, messy huddle of tavernas and houses, with little or no street infrastructure. This lack of a formal layout results in the occasional, unintentional foray through a native's backyard, often to his or her anger.

The approach road to Lendas degenerates into an unsurfaced track. This peters out on an irregular, flint surfaced, roped off vehicle park, some way distant from and elevated from the waterfront. To the rear is the relatively swept-up *Elevin Rooms Apartments*. Close by and edging one of the rough paths down to the waterfront, is the 'Bengh Exchange' where money can be changed and which doubles as a souvenir shop. Tracks connect to four tav-ernas and some houses bordering the little cove, the surrounds of which are litter bestrewn, with 'campers' to be found in most nooks and crannies. The amount of rubbish cannot be exaggerated and includes old fridges lying about - it's like Steptoe's yard. Even the tree lined backshore of the 100m grey sand and pebble beach is rubbish bestrewn, but the sea-water is sur-prisingly clear. Towards the left-hand (*Fsw*) side of the beach is the *Pink Panther* bar, painted pink (!), the public toilet, which is doorless and ready for dynamiting, and beyond that a boulderous outcrop of rock. About half-way along the edge of the shore, a few souls wild camp under the leafy arethemusa trees.

Spread around the settlement are a Supermarket-cum-Baker, signed 'Prost', which I am assured is the German for bread, a Mini-market, titled supermarket, and a fairly swept-up restaurant, the *raison d'etre* for which must be the excursion coach trade.

Although all four backshore tavernas used to have accommodation, only one or two of them can be relied upon, at any one time, to regularly offer **Rooms**. They cost about 1500drs for a double, sharing the Cycladean style toilet facilities, sited at ground floor level on the edge of the terrace patios. In fact accommodation is not that easy to come by, nor are the locals that helpful. Further round to the right (*Fsw*) of the row of tavernas, in the crook of the headland, is the *Pub Primrose*, beyond which is yet another smart outfit, smart for Lendas that is, with a stilt supported patio.

The most interesting thing about Lendas are the archaeological excavations, even if some of the scattered digs now contain a 'light dressing' of discarded drinks cans and rubbish. The main quarrying is in the angle of the southern track that makes off to the west, along the south coast. Two columns, sections of marble sculpting and a mosaic are the easily visible remains of the Temple of Asklepios. This dates back to the 4th century BC, and was tied into the then present healing springs - a far cry from the present-day, squalid little dump.

Beside the approach to Lendas are exhortations to patronise a taverna offering **Rooms**, close by a beach, to the east. So the dutiful and inquisitive are likely to bump along the unsurfaced track in that direction. The treacherous dirt road is rather higher than the 50m distant shore which it approximately parallels. The route has to cut inland to circumnavigate a gulch, and then swings back towards a stretch of fairly narrow, fine shingle and pebble beach. The 'much heralded' but closed taverna is passed by, up a spur road and on a slight rise to the left. Further along is a picturesque bay, a rocky headland and a vaguely unattractive backshore area shaded by mature arethemusa trees. In amongst the spreading branches are some wild camping bivouacs.

But that is not the end of Lendas, oh no! One of the initially inexplicable things about the place is the seeming lack of people. This problem is solved by those who bother to head along the west coast track, past a sign for the *Disco Memory* (!). A side turning, in the direction of the sea, reveals all, for here is a very fine sweep of sandy beach, broken up by small outcrops of rock, and a pebbly sea's edge. Two rustic tavernas cater for the great unwashed wild camping in tents and old camper vans. The Lendas headland blocks off the east end of the shore... and effectively shields the location from the purient gaze of the curious coach parties that drop in on Lendas.

Pressing on along the unmade coastal track passes a 'Mexican shack' of a kafeneion, set down in the middle of nowhere. The arid countryside is intensely cultivated in the manner of smallholdings, where the land is fertile enough. Once clear of the lowlands, the surrounds are mountainous, into which the route climbs. At some height above sea-level, rounding one of the crags reveals a wonderful panorama with views along the coastline, all the way to Cape Lithinon. Even at this distance, a number of circular oil storage tanks and a small islet are visible. Down below is a long expanse of beautiful, grey pebble beach at the foot of the high cliff-face. As the track commences to descend, a cliff-side rubbish dump heralds:

PLATIA PERAMATA (68km from Ag Galini) This really is a doo-hickey, widespread, agricultural hamlet, around which is an awful lot of plastic greenhousing. A faded metal sign points inland, in the direction of 'Antiskari and Iraklion'. Another sign declares the presence of a restaurant with accommodation, which probably refers to one of the 'High St' tavernas. This 'High St' is actually a summer-dry river-bed, which runs along the pebble beach backshore, narrowing down past a couple of friendly, trackside tavernas, with large trellis shaded, concrete patios.

On the grey foreshore are beached quite a number of small, glass fibre fishing boats, whilst a little chapel overlooks the west end of the beach. For those travellers who seek out the unusual, away-from-it-all locations, Peramata might well be a worthwhile consideration.

Continuing westwards leaves a nice, if small beach and taverna to the side. After this the coastal route climbs past a taverna and five or six smart chalets, some 150m above sea-level. Hereabouts is a closer seascape of the beautiful bay of:

KALI LIMENES (72km from Ag Galini) It has to be admitted that the islet mounted storage tanks do little to enhance the irregular shaped, rocky bay, from the waters of which project outcrops of rock. The inlet is edged by a fabulous, 30m wide, some 300m long sweep of sharp sand beach, possibly more a series of flat cove foreshores, set at the foot of cliffs. Lodged in amongst a fairly adjacent pair of part submerged reefs is a shipwreck, and on part of the eastern beach is a shipbreaker using a crane mounted barge. This *ad hoc* yard stretches up a defile around which the approach track loops. Astonishingly close to this mess of boiler plates, rusting iron and steel, is a hotel.

Closer inspection of the seashore reveals a very Greek state of affairs. In amongst the spreading branches of the mature arethemusa trees, that range along the edge of the backshore, is a shanty village of tents, as well as cardboard, plywood and tin shacks. This 'settlement' possesses a 'cardboard' public toilet and two 'cardboard' beach tavernas. The mess in amongst the trees is pretty grim, despite which the shore remains quite clean, apart from some blobs of tar. The sparkling sea-water is invitingly clear, so much so that the sea-bed pebbles are easily visible. Adjacent to the beach loo is a sign, hanging from the branches, which warns ' Please do not enter the sea when the red flag's are standing up. Thang (*sic*) you.'

The west end of the bay is enclosed by a horn of headland topped off by another hotel, with a powerful stand-by tug anchored in the crook of the land. The hotel looks directly out over the scenically unattractive islet, and its four storage tanks.

The other side of the promontory is a more permanent, if prefabricated hamlet edging a tiny cove of sharp sand and pebble. The left-hand side of the sea inlet is closed off by a fishing boat quay. There are a couple of shore bordering kafeneion/tavernas and a few of the buildings are of concrete construction, not simply sheets of asbestos board. All in all a most extraordinary place.

It is not necessary to retrace one's footsteps, or tyre marks, as there is a river-bed track that ascends towards Pompia.

Returning to Lendas, if one must, and journeying back to Ag Deka, involves a traveller in all the glorious uncertainties of Greek cartography as most road maps are inaccurate when detailing this area.

AGHI DEKA The large village, named after ten local martyrs who refused to worship Roman gods, is centred around a not very lovely, long High Street with roads off to either side. There are *Rooms*, petrol, a Post Office and a chemist, in addition to the usual cafe-bars. The village's main claim to fame is its proximity to the site of:

The Gortyna (Gortys) Excavations Gortyna came into its own, from about 800BC, as a city state controlling the Messara Plain. This was after the decline of the Minoan society, but the real fame was based on the *Gortyn Code*, a set of laws, set down in the 5th century BC. The Romans invaded, some time in 67 BC, when mopping up the island, and made it their capital. Plans were formulated to build a grand city, but these ideas were never fully implemented. Gortyna's importance continued through the Byzantine period, finally being laid low by the Saracens, in AD 820/30.

Archaeological excavations commenced in the late 1800s and have continued, spasmodically, up to recent times. The remains are not visually very impressive and it is easy to accidentally drive past them.

The Main road back to Ag Galini passes through via **Mires** (Tel prefix 0892), yet another busy, dusty, agricultural Messara Plain town. There is accommodation available at the *Olympic Hotel* (Class D, tel 22777), where the rooms share the bathrooms, with a single costing 1350drs & a double room 1840drs.

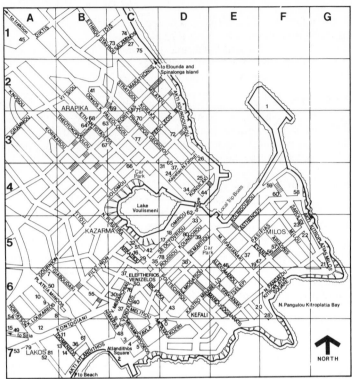

Tmr

1E/F2/3	Ferry-boat Quay	30B/C6	Snackbar
2C7	Bus Terminus	31C/D3/4	Souvlaki Snackbar
3C7	Bus Office	32C5	Airline Office
4C7	Rooms Ester	33D4/5	Commercial Bank
5C7	Pension Atlantis	34D4	General Hellenic Bank
6B/C6/7	Pension Elpida	35C/D5/6	National Bank of Greece
7A5/6	Pension Magda	36B7	Babis Scooter Hire
8A/B6/7	Hotel Apollon	37	Bread shops
9A6	Hotel Iris	38D5/6	OTE
10A6	Hotel Elena	39D5	Chapel
11A/B7	Pension New York	40C6	Cathedral
12A7	Hotel Kera	41B2	Museum
13A/B7	Hotel Zefiros	42C/D5	Post Office
14A/B7	Hotel Sunrise	43C/D6/7	The Green House Rooms
15A7	Hotel Dias	44D/E4	Port Police/Municipal
16C5	Hotel Cronos		Tourist Office
17C/D5	Hotel du Lac	45A1	Hospital
18C/D5	Hotel Akratos	46E5/6	Ikaros Hotel
19E/F5/6	Hotel Levandis	47E/F5/6	Hotel Irene
20E/F6/7	Hotel Sgouros	48C7	Rooms Info'/Rent A Bike
21G5/6	Hotel El Greco	49A7	Hotel Maria
22F/G5	Hotel Kreta	50A6	Hotel Arion
23F/G4/5	Pension Pergola	51C5	Pension Limni
24C/D3/4	Pension Marigo	52A7	Hotels Triton/Vlassis
25D/E4	Youth Hostel	53A7	Hotel Nikos
26D/E3/4	Hotel Alcistis	54A6/7	Hotel Mavroforos
27C1	Pension Perla	55B6	Hotel Zeus
28E/F6/7	Restaurant Noufara	56E/F5	Pension Mary
29C5/6	Kafeneion	57F5	Hotel Alfa

58F4	Hotel Odysseas
59E/F4	Hotel Panorama
60F4	Pension Istron
61B7	Hotel Aphrodite
62D4/5	Hotel Aegeon
63B/C3	Town police
64B3	Rooms Sunbeam
65D3/4	Hotel Amalthia
66C3/4	Pension Galini/Tave
	Klimataria
67B/C3	Hotel Kouros
68B2/3	Pension Diana
69B/C2/3	Hotel Zina
70C2/3	Mediterranean Roo
71C2/3	Katerina's Rooms
72D3	Pension Eva
73B/C1	Rooms Marilena
74C1	Hotel Carol
75C1	Hotel Hermes
76C6	Alexis Kafeneion
77C3	Taverna Aouas
78C/D5/6	Bookshop
79A7	Supermarket Lato
80D5	Massaros Travel
81A/B7	Self-service Laundr

Tmr = Town map reference
Fsw = Facing seawards
Sbo = Sea behind one
Fbqbo = Ferry-boat Quay behind

Illustration 20 Ag Niklaos

8 AGIOS NIKOLAOS (Aghios, Ayios Nikolaos)

Still very attractive, hilly harbour town & package holiday resort; massed tourists, discos & glitzy cocktail bars; mosquitoes.

GENERAL (Illustration 20) Tel prefix 0841. Unusually, for Crete that is, Ag Nikolaos has little history of note. The modern town is a comparatively recent, 19th century development. Not only are there few Hellenistic or Roman bits and pieces, but Ag Nikolaos lacks the commonplace breadth and depth of Minoan remains, churches, as well as Venetian and Turkish buildings. Mind you, the site was the harbour for the relatively adjacent, ancient Lato City (*See* **Excursion to Ag Nikolaos Surrounds**). Furthermore the clean, lovely, tree lined avenues, pretty lake and port adequately compensate for the lack of these usual historical prerequisites.

Most of the growth of this once backwater town, with a present-day population of some 6500, has occurred since the 1960s. Ag Nikolaos has undoubtedly made up for lost time and is probably the most tourist developed, or ravaged, depending upon your viewpoint, of all the Cretan holiday resorts. The town certainly is a conundrum, perhaps more correctly (but ungrammatically) it could be described as a schizophrenic settlement. Undeniably it is a tourist trap, with all the shortcomings that intense exposure to the holiday industry brings about. Despite this, in the strata beneath the annual invasion, and not totally submerged, is a delightful, interesting sea port and town.

There are a number of glaring examples of the unacceptable level of tourism. These include: a high incidence of souvenir shops, embracing 'ethnic' products and jewellery outlets; 'fast-food' snackbars; parking restrictions; Greek voices in a minority; waiters who will not hear out customers' halting efforts in Greek; an inability to purchase a cup of Greek coffee; and the 'Costa Brava' ambience. It is to be hoped that, as the Cretans did not allow the Venetians or Turks to gain the upper hand, a plethora of sunburnt, obese, swinging, fun-loving tourists will not entirely sublimate the locals natural characteristics. So say all of us!

Ag Nikolaos, which is larger than at first appears to be the case, is the subject of an all-embracing one-way road system. The usual approach to the town is via the south-western corner, leaving the Bus terminus, Plateia Atlandithos (*Tmr* 2C7), to the right. The route then ascends Odhos S Venizelos to Plateia Eleftherios Venizelos (*Tmr* C6), which Main Square crowns the hill dominating the town. From the far side, the High St, Odhos Roussou Koundourou, plunges down to the Harbour Esplanade. At this junction, a left-hand turning crosses over the bridge spanning the Lake Voulismeni sea inlet. From here Odhos K Paleologou climbs steeply out of town, towards the Iraklion road. Incidentally, the lake is supposedly bottomless, but research has established a depth of some sixty metres.

ARRIVAL BY BUS The buses park at the rather constricted terminus on Plateia Atlandithos (*Tmr* 2C7), to the south of the town.

ARRIVAL BY FERRY The style, layout and size of the harbour is surprisingly similar to that of a small Aegean island. The ferry-boats dock on the right-hand side (*Fsw*) of the port (*Tmr* 1E/F2/3). A short walk along the quay road of Akti Koundourou, towards the centre of the waterfront, leads past a row of restaurants and shops, the latter including 'traditional' Cretan art, music and gift shops, as well as Rent-A-Car offices.

THE ACCOMMODATION & EATING OUT

The Accommodation As Ag Nikolaos is 'package holiday territory', many of the pensions and hotels are block booked by tour operators. This, plus the many other demands, results in the town's available accommodation quickly filling up, in the height of summer months. Apart from mosquitoes being a problem, the biggest drawback is that many of the hotel and pension owners request a substantial 'premium' for their rooms, over and above the 'officially' approved figure. *C'est la vie.*

There are a number of 'hot spots' for accommodation, such as the *Lakos Quarter* (*Tmr* A/B6/7), in the area around the Bus Sq and the side-streets that climb up from Plateia Atlandithos (*Tmr* 2C7), towards the *Kefali Quarter*. Some of the houses have beautiful views over the bay and hereabouts are *Rooms Ester* (*Tmr* 4C7), immediately across the side-street from the Bus office, and:

Pension Atlantis (*Tmr* 5C7) (Class C)   Tel 28964
Directions: Up Tavla St, from Atlandithos Sq, first right on to Odhos Metamorfoseos, and on the right.
    Only double rooms are available. Those sharing a bathroom cost from 1400drs & those with an en suite bathroom from 2100drs, rising to 1700drs & 2500drs (16th June-30th Sept).

Continuing up Odhos Tavla, across crossroads alongside a church, and on the right is a nice looking *Rooms*, where a bedroom for two is charged at 2000drs. A few paces on, opposite the junction with Odhos Nik Foka, is the:

Green House Rooms (*Tmr* 43C/D6/7) 15 E Modatsou   Tel 22025
Directions: As above.
    Green is appropriate as the ground floor of this doo-hickey, hostelish establishment is a veritable 'garden centre' of flowers and plants. The multilingual lady proprietor is of a very smiley, if not eccentric dis- position. A double room, sharing the bathroom, costs 1500drs, a rate that can be 'negotiated', out of the height of season months.

Much further north-east along Odhos E Modatsou, and right on Alexomanoli St is the:
Hotel Ikaros (*Tmr* 46E5/6) (Class B) 11 Alexomanoli   Tel 28901
Directions: As above.
    A single room, with an en suite bathroom, is charged at 2010drs & a double room 3030drs.

Keeping to Odhos Alexomanoli, in a south-east direction, at the next junction, with Tselepi St, turn left to descend to M Sfakianaki St. On the left-hand corner, of this 'main' street to Kitroplatia Beach, is the expensive:

Hotel Levandis (Leventis) (*Tmr* 19E/F5/6) (Class B) 15 M Sfakianaki   Tel 22423
Directions: As described.

The cocktail bar has a juke-box that belts out the old favourites - oh goody! Probably much of the accommodation is booked by smaller tour operators. Rooms have en suite bathrooms, with singles charged at 3330drs & doubles 3990drs. These charges rise to 3990drs & 4785drs (16th May-30th Sept).

Still on now ascending Tselepi St, and half-way along the block, on the left, is the:
Hotel Irene (*Tmr* 47E/F5/6) (Class E) Tselepi   Tel 23860
Directions: As above.
All rooms have en suite bathrooms, with a single priced at 2800drs & a double 3000drs, which prices increase to 3000drs & 3500drs (1st June-20th Sept).

Heading towards the *Milos Quarter*, still on Odhos Tselepi, across the lateral street of Odhos Evans, and on the left, is:

Pension Mary (*Tmr* 56E/F5) 13 Evans   Tel 23760
Directions: As above.
The mid 30s landlady is nice, smiley and speaks English. Double rooms cost between 2600-3000drs, and a breakfast 300drs per head.

There are a number of extremely smart, expensive hotels that border Plateia N Pangalou Kitroplatia and Akti Kitroplatias Milos, the latter circumscribing the eastern peninsula, all the way round from N Pangalou Kitroplatia Sq to the Harbour Esplanade, Akti Koundourou. In the main, they are block booked by the package tour companies but enquirers sometimes can find space, in the out of season months,   noting that the Ag Nikolaos season starts at the beginning of May and   goes on to the middle of October. These hotels include the: *Sgouro* (*Tmr* 20E/F6/7) (Class C, tel 28931), with singles priced from 3025drs & doubles from 3730drs; El Greco (*Tmr* 21G5/6) (Class B, tel 28894); *Kreta* (*Tmr* 22F/G5) (Class C, tel 22518); *Pension Pergola* (*Tmr* 23F/G4/5) (Class C, tel 28152), with a single room charged at 1595drs & a double 2090drs, both sharing the bathrooms, whilst en suite singles cost 2015drs & doubles 2680drs, rates that increase, respectively, to 2130/2780drs & 2590/3090drs (1st July-30th Sept); *Odysseas* (*Tmr* 58F4) (Class B, tel 23934); and still further on round, on Akti Koundourou, the *Hotel Panorama* (*Tmr* 59E/F4) (Class C, tel 28890), where all rooms have en suite bathrooms, with a single costing 2440drs & doubles 2710drs, increasing to 3160drs & 3620drs (1st June-30th Sept).

Whilst in this neck of the woods, clambering up the abrupt steps of the pretty area alongside the *Panorama*, ascends, at the top, to the much more reasonably priced:
Pension Istron (*Tmr* 60F4) (Class C) 4 Sarolidi   Tel 23763
Directions: As above.
All rooms share the bathrooms, with a single charged at 1000drs & a double at 1330drs, increasing to 1250drs & 1700drs (1st June-30th Sept).

Back at the Bus terminus (*Tmr* 2C7), close to the corner with Odhos S Venizelos is a *Rooms Information-cum-Rent-A-Bike* outfit (*Tmr* 48C7). Across Odhos S Venizelos, on Himaras St, is the *Pension Elpida* (*Tmr* 6B/C6/7). Turning right, or north on Kontogiani St, and then left at the bottom of V Merarchias St, leads into a side-street whereon are the *Hotel Zeus* (*Tmr* 55B6) and, a metre or so on, a house with **Rooms**, both on the left-hand side of the road. Continuing to the end of this street, turning left down the steps, and taking the first right, on to Odhos Giaboudaki, and then left on to Odhos Gournion, leads to the:

Pension Magda (*Tmr* 7A5/6) (Class B) 13 Gournion   Tel 23925
Directions: As above.
    Although advertising itself a hotel, the Magda is licensed as a pension, despite which prices are rather expensive. All rooms have en suite bathrooms, with a single starting off at 2590drs & a double 3390drs, increasing to 2990drs & 3990drs (1st June-30th Sept).

Around the corner from Odhos Gournion is elongated Plateia   Minoos, with central aisle gardens. Spaced out around this Square, which stretches along to the main south-western road out of Ag Nikolaos, Odhos Kontogiani, are some smart hotels, as well as a few bars and shops. These hotels all have en suite bathrooms, are block booked for most of the summer months and include the:

Hotel Arion (*Tmr* 50A6) (Class C) 14 Minoos Sq   Tel 23778
Directions: As above.
    A single room is priced at 2450drs and & double 3100drs, charges that increase to 2900drs & 3650drs (16th June-15th Sept).

Across the Square are the:
Hotel Elena (*Tmr* 10A6) (Class C) 15 Minoos Sq   Tel 28189
Directions: As above.
    A single room costs 2080drs & a double 2620drs, which charges rise to 2400drs & 3620drs (1st June-30th Sept).

Hotel Iris (*Tmr* 9A6) (Class B) Minoos Sq   Tel 22407
Directions: As above, on the corner of the side-street Odhos K Loukareos.
    Actually categorised as a pension, with singles costing 1600drs & doubles 2500drs, increasing to 1800drs & 2800drs (1st June-30th Sept), but note that actual prices quoted may well exceed these listed by some 300/500drs.
and the:
Hotel Apollon (*Tmr* 8A/B6/7) (Class C) 9 Minoos Sq   Tel 23023
Directions: As above.
    Singles cost 2210drs & doubles 2950drs, rising to 2710drs & 3485drs   (1st June-30th Sept).

Bordering the noisy Kontogiani St are the:
New York (*Tmr* 11A/B7) (Class C) 21a Kontogiani   Tel 28577
Directions: As above and 'on the south side'.
    Classified as a pension and likely to have rooms available, not being on the package tour operators rota. This is not surprising as the establishment fronts on to 'downtown' Ag Nikolaos. Rooms are available, with or without en suite bathrooms, and the rates requested are the average for this style of place.

Hotel Kera (*Tmr* 12A7) (Class C) 34 Kontogiani   Tel 28711
Directions: Across the road from the *New York*.
    Only en suite double rooms are available, at a cost of 2550drs, increasing to 3000drs (1st June-30th Sept).

A little further along the Main road, right at the fork in the road, in the direction of Sitia, and on the right is the *Hotel Maria* (*Tmr* 49A7), followed by the:

Hotel Dias (*Tmr* 15A7) (Class C) 2 Latous   Tel 28263
Directions: As above.
    En suite rooms with singles charged at 2110drs & doubles at 2760drs, rising to 2610drs & 3760drs (1st July-30th Sept).

Instead of forking right from Odhos Kontogiani, turning left leads past the:
Hotel Nikos (*Tmr* 53A7) (Class C)   Tel 24464
Directions: As above, and on the left.
   En suite double rooms only available, at a cost of 3525drs,   increasing to 3875drs (1st June-31st Oct).

Back along Kontogiani St and around the corner is the:
Hotel Mavroforos (*Tmr* 54A6/7) (Class C) Hortatson   Tel 23714
Directions: As above, and on the left. All rooms have en suite bathrooms, with a single priced at 1870drs & a double at 2710drs, increasing to 2780drs & 3885drs (1st June-30th Sept).

To the south of Kontogiani St, in the side-streets that run down to the waterfront, is a plethora of choice including the:
Hotel Zefiros (Zephyros) (*Tmr* 13A/B7) (Class C) Idomeneos   Tel 23631
Directions: As above, and on the right (*Fsw*).
   All rooms have en suite bathrooms, with a single costing 2100drs & a double 2600drs, which rates increase to 2600drs & 3500drs (1st July-30th Sept).

Hotel Sunrise (*Tmr* 14A/B7) (Class B) 1 Idomeneos   Tel 23564
Directions: A few buildings down from the *Zefiros*, and classified as a pension.
   All rooms are en suite, with singles costing 2000drs & doubles 3000drs. These rates rise to 2400drs & 3500drs (1st June-30th Sept).

In the parallel street to the right (*Fsw*) of Idomeneos are the side-by-side *Hotel Vlassis* (Class C) and *Hotel Triton* (*Tmr* 52A7), whilst on the next street to the left is the *Aphrodite* (*Tmr* 61B7), which offers apartments, not bedrooms.
   From Odhos Kontogiani, proceeding up Odhos V Merarchias, or the parallel street of S Venizelos, leads to the top of hill and Plateia El Venizelos. Across this Square, to the left and along the side-street of Arkadiou is the *Hotel Cronos* (*Tmr* 16C5) (Class C, tel 28761), which is tour operator block booked. In the parallel street of Odhos N Plastira, edging the south-west cliff-edge of Lake Voulismeni, is the *Pension Limni* (*Tmr* 51C5, tel 22173). From El Venizelos Sq, the two parallel streets of 28th October (Octovriou) and Roussou Koundourou plunge down to the harbour front. Odhos 28th October passes by the:

Hotel du Lac (*Tmr* 17C/D5) (Class C) 17, 28th October   Tel 22711
Directions: A third of the way down from the Main Sq, in a superb position overlooking the small, sea-connected lake in the centre of the town.
   All rooms have en suite bathrooms, with single rooms costing 1990/2260drs & double rooms 2530/3340drs. These rates rise, respectively, to 2260/2710drs & 2800/3390drs (16th June-30th Sept). Breakfast is charged at 380/425drs.

Continuing down Odhos 28th October, beyond a side-street, is the usually block booked *Hotel Akratos* (*Tmr* 18C/D5). At the bottom of Odhos 28th October and on the left, overlooking the bridge, in a marvellous if somewhat noisy location, is the:

Hotel Aegeon (*Tmr* 62D4/5) (Class E) 2, 28th October   Tel 22773
Directions: As above.
   A great example of the dry-rot riddled, dark and dusty, worn linoleum, provincial hotel of yesteryear, wherein a couple of the double bedrooms, sharing the bathroom, overlook the bridge and cost 1360drs a night! I'd love to hear from any reader who manages to stay here, before it falls down.

Down at the Harbour, a bridge spans the small inlet connecting the sea to Lake Voulismeni and allows easy access from the east to west of the town. On the west side of the bridge is Odhos K Paleologou and the Esplanade, Akti Koundourou, the latter leading out along the coast to the Minos and Elounda beaches, as well as Spinalonga islet. Both roads lead to 'parcels' of accommodation. Prior to ascending Odhos K Paleologou, the first turning to the right, from the north side of the bridge, is between a Taxi rank and the General Hellenic Bank. It advances along the narrow lane of Odhos Kondilaki to a junction with Odhos Koraka and, on the left, the:

Youth Hostel (*Tmr* 25D/E4) 3 Stratigou Koraka   Tel 22823
Directions: As above, with a Taxi rank alongside the building.
A very youth-hostelish hostel, if you see what I mean. There are lots of signs splashed about, which can't conceal that it is a bit of a dump. Rumour, only rumour, suggests that there could be bed bugs in the mattresses. For this congenial squalor, a dormitory bunk costs 500drs a night. The establishment can also offer the dubious, added attraction of 'open air' beds in the still unfinished, concrete pillar dotted rooms at the top of the building. Certainly cool, but what about the mosquitoes? There is a bar.

Pension Marigo (*Tmr* 24C/D3/4) (Class B) K Paleologou   Tel 28439
Directions: From the bridge, a few metres up Odhos K Paleologou and on the right, opposite one of the town's car parks, on the corner of a row of tavernas and a souvlaki snackbar. The car park tends to obscure views of the lake.
The *Marigo* is part and parcel of another pension, the *Amalthia*, which is just around the corner. Only double rooms, with en suite bathrooms, are available at a cost of 2500drs, increasing to 3000drs (1st June-30th Sept).

Pension Amalthia (*Tmr* 65D3/4) (Class B) 13 Pringipos Georgiou   Tel 28914
Directions: As above.
All rooms have en suite bathrooms, with a single room costing 2420drs & a double room 3100drs, which charges increase to 2860drs & 3630drs (16th June-15th Sept).

In the parallel streets either side of Odhos K Paleologou are a number of possibilities, including, on Odhos Ethnikis Antistaseos, the *Pension Galini* (*Tmr* 66C3/4) and the:

Hotel Kouros (*Tmr* 67B/C3) (Class C) 17 E Antistaseos   Tel 23264
Directions: As above.
All rooms have en suite bathrooms, with a single costing 2200drs & a double 2700drs, rising to 2500drs & 3000drs (1st June-30th Sept).

Further up the street, across the lateral side-street of Odhos Nikonos, and on the left is *Rooms Sunbeam* (*Tmr* 64B3), whilst on the opposite side is the:

Pension Diana (*Tmr* 68B2/3) (Class B) 28 E Antistaseos   Tel 22694
Directions: As above.
A single room, with an en suite bathroom, is priced at 2700drs, a double sharing the bathroom 2100drs & a double en suite 3400drs, prices that rise, respectively, to 3400drs & 2800/4100drs (1st July-30th Sept).

By proceeding along Odhos Nikonos, in a north-east direction, across Odhos K Paleologou, and on the right is the:

Pension Zina (*Tmr* 69B/C2/3) (Class B)   Tel 22210
Directions: As above.
   All rooms have en suite bathrooms, with a single charged at 2240drs & a
double 2800drs, increasing to 2720drs & 3400drs (1st June-30th Sept).

Further down towards the harbour, along Koritsas St, from Odhos K Paleologou,
and to the right on Pringipos Georgiou St is the nice looking *Mediterranean
Rooms* (*Tmr* 70 C2/3). Close by, on Koritsas St is *Katerina's Rooms* (*Tmr*
71C2/3), whilst even lower down Odhos Stratigou Koraka and on the left, close
by the junction with Kantanoleontos St, is the *Pension Eva* (*Tmr* 72D3) (Class
B, tel 22587).

Back at the Harbour Esplanade, Akti Koundourou, which makes off in a
north-west direction, edges the seafront past:
Hotel Alcistis (Alkistis) (*Tmr* 26D/E3/4) (Class C) 30 Koundourou   Tel 22454
Directions: From the bridge, turn past the office of the Port police, following the
quay wall round along the Spinalonga coast road.
   Well situated, but at the outset of a very busy stretch of 'corniche'. All rooms
have en suite bathrooms, with singles starting off at 1980drs & double rooms
3080drs, which charges rise to 2475drs & 3740drs (1st July-30th Sept). Breakfast
is listed at 370drs.

Beyond a number of precipitous flights of steps up from the Esplanade, are the
extremely smart hotels *Rea* (Class B, tel 28321), *Hermes* (*Tmr* 75C1) (Class A,
tel 28253) and *Coral* (*Tmr* 74C1) (Class B, tel 28363), which follow on the
'foyer' of each other. Naturally charges reflect their delightful siting and classi-
fication. Additionally the ambience is heavily weighted towards the Aegean,
fun-loving, swinging disco, jet-set, package tourist holiday-makers, rather than
Greek traditional.

Not all is lost though, for situated hereabouts is the:
Pension Perla (*Tmr* 27C1) (Class C)   Tel 23379
Directions: On the corner of Koundourou and the steeply ascending Salaminos St.
   A pleasant, family owned, clean, well furnished pension, which must rate as a
find, if only because of the comparatively reasonable rates charged - reasonable
for Ag Nikolaos that is. Despite the family living elsewhere, someone is always
in attendance, even if it is one of the disinterested teenage children. The *Perla* is
located in a fashionable, well-placed position. The front facing rooms have a
balcony overlooking the sea but the downstairs rooms, at the rear of the building,
can be a bit smelly, due to their proximity to the toilets. Rooms are available
sharing the bathrooms, or with rather 'bolt-on' en suite bathrooms. A single
room sharing is priced at 1100drs & en suite 1600drs, whilst doubles sharing are
1600drs & en suite 2000drs, which rates increase, respectively, to 1400/1900drs
& 1900/2300drs (1st June-30th Sept).

Whilst hereabouts, it is a pity that the Esplanade fronting *Perla* basement bar is
owned by a 'prissy' couple. To maintain the 'just so' atmosphere, necessary to
ensnare clients from the nearby hotel glitz, their customers must be properly
dressed, sit-up straight, and not play cards (which is my real gripe!). If that were
not enough, even for Ag Nikolaos, their prices are pitched at the 'cocktails and
adultery' level. The establishment is very reminiscent of those located adjacent
to countless, eminently forgettable numbers of Spanish Costa hotels.

At the top of Salaminos lane, and on the right (*Sbo*) is *Rooms Marilena* (*Tmr* 73B/C1). Those prepared for a longer walk still, have more choice as there are additional *Rooms*, pensions and hotels spread out along the Elounda road. Options include *Rooms Poppi*, followed by the exclusive *Minos Beach*, *St Nicholas Bay Hotel Bungalows* and the *Minoos Palace*.

THE EATING OUT

The Eating Out There is no shortage of eating places, which range from 'tost', 'fast food' hamburger and souvlaki snackbars, through to swanky tavernas and restaurants accepting most credit cards. What is lacking are reasonably priced, quality establishments. In fact charges are generally 'hurtful'! Thus, in this 'plethora of cooking oil', only a few offerings are listed, out of the dozens and dozens of troughing places that range around the edge of Lake Voulismeni, the quay and coastal road of Akti Koundourou, Plateia N Pangalou Kitroplatia, and along Odhos M Sfakianaki. A number of the tavernas on Odhos K Paleologou and overlooking the Lake, claim to be that used by the cast of one or two British television thriller series, filmed in Ag Nikolaos, some years ago.

Now that the '*Papas Kafeneion* ' has disappeared from Plateia El Venizelos, I am pleased to nominate:
Alexis Kafeneion (Tmr 76C6)
Directions: From Plateia El Venizelos descend Odhos V Merarchias, towards the Bus Sq. The cafe-bar is on the left, with a number of chairs and tables spread along the narrow pavement, opposite a building in which is a 'full-house' of pharmacy, dentist and doctor.
The place is run by a dear old lady. A nightcap of two Nes meh ghala and an ouzo cost 220drs. I have to own up to only being charged 120drs, one night ...and I also have to own up to wilting under the thought of trying to explain to her that she had undercharged me, especially as, on that occasion, she had been at the receiving end of some foreign 'so-and-so's' ignorance.

Taverna Aouas (*Tmr* 77C3)
Directions: Ascend Odhos K Paleologou, from the Harbour bridge, to beyond the extent of the Lake, and on the right, set back from the road's edge with a pleasant garden to the fore.
The owner is attentive, the reasonably priced menu varied, and the servings are more than adequate, and tasty. Can one say more? One other plus point must be the attractive garden, in amongst the bushes and trees of which are laid out the taverna's tables and chairs. Menu offerings include: chicken 348drs; moussaka 496drs; most meat dishes 650drs; a bottle of beer 99drs; and a Nescafe 60drs. A meal, for two, of 2 servings of liver & chips (308drs each, and tasty with plentiful chips), 1 gigantes beans (190drs, appetising and a good helping), 1 fried courgettes (150drs, not over generous but very palatable), 2 kortaki retsina (140drs each), bread & service (20drs each), cost a total of 1276drs. Another meal, for two, of 1 Greek salad (250drs, good and plentiful), 1 chicken dish (348drs), 1 plate of kalamari (350drs), 1 bottle of retsina, and bread, was charged at 1128drs.

An additional establishment, that has an acceptable menu, is the *Taverna Klimataria* (*Tmr* 66C3/4), to the left of Odhos Ethnikis Antistaseos, just up from the car park alongside the Lake.

The one-time El Venizelos Sq kafeneion is now round the corner, on 28th

October St. It is run by an old lady, who, unless pressed, serves tins of export beer, not bottles. She advertises accommodation, but it is a performance to obtain directions, and it is not inexpensive, even at the 'special price' of 2300drs.

The rip-off nature of many of the popular locations is no better exemplified than by the Kafeneion, alongside the *Taverna To Limani*, close by the General Hellenic Bank (*Tmr* 34D4). Here the only beer available is a small bottle of Tuborg lager, not an Amstel, which with a coffee costs 250drs! Incidentally just around the corner, on Odhos Kondilaki, is the *New Dragon Chinese* Restaurant. Very Greek!

THE A TO Z OF USEFUL INFORMATION

AIRLINE OFFICE & TERMINUS (*Tmr* 32C5) The Olympic office is on Odhos Plastira, which street skirts the cliff-edge, overlooking the south end of Lake Voulismeni. The office is open Monday to Saturday, between 0800-1530hrs.

BANKS The **Commercial Bank** (*Tmr* 33D4/5), at the bottom, harbour end of Odhos 28th October, not only opens normal banking hours, but also on summer month Saturday mornings, between 0900-1200hrs. Other Banks include the: **General Hellenic Bank** (*Tmr* 34D4), on the right of the outset of Odhos K Paleologou, on the corner of Kondilaki St; **National Bank** (*Tmr* 35C/D5/6), at the top of Odhos Roussou Koundourou, just down from Plateia El Venizelos; **Ionion Bank**, beside Plateia El Venizelos, on the corner of Politechniou St; and, across the Square, alongside a green shuttered Baker's, the **Macedonia & Thrace Bank**.

BEACHES In truth, there is a paucity of beaches for a town with this number of tourists. Plateia N Pangalou Kitroplatia (*Tmr* F6) gives access to a fairly small, grey sand, stony beach fringing the bay, to the east of Ag Nikolaos. The foreshore is mainly large pebbles. Apart from beach beds, there is a ski-run and ski-jump. The trees that edge the backshore allow satisfactory shade and the very small rubbish bins provided are emptied every morning, even if they do overflow during the day.

The other beach is the very narrow strip of fine pebble that borders Akti Atlandithos (*Tmr* B7) for about 150m, and runs south of Plateia Atlandithos, the Bus Square (*Tmr* 2C7). There is some tree cover at the far, south end.

The only other bathing areas are off the large, flat platforms that edge Akti Koundourou, along the stretch from about north of the Marathonos St junction (*Tmr* C/D1/2). Steps lead down to these concrete and rock stagings, but watch out for the sea-urchins.

BICYCLE, SCOOTER & CAR HIRE The northern Esplanade, from about the *Hotel Alcistis* (*Tmr* 26D/E3/4) is 'awash' with scooter, motorbike and car hire firms. **Adonis Rent A Bike** (Tel 23407), next door to the *Oasis Bar*, is run by a couple of youngish 'Arthur Daley's', and carries on about being the cheapest in town. An old favourite of mine was **Babis Scooter Hire** (*Tmr* 36B7), which has smartened up no end, and is now located in a side-street off Idomeneos St, to the west of the Bus Sq.

BOOKSELLER (*Tmr* 78C/D5/6) A very good shop is located on 28th October, or Roussou Koundourou, just down from Plateia El Venizelos, the shop stretching laterally between the two streets.

BREAD SHOPS There are Bakers on the streets of: M Sfakianaki (*Tmr*

37E/F5/6); Kontogiani (*Tmr* 37B/C6/7), close to the junction with V Merarchias; Kapetan N Fafouti (*Tmr* 37C/D3/4); and the west side of Plateia El Venizelos (*Tmr* 37B/C5/6). The latter shop is recognizable due to its green shutters, and noteworthy because this Baker still uses old, wood-fired ovens.

BUSES The Buses park on Plateia Atlandithos (*Tmr* 2C7), on the edge of which is the Bus office (*Tmr* 3C7).

Bus timetable
Ag Nikolaos to Iraklion via Malia
Daily   0630, 0730, 0800, 0830, 0900, 0930, 1000, 1030, 1045, 1100, 1115,
               1130, 1200, 1230, 1300, 1330, 1345, 1400, 1430, 1500, 1530, 1545,
               1615, 1630, 1700, 1745, 1800, 1830, 1900, 2000, 2100, 2130hrs
Return journey
Daily   0630, 0730, 0800, 0830, 0900, 0915, 0945, 1000, 1015, 1030, 1100,
               1130, 1200, 1230, 1300, 1330, 1400, 1430, 1500, 1530, 1600, 1630,
               1700, 1730, 1745, 1800, 1830, 1930, 2100hrs
One-way fare: 480drs; duration 1½hrs; distance 69km.

Ag Nikolaos to Elounda via Schisma
Daily   0715, 0800, 0900, 1000, 1100, 1200, 1300, 1400, 1500, 1600, 1700,
               1800, 1915, 2000, 2100hrs
Sat & Sun   1200, 1300, 1400, 1500, 1700, 1800, 1900, 2100hrs
Return journey
Daily   0745, 0820, 0920, 1020, 1120, 1230, 1320, 1420, 1620, 1720, 1820,
               1945, 2020, 2120hrs
Sat & Sun   0735, 0950, 1020, 1150, 1220, 1350, 1420, 1550, 1750, 1820, 1940,
               2120hrs
One-way fare: 80drs; duration 20mins; distance 11km.

Ag Nikolaos to Kritsa (Kera Monastery)
Daily   0600, 0700, 0800, 0900, 1000, 1100, 1200, 1300, 1400, 1500, 1600,
               1700, 1800, 1900, 2000hrs

Sat & Sun   1200, 1300, 1400, 1500, 1600, 1700, 1930hrs
Return journey
Daily   0615, 0715, 0815, 0915, 1015, 1115, 1215, 1315, 1415, 1515, 1615,
               1715, 1810, 1915, 2015hrs
Sat & Sun   0630, 0730, 0815, 1015, 1115, 1215, 1315, 1415, 1515, 1630, 1715,
               2000hrs
One-way fare: 80drs; duration 15mins; distance 11km.

Ag Nikolaos to Lassithi Plateau
Daily   0830, 1400hrs
Sat   0830hrs.
Return journey
Daily   0700, 1400hrs
Sat   1400hrs
One-way fare 380drs; duration 2 hrs; distance 55km.

Ag Nikolaos to Ierapetra via Istron & Gournia
Daily   0630, 0830, 0900, 1000, 1100, 1200, 1300, 1400, 1500, 1700, 1830,
               2000hrs
Return journey
Daily   0630, 0830, 1035, 1230, 1400, 1430, 1530, 1700, 1900, 2030hrs
One-way fare: 250drs; duration 1hr; distance 36km.

Ag Nikolaos to Sitia via Istron & Gournia
Daily   0630, 0830, 0930, 1000, 1200, 1400, 1630, 1900hrs

Return journey
Daily   0615, 0915, 1115, 1215, 1430, 1445, 1645, 1915hrs
One-way fare: 550drs; duration 1½hrs; distance 74km.

Ag Nikolaos to Plaka via Elounda
Daily   0900, 1100, 1300, 1500, 1700, 1915hrs
Return journey
Daily   0940, 1140, 1340, 1620, 1740, 1955hrs
One-way fare: 550drs; duration 1½hrs; distance 74km.

There is an Elounda bus stop on the Harbour quay, by the Lake bridge, opposite
the Municipal Tourist office (*Tmr* 44D/E4).

COMMERCIAL SHOPPING AREA No specific district. Most grocery, fish,
fruit & vegetable, meat, general stores and shops, are centred on the parallel
streets of V Merarchias and S Venizelos (which are attractively lined with mature
trees, down both sides), and on the right-hand side of the top of Roussou
Koundourou St, from Plateia El Venizelos.
    The Supermarket Lato (*Tmr* 79A7), in downtown, south-west Ag Nikolaos, on
the left of Odhos Kontogiani, is a workmanlike job and may well be open on
Sunday mornings. In this area of town is a most interesting drink shop edging
Plateia Minoos, north of the *Arion* (Tmr 50A6). Inside the shop resembles a
small garage and advertises the cheapest prices, with a litre of ouzo, and a little
present, costing 480drs - I should think the present is a doctor's certificate!
Naturally, Ag Nikolaos is not short of gift, traditional wear or jewellery shops.

DISCOS No problem!

FERRY-BOATS Quite a busy port, with a number of well-worthwhile
connections to various other Greek islands.

Ferry-boat Timetable (Mid-season)

Day	Departure time		Ferry Ports/Islands of Call
Mon	(After) 2200hrs	Ikaros	Sitia, Kasos, Diafani (Karpathos), Chalki, Rhodes, Simi, Tilos, Nisiros, Astipalaia, Katapola (Amorgos), Paros, Piraeus(M).
Tues	0830hrs	Ierapetra	Sitia, Milos, Piraeus(M).
Wed	0600hrs	Olympia	Sitia, Kasos, Diafani (Karpathos), Chalki, Rhodes.
Thur	0830hrs	Ierapetra	Sitia, Milos, Piraeus(M).
	1100hrs	Olympia	Anafi, Santorini, Piraeus(M).
Sat	0600hrs	Olympia	Sitia, Kasos, Diafani (Karpathos), Chalki, Rhodes.
	0830hrs	Ierapetra	Sitia, Kasos, Karpathos, Rhodes.
Sun	0545hrs	Olympia	Milos, Piraeus(M).
	1100hrs	Olympia	Anafi, Santorini, Sikinos, Folegandros, Milos, Piraeus(M).

FERRY-BOAT TICKET OFFICES
Massaros Travel (*Tmr* 80D5) 29 Roussou Koundourou   Tel 22267
Directions: On the left, on the way down from Plateia El Venizelos.

Mr Massaros must be one of the most helpful vendors of tickets in all of the Greek islands. Almost unbelievably, he has produced typed schedules of ferry-boats arriving and departing, not only from Ag Nikolaos but Iraklion, Souda (Chania), Kastelli and Sitia. The office also carries out exchange transactions.

The first section of Akti Koundourou, north of the Harbour bridge, is awash with tour offices, in amongst which is **Nostos Tours**, at No 30. This firm acts for most, if not all the ferry-boat companies.

LAUNDERETTE (*Tmr* 81A/B7) More a self-service laundry in which a more usual laundry business has a couple of do-it-yourself machines. The doors are open Monday, Wednesday & Saturday, between 0800-1400hrs, Tuesday, Thursday & Friday, between 0800-1400hrs & 1700-2000hrs, and is closed on Sundays.

MEDICAL CARE
Chemists & Pharmacies There are quite a number on the major streets.
Doctors There is a surgery across Odhos 28th October from the Post Office (*Tmr* 42C/D5), as well as another opposite the *Alexis Kafeneion* (*Tmr* 76C6), in the same building as a Dentist and Chemist.
Dentist *See* Doctor.
Hospital (*Tmr* 45A1) A large facility at the top of Odhos K Paleologou.

NTOG (*Tmr* 44D/E4) More a Municipal office, situated in the same building as the Port police, but facing directly on to the Lake bridge. The staff are very pleasant, friendly and helpful. Apart from a wealth of information, including ferry-boat details, currency is exchanged. The office opens daily, Monday to Saturday, between 0800-2100hrs, and Sundays, between 0800-1500hrs.

OTE (*Tmr* 38D5/6) Halfway down Odhos Roussou Koundourou, from Plateia El Venizelos, and one street to the east. The turning is to the right, along Odhos K Sfakianaki. Open daily, between 0600-2400hrs.

PETROL There are a pair of pumps on Odhos V Merarchias, as well as a number of petrol stations spread about the outskirts of the town.

PLACES OF INTEREST
Cathedral & Churches A lovely little chapel (*Tmr* 39D5) is sandwiched in between the tourist dross, towards the bottom of Odhos Roussou Koundourou, and comes as a complete surprise. The Cathedral is situated on Odhos S Venizelos (*Tmr* 40C6).
Museums
Archaeological Museum (*Tmr* 41B2) A small collection of exhibits housed in a new building, towards the top of Odhos K Paleologou. Open daily, Monday to Saturday, between 0830-1500hrs, and Sundays/holidays, between 0930-1430hrs, with admission costing 250drs.
Folk Museum Located in the same building as the Tourist office/Port police (*Tmr* 44D/E4). Open daily, between 0830-1300hrs & 1700-2100hrs, with admission costing 100drs.

There are some pathetic bird cages alongside the steps that ascend from Lake Voulismeni to Odhos N Plastira.

POLICE
Port (*Tmr* 44D/E4) In the corner of the building opposite the Lake bridge.

Town (*Tmr* 63B/C3) The Tourist and Town police are merged in an office, on the left of Odhos K Paleologou, as it ascends north-west from the Lake bridge.

POST OFFICE (*Tmr* 42C/D5) Down 28th October St, from Plateia El Venizelos, and on the left. Perhaps because there isn't a Post Office portacabin, unusually this facility is not only open weekdays, between 0730-2000hrs, but Saturdays, between 0730-1415hrs, and Sundays, between 0900-1330hrs.

SPORTS FACILITIES Apart from the more usual water sports, there is a Horse Riding centre at **Exo Lakkonia**, up in the hills, off the road to Kritsa.

TAXIS The main rank is beside the street close to the Municipal Tourist office (*Tmr* 44D/E4). There used to be a board displaying the charges to various destinations, but this has disappeared. If possible, ascertain the 'going' rate and negotiate with taxis at other points in the town, including the Squares of El Venizelos, Atlandithos and Minoos. This may well result in a lower quote.

TELEPHONE NUMBERS & ADDRESSES

Hospital (*Tmr* 45A1) K Paleologou	Tel 22369
Municipal Tourist office (*Tmr* 44D/E4)	Tel 22357
Olympic Airways (*Tmr* 32C5) Plastira	Tel 22033
Taxis 24hr rank	Tel 24000/24100
Tourist police (*Tmr* 63B/C3) 17 K Paleologou	Tel 22321

TRAVEL AGENTS Creta **Travel**, as remarked elsewhere in the book, offer an unequalled and extensive range of tours. They have an office on Odhos K Paleologou, across the street from Lake Voulismeni. **Massaros Travel** (*Tmr* 80D5) have an office at 29 Roussou Koundourou, and their attributes are eulogised about under **Ferry-boat Ticket Offices**.

EXCURSION TO AG NIKOLAOS SURROUNDS

Excursion to Kritsa, Lato & Kroustas (about 16km) Proceed along the Sitia road from Ag Nikolaos but instead of turning on to the Main Highway, cross over it and head for the hills. The initial stretch of the route, still in the 'shadow' of Ag Nikolaos, is a mess of light industry. Beyond **Mardati** village, and its taverna, is a sign to the right to:

Panaghia Kira (about 10km from Ag Nikolaos) A very lovely, simple, white-washed, Byzantine church. It is flanked by cypress trees, surrounded by a white-washed wall set in olive groves, not far distant from the roadway. The original 14th century central nave was supplemented, in the 15th century, by an aisle to each side. Admission from Monday to Saturday is between 0900-1500hrs and on Sunday between 0900-1400hrs. Entrance costs a princely 200drs, but the magnificent, richly executed, wall-to-wall frescoes are supposedly some of the best in Crete. Surprise, surprise, there is a small cafe-bar on the far, west side of the church. The owners sell icons, as well as yoghurt with honey, and postcards.

Lato Excavations (14km from Ag Nikolaos) The right-hand turning from the Main road is immediately prior to Kritsa village. The signpost points along a 3km rough track, and takes about an hour and a half to walk. The signs also indicate the 'Kritsa Gorge'.

There are substantial remains of the ancient city, which some authorities consider to have been one of the finest in Crete. It started to take shape in the 18th/17th century BC, with building proceeding until about the 3rd century BC. Lato was constructed between two hills, with extensive views out over the Gulf and the then City's harbour, now the site of modern day Ag Nikolaos. Well worth a visit.

KRITSA (11km from Ag Nikolaos) At the outset to this attractive mountain village, famed for local handicrafts, is a one-way road system. How quaint! Kritsa is now on the coach excursion schedules, as well as the busy, local bus route. Despite this it is still billed as an 'authentic', rural village, untouched by the (destroying) hand of tourism. Oh yes! And visitors should note that buses to this 'quiet, Cretan Eden' get very crowded.

The last part of the steep ascent into the village narrows down past *Rooms Argero*, on the left, a parking sign, on the right, the bus stop and a petrol station, close to a church and the Main Square. Alongside the Square is a fork in the road. The left-hand turning is to Kroustas, whilst the right-hand choice becomes Kritsa High St. The latter climbs up past a butcher with **Rooms** over the shop, and a fruit & vegetable store. The first floor balconies and vine covered trellises of the private houses are, in the main, draped with woven rugs and crocheted table clothes.

The Main St scrabbles along to a small, one tree-shaded village square edged by the Post Office, on the right. The latter reveals the extent of the tourist exposure as it is not only open weekdays, but Saturdays, between 0730-1415hrs, and Sundays, between 0900-1330hrs. Beyond the Post Office is a baker, also on the right, selling quite large, round cheese pies for 85drs. Where the High St levels out, so the tavernas and cafe-bars line up to compete with the numerous shops flogging the crochet work, for which the village is famed. There is some pressure-selling and a few instances of straightforward begging. In case any of the teeming hordes, that are bussed here, should fall ill, Kritsa boasts a Doctor.

Despite the despoiling waves of tourists (who daily 'assault' the village to plunder the not always genuine, local-grown wares), sanity returns as nightfall approaches. For those prepared to sit it out, there are several pensions and some *Rooms*, the rates for which are a little less expensive than those demanded in Ag Nikolaos. Most of the taverna/restaurants are located on the High St and their prices 'reflect' the situation.

There are spectacular views out over the rooftops of the serried houses as far as the Gulf of Merambellou. The village was the setting for the filming of one of Nikos Kazantzakis' novels, but there is some confusion as to which one!

Selecting the left-hand turning at the Main Square, ascends along a gently snaking road which narrows down and bends round a small, three barrel roof chapel, on the right. Five kilometres can make quite a difference and nowhere more so than the 5km separating Krista from:

KROUSTAS (15km from Ag Nikolaos). This delightful, tree lined, typical, unwhitewashed Cretan village boasts three kafeneions and a taverna, at the outset of the settlement, but no accommodation. The older women's everyday dress is the traditional garb, even when going about their common tasks and daily rounds. In the autumn this includes cracking piles of nuts.

Kroustas remains totally unsullied by the hordes that descend on nearby Kritsa, a state of affairs that will remain substantially unchanged if the inhabitant's present disinterested, if not dismissive attitude is any indicator to the future.

ROUTE NINETEEN To Sitia via Pachia Ammos (some 70km) The seabord from Ag Nikolaos, round the Gulf of Merambellou, as far as and beyond Istron, is 'Villa Country'. The coast is gently rugged, with little sandy coves here and there. The views are magnificent, with distant headlands to east and west curving round like the horns of a bull. The problem with holidaying . in an apartment hereabouts would be the comparative isolation - any cost calculations would have to include an allowance for taxi fares or vehicle hire. There are buses, but the timetables are limited, so be warned. One other point to bear in mind is that the daily traffic flow along this route is similar to being beside the M25, many of the scooters, motorbikes, jeeps, and cars being hired by happy holiday-makers.

Almiros has few hotels, after which the coast road climbs, winds and descends, in and around the various bays. At **Ammounda** there is a small bay, the rocky coast is beset by olive groves and the villas 'start in earnest'. The first turning off to the right, by a bridge, is for **Pirgos**, the junction being marked by some tavernas and flowers. In this area are a number of fashionable villas, in amongst which are dotted about the occasional old family house. At a major junction (12km) is a right-hand road up to **Kalo Chorio** village (13km from Ag Nikolaos, tel prefix 0841), backed by a pyramid shaped hill.

ISTRON (13km from Ag Nikolaos) A spaced-out swathe of a resort through which the main road thunders. The thoroughfare is edged by typical, everyday facets of Greek life - mini-markets, cafe-bars, tavernas, restaurants, a police office, petrol station, ladies hairdresser, supermarkets, a tour office or two, Rent-A-Vehicle, and souvenir shops. Mmmh!

From the left-hand side of the main road, alongside a taverna, is a backwards angled, surfaced track. This potters past the *Villa Ariadne*, through well-watered, cultivated fields, passing by a sandy football pitch, edged by bamboo groves, and opposite which is the smart *Rooms Dhomna*, surrounded by loads of old plastic.

The passageway emerges towards the right-hand side of a gently curving shore, close by a Cantina. On the far curve of the bay are two rather derelict boat houses and a neat, small chapel secured by a stone retaining wall. The seashore stretches away to the left, bordered by an arethemusa tree lined backshore, about centre of which is a wartime pillbox. The beach is a lovely sandy sweep with a pebbly middleshore.

The authorities have selected this location for one of those Ministry of Mercantile Marine signs - a directive for bathers headed 'The sea is waiting for you, are you ready?' The eight cartoons variously depict: a shipwreck (?); a drowning, whilst others chat away unaware; a speedboat rounding a swimmer; a sunbather toasting to a crisp; a litter lout; then a pictorial representation that means I know not what; a diver 'head-firsting' on to some rocks; and two men who appear to be kissing each other...!

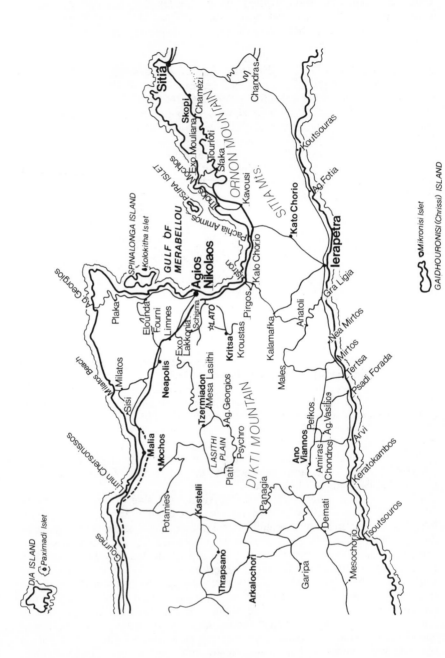

Illustration 21 Crete centred on Ag Nikolaos

Back at the main road is the *Hotel Golden Bay*, followed by the outskirts of the resort.

Hotels include the: *Elpida* (Class C, tel 61403), where an en suite single costs 2700drs & a double 3070drs, rising to 3620drs & 4520drs (1st June-30th Sept); *Golden Bay* (Class C, tel 61202) with en suite single priced at 2650drs & a double 3700drs, increasing to 3100drs & 4400drs (1st June-30th Sept).

Around the next low headland is a pretty, indented bay, bordered by a super, 100m long, sandy if narrow beach. The shore is overlooked by the massive, ugly, two-tone *Mistral Hotel*, clamped limpet-like to the cliff-face, on the inland side of the road. Either side of the *Mistral* are a couple of restaurant bars and a row of hill-hugging villas. As there isn't a Cantina down below, any beach buff, requiring a daytime snack or a drink, will have to climb up and cross the road. I suppose it would be possible to hire one of the pedaloes and 'motor' round to Ag Nikolaos!

Next along is the remarkable:
Istron Bay Hotel (Class L, tel 61303). This de luxe emporium is built on the sea side of a vertical cliff-face. The swimming pool and tennis court are spread around a small, sand and pebble beach, set in a lovely little cove, which the hotel almost totally fills. Not that I would like readers to be under the misapprehension that the facilities only include a swimming pool and (floodlit) tennis court. Oh no, there is a night club, in addition to the pool bar, boutique, jewellery shop, games rooms, complete with table-tennis and billiards, children's pool, water-skiing, sailing, pedaloes, canoes, a hotel caique, wind surfing and skin diving, to name but a few! Mark you, the charges reflect these small trifles, to which I must not forget to add air conditioning. Single room rates vary between 4220-7600drs, whilst double rooms cost between 5060-9120drs, and this is not per week. No, these are the daily rates.

This coast road is quite dramatic but alters, quite suddenly, on the approach to Gournia, where the scenery changes to moorland terrain. Prior to arriving at the archaeological site, a signboard declares the existence of:

Gournia Moon Camping (Tel (0842) 93243) The site is set down in a fairly exposed dip in the hillsides, which leads to a nice, little but rocky cove. The management have made up for the lack of a natural shore by creating an enclosed rectangle of sand. The rather strange little man on the reception desk speaks no English, but there is book exchange.

Gournia Site (21km from Ag Nikolaos) The contrast between the campsite and the archaeological remains could not be more extreme, if it was not such a ridiculous concept. The first time I viewed the ancient Minoan town of Gournia was when driving over from Ierapetra. The coastal plain, edged by the sea to the north, and surrounded by hills on every other side, spreads out down below, with the site laid over a small hillside. From a distance and height, it requires several long looks to establish that Gournia is not a comparatively recently abandoned village, but a place of great antiquity. This helps prove what I have always suspected, namely that not a lot has changed in Greek architectural development from Minoan times to the present day.

The approximate area of Gournia was initially pinpointed by Sir Arthur

Evans and taken up by a young American lady, in 1901. She almost completed the task of excavation by 1904. It appears to have existed as a working, self-supporting community, with harbour installations in the bay, the latter now submerged and lost. The opening and closing times are somewhat superfluous as entry can be gained with ease!

The main road drops down from the hills, past *Rooms* to the nearside of:
PACHIA AMMOS (22km from Ag Nikolaos) Tel prefix 0842. The dusty, dirty seaside village, and small port, spreads around a long, flat bay. In the background, to the east, are the towering Sitia and Ornon Mountains. Despite the setting and a sandy beach, Pachia Ammos has managed to make a real mess of things.

The main road/High St, which parallels and is some 100m distant from the waterfront, is edged by a large, inexpensive supermarket, on the left, *Marcos Rooms* signposted to the right, the smart *Hotel Zenios Zeus*, also on the right, and a petrol station, as well as remains of plastic agriculture, and old skeletal windmills.

The principal street down to the sea is at the west end of the settlement. It passes *Rooms*, prior to emerging on the waterfront in front of a 'sort-of' breakwater, alongside the fish taverna *Mouragio*, with the harbour quay to the left. The sandy shore, which becomes pebbly the further east one progresses, is comprehensively covered with a thick layer of rubbish - yes, a thick layer of rubbish. Clumps of bamboos appear here and there and a few fishing boats are 'dejectedly' moored alongside the harbour quay and mole. A solitary beach shower forlornly spits water at no one in particular.

Accommodation includes the:

Hotel Xenios Zeus (Class D)   Tel 93289
Directions: Beside the High Street.

Despite its grand sounding name, size and appearance, it is only a D class hotel, although all rooms have en suite bathrooms. Single rooms cost 2500drs & double rooms 3500drs. Some might say that clients should be paid to stay in this particular establishment!

Hotel Golden Beach (Class C)   Tel 93278
Directions: The Golden Beach is ineptly, if not ludicrously named, being located across the road from one of the greyest, filthiest beaches it has ever been my privilege to witness.

All rooms have en suite bathrooms, with a single costing 2000drs & a double 2500drs, which rates increase to 2500drs & 3000drs (1st July-15th Sept).

Not far to the east of Pachia Ammos is the junction with the turning off across the island, to Ierapetra. Offshore is a small, lighthouse topped islet. Hereabouts the main road veers away from the coastline, past an unusual stone chapel and a large petrol station, through an absolute sea of olive trees, on the way to the very pretty village of:

KAVOUSI (28km from Ag Nikolaos) A pleasurable, beautifully flower and tree lined settlement, which lies snuggled at the foot of the mountains. Apart from a *Pub Fish* (!), there are *Rooms* and a baker.

In Kavousi village is a sharply angled turning signed to Paralia Tholos. The tarmacadamed, olive tree edged road is overlooked by a massive, 'pebble-dash' mountain. The almost sheer-faced surface of the latter, which is broken up by regularly spaced outcrops of trees, slopes down for the 4km, drive to the right-hand side of the lovely, untouched if shadeless bay of:

Paralia Tholos The sandy foreshore of the quite wide beach becomes pebbly sand towards the levelled off backshore. There is some tree cover, a 'No Camping' sign, two or three small boats pulled up on the shore, four or so rubbish bins, and, curiously, 2-3 beached pedaloes. They have probably escaped from Ag Nikolaos!
The bay is overlooked by a dwelling, built on the soft slopes to the right, and a chapel and ruined building to the left. The seaward aspect appears to be almost blocked off by **Psira islet**, resulting in the erroneous impression of a channel to either side of the blob of land. This islet was an important Minoan port, with the remains of the settlement still extant.

From Kavousi the route commences on a long, steep climb, initially edging a dramatic, oleander filled canyon. Trees and flowers line the road all the way up the sharp ascent, which dramatically ends at the viewpoint platform of **Platanos**. A cafe-bar taverna snuggles up alongside a chapel with a rather unusual bell-tower. But the vista... The sea-views out over the steepling cliff-face, the base of which is constantly washed by the waves, take in Psira islet encircled by the bright blue, shimmering sea.
The route passes by a minor, unmade turning to Mochlos on the way to **Lastros**. The village stretches out to the left, along a spiny mountain projection edged by a gorge. At the next settlement of **Sfaka**, which similarly clings to a mountain ridge, is the main turning off to:

MOCHLOS (47km from Ag Nikolaos) Tel prefix 0843. The narrow, winding, dusty, descending, ripple-surfaced track crosses a pretty, agricultural plain. The road would appear to be in danger of being tarmacadamed. Maybe this is because of the rather plush holiday development that languishes alongside the thoroughfare, complete with swimming pool and tennis courts. Further on can be seen the main body of the fishing hamlet, tucked into the far side of a small headland, across the water from which is **Mochlos islet**.
Where the undulating, part-metalled road starts to parallel the shoreline, there is a wide, summer-dry river gulch, on the right. To the left is a sign indicating the presence of the *Blue Sky Villa & Rooms*, which are followed by *Villa Voula Rooms*, close to a small taverna. Beyond a grove of olive trees and vines is another doo-hickey taverna and, as a strict contrast, the *Club Aldiana Kreta*.
The general aspect of the countryside is similar to that of the west coast of Ireland, that is if the polythene greenhouses and occasional skeletal windmill are ignored!
At the outset to the settlement, and on the left, is the *Pension Restaurant Arethusa*, then the *Club Aldiana Water Sport* hut, alongside which is a stack of windsurfers, beside a rocky outcrop that forms a launch-way for the local fishing boats. The heart of this nicely off-beat hamlet edges a serpentine, concrete surfaced street bordering a rubbish strewn, steeply shelving,

pebble shoreline. This 'Esplanade' is pleasantly shaded by mature, pollar-
ded arethemusa trees and leads past a number of establishments. These
include the *Hotel Sophia Tavern*, of ethnic appearance, *Rooms/Cafe
Restaurant Kavouria*, run by a nice smiley lady, opposite which is a mini-
market-cum-tourist shop, and then *Rooms/Taverna Kokalia*. The Mochlos
menu prices are a good 10drs cheaper than 'town' charges.

Two hundred metres from the foreshore is the small, bold, barren islet
named after the settlement. A chapel nestles on the mountainside facing the
port and the sound between the two hosts a number of fishing vessels. The
islet's historical importance was as a Minoan harbour. Excavations have
turned up some dwellings and important burial tombs which, in their turn,
yielded a number of interesting artifacts.

Hotels include the: *Sophia* (Class D, tel 94240), where en suite double rooms
cost 2500drs; and the *Mochlos* (Class E, tel 94205), where bedrooms share the
bathrooms, a single costing 1350drs & a double 2300drs.

Back on the Cretan corniche of a main road, the thoroughfare winds past
Tourloti, perhaps the most dramatic of the rock-spine draped villages that
frequent this area, and then **Myrsini**, again set to one side of the highway.
Hereabouts is a magnificent view of the bays below, with soaring eagles,
seemingly suspended over the junction of cliff-edge and sea. The road
descends past another turning down to Mochlos, **Mesa Mouliana**, where
petrol is available, and **Exo Mouliana**, which straddles the road and is a
mix of dusty, old and new buildings.

The white blob of Sitia now hoves into view and the slow, winding, circuitous, rising and falling route, poorly surfaced in places, proceeds past
the Turkish-like, hill-hugging village of **Chamezi** overlooking a valley
plain. In an attempt to beautify the vista, the road edge has been prettily
planted with oleanders. Despite all the intrusions of the 20th century, a still
commonplace sight is men astride donkeys, pulling along reluctant goats
and sheep. Not all is Japanese trucks!

Next along, to the right and below the terraced olive grove lined road, is
the large, rambling, flat-roofed town of **Skopi**. Beyond this is yet another
'thought-provoking', dramatic section of road and ravine, that proceeds all
the way to Sitia.

**ROUTE TWENTY To Tsoutsouros via Kalo Chorio, Anatoli, Mirtos,
Arvi, Keratokambos** (about 106km) Take **Route Nineteen** to the Kalo
Chorio junction, where turn right on to the narrow, winding road which
passes through the large village of **Kalo Chorio**. Once past the side turning
to **Meseleri**, the road improves. This amelioration enables a traveller to
concentrate on the scenic delights of the comparatively lush country-side, to
admire the mountain vistas and trees... despite the bends.

Prina is a small settlement clinging to the hillside, rich in fruit and
vegetables, as well as grazing animals. Between Prina and the village of
Kalamafka (25km from Ag Nikolaos), nestling in the mountains, it is possible to observe the sea to the north and south of Crete, that is as long as
roamers are able to drag their eyes away from the now narrow, potholed
road. Unusually the culverts run with water, but from hereabouts

the beautiful views are marred by the familiar plastic. The road descends past a vast quarry works, where the surface of the thoroughfare is very bad, probably due to the weight of haulage traffic, and litter and dust are every-where. The route bends round a hillside, past the most unusual sight of a damned lake (no aunty not damned as in...). The land at the foot of the dam wall is littered with a mishmash of derelict quarrying equipment. A new stretch of as yet unsurfaced road approaches the sea   through acres of plastic, almost more dust than there is in the Sahara, as   well as great spaghetti junctions of irrigation piping. Incidentally, nowhere else on Crete is this trend to pressure artesian well-heads more apparent.

The western outskirts of Ierapetra, all the way to **Gra Lygia** (44km from Ag Nikolaos), are an absolutely appalling mess of quarries, bamboo, plastic agriculture, construction work, car breakers, and repair yards. The seashore is about 60-70m to the left, the backshore separated from the roadside by a sprawl of buildings, with plenty of petrol stations   scattered about. Truly speaking the dusty, rapidly developing Gra Lygia is really no more than a suburb of Ierapetra. It has a grey pebble, squalid, litter strewn beach, the backshore of which is planted with arethemusa trees, naturally interrupted by outcrops of plastic. Gra Lygia itself runs into **Stomio**. From hereon the road arrows over a flat plain bordering the sea, with *Rooms* and villas in amongst the sprawling ribbon development, and acres of plastic, all the way to **Nea Anatoli**, with its large church. The roadway is anything up to 120m from the sea's edge and 'drenched' in intensive polythene agriculture. It is interesting to note that mere plastic is beginning to make way for the com-parative permanence of acrylic sheeting. The countryside, now viewed from a plentifully tree bordered route, opens out on to not very attractive, cream-like, light brown soil, which appears to have been, and continues to be chewed by machinery. Where the road drops over a hillside, there is a pleasant, beautifully positioned chapel mounted on a knoll, adjacent to an olive grove but, naturally, almost completely surrounded by plastic.

Close to the route skirting a slender thread of a big pebble and rubbish strewn shore, with polythene greenhouses precariously balanced right up against the backshore, is a sign indicating a Minoan archaeological site. This is to the inland side of the road and is one of two adjacent to **Nea Mirtos**. Beyond these is a wide, stony, summer-dry river-bed and the turning down to:

MIRTOS (52km from Ag Nikolaos) Tel prefix 0842. The junction is alongside a lovely bougainvillea and the nice looking *Hotel Esperides* (Class C, tel 51207). Here all rooms have en suite bathrooms, with a single costing 2750drs & a double 3450drs, increasing to 3300drs & 4130drs (16th June-30th Sept).

The narrow streets of the 'fly-friendly' village are laid out on a grid pattern profusely planted with flowers and trees, as well as green rubbish bins. The settlement extends along the fairly elongated, not very wide, grey sand but predominantly pebble beach, edged by a surprisingly formal, concrete surfaced pedestrian Esplanade. There are at least three *Rooms* signed from the waterfront, including *Nikos*, whilst the *Straight Pub*, alongside the *Taverna Akti*, opens between 2100-0900hrs. A few small fishing boats are anchored off the beach.

Apart from the Esplanade accommodation, where a double bedroom costs from 1500drs, the 'High St', which parallels and is some three streets back from the sea, contains the *Myrtos Hotel* (Class C, tel 51215). Close to the *Myrtos* is a periptero and a taxi rank. Adjacent to the latter is a shop with **Rooms**, and a window notice 'At the primary school in our village there is a museum of   traditional art. Entrance is free. You are welcome to visit it 1900-2230hrs'. To the west of the *Myrtos*, along the High St, is a baker offering accommodation, as does the fruit & vegetable shop next door. Yet further on is the *Villa Mare*.

In one of the side-streets is the agreeable *Kafeneion Ermioni*, a favoured hang-out with both locals and expatriates, whilst another popular rendevous is the *Restaurant Botsalio*. On the bypass is the swept up *Kastro Studio Apartments*, alongside a church.

The pretty and pleasant village has won its long struggle to repel an unsavoury invasion by the 'great unwashed'. Despite this a few still lurk and the resultant, if occasional, fairly violent disagreements are resolved in a very Cretan fashion - a nod's as good as a wink. Perhaps the fact that the Germans destroyed the village, disposing of all the males, stiffened the residents resolve against any blitzkrieg by modern day undesirables!

Mirtos heralds the outset of a coastal stretch largely devoid of tourist intrusions, a welcome, if unexpected return to a swathe of the Crete of old.

The road climbs westwards, turning inland and gently winding up through fire wracked countryside. The brown foothills of Mount Dikti lie to the right. The turning for by-passed **Sikologos**, advances along a neatly signposted but appallingly surfaced track to a fork. Here the left choice descends to the simple, agreeable looking, reasonable expanse of pebble beach at **Tertsa** (65km from Ag Nikolaos). Next along is:

PSADI FORADA (68km from Ag Nikolaos) A simple, seaside hamlet which lacks any 'support' facilities, that is apart from the taverna at the junction of the access road with the wide winding track bordering the backshore. This is rather surprising as there is a super, broad sweep of fine grey sand beach, with a fine pebble foreshore edging a beautifully clean sea. Large arethemusa trees are spaced out along the edge of the beach. The east end of the shore peters out in amongst a clutter of boulders and a cliff remnant, whilst the west side is shut off by a rocky headland. Incidentally the owner of the reasonably priced taverna speaks fair English.

There is a choice of routes to Arvi. One involves returning inland to the mountain hugging main road, via **Kalami** village, in the area of which are a number of beehives amongst the hillside lemon groves. At **Pefkos** there is petrol, some tavernas and a turning off to **Ag Vasilios**, high above a green ravine. Apart from a bus stop in the latter village, there are kafeneions and **Rooms**, with caves looking down on the road and pomegranates in the trees. The loop road curves back towards the main route, via the narrow, old village of **Amiras**. Here is the tightly twisting, downward plunging road to Arvi, which runs out on a poorly surfaced track edging the backshore of a big pebble, rubbish littered shore. Turn left, or east for the still unspoilt, seaside village, past a sign which exclaims 'Have a nice trip'! Dear God.

The alternative route is the dusty, scrubbly, coastal track that ploughs on through a riot of plastic agriculture, the occasional outcrop of domesticity, and bursts of flowers. *En route* this choice passes a pleasing pebble beach close to the tiny hamlet of **Faflangos**. The basic terrain resembles that of creamy, gnawed moon rock. Hereabouts the track cuts inland in a horse-shoe of a curve to circumnavigate a valley gorge. The kerbside is edged by bamboos as well as the occasional wrecked motor car, which is not really that surprising considering the state of the track. The route closes with a boulderous seashore, broken up by scattered outcrops of pebbly shingle. The sea-bed is liberally sprinkled with rocks and there is despoiling poly-thene, everywhere. Random dwellings, almost hidden by abundant bougainvilleas, are passed by, after which another inland loop circles round a small plain crammed full of plastic greenhouses. The track runs on to a surfaced section of road, some 50-60m above a pebble beach, prior to:

ARVI (81km from Ag Nikolaos) Tel prefix 0895. A pleasant, 'halfway village', halfway between the isolation of nearby Keratokambos and the busier, if very Greek, Yukon-style, doo-hickey, 'prefabricated' resort of Tsoutsouros. Arvi is spaced out either side of a High St, which runs parallel to and is separated from the seafront by a continuous row of buildings. The shore is a narrow strip of mainly pebble, with some grey sand, bordering a clean sea washing over a large, rounded pebble sea-bed. There isn't an Esplanade, as at Mirtos, more a string of interconnected patios and terraces of the various tavernas and accommodation establishments that line the sea-wall. Similarly to Mirtos, Arvi lacks a harbour and the few large fishing boats lie anchored close to the foreshore.

The eastern approach crosses a summer dry river-bed, passing by goats tethered to homestead railings, riots of bougainvillea, plastic greenhouses cheek-by-jowl with modern apartments, a kafeneion and a store. The road makes a junction, opposite a periptero, with the approximate centre of the confined, rather canyon-like High St.

To the left (*Fsw*) along the High St is a cafe-bar souvlaki place, followed by the *Taverna Pub Valentino BBQ*, also on the sea side of the street, then the *Taverna Diktina*, which specialise in vegetarian foods, fresh fish and break-fasts, and beyond which the High St 'sort of' runs out. A sign indicates *Rooms Galaxy* and there is yet another *Rooms* at this end.

To the right along the High St are *Rooms*, a restaurant and a kafeneion, all on the left, a small store, on the right, the *Rooms/Restaurant Alkion* and *Gorgona Rooms*, both on the left, a mini-market with accommodation, on the right, another store labelled 'supermarket', across the road, a restaurant, on the right, and, on the left, the *Hotel Ariadne* (Class C, tel 71300).

All the hotel rooms have en suite bathrooms, with a single costing 2059drs & a double 2575drs, increasing to 2405drs & 3300drs (16th July-15th Sept). Of the eating places, the *Beside The Sea Restaurant* is an interesting, 'local bandit' rendezvous, with a pleasantly positioned patio looking out over the boulderous sea. The *Fast Food Shop* offers both 'perked coffee' and 'breaded lab chops' (*sic*). I have, in the past, favoured the rather untidy but interesting *Restaurant/Rooms Kyma*. The interior is festooned with various impedimentia, including bits of fish, sea shells, crabs, crayfish and a turtle shell. An old-fashioned juke-box adorns the ground floor, as does a litter of wicker chairs and circular fishing baskets, the latter edged with cork into which are stuck the sharp hooks. Mine hostess speaks English and her double rooms, sharing the bathroom, cost 2000drs, or 2500drs with breakfast. A meal, for two, of 2 plates of small dab-like fish (350drs each), an enjoyable cabbage salad with feta cheese (250drs), a bottle of retsina (110drs), and bread, was charged at 1100drs.

From Arvi, the more sober-minded citizens will retrace their 'wheel marks' to the main road, beyond Amiras, and turn left for the appealing, spectacularly mountain clinging village of **Ano Viannos**. A left here turns down and along the pretty route to attractive, but not so spectacular **Chondros**, from whence the road is asphalted all the way to Keratokambos.

On the other hand... instead of rejoining the main road, it is possible to journey from Arvi along the coast, on a rather daunting, unmade, rocky, dusty donkey route. This roughshod track wanders through a poorly signposted, pretty but plastic greenhouse littered landscape. It passes a number of chapels and numerous German handwritten indicators for a beach, which is disappointingly nothing more than shingly pebble. The inland mountains are Nevada-like. After the possibility of a few false trails, alongside some sort of concrete gas holder, the route makes a junction with the well signposted road between Ano Viannos and:

KERATOKAMBOS (90km from Ag Nikolaos) The main road from Chondros spills out on the tiny seaside hamlet's 'Esplanade/High St'. This mature arethemusa tree lined tarmacadam strip edges a long, narrow, mainly pebble beach, in which there is some sand, that stretches away to left and right. Since I first wrote about Keratokambos, despite detailed changes, it has remained largely undeveloped and I still regard it as unspoilt, if delightfully messy, straggling, tawdry Shangri-la. I have to admit that one person's idea of beauty, desirability, or heaven on earth, is not necessarily that of another observer. For instance, visitors might find the overwhelm of chickens, that scratch their way from one end of the settlement to the other, rather too rural. Those readers who think they could learn to love Kerato-kambos, as it stands, should visit before it is too late.

Close by the centre of the settlement, at the Chondros road T-junction, is a small square dominated by a twin barrel roofed chapel, standing back on the west corner of the plateia. Opposite the chapel is a well organised looking beach shower and water point. A few paces up the access road is a *Rooms*, whilst to the left (Fsw) are three side-by-side tavernas. In 'line order' they are, respectively, the *Cafe-bar Kokolas*, the *Fish Taverna Grill Stube* - 'We speak German', and the *Taverna Kionossos*, all offering simple meals, with the latter two having unsophisticated Rooms. Incidentally my selection out of the three (based on boring old Geoffrey's reminisces, about which I will tell anybody who is prepared to listen) is the middle of the trio, run by Nikitas.

English is not a language suit to be long in - German appears to be a better bet, and the average charge for a double room, sharing a bathroom, is 1500drs. A metalled road runs along the edge of the shore to the east, passing by the three aforementioned tavernas, alongside the last of which are a row of polythene green houses. They are followed by three or four modest villas and a wasteland, which continues to evince some signs of development, one day. The trees edging the backshore of the two metre wide sand and pebble beach almost entirely thin out, and at about 200m there is a spit that projects into the sea.

Along the surfaced road to the west, or right (*Fsw*) of the village, in the direction of Tsoutsouros, is a doo-hickey cocktail bar, then a mini-market, followed by the *Morning Star Taverna/Rooms*. This latter accommodation is more often than not fully booked by Germans.

To the west *en route* to Tsoutsouros, the road's surface disappears, degenerating to become nothing more than a rugged, stony track. This borders the coastline, passing through the shadeless, rural outskirts of Keratokambos, all chickens, goats, donkeys and dust. After some 200m there is a cluster of dwellings, including the *Pension/Fish Taverna Kastri*, edging a large pebble shoreline and overlooked by a couple of very smart, hillside villas.

The route serpentines and switchbacks round a rocky headland, about 80m above a beautiful bay and gorgeous, sandy beach, before dropping down to a narrow, sandy coastal plain, rimmed by rather barren hillsides. Unexpectedly, in the middle of this wilderness of salt flats and olive groves, set in a sea of agricultural plastic, is an unattractive, brown dapple coloured little cafe. The direction to take becomes distinctly problematical hereabouts. If it's any help, after 5km turn left and then swing inland, cross over a rudimentary bridge and veer left again, passing by an appalling mess of a shanty settlement bordering a wide, summer-dry, valley river-bed. The commercial *raison d'etre* of this dust covered 'Soweto' appears to be a cement ring making plant. But the riveting focus of attention must be the fact that the privies, or 'tai-bach's'of the hamlet are lined up on the bank of the river-bed! (I hope this is the correct plural of the Welsh 'Ty-bach', or 'the little house'). It must be reiterated that the surface, or more correctly the lack of any surface of this route, would severely test a well-heeled tank, let alone an ordinary vehicle. The flat plain, across which the track forges, supports olive trees, bamboos and giant shrubs. At a fork, to the left simply finishes up on a sweep of pebble beach. To the right, the part tree shaded route climbs steeply away from the coastline to cross over a small, red soil, polythene littered plateau. Beyond this, the track proceeds through another olive grove to round a small bay, past a lot of plastic rubbish as, in the distance, is sighted:

TSOUTSOUROS (101km from Ag Nikolaos) The final approach is along an extremely rough surface, as is the street even in the confines of this messy, disappointing, very Greek seaside settlement. The two and three storey, prestressed concrete, backwoods development has been 'thrown up' on a narrow area edging a small, flat bay and surrounded by steep mountainsides, to the west.

The resort, if it can be so named, becomes extremely busy in the height of the season, being very popular with the Greeks (what do they know that I don't?). Most of the buildings look out over the broad sweep of gritty sand beach, in which is mixed a lot of pebbles, with a very fine pebble foreshore. Some sickly trees have been planted on the backshore, to supplement the more mature arethemusas close to the heart of Tsoutsouros. A number of fishing boats are moored to the beach, which is bordered by an Esplanade of sorts.

In and about the centre of the place are *Preassos Rooms* and the *Hotel Georgios*, whilst moving west, towards a spit pleasantly covered with trees, passes a cafe-bar, a mini-market, **Rooms**, a restaurant or two, *Venetia Rooms*, *Rent Rooms* and a kafeneion.The sight of a post box in such out-of-the-way places always makes me wonder when and by whom these widely scattered receptacles are emptied.

To the right are the remnants of the original fishing hamlet, whilst beyond the spit is a pebble cove and the very smart, two storey *Apartments Sophia*.

Instead of travellers retracing their steps, it is possible to take the serpentine, dramatically ascending dirt track towards the north. The road edge is rubbish littered at certain spots, a blight more than adequately compensated for by the magnificent views. That is assuming one's nerves are up to taking time to appreciate the great panoramic sweeps. Once the mountains have been topped, there are even more amazing landscapes, this time of the green, cultivated valleys ringed by the great mass of the looming Dikti Mts. A strange feature is the extraordinarily symmetrical outlines apparently traced on the distant slopes, probably something to do with regularly planted olive groves. Altitude pills might be a help on these heights!

The still unsurfaced but wide road, apparently in danger of being metalled, descends to the doo-hickey village of **Kato Kastelliana**, possessed of an inordinately large chapel, and positioned on an east-west road. To the right is the settlement of **Demati**, to the left is the village of **Ano Kastelliana**, wherein a petrol station, and beyond which the road is surfaced.

Those who do not want to return to Ag Nikolaos, but wish to cross over into another region, can continue in a westerly direction through pleasant, deep Cretan countryside. The first village, where fuel is available, is **Mesochorio**, quite dramatically poised on the Kofinas Mt range, with views out over a huge, flat plain, mainly filled with olive trees. Next along is the spread out, hillside clambering **Rotasi**, followed by the quite large village of **Pirgos**. Herein are *Rooms*, a pharmacy, the *Restaurant O Memas*, a Post Office, more *Rooms*, and a zacharoplasteion. The only easily visible signpost is that for **Prinias**, which is along a minor road to the south. The required route is to the west, which becomes unsurfaced on the way to **Charakas**. The savagely potholed road is surfaced through this latter village, as is often the case, but becomes unmetalled on the far side of the settlement, at **Ag Fotia**, which appears almost deserted and has a pretty chapel. On the outskirts of the rather scrubbly, 'wild west', water-abundant village of **Sternes** (133km from Ag Nikolaos) is a vast Texaco petrol station. The latter is alongside the junction with the tarmacadamed **Asimi** road. Beyond the next, cramped village of **Panagia**, the roadway follows a watercourse, of sorts, all the way to the rubbish littered settlement of **Dionisio**. The road then becomes unsurfaced in hillier, grassland countryside. At **Stavies**, which is quite old in places, there is petrol. Spaced out **Fournofarango** has narrow little streets, from which a roughly surfaced track passes a cemetery on the way to **Loukia**. This, as my notes so succinctly put it is 'real honey of a little place' - a fascinating village with bread ovens easily visible, as are the remains of one of those vertical, revolving stone wheel, grain crushing devices. The back streets are worth poking about. To the west the surfaced road is bordered by olive groves, all the way to the narrow streets of **Vagiona**. This village is large, has a cafe-bar, taverna and not one, but two petrol stations. On the far side of Vagiona are low hills supporting groves of olives. The signposting hereabouts is dreadful. Next along the now unmade road is **Flathiakes**, assuming a traveller is fortunate enough to get the direction correct, beyond which is the village of **Apesokari**, whereat is the junction with the road that leads to Lendas, *et al.*

ROUTE TWENTY ONE
To Plaka & beyond via Elounda & Spinalonga (16km) The road from the centre of Ag Nikolaos follows the coast hugging Esplanade to the north, through the widespread suburbs of the town. Close to the *Mirabello* is a 'Water Sports Centre', where buffs can do almost anything to all and any piece of floating kit. This route passes by numerous hotels, pensions and *Rooms*, all the way to **Ammoudi**, where there is a prominent headland. Amongst these accommodation possibilities are *Rooms Poppi, Minos Beach*, and the *St Nicholas Bay Hotel Bungalows*.

On the seaward side, a branch road skirts a sound in which are anchored a wildly disparate number of craft, this bay formed by an isthmus and a headland bulge. The side road becomes a paved strand, which continues on to encircle the southern section of the promontory to come to an end, up against a flight of steps. Beyond these, the grockles have forced their way through the fence of the luxury *Minos Palace Hotel*, thus pedestrians can wander on for a bit, to be able to look at the sea from close by the hotel's green lawns.

The main coast road continues to chicane along the coast, past inland hillsides well and truly despoiled by the Ag Nikolaos overspill. It then sets out on the ascent towards **Hera** village, sited halfway up the mountainside. Hera may now have been invaded by one or two hotels, as well as some villa development, but from the vantage point there are still amazing views. These panoramas look out over the elongated peninsula of **Megala Spinalonga** (to distinguish it from the like-named, tiny islet to the north) and the narrow causeway linking the 'offshore' land to the 'mainland'. In the way of this isthmus are extant some windmills, even if the original salt flats have all but disappeared.

The main road descends from the heights to pass through clean countryside dotted with isolated hotels, cafes and bars, olive groves, some old houses, classy apartments, a number of *Rooms*, the *Astia Palace*, and *Christine Rooms*. Prior to gaining the centre of Elounda, a signpost to the right indicates the route to the ancient site of **Olous**, and the Spinalonga causeway. Olous was a port and important city, but little now remains, although there is an early Roman mosaic and basilica in the area.

ELOUNDA (11km from Ag Nikolaos) Tel prefix 0841. Once a simple fishing port, Elounda has, for many years, been a smart, international holiday resort, exuding an air of quite dignity. This ambiance is even more noticeable when compared with the razzamatazz of nearby Ag Nikolaos. Furthermore it is a pleasant surprise to observe some old buildings have survived the explosion of luxury and Class A hotels, the latter providing an adequate testament to the swept-up nature of the seaside haven. To further preserve the widespread acclaim and acceptability of the location, there are a few discos and night clubs.

In and around the Main Square are: an OTE hut, close to the prominent clock tower and a church; a Post Office, one block north of which is the Police station; and the National Bank of Greece. The Square is situated adjacent to the rocky seafront harbour, in which are moored private craft, fishing boats and some excursion craft.

Immediately to the north of the Main Square are a pair of *Rooms*, on opposite sides of the street, followed by a wide Esplanade backing the resort's shadeless beach. This is an agreeably sandy, if small shoreline, the sea-bed of which shelves quite steeply. As yet, sun-beds and umbrellas are noticeable by their absence, despite which water skiing is available. Unless I am very mistaken, the beach has been truncated by extensions to the harbour works.

From the centre of Elounda, the coastal road to the north snakes along the edge of the sea. At the north end, the *Taverna Alasia* has accommodation and a little further on is a tiny, pocket-handerkerchief of sand, followed by *Rooms Despina*. This is a quieter, prettier area of Elounda, with boats moored in and amongst tree planted little inlets and headlands. The sound formed by the mass of Megala Spinalonga and the shore is very attractive.

Elounda was the location for the BBC TV series *Who Pays The Ferryman*, a fact that is used to advertise the various hostelries once favoured with the crew and cast's patronage.

Accommodation available includes the following hotels and pensions, all with en suite bathrooms: *Korfos Beach* (Class B, tel 41591), with singles priced at 1945drs & doubles 2530drs, rising to 3430drs & 3845drs (1st June-30th Sept); and the *Hotel Maria* (Class C, tel 41335), where a single costs 2000drs & a double 2600drs, increasing to 2200drs & 2800drs (15th May-15th Sept).

Cheaper accommodation is located at **Schisma**, immediately prior to Elounda, which includes the: *Hotel Aristea* (Class C, tel 41300), with singles at 2800drs & doubles at 3800drs, rising to 3300drs & 4400drs (1st June-30th Sept); *Hotel Calypso* (Class C, tel 41367), where singles cost 2240drs & doubles 3440drs, increasing to 2990drs & 4180drs (1st May-30th Sept); the *Krini* (Class C, tel 41602); *Maria* (Class D, tel 41335), with singles at 2000drs & doubles at 2600drs, rising to 2200drs & 2800drs (15th May-15th Sept); and the *Hotel Olous* (Class E, tel 41357).

A branch road off to the left, through the 'old quarter' of Elounda, winds up to the pretty village of **Fourni**, surrounded by stone-walled vineyards and with no concessions to tourism. From Fourni the road, lined with a lovely avenue of white trunked eucalyptus trees, advances to the pretty little village of **Kastelli** (not western Crete Kastelli), where there is petrol and a post box. Continuing on in this direction leads westwards to Neapolis.

Returning to the north coast road, in the direction of Plaka, it passes through some nicely stone wall divided olive groves, in which are embedded the occasional outcrops of luxurious development, as well as a scattering of *Rooms*. About half-way along this route are some magnificent views of the fortress isle of Spinalonga, with Megala Spinalonga peninsula to the south and, to the north, the headland of Cape Ag Ioannis rearing up in the background.

PLAKA (16km from Ag Nikolaos) Alongside the approach is a further 'Watersport Centre'. Immediately before the hamlet and tiny fishing boat port is a crescent of pebble beach, backed by a gently rising, scrubbly area of land, with not a villa or hotel in sight. Next along is a lovely little chapel, beyond which, and before the settlement, is a foreshore, well shaded by mature arethemusa trees.

Attractive, quiet, part-crumbling Plaka is draped over a red soil headland projecting into the sea. Close to where the Spinalonga islet boats dock, is *Rooms Kadiana*, in the same building as the Karva Mini-market Kastello. The various restaurants and tavernas include *Le Gaulois Restaurant*, as well as a low key motorbike and car hire business, Motor Myrima. At the north end is a large pebble beach edged by the main road.

There is no doubt that Plaka becomes busy during the day... but at night-time reverts to a lazy, restful most pleasant place to stay.

Local fishermen have made an alternative living by ferrying people (600drs each) to and from:

Spinalonga Islet Known as 'the island of the living dead', whilst a leper colony. The fortress was built by the Venetians, in 1579, and the structure proved so impregnable that they managed to hold out against the all-conquering Turks until 1715 (the rest of Crete having fallen by 1669). The Turks, in their turn, stayed in occupation of this remarkable outpost for some years after they had departed 'mainland' Crete. Some time in 1904 it became a leper colony, which finally closed in 1957.

To the north of Plaka the road winds away from the coastline rising steeply on a metalled surface, whatever the maps may indicate. As the route bends back towards the cliffs of the massive headland and climbs, the views become more and more dramatic. There are wonderful seascapes out over Spinalonga islet, past a line of 'dead' Cretan shaped windmills, in the midst of which is a chapel. These windmills overlook the village of **Vrouchas**.

Somehow up here is a feeling of shaking off the excesses of tourism, a reversion to the Greece of old, and a pleasant, welcoming ambiance. The moorland countryside is dominated by narrow, small fields enclosed by stone walls. The still-paved, country lane-wide route passes through and by a number of lovely hill settlements, which include **Selles, Kato Loumas, Pano Loumas** and **Skinias**. Apart from one or two windmills that are almost in one piece, the multitudinous water wells are interesting in that they are fenced off with railings. It is also noteworthy that hereabouts the old roads are clearly visible, even if they are more wide paths than roads, edged by stone walls... as is everything up here.

At the junction where Valtos, Finokalia and Neapolis are signposted to the left, is the now concrete surfaced track. This descends on to a wide, surprisingly long agricultural plain, stretching out beside the rocky, northern coastline, and on which lies the scattering of dwellings that make up the hamlet of:

AG GEORGIOS (approx 26km from Ag Nikolaos) The track loses its surfaced coating as it wanders across the shabby, not overly fertile landscape, around which are scattered a number of quite noticeable, concrete water cisterns.

Fishermen lift their craft in and out at a small cove, by which is a rural kafeneion. This is not a location at which to get stranded, at the end of the day, without the means to make a return to larger céntres of opportunity!

9 SITIA (Siteia)

A Cycladean island 'look-alike' Chora & port; a busy town awash with steps & white cubic houses; a lack of Venetian or Turkish remains; biting flies.

GENERAL (Illustration 22) Tel prefix 0843. The population is about 6500.

The harbour town probably has connections with the Byzantium Eteia and was named La Sitia by the Venetians, who built a fortified wall and castle. Otherwise history appears to have side-stepped the area, apart from the occasional earthquake and pirate raid.

The town to the north of the Main Square, Plateia El Venizelou, is pure island harbour charm, with the higher sections rather reminiscent of the upper flights of Syros. The terraces of square, white houses are interspaced with steep, broad steps, both of which climb upwards, seemingly ever up-wards. The 'Chora' hillside is topped, to one side, by a fort and chapel cemetery, overlooking the old ferry-boat quay, a long, triangulated water-front square and the Esplanade. In strict contrast, the areas to the south and the east are generally messy, urban sprawl.

Here at Sitia, the more usual tidal flow of holiday-makers is still only a mild swell, but the causes for the comparatively slow infiltration by the tourist industry are difficult to fathom. Certainly one of the main reasons must be the extreme distance from Iraklion airport. The relative remoteness is accentuated by the fact that much of the main road, although fairly well surfaced, is of a sinuous, 'island quality' after the National Highway runs out, just beyond Ag Nikolaos.

The usual approach is from the direction of Iraklion. This road drops down from low, gentle hills to the south-west of the town. Once on the out-skirts, the descending route curves fairly sharply past the Ierapetra turning, along a dual carriageway to the junction with the waterfront Esplanade. To the right (or south-east) advances out of Sitia towards Vai, Paleokastro and Zakros, alongside a very long, gently curving shore of several miles length. To the left of the junction leads immediately into the town proper. At Plateia El Venizelou the broad quayside Esplanade makes an 'L' shaped angle, running away to the right (*Sbo*) and edged by house, shop, taverna and restaurant fronts, on the left, and, on the right, by awning covered terraces lining the harbour quay wall.

Unusually, little Venetian or Turkish influence is visible, apart from the fort. In fact the houses are in the style of the Cycladean islands, being coloured cubic shapes. Certainly Sitia might well be considered an ideal seaside resort for it possesses: a splendid beach; an interesting old town; a fishing, cargo and ferry-boat port; and a picturesque waterfront packed with lively tavernas. At night the north Esplanade, Leoforos El Venizelou, is closed off to traffic.

The town is famed for its sultanas and there is a rave-up - no, no, a fes-tival, held in the month of August to celebrate the fruit. A ticket allows visitors to drink as much of the local wine as can be consumed, whilst watching Cretan folk dances.

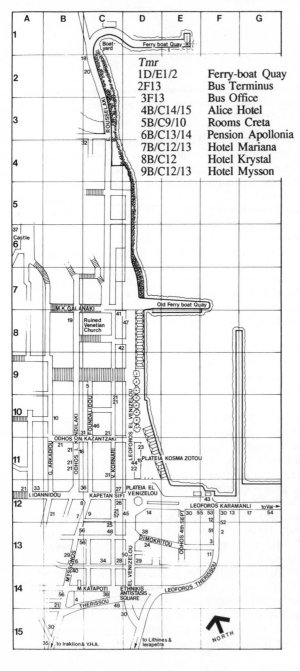

Tmr	
1D/E1/2	Ferry-boat Quay
2F13	Bus Terminus
3F13	Bus Office
4B/C14/15	Alice Hotel
5B/C9/10	Rooms Creta
6B/C13/14	Pension Apollonia
7B/C12/13	Hotel Mariana
8B/C12	Hotel Krystal
9B/C12/13	Hotel Mysson

10B10	Hotel El Greco
11E/F13/14	Hotel Via
12E/F12/13	Hotel Helena
13F/G12	Hotel Flisvos
14D12	Hotel Itanos
15D11	Hotel Denis
16B/C11	Rooms Maria
17G12	Hotel Akrogiali
18B/C1/2	Hotel Nora
19B8	Hotel Arhontica
20B/C2	Hotel Castello
21	Rooms
22D11	Souvlaki Snackbar
23D10/11	Zorba's Restaurant
24D13	Taverna Ouzeri Ergan‹
25C12/13	Cafe-Taverna Baclava‹
26C/D12	Commercial Bank
27C/D11/12	National Bank
28C/D13/14	Bank of Crete
29	Supermarkets
30	Petrol Stations
31	Bread shops
32B/C3/4	Hotel Stars
33A12	Hospital
34C13/14	Supermarket/General Store
35A/B15	Hotel Minos
36B/C11/12	OTE
37A6	Venetian Fort
38D13	Post Office caravan
39C14	Post Office
40B13/14	Town police
41C/D7/8	Port police
42C/D8/9	Ferry-boat ticket Offi‹
43E/F12	Public lavatories (dea‹
44D11	Olympic Airways Ag‹
45C/D12	Kafe Zackro
46C10	Taverna Kali Karda
47C/D8	Kafeneion Taverna To Kyma
48C12/13	Kafe-Bar
49C14/15	National Bank
50C/D13	Ionian & Popular Ban‹
51F13	Petras Moto
52F12/13	Kazamias Rent A Car & Bike
53F12	Sitia Rent A Car
54G12	Car Hire (various)
55E/F12	Hermes Car Hire
56	Ladies Hairdressers
57C12/13	Dentist

Tmr = Town map reference
Fsw = Facing seawards
Sbo = Sea behind one
Fbqbo = Ferry-boat Quay behind or‹

Illustration 22 Sitia

ARRIVAL BY AIR The airport, which is about 1km to the west of Sitia, is rather difficult to locate and the street leading to it is very narrow. Perhaps this accounts for the fact that, unusually, there isn't an Olympic Airways bus, it being necessary to walk, or to catch a taxi. There was a rumour, in 1989, that the Swedish airline, *SAS*, was taking over the facility, as they had acquired a stretch of southern coastline, between Makri Gialos and Ierapetra.

Whatever the future holds, currently the only flight connections are with the Dodecanese islands of Karpathos, Kasos and Rhodes.

ARRIVAL BY BUS The Bus Terminus (*Tmr* 2F13) is sited on the right of the Main road into Sitia, close to the seafront. Incidentally, Leoforos Therissou is a rather featureless, drab, dual-carriageway, although the central island has been landscaped and planted with flowers and shrubs.

ARRIVAL BY FERRY The Ferry-boat Quay (*Tmr* 1D/E1/2) is at the far, north end of the town. After disembarking it is a maximum of a ten minute, dusty walk to the centre of Sitia.

THE ACCOMMODATION & EATING OUT
The Accommodation There is a surprisingly wide choice and variety, at both the bus (south) and ferry-boat (north) end of the town.

For those who arrive by ferry, on the right of Odhos E Rousselaki, quite close to the quay, there are the *Hotel Nora* (*Tmr* 18B/C1/2) (Class D, tel 23017), the *Hotel Castello* (*Tmr* 20B/C2) (Class C, tel 23763), and the:

Hotel Stars (Astra) (*Tmr* 32B/C3/4) (Class D) 37 M Kalivaki   Tel 22917
Directions: As above.

Not only convenient to the Ferry-boat Quay, and away from the general hurly-burly, but probably the best value in town. The old lady owner really is a dear, more often than not sitting down new guests with an ouzo and a slice of apple - a proper *xenos* welcome. Double rooms, sharing the bathrooms, are charged at 1475drs, plus 150drs each for the use of the hot water shower. Incidentally the water is hot, all day, and the best rooms are at the front, facing towards the harbour, which can be seen over the roofs. The lateral street, also to the front of the building, is incredibly steep, despite which the locals persist in driving up the incline, with varying degrees of damage to their vehicle's clutch.

The 'Chora' is a warren of streets in a grid layout, in amongst which are a good selection of **Rooms** (*Tmr* 21). Those lanes richest in accommodation, all parallel to the waterfront down below, are Odhos I Kondilaki, Foundalidou and V Kornari. A sampling of these typically disorganised, 'Greek family ethnic' offerings are the:

Hotel Arhontica (Archontikon) (*Tmr* 19B8) (Class D) 16 Kondilaki   Tel 28172
Directions: From the north end of the waterfront, turn up the steep flight of steps, Odhos M K Galanaki, alongside the Port police office (*Tmr* 41C/D7/8). At the first lateral street of I Kondilaki turn left (*Sbo*) and the hotel is almost immediately on the right.

Neat and of pleasantly provincial appearance, with double rooms only, sharing the bathrooms. Rates start off at 1590drs, rising to 1650drs.

Rooms Creta (*Tmr* 5B/C9/10) 37 Foundalidou   Tel 28743
Directions: Continue on along Kondilaki St, south from the *Arhontica* and left
down the second, main flight of broad steps, first right on to Foundalidou St, and
the place is on the right.
Reasonably priced at 1800drs for a mid-season double room.

Rooms Maria (*Tmr* 16B/C11) 35 Kondilaki   Tel 22768
Directions: Back on Odhos I Kondilaki and on the east or sea side of the street.
A very nice, smiley lady who offers double rooms, sharing the bathroom, at a
mid-season price of 1800drs.

The other side of the street, almost opposite *Maria's*, is **Rooms** (*Tmr* 21B10/11),
at No 54. This is a 'perfect' example of the 'Greek family, disorganised, ethnic
accommodation'. The rooms are jumbled up with the owners' living quarters and
the washing machine is in the guests' bathroom. Despite the above, prices are not
commensurately cheaper than the 'good, average' charges.
Also on this side of the street are **Rooms** (*Tmr* 21B11), at No 58, followed by,
and one building to the south, the *Venus Rooms*.

Back at the junction of I Kondilaki and N Kazantzaki, turning west up Odhos
Kazantzaki passes *Rooms Apostolis* (*Tmr* 21B10/11), at No 27. At the
T-junction with Odhos G Arkadiou, turn right (*Sbo*) and on the right is the:

Hotel El Greco (*Tmr* 10B10) (Class C) Arkadiou   Tel 23133
Directions: As above.
All rooms have en suite bathrooms, with a single costing 1900drs & a double
2440drs, increasing to 2500drs & 3250drs (1st July-30th Sept).

For those prepared to climb up Odhos Kapetan Sifi, from Plateia El Venizelou
(*Tmr* D12), past the Hospital (*Tmr* 33A12), and on the right is **Rooms** (*Tmr*
21A12, tel 23868).
Crossing over to the Bus terminus side of town, leads to a number of smarter,
more expensive options than the more traditional rooms. These include the:
Hotel Vai (*Tmr* 11E/F13/14) (Class C) Leoforos Therissou   Tel 22528
Directions: On the left (*Fsw*) of the Main road into Sitia, at the junction with
Odhos Dimokritou.
Smart and expensive, despite its Class C rating, and all rooms have en suite
bathrooms. Singles start off at 2800drs & doubles 3000drs, which charges in-
crease to 3300drs & 3500drs (1st July-30th Sept).

Hotel Helena (*Tmr* 12E/F12/13) (Class C) Leoforos Therissou   Tel 22681
Directions: Further on along the avenue from the *Vai*, almost at the T-junction
with the Esplanade.
The rooms have en suite bathrooms, with singles charged at 2720drs &
doubles 3160drs, rising to 3340drs & 3620drs (1st July-3Oth Sept).

At the Esplanade T-junction, to the right (*Fsw*) along Leoforos Karamanli, in the
direction of Vai, are a number of opportunities, including the:
Hotel Flisvos (*Tmr* 13F/G12) (Class D) 4 Leoforos Karamanli   Tel 22422
Directions: As above.
It may have a good seafront view, but this is a busy, noisy road. Single
rooms, sharing the bathroom, cost 1300drs & doubles sharing 1800drs, whilst en
suite double rooms cost 2150drs, charges that rise, respectively, to 1400drs,
2100drs & 2500drs (16th July-30th Sept).

Hotel Akrogiali (*Tmr* 17G12) (Class E) 10 Leoforos Karamanli   Tel 22357
Directions: As above.
Only double rooms available, with those sharing the bathrooms priced at 1800drs & those with an en suite bathroom 2300drs, increasing to 2000drs & 2700drs (1st June-15th Sept).

A little further along the road is the *Hotel Elysee* (Class C, tel 23427).
From the Esplanade T-junction and to the left (*Fsw*), towards the Main Square, and on the left is the:
Hotel Itanos (*Tmr* 14D12) (Class C) El Venizelou Sq   Tel 22146
Directions: As above.
Smart but booked by rambling groups and coach parties, amongst others. Naturally (at these prices) all rooms have en suite bathrooms, with a single costing 2800drs & a double 3300drs per night. These rates rise to 3200drs & 3800drs (1st July-30th Sept). Breakfast costs 350drs & lunch/diner 1000drs.

Hotel Denis (*Tmr* 15D11) (Class B) 60 El Venizelou Sq   Tel 28356
Directions: At the west end of Leoforos Karamanli is a raised, small round-about. This 'hosts' a stone memorial, in the shape of a recumbent soldier, and four large palm trees. To the right, where the road divides, is a fairly large block of buildings. The hotel is behind a cafe-bar.
Although categorised B Class, this is an old-fashioned pension and the bed-rooms all have to share the bathrooms. A single is priced at 2000drs & a double 2600drs, increasing to 2200drs & 3200drs (1st July-30th Sept).

The Hotel Krystal (*Tmr* 8B/C12) (Class C) 17 Kapetan Sifi/Myssonos Tel 22284
Directions: Up Odhos Kapetan Sifi and in the third block west from Plateia El Venizelou, on the left.
A modern, stylish hotel wherein all rooms have en suite bathrooms. A single room costs 2900drs & a double room 3200drs, which rates rise to 3400drs & 3800drs (1st July-30th Sept). Breakfast costs 450drs.

The Hotel Mysson (*Tmr* 9B/C12/13) (Class D) 82 Myssonos   Tel 22304
Directions: Almost opposite the *Krystal*, in the side-street of Odhos Myssonos.
Clean, sparse and very Greek provincial, as might be expected of a Class D hotel. Mid-season doubles cost from 1600drs, sharing the bathroom.

Hotel Mariana (*Tmr* 7B/C12/13) (Class C) 67 Myssonos   Tel 22088
Directions: On the other side of the road from the *Mysson*.
All bedrooms have en suite bathrooms, with single rooms charged at 2500drs & double rooms at 3200drs, which prices increase to 3000drs & 3800drs (1st July-30th Sept).

Further along Odhos Myssonsos, in a south-westerly direction, there is accommodation at:
Pension Apollonia (*Tmr* 6B/C13/14) 22, off Odhos Myssonos.
Directions: As above and on the left, a block before the Police station. The building is on the corner of Myssonos St and the side-street.
Picturesque, literally, with murals here and there. Steps from the side-street lead to the bedrooms and a pleasant balcony, off which are a washroom and toilets. Singles cost about 1200drs & doubles 1800drs.

Across the street from the 'Copshop' (*Tmr* 40B13/14) is a snackbar with **Rooms**.
Alice Hotel (*Tmr* 4B/C14/15) (Class C) 34 Papanastassiou   Tel 28450
Directions: Close to the top of Myssonsos St, adjacent to the main Iraklion road.

A modern hotel in which all rooms have en suite bathrooms, with a single costing 2900drs & a double 3200drs, which rates rise to 3400drs & 3800drs (1st July-30th Sept).

Also at this end of the town are the:
Hotel Minos (*Tmr* 35A/B15) 31 Therissou   Tel 28331
Directions: As above, at the outset of the Iraklion road 'proper'.
    Rather more 'pensionish' than a hotel, and a 'little rough and ready', but all bedrooms have en suite bathrooms. A single starts off at 1450drs & doubles 2000drs, increasing, mid-season, to 1700drs & 2300drs.

Not more than a couple of hundred metres up the Iraklion road is the:
Youth Hostel 4 Therissou   Tel 22693
Directions: As above and on the left.
    Well spoken of, with a very friendly, 'camp fire' atmosphere (as have many Cretan Youth Hostels). The sexes are only divided by hand-painted signs, so God help the population explosion amongst friendly hostellers! An iron dormitory bunk costs 450drs a head... and the best of luck.

The Eating Out The Gallic presence and bias is most noticeable, and welcome - and why not? At least it's a change from the more usual German this and that. 'For instances' are menus in French and restaurant dishes that include snails, bouillabaisse and *petit dejeuner*.
    A plethora of waterside taverna tables and chairs, shaded by bright awnings, stretch north from Plateia El Venizelou, all the way to the old ferry-boat quay. Their fare is extremely well presented, breakfasts are a speciality, and the standard of fish dishes excellent. Naturally clients must have deep pockets to order fish, but this maybe one of those occasions and locations at which to give into the temptation to shell out (whoops) the extra drachmae. Possibly it is unfair to select one particular establishment from the pack, but at the Plateia El Venizelou end of this attractive row of diners is:

Zorba's (*Tmr* 23D10/11)
Directions: In the same block as the *Cafe Tsirilakes/Hotel Denis*.
    A wide range of dishes to fit most pockets and sensibilities.

At the other end of the spectrum, from the sublime to the ridiculous, is the:
Souvlaki Snackbar Ostellios (*Tmr* 22D11)
Directions: Sandwiched (must one!) between the *Cafe Tsirilakes/Hotel Denis*, the other side of the building to Plateia Kosma Zotou.
    Serves a good quality souvlaki pita and is an extremely popular establishment. The locals who crowd in are a noisy testament to the quality.

The *Ostellios* is no longer on its own, their being some 2 or 3 other snackbars across the street, one being the *Fast Food Tsak Cafe-bar*.

Taverna Erganos (*Tmr* 24D13) Dimokritou
Directions: From Plateia El Venizelou proceed in a southerly direction along Odhos El Venizelou, past the Public Garden, and the first street on the left slants down past *Erganos*.
    The ownership changed late in 1989, so I can only wish the new, young owner all the best and hope his high aspirations succeed. Across the street from the building is an awning covered terrace where the BBQ's are cooked and summer

months clients sit outside. The service is slick, the menu offerings are good, the helpings generous, a local retsina is available, but the meals may well be served cool, if not cold. Sample dishes and prices are as follows: tzatziki 200drs; cucumber/tomato salad 120drs; Greek salad 225drs; kalamares 300drs; meat balls 350drs; octopus 450drs; chicken 350drs; rabbit 600drs; grills 700drs; a bottle of beer 95drs; a kortaki retsina 140drs; and bread & service 20drs.

Kafe Zackro (*Tmr* 45C/D12)
Directions: Edging Odhos El Venizelou, south of the Main Sq. A friendly, popular daytime cafe-bar, with a usually crowded, awning covered patio edging the pavement on the other side of the road.

They serve Nes meh ghala (75drs), a solid cheese pie (80drs), bread, doughnuts, as well as the more usual cafe-bar zacharoplasteion type food and drink.

One shopfront to the east of the *Itanos* (*Tmr* 14D12) is a glitzy, sit-down or takeaway, soda-pop style snackbar, where they have a space-age machine to make loukoumades. A helping for one is enough for two, at a cost of 120drs.

Beside Foundalidou St is the 'locals' *Taverna Kali Karda* (*Tmr* 46C10).

Cafe-Bar Taverna To Kyma (*Tmr* 47C/D8)
Directions: At the far, north end of Leoforos El Venizelou, close to the old ferry-boat quay, with a covered patio across the Esplanade. It is the last but one, beyond the Air Force Club, yes the Air Force... who have their own building and section of quayside terrace.

A meal, for two, at the down-to-earth *To Kyma*, of 1 tzatziki (180drs), 2 helpings of liver (300drs each & absolutely excellent), a Greek salad (230drs, very good & plenteous), 1 bottle of kortaki retsina (140drs), bread & service (20drs each), cost a total of 1190drs. Other dishes available include fresh fish, omelettes, cutlets and beefsteak. Apart from meals, I rate this an excellent spot at which to sup a postprandial drink. Mark you, it depends on who does the addition, Mother, who errs on the 'light side', or the son, who might 'weight' bills a little. A couple of 'meaty' Nes meh ghala and an ouzo costs 250drs.

Two almost side-by-side, low-ceilinged, old-fashioned, not inexpensive establishments lurk on the street one back and parallel to Odhos El Venizelou, south of Odhos Kapetan Sifi. They are 'local' haunts, both of which have attempted to establish a distinctive style with their advertising slogans and owner's 'point of sale' offers. The first is the *Cafe-bar Delicious Foods Restaurant Baclava* (*Tmr* 25C12/13). This advertises *Rooms*, and is a 'bit of a hole', sporting numerous youth hostel style signs and a board declaring 'If You Don't Like The Food You Don't Pay'. I presume diners who make a habit of 'not liking' are discouraged from future patronage. The next along is the *Kafe-Bar* (*Tmr* 48C12/13), a more ethnic joint that advises 'In a friendly Cretan atmosphere - enjoy'. Yes!

There are signs in the Esplanade trees advertising the *Taverna Narromilos*, Ag Fotia, which is 3km from Sitia and reckons it is the best taverna in the world!

THE A TO Z OF USEFUL INFORMATION
AIRLINE OFFICE & TERMINUS (*Tmr* 44D11) More an Olympic agent, at No 56 Leoforos El Venizelou (Tel 22270), north of Plateia El Venizelou. The office is open Monday-Saturday, between 0830-1300hrs & 1700-2030hrs.

There are no airport buses to the 'small island' airport, thus it is necessary to take 'Shanks pony' or a taxi (200drs). Flights do not connect to Athens, but very conveniently make a link with three of the Dodecanese islands.

Aircraft timetables

Day	Departure time	Islands	Arrival/Departure time
Tues & Thurs	1110hrs	Kasos	1140hrs
		Karpathos	1215hrs
		Rhodes	1315hrs
Sat & Sun	1145hrs	Karpathos	1220hrs
		Rhodes	1320hrs

One-way fares: to Kasos   3470drs, duration 30mins.
to Karpathos 4510drs, duration (via Kasos) 1hr 5mins.
to Rhodes   8770drs, duration (via Kasos & Karpathos) 2hrs 5mins.

BANKS The Commercial Bank (*Tmr* 26C/D12) and the National Bank (*Tmr* 27C/D11/12) span the entrance to Odhos Kapetan Sifi, alongside Plateia El Venizelou. South of the latter Square are the Bank of Crete (*Tmr* 28C/D13/14) and the Ionian & Popular (*Tmr* 50C/D13), almost side by side on Odhos El Venizelou, whilst the National has another branch office (*Tmr* 49C14/15), alongside Odhos Therissou.

BEACHES The town's sandy beach describes a gentle curve for a mile or so, in an easterly direction, and is edged by the Vai road. Once in the water,there is a stretch of pebble and an unexpected dip in the sea-bed surface, probably caused by wave action.

BICYCLE, SCOOTER & CAR HIRE There are any number of car and scooter hire businesses 'gathered together', in and around the junction of Leoforos Therissou with the Esplanade, Leoforos Karamanli, from whence they also stretch along the Vai road. Firms include Hermes Car Hire (*Tmr* 55E/F12), Petras Moto (*Tmr* 51F13), Kazamias Rent A Car & Bike (*Tmr* 52F12/13), Sitia Rent A Car (*Tmr* 53F12), as well as Kazamias (again), Interrent Europe Car, Apollon Rent A Car, and Vai Rent A Car, in a bunch bordering the Vai road (*Tmr* 54G12). Petras are a fairly 'switched on' outfit, where a 50/80cc moped costs 700drs a day and a 125/160cc scooter 1300drs. Strangely enough, considering their proximity, Kazamias, across the road, demands 1700drs a day for a 50cc machine, reducing that fee to 5000drs for 3 days and 10000drs for one week, despite which they are still damned expensive, compared to Petras. Cars are the usual exorbitant rates.

BREAD SHOPS The Bakers definitely hide their bushel in Sitia... From Plateia El Venizelou climb Odhos Kapetan Sifi and turn right (*Sbo*) on to Odhos Kornari. On the left is a tiny Bread shop (*Tmr* 31C11/12), at No 85, with a post box on the wall alongside. Continuing along Odhos Kornari, left on N Kazantzaki St, across the crossroads with Odhos Foundalidou, and on the right is a 'hole-in-the-wall' Bread shop (*Tmr* 31B/C10/11).

BUSES The Bus Terminus (*Tmr* 2F13) is located on the right (*Fsw*) of Leoforos Therissou, close to the waterfront. The Bus office (*Tmr* 3F13) is diagonally across the Avenue and apart from tickets, pies can be purchased.

Bus timetable
Sitia to Iraklion via Ag Nikolaos, Malia, Iraklion
Daily   0615, 0915, 1115, 1215, 1445, 1645, 1915hrs
Return journey
Daily   0800, 1030, 1230, 1500, 1730hrs
One-way fare: 1000drs; duration 3½hrs; distance 143km.

Sitia to Vai via Paleokastro
Daily   0900, 1000, 1100, 1200, 1415, 1600, 1815
Return journey
Daily   1000, 1100, 1200, 1300, 1515, 1700, 1900hrs
One-way fare: 210drs; duration 1hr; distance 29km

Sitia to Kato Zakros
Daily   0615, 1115, 1430hrs
Sun & hols   1115, 1430hrs
Return journey
Daily   1230, 1700hrs
Sun & hols   1230, 1700hrs
One-way fare: 350drs; duration 1hr; distance 50km.

Sitia to Ierapetra via Makri Gialos
Daily   0615, 0900, 1200, 1415, 1700, 2000hrs
Return journey
Daily   0630, 0800, 1000, 1200, 1415, 2000hrs
One-way fare: 430drs; duration 1½hrs; distance 61km.

COMMERCIAL SHOPPING AREA Not only is there no central market but, generally speaking, Sitia is a difficult town in which to shop, it being necessary to incur much 'to'ing and fro'ing'. On the other hand matters have improved in recent years with the opening of several Supermarkets (*Tmr* 29D13/14 & 29B13), one each almost directly opposite the junction of the side-street that runs between Odhos El Venizelou and Myssonos. In this latter side-street is located the original, busy Supermarket, more a General store (*Tmr* 34C13/14).

Close to the Therissou St National Bank (*Tmr* 49C14/15) is a Fruit & Vegetable shop/store. At the outset to Odhos V Kornari, which branches off Kapetan Sifi (*Tmr* C/D12), are a number of Fruit & Vegetable shops. If there is a 'Market' St, it is Odhos Foundalidou, between the junction with Kapetan Sifi and the crossroads with N Kazantzaki St (*Tmr* B/C10/11), wherein are Fish merchants, Butchers, Fruit & Vegetable shops, *et al.* The southern continuation of Odhos V Kornari, as well as the south end of the parallel street of El Venizelou, are the dress and shoe shop area. Shops generally do not open on Sunday, and useless information is that Sitia must have more barbers than bars.

DISCOS The faintly menacing *Rock Bar Kazamia* (*Tmr* C6) is in a stepped alley angled off the south, old ferry-boat quay end of Odhos E Rousselaki. Alongside M K Galanaki, the steps up from the old ferry-boat quay, is another strobe-light flashing rock pub, with a further selection of the same along the Vai road.

FERRY-BOATS The new Ferry-Boat Quay (*Tmr* 1D/E1/2) is to the north. It seems strange that, in building the facility, the berthing arrangements were not made easier. The quay is a tight fit for the larger craft, which have to have the assistance of a rowing boat in order to dock. This is to aid the positioning of the starboard hand stern line and the bow mooring rope, the latter having to be taken over to the seashore edging the approach road, Odhos E Rousselaki.

Ferry-boat timetables (Mid-season)

Day	Departure time	Ferry-boat	Ports/Islands of Call
Mon	2400hrs	Ikaros	Kasos, Karpathos, Diafani (Karpathos), Chalki, Rhodes, Tilos, Nisiros, Astipalaia, Amorgos, Paros, Piraeus(M).
Tues, Thurs & Sun	1500hrs	Ierapetra	Ag Nikolaos(Crete), Milos, Piraeus(M).

Ferry-boat timetables (Mid-season)

Day	Departure time	Ferry-boat	Ports/Islands of Call
Wed	0800hrs	Olympia	Kasos, Karpathos, Diafani (Karpathos), Chalki, Rhodes.
Sat	0800hrs	Olympia	Kasos, Karpathos, Diafani (Karpathos), Chalki, Rhodes.
	1030hrs	Ierapetra	Kasos, Karpathos, Rhodes.

FERRY-BOAT TICKET OFFICES
K Tzortzakis (*Tmr* 42C/D8/9) 183 El Venizelou   Tel 22631
Directions: Half-way along the northern Esplanade.
When the office is not open, there are chalk-written boards with the latest shipping information.

HAIRDRESSERS Apart from the barbers, there are at least three Ladies Hairdressers (*Tmr* 56B/C12/13; 56B/C13 & 56B14) clustered on or around Odhos Myssonos.

MEDICAL CARE
Chemists & Pharmacies Plentiful, including one across M Katapoti St from the Post Office (*Tmr* 39C14), and another alongside the Commercial Bank (*Tmr* 26C/D12). A rota system operates.
Dentist (*Tmr* 57C12/13) The surgery is in the street one back and parallel to Odhos El Venizelou. The doors open weekdays, between 0900-1330hrs & 1700-2030hrs.
Hospital (*Tmr* 33A12) This is quite a large facility, in a busy little upper quarter of the Town, reached by ascending Odhos Kapetan Sifi, which becomes I Ioannidou St, and is on the right (*Sbo*).

NTOG None.

OTE (*Tmr* 36B/C11/12) At 22 Kapetan Sifi St and only open Monday to Friday, between 0730-2200hrs.

PETROL There are a number of petrol stations (*Tmr* 30C/D14/15; 30E12; 30F12 & 30A/B15) in the south-east segment of Sitia. The Petrol station (*Tmr* 30F12), alongside the junction of the Esplanade and Leoforos Therissou, appears to close for siesta early every day, as well as Sundays, holidays and high days. The 'in place' (*Tmr* 30E12), on the corner of the Esplanade and Odhos 4th September, is inconveniently sited, causing many a traffic-jam.

PLACES OF INTEREST There is a shortage of the usual offerings, but all is not lost.
Pelican Sitia has acquired a resident pelican, for which the worthy burghers have erected a 'Pelican kennel', at the outset to the old ferry-boat quay. He (or she, I am no pelican sexer) is an autocratic bird and wanders about, disdainful of people and traffic alike. So as to minimise the mayhem the bird can cause, his ex officio minder shuts the pelican away in the kennel at nights.
Folklore Museum Rustic but interesting exhibits used to be displayed in a build-ing on Odhos Arkadiou but, in 1989, its 'home' had moved. Conflicting sign-posting points up the steps at the top of Odhos I Ioannidou, beyond the Hospital (*Tmr* 33A12), despite which the exact location defeated me.
Sultana Factory "Did you know"... there is one edging Odhos Foundalidou,

reminiscent, in a sunny way, of a British, northern industrial town backstreet warehouse. It may look dead but do not be fooled.

Venetian Fort (*Tmr* 37A6) Built in 1204, it is small and plain with extensively restored walls and a pleasant keep. The elderly attendant may still possess a piece of paper with, written on it, the following dates: 'Spanish pirates 1538: Turks 1651; Greek 1870'! Were that all history lessons were that easy!

POLICE
Town (*Tmr* 40B13/14) In Myssonos.
Port (*Tmr* 41C/D7/8) Above a gift shop on the corner of a building facing the old ferry-boat quay.

POST OFFICE (*Tmr* 39C14) In the same wedge of buildings as the *Alice* and open the usual hours. There is a Post Office caravan (*Tmr* 38D13) beside Odhos Dimokritou, which opens weekdays and Saturday, between 0800-2000hrs, and Sunday, between 0900-1800hrs. Without doubt, the introduction of this service, to the more busy resorts, must be voted one of the most tourist friendly innovations of many a year.

SPORTS FACILITIES The French connection is nowhere more evident than at the *boule* pit, close to the bridge on the Vai road. Also along the Leoforos Karamanli (the 'Ocean Side Drive' road to Vai) and by the (last) Beach Bar, on the left, is a Windsurfing School. Not to be forgotten is the Sitia Body-building set-up, close to the BP Petrol station (*Tmr* 30A/B15), alongside the Iraklion road out of town.

TAXIS There are taxis ranked in front of the Post Office (*Tmr* 39C14) and alongside the Public Garden, on Plateia El Venizelou.

TELEPHONE NUMBERS & ADDRESSES
Olympic agent (*Tmr* 44D11) 56 El Venizelou   Tel 22270
Town police (*Tmr* 40B13/14) 24 Myssonos   Tel 22266

TRAVEL AGENTS *See* Ferry-boat Ticket Offices.

TOILETS There is an 'at the moment' closed, quay toilet block (*Tmr* 43E/F12), almost opposite the junction of Leoforos Therissou and the Esplanade.

ROUTE TWENTY TWO To Kato Zakros via Erimoupolis, Vai, Paleokastro & Zakros (59km)

The poorly surfaced road leaves Sitia over an almost makeshift bridge. The inland countryside is littered with bamboo, trees, backyards, allotments and the occasional holiday development. The left, or sea side of the road borders the backshore of a very long, grey, shelving, sandstone beach, edged by groves of trees. Many of these have been recently uprooted, thus somewhat despoiling the scenic effect. At the far end the seashore degenerates into slabs of rock, about which are scattered some patches of gritty sand, and overlooked by polythene greenhouses.

The road now rises to some 50m above the rocky coastline. In amongst this rather desolate, quarried, lunar scenery are dotted about even more plastic greenhouses, as well as signposts to this or that holiday bungalow and villa. Where **Roussa Eklissia** is indicated to the right, the route wanders away from the sea's edge. At the village of **Ag Fotia**, to the inland side of the road, are **Rooms**, small apartment developments and villas to let. Visitors who choose to holiday in this area would almost certainly have to hire a car, and have the use of a swimming pool. In 1971 a Minoan cemetery was discovered.

The Main road now tucks back towards the boulderous coast, with outbreaks of new building in progress - goodness only knows why? Close by a fire-gutted petrol station, the thoroughfare describes a large loop, allowing views back over Sitia. As the route progresses eastwards, the countryside changes from the mountainous ravines, to the west of Sitia, to gentle, sloping, scrub-covered, sandy hillsides. The road serpentines about, winding backward and forward over the dramatic 'Minoan/West coast Irish' panorama. At about 10km the highway hooks around a sandy but rubbish strewn, shadeless cove, whereon are a couple of very isolated villa apartments. Oh dear me, what would a holiday-maker do out here?

Twelve kilometres from Sitia is a fork in the road (right for Paleokastro, left for Vai), where there are some quite strange chalets lining the junction. I ask you, what on earth are they thinking about? Perhaps they are overgrown beehives!

Selecting the left-hand fork, in the direction of Vai, the road climbs in a series of steep zig-zags on to the top of the hills. This viewpoint allows seascapes out towards the group of islets that make up the **Dionisiades Islands**. The highway now veers inland, on an appallingly surfaced road, with badly eroded edges, past a windmill, to:

Toplou Monastery (17km from Sitia) The strange looking building, a fortified Venetian monastery, is built on a sparse, bare and isolated location. This is the site of a much earlier religious building, but earthquakes and human predators caused the location to be rebuilt in the 16th century. The interesting nomenclature *Toplou* is derived from the Turkish for canon ball and on display in the Museum are some intriguing relics, historical documents and icons. The Monastery buildings, usually surrounded by grazing herds, are supplemented by a cafe and gift shop, but frankly the chapel on the other side of the road is prettier than Toplou.

From hereon the landscape is bleak, rolling moorland, all the way to the Vai/Erimoupolis choice of routes, a junction marked by a car park and Cantina. The northern road of the two advances to:

Erimoupolis Beach (24km from Sitia) The location is also known as Itanos, after the presence of a Minoan settlement that, unusually, retained its importance and expanded during the Roman and Byzantine era's. Observing the now deserted, if attractive site, the latter seems rather unbelievable, but there you go.

The approach runs out close by an informal vehicle park, a grove of trees and a small, gritty sand cove, with a few boulders scattered about and some angled biscuit rock. Beneath one of the trees, a fisherman, or shepherd, has fashioned an open-air 'drawing room', equipping it with an old fridge, secured by a guy rope, and used as a larder, as well as a BBQ grill. 'Our man' is not very tidy - perhaps the housekeeper has been ill!   At a quick glance, the nibbled grass to the rear of this 'domicile' appears to be rather lawn-like.

Over the headland to the left (*Fsw*), is a much larger but shadeless cove, with a lovely sandy sea's edge and a fine, gritty sand beach.

To the right is an outcrop, on which are still visible the remains of some now unidentifiable foundations. On the far side is yet another, small, sandy beach cove. The bundy has been put to use as an outdoor toilet, and the whole area is littered with rubbish, especially discarded bottles and tins. These indicators of the 'great unwashed' usually betoken their presence, but they would have appear to have flown the coop.

The setting is magnificent, with **Elasa islet** to the east and the **Cape of Sideros** curving away in the distance. No further exploration to the north can be undertaken, as the Greek Navy occupy the rest of the peninsula.

A hop, skip and a jump leads back to the junction, and the palm tree bordered approach to:

Vai Beach (some 24km from Sitia) More correctly named Finikodasos. This renowned, seaside beauty spot has a gritty sand beach, the backshore of which is edged by groves of palm trees, giving the appearance of a tropical location. That is, a much-visited, excursion-crowded, beach-bar, car park-encircled, highly overrated tropical location.

There is a large toilet block where the vehicles pull up, as well as a vendor of bananas. The beach is gated off, as this area is a National Park. Despite this designation, immediately on the left is a beach bar chalet, to which a track of duckboards allows ease of access over the sand. Here a Nes meh ghala costs 75drs and a Coke 80drs. The 'deserted' beach sports a Watersports Centre, at the left-hand end, where charges per hour are as follows: 300drs for a canoe; 800drs for a pedalo; 1000drs for a windsurf board; and 5000drs for scuba diving.

Returning to and selecting the Paleokastro turning, the countryside is more pleasing, even if it is rather 'Army range' in character. Unbelievably there are holiday-let villas in this comparatively deserted expanse. To the left is signposted a rough track down to:

Kouremonos Beach (31km from Sitia) The track sweeps past the backshore of a pleasant expanse of sand and pebble beach with a sandy sea's edge bordering a rather wild bay. The shoreline keeps on to the right (*Fsw*) and about a 100m distant is a 'dead' bus, seemingly abandoned in the scrub.

The track continues on, cutting over a hillside to the left, to come to a halt alongside a small caique harbour. The only things present, in these barren surrounds, are a couple of fishermen's huts and what appears to be literally hundreds of pre-cast concrete, sea-water breakwater 'knucklebone' fabrications. I wonder how many years it will be before this delightful, if deserted spot receives the 'treatment'.

Back on the main route, the road swings past various signs, amongst which are 'Next Summer Vai Camping' and *Rooms*, as well as a signpost, in the direction of the coast, indicating Angathia and Marina Village (of which more later). These precede the outskirts of:

Illustration 23 Crete centred on Sitia

PALEOKASTRO (33km from Sitia) Tel prefix 0843. The road into the centre of the large village passes by at least three **Rooms**. The Main Square is surrounded by a taxi rank, a church and a campanile/clock tower, three or more tavernas, a motorbike hire firm, a restaurant, half-a-dozen or more **Rooms** (including *Rooms Calin*), the *Why Not Pub*, and the *Hotel/Restaurant Itanos* (Class E, tel 61205). West of the Square is a petrol station, more **Rooms**, the *Restaurant Vai* and the *Discoteque Space*.

Other village hotels include the *Pension Hellas* (Class B, tel 61240) and the *Paleokastro* (Class E, tel 61235). The average single room costs 1200drs and a double 1800drs, both sharing the bathrooms.

Returning to the north end of Paleokastro and following the sign for Anga-thia/Hotel Marina Village, an unmade, dusty track makes a straight run through highly cultivated olive groves. Beneath the shady branches of these trees, sheep peacefully graze. The small village of **Angathia**, in which are **Rooms**, is to the right, whereabouts the track becomes very flinty. The *Marina Village* (Class C, tel 61284) complex, signed off to the left, is also set in the olive trees. Various confusing tracks descend to an enormous bay, hemmed in by a headland to the left (*Fsw*) and the extended finger of land of Cape Plaka, to the right. The main track emerges at the right-hand side of the rather wild, lovely, nearly deserted series of large sandy coves. Close by is the site of the Palaikastro Minoan remains, overlooked by Kastri Hill. Keeping along the track to the extreme right (*Fsw*) of the bay, on the north side of the Petsofas headland, passes by further coves.

The main, sand, gritty sand and fine pebble beach is edged by smallish arethemusa trees, in amongst which are one or two tents of wild campers. The whole bay is bordered by a wide plain, once a marshy area of saltings, now scrapped flat and levelled with scalpings.

Set back from the waters edge, in about the middle of the lowland, is the pleasantly doo-hickey *Taverna Kakavia*, ringed by tamarisk trees and con-veniently possessing a patio shower. The meals served are interesting and imaginatively presented. Fish dishes are a speciality, and the choice em-braces briam, leeks, boiled potatoes and mange-tout. I've dreamt of mange-tout! The middle-aged couple who run the place are very helpful, and smiley, even if Papa is prone to a touch of the 'temperamentals'.

There are two more tavernas, both over to the left (*Fsw*), the very far one of which is tucked into the lee of a distant, boulderous outcrop.To sea-wards, cradled in the loop of Cape Plaka, are the **Grandes islets**. Occasion-ally a laid-up tanker idly swings at anchor, between the islets and the bay.

Back at the Main road and continuing south from Paleokastro, the moorland appearance of the countryside persists. The winding route weaves on through neat groves of olives, gentle foothills, and a long valley. This is one of the prettier, if spasmodically potholed routes on Crete, a thorough-fare of gentle extremes of countryside - some pinky red soil, granite moun-tainsides, unexpected outcrops of polythene greenhouses, and rolling hills. Adding to the attractions of the itinerary are the spaced out villages: **Langada** - with a church typical of this area supplemented by a large dome and a 'bolt-on' bell tower; **Chochlakies** - as for Langada, plus cubic houses; the apparently deserted, erstwhile settlement of **Azokeramos**, beside the

roadside in the locality of which is a most distinctive, tiny, garishly coloured chapel, with an equally tiny rooftop campanile, as well as a twin barrel
roof chapel, and the first of a number of unique, dome covered, roadside
wells; and small **Kellaria** - wherein single storey, flat topped houses.

The soil hereabouts is startlingly pinky-purple, and the grazing cows
appear to be treated like household pets. They are often to be seen wearing
a twisted rope noseband and usually look in excellent condition. Next along
the 'seriously chewed' road surface is **Adravasti**, a lovely, quaint old
village, with a large number of donkeys, set in lush, heavily cultivated
surrounds. The pine tree lined route enters:

ZAKROS (Ano) (50km from Sitia) Tel prefix 0843. The still naive, somewhat expectant air, emanated by rural Zakros, does not come as a dis-
appointment, after the beauty of the preceding journey. Beside the approach
is a sign indicating spring water, to be found to the right, flowing into a
large concrete cistern.

The High Street ambles past the *Action Pub*, a baker on the right, the
Cafe-bar Restaurant Nikvlokakis and the Police station, both on the left.
Prior to the Main road curving sharply to the right, at about the centre of
the village, and on the left is the *Taverna Maestro*. This is a splendid, no-
frills establishment where an excellent home-cooked meal of the day is to
be enjoyed. The old lady, now 80 years young, advertises 'The finest Greco
cookery'. The simple but tasty meals do not let down her proud boast.

Straight ahead is a small shop, signed 'OTE, Telephonon (sic), Tele-
gram', flanked by kafeneions and close to the doo-hickey 'Town plaza'.
This square sports a fountain and periptero.

Also bordering the High St is the *Hotel Zakros* (Class C, tel 93379) at No
1 Eleftherias. The hotel is not inexpensive, considering the rather 'far
flung' position of the village. Rooms have en suite bathrooms, with a single
costing 1900drs & a double 2500drs, rates that rise to 2200drs & 3000drs
(1st July-30th Sept).

Across the street is a General store, and where the road swings round
towards Kato Zakros, is a little lane up to the right. In this is a hairdresser
and another restaurant, the *Aro To Cretos*.

The far side of Zakros is a petrol station, the track off to the right to
Xerokambos, and, beside the roadside, the signed archaeological remains
of a small Minoan house. I have to own up to the fact that these merely
look like any other ruined Greek dwelling.

The asphalted road arrows on southwards towards the downwardly distant
coastline. A side road off to the left is passed, which enters Kato Zakros,
via the 'back-door' as it were. The main thoroughfare allows lovely views
along the cliffs, to the right and left. The panorama to the left looks down
over the zig-zagging route, rapidly descending the dramatic, wild mountainside approaches to the surfaced, shore-hugging, attractively tree lined
track of:

KATO ZAKROS (58km from Sitia) Cultivated fields fill the valley that
edges the rim of the clean, pebbly beach of this sparse, outwardly attractive, sleepy, fishing boat hamlet.

The road makes a junction at about the centre of the tarmacadamed strip, the informal Esplanade, that borders the slightly curved sweep of the bay. Despite the comparative isolation of the spot, there are a surprising number of private cars present most days, say some twenty or so out of the height of season months, as well as a few caravans. Bunched up alongside the Esplanade are three tavernas, in addition to the other two spanning the back road into the settlement, at the left-hand side of the waterfront.

The latter alternative approach, which 'sneaks' into the rear of Kato Zakros, is the previously mentioned, left-hand turning off the main Kato Zakros road. This is now surfaced for much of its length, skirting an extremely steep gorge famed as a Minoan burial ground. I suppose they tipped them over the edge. You know - there goes granny in her sarcophagus. The road does degenerate to that of a sandy, bumpy, third-rate donkey track, about where it flattens out through banana and olive groves to cross a summer trickling stream, in the area of the Palace of Zakros (of which more later). Beyond these Minoan remains, the path meanders across some grassland and through the gap between the pair of backshore tavernas, to make a junction at the left (*Fsw*) end of the Esplanade.

Incidentally the waterfront tavernas not only offer sustenance, and limited accommodation, but the use of their toilet facilities. Correspondents have reported that dining at Kato can be accompanied by the strong impression of being 'ripped off'. If I had to plump for one establishment, it would be the *Restaurant Grill Maria*, on the left (*Fsw*) of the country track approach to the beach, that is at the far, east side of the Esplanade. This taverna hangs a key in a nearby tree for those who wish to avail themselves of their loos.

Further to the left, the sea's edge is broken up into small, stony beaches. The half dozen or so fishing boats, that work out of the bay, are moored here, overlooked by a string of buildings, fronted by a large patio. This 'upper' hamlet is accessed by a track that swings around from the rear of the eastern-most tavernas. In these few houses is some accommodation, the first *Rooms* being in the 'care' of probably the biggest, fattest, ginger-tom cat in Greece, if not in the world! Beyond is *Poseidon Rooms*, followed by a row of single storey, whitewashed, cell-like cubes, in one of which is the office of the Port police.

It is impossible to leave Kato without eulogising about the informal and simple remains of the:
Palace of Zakros Excavations were started at the turn of the century by one Hogarth, a British archaeologist. But it was not until after the Second World War that the Greeks realised the true potential of this marvellous site. Entrance costs 300drs.

It is possible, just possible, to avoid returning to Sitia via Paleokastro. To achieve this 'short cut', it is necessary to turn off the main road beyond Adravasti, taking an extremely rough track across a mountain range, to rejoin the main road (any main road) at Piskokefalo, to the south of Sitia.

This tank-testing 'little beauty' of a route initially serpentines up the side of a mountain. Apart from the 'difficult' state of the surface, the loosely looped, chicken wire 'armco barrier', edging the outset of the adventure, is, at best, a derisory safety measure - all that is between a driver and the 'big drop'. It goes without constant reiteration that the various vistas and panoramas, attainable from strategic points, along the journey are magnificent, if not unrivalled.

Apart from the countryside, the joy of this choice are the unspoilt, rural villages passed through and round, *en route*. The first is **Karidi**, attractive and strongly reminiscent of the Crete of yesteryear. It snuggles in a shallow valley surrounded by pocket-handkerchief sized, fertile fields; little patches of vineyards; and circular, paved threshing floors. At the appropriate time of year, the grapes are spread out on the flat house-tops. The double roofed church and campanile are noticeable, as is the War Memorial.

The next village is **Sitanos**, where there is a turning off to the left, signed Ierapetra and which bumps through **Chandras**. The right-hand possibility is the one to follow and is signposted to **Katsidoni**. The old, stone walled terraces hereabouts enclose all sorts of trees, whilst the surface of the route alternates between wide, expansive sweeps and downright hairy sections. Here and there, the road is metalled, for instance where it progresses through **Stavromenos**, beyond which are a few particularly nasty stretches of track. This is especially so the far side of **Zou**, where the surface simply reverts to bare earth. Yes, earth. The surface state changes to stony as the now wide track runs alongside a river-bed, before swooping down towards:

PISKOKEFALO (3km from Sitia) This is a very large village, through which wind narrow streets, with *Rooms* above a Main Square cafeteria.

ROUTE TWENTY THREE To Ierapetra via Piskokefalo & Makri Gialos

(59km) The first leg of the road, across the island, follows the normal pattern and mix of good and bad road surface; pretty and ugly villages; cultivated and barren countryside; valleys and mountains; chapels and yet more chapels; settlements that straddle the road, settlements that tower over the road, settlements that hide away beneath the road; and, above all, magnificent views, dramatic views, and squalid views.

Once on the south coast, I must first of all pass on my opinion that this is one of the most despoiled holiday resort stretches of Cretan coastline. Instead of concentrating the developments in high profile, localised splurges of 'Kosta'd' package horror, the authorities have allowed a lazy sprawl to envelope almost the whole of the coast, all the way from Analipsi through to Ierapetra. Any attempt to speak Greek, however little, is treated with the utmost suspicion, by 'native' staff at most of these settlements.

The first seaside village is:

ANALIPSI (32km from Sitia) Bearing in mind the overall caveat expressed in my prefacing comments, this is probably the nicest of the resorts described along this route.

The opening auguries are not good, as almost the first sight from this direction is the appallingly modern, unseemly large *Sun Wing Hotel*, which has appropriated the adjacent sandy little cove. A British company block-books this particular 'paradise'.

Analipsi has a pleasant, if small bay, with a tamarisk tree shaded, big pebble backshore, a 2-3 m wide swathe of grey, sharp sand beach, and a fine pebble foreshore. The sea is very gently shelving. Apart from surf-boards, there is the opportunity to water ski.

At Analipsi is a backward angled coast road that makes off in an easterly direction, signposted for a Monastery and Goudouras. This, in places, unsurfaced highway, tracks across a long coastal plain, distantly hemmed in by a ring of cliff-like hills, and set up a little from the sea's edge. The whole area has the aura of being a newly discovered land. The sea is beautifully coloured and the fairly flat topped **Koufonisi islet** is prominent to seawards.

At one spot, to the side of the road, is a small 'rash' of modern dwellings and plastic greenhouses. Tucked up against the foot of the adjacent hillside, is an oasis of greenery surrounding a rather uninteresting looking religious building. In amongst the domiciles are a couple of cafe-bars.

The route cuts inland, in order to steer round a gulch filled with a little pebble beach and dominated by a large blob of rock. At about this point, the outline of Goudouras village shimmers in the distance, framed by the back-drop of Cape Goudoura. Hereabouts, clinging to the cliff-face over to the left, is the 'Amorgos-like' **Monastery Kapsa**, below which is a grove of tamarisk trees.

The road sweeps past a lovely, if small bay of sandy beach, edged by a pebbly backshore and crumbling escarpment. The latter is followed by a few more sand and pebble coves, and a pint-sized, man-made harbour in which are moored some small fishing boats. A build-up of plastic greenhouses heralds the outskirts of:

GOUDOURAS (44km from Sitia) Briefly this is a dump of a shanty village, set down on a featureless, almost bowling green flat, shadeless plain, surr-ounded by arid mountains. Turning left, away from the sea, is a 'High St' between the prefabs, amongst which are one taverna and a cafe-bar. The last mentioned announces 'Delicious food cooked here'.

Returning to Analipsi, the latter almost, no, let's not prevaricate, it does merge with:

MAKRI GIALOS This settlement is based on an older, dusty hamlet. In fact with all the new construction going on, it is difficult to determine what is old, but being pulled down, as distinct from that which is new, and going up! This presence of a core village allows something of the original Greece to 'intrude'. An example is to be found close to the junction with the **Ag Stefanos** road, along which, a pace or ten, is the *Cafe/Ouzerie Melissa*. Here, in strict contrast to the more usual cocktail rock-bars, it is possible to sit down for a bottle of retsina and a plate of mezes. Golly gosh!

The bay is quite large and pleasant, with a rather shadeless beach of sharp, grey sand and a very fine pebble sea's edge.

The flats, apartments and *Rooms* are supplemented by a ladies hair-dresser. At the western end, dominated by polythene greenhouses, is another, smaller bay with a similar beach to the previous one, but with even less shade.

KOUTSOURAS (37km from Sitia) A once rural site which is now nothing more than a messy sprawl of both civil engineering and agricultural development. At times it is difficult to distinguish between house or hotel construction, and the race to cover large areas of this coast with plastic greenhouses! Koutsouras possesses a National Bank, a super-duper Post Office, a policeman, a bus stop, a couple of petrol stations, a gift shop, almost dozens of *Rooms*, some hotels and tavernas, as well as a timber yard.

The foreshore alternates between 'the very boulderous' and sloping flat rock, broken up by little coves of grey sharp sand, and along the length of which extends the ribbon development, seemingly for ever.

West of Koutsouras is prettier and greener, with fruit and flowers growing, some alongside the roadside. In fact this is an oasis, a 'Green belt' - well more the *National Pines Park & Red Butterfly Gorge*, complete with a tourist camping office. It has to be admitted that beyond this conservation effort is a football pitch, followed by an ugly quarry, then a countryside unsullied by even the hint of prestressed concrete. A rather unusual, blue and white double chapel is perched above the road, to the right, across from which is a pleasant, tiny cove of pebble beach. Thereafter follows more plastic, a restaurant/bar or two, a pebbly beach, and yet another bay, complete with a taverna, a sandy pebbly beach, *Rooms*, a pension and a petrol station.

AG FOTIA (46km from Sitia) This little bay is circumscribed by a huge loop of road and lies in a wide ravine edging a grey, gritty sand, airless beach. The signpost off the Main road, for the steep slope down to the track, that winds through the undergrowth of the lowland, is alongside a wrecked bus shelter and the sizeable *Hotel Mare*.

The once olive tree and vine filled, tiny agricultural plain is now being filled with the buildings offering accommodation, a restaurant as well as a taverna or three. I just love the sign that forbids backshore camping, alongside which are usually to be found up to half-a-dozen tents.

Two kilometres further on is:
FERMA Notable for several, pretty massive hotel developments... and nothing else. Ferma is one of those locations where there was no original infrastructure, 'not nothing', apart from the omnipresent olive trees. I would not wish to give the impression that the hotels stand in splendid isolation, as other facilities embody a supermarket, a cafe-bar restaurant and a petrol station.

KOUTSOUNARI (52km from Sitia) Once again there is little evidence of an original fishing boat hamlet, a fact that has not stopped the despoilers - hush my mouth. Oh no! Hard by a little cove of pebble beach is a resort development and suburbs, in amongst which is the *Litos Beach Hotel*.

A larger, wildish beach further to the west, is backed by sand dunes, across the road from which, on an inland plain, is an unattractive splash of speculative villa development. Edging the beach backshore are not one, but two campsites: *Camping Ierapetra* (Tel 0842 61351) and *Camping Koutsounari* (Tel 0842 61213). Both charge 450drs per head and 250drs for a tent. There is also accommodation at *Villa Rooms Mary*.

From hereon, in amongst a landscape that is pitilessly devoid of any shade and is a rough, uneven mix of Army firing range and lunar terrain, are plonked down a number of holiday villas and smart hotels, representative of which is the *Hotel Blue Sky*. Apart from the undeniably ugly country-side, the foreshore is, in the main, angled slabs of biscuit rock that stretches on, almost all the way to the rubbishy suburbs of Ierapetra.

IERAPETRA

A scattered, messy, industrious seaside town; lack of charm and a discernible centre; a very small Old Quarter and fort

GENERAL (Illustration 24) Tel prefix 0842. The population now totals some 12500 inhabitants. The modern town is sited on the ancient seaport of Ierapytna, which had substantial trade links with North Africa. The Romans established a large development, of which there are a few remains extant. Naturally enough, the Venetians and Turks occupied the site, as evidenced by the Venetian fort and the Turkish mosque and minaret.

The outer suburbs and immediate surrounds of Ierapetra are horrifyingly squalid, and the town is no great shakes either. It is not particularly diffi-cult to select a number of reasons for this overall lack of desirability, charm and ability to captivate. Certainly its large size, modernity and comparative lack of shade do little to encourage a feeling of intimacy, and are no help to the plus column of the ledger. In addition the lack of a substantial Old Quarter is a negative entry, as are the absence of a coherent street layout and a 'proper' town centre.

Despite being the only settlement of any size on the south coast, Ierapetra remained a backwater. That is until it was overtaken by rapid growth, in the 1960s, due to the wealth generated by the deployment of polythene green-houses. The plastic is used to force aubergines, bananas, cucumbers, tom-atoes and zucchinis. Much of this produce finds its way to Germany - which may well explain why 'Deutsche' appears to be the second language here-abouts. The agricultural bonanza was followed by the general realisation that Ierapetra was a potential holiday resort.

I own up to failing to appreciate the attributes, the magic ingredients that achieved this transmogrification, apart from the abundance of sand, sea and sun. Why spoil the squalor with an overlay of tourist requisites? Most of the hotel development has taken place along the wide, pedestrian way Esplanade, that stretches along the eastern beach backshore. At the western end is: the small Old Quarter; a Venetian fort; a Turkish mosque and minaret; a clock tower; and a small cargo ship harbour.

ARRIVAL BY BUS The Bus Terminus (*Tmr* 1C1) is on the outskirts of Ierapetra, alongside the dual carriageway Leoforos Lasthenous. The adja-cent bus ticket office not only houses a cafe-bar, but some toilets.

THE ACCOMMODATION & EATING OUT

The Accommodation Particularly helpful is the excellent Municipal tourist office (*Tmr* 2B/C2/3), where are handed out a list of *Rooms*, as well as the more usual hotel details. The average en suite double room costs 2000drs per night in a private house, and 2800drs in a pension.

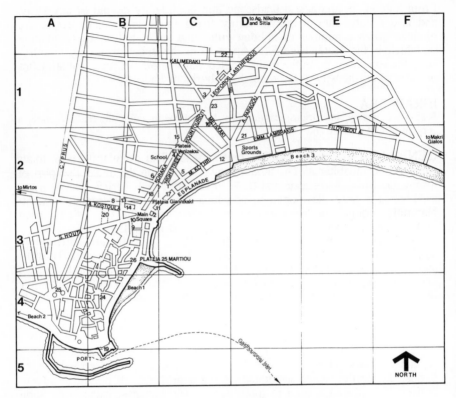

Illustration 24 Ierapetra

Turning towards the Main Square from the Bus Terminus, the *Four Seasons Rooms* (*Tmr* 3C1) are on the right.

Hotel Creta (*Tmr* 4C2) El Venizelou Sq   Tel 22316
Directions: The hotel is above the Ionian & Popular Bank, overlooking Plateia El Venizelou, towards the north end of the High St, Odhos Kountourioti.
  All rooms have en suite bathrooms, with a single charged at 2600drs & a double 3800drs.

Continuing south-west along the High St, the next side street off to the left, leads to the:
Hotel Camiros (*Tmr* 5C2) 17 M Kothri   Tel 28704
Directions: As above, and on the left.
  Once again all rooms have en suite bathrooms, a single priced at 2780drs & double at 4565drs.

Across the street from the *Camiros* is *Rooms* (Tel 28249).

Returning to Plateia El Venizelou, instead of keeping to the High St, it is possible to veer to the right along Odhos Koraka. This parallels the High St and advances across an elongated Square edged by the OTE (*Tmr* 6B/C2), as well as a *Rooms*. Still heading towards the Main Sq, beyond the 'OTE Sq' and to the right is a narrow, short lane, on the left of which is the *Hotel Ipnou* (*Tmr* 7B2/3), a very old fashioned little prospect.

From the Main Sq radiates a number of possibilities, including the:
Hotel Ligia (*Tmr* 9B3) (Class C)   Tel 28881
Directions: Behind the Main Sq Post Office, and down an alley.
  All rooms have en suite bathrooms, with a single priced at 1830drs & a double at 2450drs, which prices increase to 1930drs & 2800drs (21st June-20th Sept). Breakfasts cost 300drs extra per head.

Selecting the Mirtos road from the Main Sq, and on the right is the:
Hotel Zakros (*Tmr* 8B2/3) (Class C) A Kostoula   Tel 24101
Directions: As above.
  A modernish hotel with en suite bathrooms, a single costing 2750drs & a double 4000drs.

Behind the Municipal Tourist office (*Tmr* 2B/C2/3) and the Police station is the Esplanade, which edges the sea round to the north-east. The cluttered outset of this initially smart, paved way is bordered by all sorts, sizes and shapes of shops and schlepping restaurants, passing *Rooms Leon* (Tel 28577).

Hotel Katerina (*Tmr* 12C/D2)   Tel 28345
Directions: Almost at the far, shadeless end of the Esplanade, close to the outset of the main, eastern beach.
  Really more a pension than a hotel, but the whole place is a bit of a surprise as it is a fairly modern, six storey high, apartment type building. Those who elect to have one of the upper rooms will, on a clear day, probably be able to see Libya! In fact Katerina's could hardly be better situated, being only some 30-40m from the beach. The nice, smiley lady has little English. There is a rather musty smell to some of the bedrooms, but iced water is on tap (sorry) and breakfasts are served in a tiny dining room. A double room, with en suite bathroom, costs 2800drs in the mid-season months.

Camping The two closest sites are some 10km to the east of Ierapetra, at the south coast resort of Koutsounari, despite the older of the two being named *Ierapetra*. For details refer to **Route Twenty Three.**

The Eating Out Most of the bars, restaurants, tavernas, and their chairs and tables, are grouped along the Esplanade. Menus and prices tend to be 'much-of-a-much'.

For those seeking a reasonably priced, 'different' diner, there is no need to look any further than the:

Restaurant O Dimitrios (*Tmr* 13B2/3)
Directions: To the west of the Main Sq, a few metres along Odhos A Kostoula and in a cramped square behind the Town Museum (*Tmr* 14B2/3).

Really rather more a cafe-bar-cum-souvlaki place than a restaurant - but what's in a name? They serve sit-down or takeaway souvlaki, both pita and stick. A lunch-time meal, for two, of 3 souvlaki pita (I must own up to being the pig who ate 2 of them), and 2 bottles of beer, cost 600drs. Salad is also on offer.

One other establishment of interest, if only out of curiosity, is the *Restaurant Rex* sited in an abandoned cinema, on the edge of Plateia El Venizelou.

THE A TO Z OF USEFUL INFORMATION
AIRLINE OFFICE (*Tmr* 15B/C1/2) The office borders Plateia El Venizelou.

BANKS There are any number of Banks, amongst which are the: Agricultural (*Tmr* 16C1/2) on Odhos Metaxaki, quite close to the Bus Terminal, and which conducts the usual tourist requirements; **Ionian** (*Tmr* 4C2) on El Venizelou Sq; **National** (*Tmr* 17B/C2/3), edging Plateia Giannikaki; and the **Bank of Crete** (*Tmr* 18B/C2/3), beside Odhos Koraka, across the street from an ANEK ferry-boat ticket office.

BEACH One heading under which Ierapetra certainly is not deficient is that of beaches - there are three of them.
Beach 1 South of the Main Sq, and extending south from Plateia 25th March, almost as far as the Venetian Castle (*Tmr* 19A/ B4/5). This is a nice, wide, if gritty sand shore edging clear seas.
Beach 2 To the west around the corner from the Venetian Castle and Port headland. This is a long stretch of dirty grey coloured pebble beach, with a tiny pebble foreshore and sea-bed. Pleasantly mature arethemusa trees and various discretely spaced, small, canopied cafeterias are spaced out along the backshore, giving shade from both the sun and the wind.
Beach 3 Starts out from the east end of the Esplanade and, at first glance, appears rather desirable, but is actually pebbly with angled slab and biscuit rock at the sea's edge. Additionally there isn't any shade. Beyond the Sport's Ground is a Second World War pillbox. Well, I thought readers would like to know! Another piece of less useless information is that this beach improves, at the very far, east end.

BICYCLE, SCOOTER & CAR HIRE Generally charges are at the top end of the pricing scales. Is this because most of the visitors are desperate to get away?

BOOKSELLERS A bookseller and gift shop is located on the left (*Sbo*) of the High St, to the north of Plateia Giannikaki.

BREAD SHOPS A Baker is hidden away to the side of the Fruit & Vegetable Market (*Tmr* 20A/B2/3).

BUSES The Terminus and ticket office is at the edge of the Town (*Tmr* 1C1).

Bus timetables
Ierapetra to Iraklion via Istron & Gournia
Daily   0630, 0830, 1030, 1230, 1430, 1530, 1700, 1900, 2030hrs
Return journey
Daily   0730, 0830, 0930, 1130, 1330, 1530, 1700, 1830hrs
One-way fare: 750drs; duration 2½hrs; distance 105km.

Ierapetra to Iraklion via Mirtos & Viannos
Daily   1030, 1630hrs
Sun/hols   None
Return journey
Daily   0630hrs
Sun/hols   None
One-way fare: 750drs; duration 3hrs; distance 106km.

Ierapetra to Sitia via Makri Gialos
Daily   0630, 0800, 1000, 1200, 1415, 2000hrs
Return journey
Daily   0615, 0900, 1200, 1415, 1700, 2000hrs
One-way fare 430drs; duration 1½hrs; distance 61km.

Ierapetra to Makri Gialos via Ag Fotia & Koutsouras
Daily   0630, 0800, 1000, 1200, 1415, 1700, 2000hrs
Return journey
Daily   0630, 0930, 1030, 1445, 1730, 2030hrs
One-way fare: 190drs; duration ½hr; distance 27km.

Ierapetra to Mirtos
Daily   0630, 1030, 1200, 1345, 1630, 1930hrs
One-way fare: 100drs; duration ½hrs; distance 15km.

COMMERCIAL SHOPPING AREA There is a Market building (*Tmr* 20A/B2/3). For some obscure reason, probably only known to a now long dead worthy, this is labelled the Fruit and Vegetable Market. Despite this subterfuge, the excellent Market, which is on A Kostoula St, is packed with stalls selling almost everything. In addition there are any amount of shops, stores and supermarkets, including a pair of Supermarkets, one either side of the Market building. The majority of the shops and stores are spaced out along the High St and the parallel street of Odhos Koraka. Sundays and siesta are strictly observed.

DISCOS Yes.

ELPA The Greek equivalent of the United Kingdom *AA* has an office beside the Mirtos road.

FERRY-BOAT TICKET OFFICE The *ANEK* line maintains an office on the 'OTE Sq'.

LAUNDRY There is a Launderette (*Tmr* 21C/D1/2) rather inconveniently tucked away towards the east end of the Town, to the rear of the Sports Ground.

MEDICAL CARE
Chemists & Pharmacies Plentiful, one of which, in the area of the Post Office (*Tmr* 10B3), sports a window sign 'Italiano, Deutsche and English'.
Hospital (*Tmr* 22C/D1) To the left (Sbo) of the main Ag Nikolaos road, just beyond the Bus Terminus.

NTOG (*Tmr* 2B/C2/3) Close by the Main Sq and actually a Municipal operated facility, but who cares about the title? Without doubt this office offers an excellent service, handing out any amount of useful information and assiduously answering most enquiries. In addition the doors are open weekdays, between 0900-2100hrs, and weekends, between 0900-1500hrs.

OTE (*Tmr* 6B/C2) Borders Koraka St, and opens weekdays only, between 0730-2200hrs.

PETROL Apart from the garages spread about the 'suburbs', there is a petrol station (*Tmr* 23C1) at the junction of the High St and Odhos Metaxaki.

PLACES OF INTEREST These include the: Venetian Castle (*Tmr* 19A/B4/5); Mosque and Minaret (*Tmr* 25A4); Museum (*Tmr* 14B2/3); a Turkish fountain; and 'Napoleon's' House (*Tmr* 24A/B4). The latter is where Napoleon is rumoured to have stayed for a night, on his way to campaign in Egypt, in June 1798.
Archaeological Museum (*Tmr* 14B2/3) A single storey, Turkish building which, amongst other exhibits, houses a remarkable Minoan sarcophagus with painted hunting scenes.
Gaidhouronisi islet *See* Travel Agents...

POLICE
Town (*Tmr* 11B/C2/3) They are housed in a building to the east of the Tourist office, close to the seafront.

POST OFFICE (*Tmr* 10B3) Alongside the Main Sq.

TAXIS (*Tmr* T) The main rank is situated on Plateia Giannikaki, close to the Main Sq. They also 'lay in wait' adjacent to the Bus Terminus (*Tmr* 1C1).

TELEPHONE NUMBERS & ADDRESSES
Hospital (*Tmr* 22C/D1)	Tel 22252
Police (*Tmr* 11B/C2/3)	Tel 22560
Tourist office (*Tmr* 2B/C2/3)	Tel 28658

TRAVEL AGENTS & TOUR OFFICES There are any number of offices throughout Ierapetra. One of the most convenient, specialising in the Gaidhouronisi islet excursion, is **Zanadu Enterprises** (*Tmr* 26B3/4),which office borders Plateia 25th March. The caique trip to Gaidhouronisi sets out every day, at 1000hrs, during the summer months, weather permitting. The islet, famed for its crushed-shell beaches, is confusingly known by any number of alternative names, such as Chryssi, Gold and or Donkey. Whatever the nomenclature, the sea voyage is some 15km, the islet is 6km in length, and 2½km from top to bottom. There is an informal campsite and a few beach tavernas.

> I was with Hercules and Cadmus once,
> When in a wood of Crete they bay'd the bear
> With hounds of Sparta; never did I hear...
> So musical a discord, such sweet thunder.

Omission
This is relevant to pages 153 & 159.

'By proceeding west to the deserted village of **Aradena** it is possible to explore a gorge which runs down to the sea, spilling out on to **Marble Beach**. While on a smaller scale than the Samaria Gorge, it is still extremely impressive, and more importantly, deserted! One snag is that there is a spot in the descent where explorers have to lower themselves down a 15-18m cliff, using ropes. The ropes are in position, if a bit dodgy! This abseiling is not exceptionally difficult for the fit and fearless, but is not for the weak of resolve!'

ACKNOWLEDGMENTS Apart from those numerous friends and confidants we meet on passage, there are the many correspondents who are kind enough to contact me with useful information, all of who, in the main, remain unnamed.

Rosemary who accompanies me, adding her often unwanted, uninformed comments and asides, requires especial thanks for unrelieved, unstinting (well, almost unstinting) support.

Although receiving reward, other than in heaven, some of those who assisted me in the production of this book require specific acknowledgement, for effort far beyond the siren call of vulgar remuneration! These worthies include Graham Bishop, who drew the maps and plans; Ted Spittles who does clever things with the process camera and other bits and pieces; and Viv Hitie, who now not only controls the word processor, but the laser printer. Soon she will write the wretched things! During the end- less months while the year's books are in preparation, Viv's 'playmate' must wonder why she doesn't pick up her bed and move into Bridge House!

In passing, an old chum of mine, Bob Bingham, is sure he took my mug shot and has been carrying on and on about a credit. Similarly in the second edition of Crete I omitted to acknowledge Anne Merewood in respect of some photographs, for which apologies.

I would, this year, like to include a general apology to chums and more especially my Mother & Father, for the endless times I have had to forego an invitation or a visit... due to the all time consuming demands of authorship. Lastly, and as always, I must admonish Richard Joseph for ever encouraging and cajoling me to take up the pen, surely the sword is more fun?

Artwork: Ted Spittles &
    Geoffrey O'Connell
Packaging: Willowbridge
    Publishing
Plans & Maps: Graham
    Bishop & Geoffrey
    O'Connell
Typeset: Disc preparation
    Viv Hitie & Willowbridge
    Publishing.

TWO ABSORBING NEW TITLES BY OLIVER BURCH, AS RECOMMENDED BY GEOFFREY O'CONNELL

UNDER MOUNT IDA
A Journey into Crete

A refreshing and original look at this most popular and historic of Mediterranean islands. Oliver Burch skilfully evokes the full character of both people and place, from the bleached hillside villages to the sun-drenched tourist beaches. Tales from Crete's turbulent past combine with sometimes hilarious, sometimes sad encounters with the less-noble present to produce a fascinating portrait of this beautiful island under seige.

HB   £13.95   ISBN 1 85253 202 5

THE INFIDEL SEA
Discovering Turkish Cyprus

Despite its obvious attractions – Crusader castles, unspoiled beaches, temperate climate, welcoming people – northern Cyprus has remained neglected as a tourist destination, passed over in favour of the teeming resorts of the south. Now Oliver Burch attempts to redress the balance, discovering the unchanging beauty and unique character of this troubled region. He unravels the complex but absorbing history of this 'orphaned realm' set in an 'infidel sea', creating an ideal companion for both the interested holiday-maker and armchair traveller alike.

HB   £12.95   ISBN 1 85253 232 7

Oliver Burch displays a breadth and depth of writing about his chosen travel subjects that I find quite absorbing. After but a few pages of Under Mount Ida *I was totally engrossed and chose to read the book as a pleasure, not a job of work. Suffice to say I envy Oliver Burch his literary skills and ability to craft an absolutely compelling narrative.*
Geoffrey O'Connell

Available from all good bookshops or direct from Ashford, Buchan & Enright, 1 Church Road, Shedfield, Hants SO3 2HW. Telephone: (0329) 834265. Fax: (0329) 834250.